Accession no.
36124453

D1588800

WITHDRAWN

The Oxford Guide to
Etymology

For my parents

The Oxford Guide to Etymology

Philip Durkin

LIS LIBRARY	
Date 2717	Fund LA
Order No 2142077	
University of Chester	

OXFORD
UNIVERSITY PRESS

OXFORD

UNIVERSITY PRESS

Great Clarendon Street, Oxford OX2 6DP

Oxford University Press is a department of the University of Oxford.
It furthers the University's objective of excellence in research, scholarship,
and education by publishing worldwide in

Oxford New York

Auckland Cape Town Dar es Salaam Hong Kong Karachi
Kuala Lumpur Madrid Melbourne Mexico City Nairobi
New Delhi Shanghai Taipei Toronto

With offices in

Argentina Austria Brazil Chile Czech Republic France Greece
Guatemala Hungary Italy Japan Poland Portugal Singapore
South Korea Switzerland Thailand Turkey Ukraine Vietnam

Oxford is a registered trademark of Oxford University Press
in the UK and in certain other countries

Published in the United States
by Oxford University Press Inc., New York

© Philip Durkin 2009

The moral rights of the author have been asserted
Database right Oxford University Press (maker)

First published 2009

All rights reserved. No part of this publication may be reproduced,
stored in a retrieval system, or transmitted, in any form or by any means,
without the prior permission in writing of Oxford University Press,
or as expressly permitted by law, or under terms agreed with the appropriate
reprographics rights organization. Enquiries concerning reproduction
outside the scope of the above should be sent to the Rights Department,
Oxford University Press, at the address above

You must not circulate this book in any other binding or cover
and you must impose the same condition on any acquirer

British Library Cataloguing in Publication Data

Data available

Library of Congress Cataloging in Publication Data

Data available

Typeset by SPI Publisher Services, Pondicherry, India
Printed in Great Britain
on acid-free paper by
CPI Antony Rowe, Chippenham, Wiltshire

ISBN 978–0–19–923651–0

1 3 5 7 9 10 8 6 4 2

Contents

Acknowledgements

As my 'day job' I lead the team of specialist editors researching, writing, and revising etymologies for the new edition of the *Oxford English Dictionary*. As a result my first debt of gratitude must be to all of my colleagues, past and present, for their deep expertise, stimulating questions, and very good company, over (so far) fourteen years of highly enjoyable and rewarding collaborative research.

I am very grateful to the following people and institutions for kind invitations to give lectures and papers which drew extensively on draft chapters of this book: Derek Britton and the Institute for Historical Dialectology at the University of Edinburgh; Hans Sauer and the University of Munich; Ursula Lenker and the University of Eichstätt; Hans Sauer and Ursula Lenker and the Fifteenth International Conference on English Historical Linguistics, Munich, 2008. To the audiences at each of these papers I am grateful for many helpful suggestions and observations, and not least for confirming that there is an audience for a book of this sort.

I am enormously grateful to all of those who have commented on parts of this book in draft: Kathryn Allan, Joan Beal, Alan Durant, Anthea Fraser Gupta, Christian Kay, Peter McClure, Inge Milfull, Nicholas Sims-Williams; and to the following who were generous and brave enough to read drafts of the whole book: Anthony Esposito, Meg Laing, Roger Lass, Anna Morpurgo Davies, John Simpson, and Edmund Weiner. The book as it stands today has benefitted enormously from the keen eyes and still keener intellects of all of these people. Needless to say, all errors and omissions are to be laid, with complete justice, entirely and exclusively at my own door.

I am hugely grateful also to John Davey at OUP for his help, advice, and encouragement at every stage in the process of shaping, writing, and producing this book. Elmandi du Toit, Malcolm Todd, and Lesley Rhodes provided expert input on the production of the book.

I would also like to thank Kathryn Allan a second time, for putting up with me on the many days when even brimming pots of coffee were not enough to focus the mind and drive away irritation. And finally I would like to thank the dedicatees of this book for tolerating a child's at times rather obsessive interest in very old documents and even older words.

About this book

Etymologies appeal to people with a very wide variety of interests and intellectual backgrounds. A very few people, such as myself, spend most of their time researching etymologies. A slightly larger number do so very occasionally. Many, many more people look at etymologies, but have never researched any themselves. Some people will never even have thought of etymologies as things which need to be researched. Particularly when etymologies are encountered in the compressed form found in many dictionaries, they can seem to be a given, rather than the (often very tentative) results of extensive research.

This book is intended for anyone who has taken the important first step of realizing that etymologies are the result of research, and would like to discover something about the nature of that research, and the principles and methodologies which underlie it.

I have attempted to frame this book so that it is addressed most centrally to someone who has an interest in historical linguistics, the study of how languages change and develop over time. Etymology is a part of this wider field, and anyone's understanding of etymology will be greatly enriched by at least some acquaintance with the broader concerns of the discipline as a whole. Readers who are entirely new to this field may find that they get much more out of this book if they read it in conjunction with one of the many excellent general textbook introductions to historical linguistics, such as Schendl (2001) or, in slightly greater depth, Millar (2007, which is a revised edition of Trask 1996) or Campbell (2004); for an excellent introduction to a wide variety of linguistic topics focussing on the vocabulary of English see Katamba (2005).

When deciding what to cover in this book and in how much detail, I have tried to pay particular attention to those areas which are important for etymology but which receive relatively little attention in most introductory books on historical linguistics. Nonetheless, I have also endeavoured to ensure that the book provides a balanced account of all aspects of etymology, especially for readers who are prepared to follow up references to fuller discussions of any topics which may be new or unfamiliar.

Most of my examples will be drawn from English, since this is the one language that any reader of this book will necessarily have some knowledge of. However, my aim has been to assume no particular knowledge about the history of the English language, beyond the explanations and further references given in the text. Drawing examples from the history of English also brings the advantage that I have in many cases been able to make use of very recent research for the new edition of the *Oxford English Dictionary* with which I have been involved personally.

There are no exercises, but at various points in the text I have listed further examples of the phenomena discussed, which readers can pursue if they wish in etymological dictionaries. Access to a good etymological dictionary of English would be of great benefit to anyone reading this book. In particular, access to the full *Oxford English Dictionary*, especially in its online version (www.oed.com), would be of especial benefit, so that many examples given here in summary form can be pursued in greater detail. (The dictionary can be accessed online via most institutional libraries and many public libraries.)

1

Introduction

1.1 What is etymology?

As we will see in this chapter, etymology can tell us that English *friar* was borrowed from Old French *frere* 'brother', which in turn developed from Latin *frāter* 'brother'. It can also tell us, perhaps rather more surprisingly, that Latin *frāter* is ultimately related to English *brother*, and that English *foot* is related to Latin *pēs* 'foot' and Armenian *otn* 'foot'. Just as surprisingly, it can tell us that, in spite of the resemblance in form, English *care* and Latin *cūra* 'care' are definitely not related to one another, nor are Latin *deus* 'god' and Greek *theós* 'god'. Etymology can also trace dramatic changes in meaning: for instance, English *treacle* originally had the meaning 'medicine', and comes ultimately from a Greek word which originally meant 'antidote against a venomous bite'; *sad* originally had the meaning 'satisfied'. How we trace such developments, and what they tell us about linguistic history, will be the topic of this book.

Etymology is the investigation of word histories. It has traditionally been concerned most especially with those word histories in which the facts are not certain, and where a hypothesis has to be constructed to account either for a word's origin or for a stage in its history. That might be a stage in its meaning history, or in its formal history, or in the history of its spread from one language to another or from one group of speakers to another. The term is also used more broadly to describe the whole endeavour of attempting to provide a coherent account of a word's history (or pre-history). As we will see in the course of this book, many of the basic methodological assumptions made in etymological research are the same regardless of whether we are looking at well-documented periods of linguistic history or at periods earlier than our earliest documentary records. Indeed, even someone who is primarily concerned only with attempting to solve hitherto unresolved difficulties of word history can only do so by building on the knowledge of many other word histories which have been much more securely established. For this reason, very many of the illustrative examples in this book will come from word histories which are very secure and not in any doubt, since they often provide the surest foundation for further investigation. Nonetheless, we will also look at some rather more difficult cases along the way.

Etymology forms part of the wider field of historical linguistic research, that is to say of attempts to explain how and why languages have changed and developed in the ways that they have. However, it does not concern itself exclusively with a particular linguistic level, as does for instance historical phonology (the study of speech sounds and of their deployment in ways which convey distinct meaning), historical morphology (the study of word forms as used to convey grammatical relationships), historical semantics (the study of the meaning of words), or historical syntax (the study of the meaning relations between words within a sentence). This is not to suggest for a moment that historical phonologists, morphologists, semanticists, or syntacticians never pay any attention to anything other than phonology, morphology, semantics, or syntax respectively. However, etymology is rather different, in that an individual word history will almost never be explicable in terms of only one linguistic level. Typically, some arguments or at least tacit assumptions about word form, probably involving issues of both historical phonology and morphology, will be combined with some arguments or assumptions about word meaning. In fact, etymology can be defined as the application, at the level of an individual word, of methods and insights drawn from many different areas of historical linguistics, in order to produce a coherent account of that word's history. One of the most exciting aspects of etymology is that this sort of detailed work on individual word histories sometimes throws up interesting results which can have a much broader significance in tracing the history of a language (whether that be with regard to phonology, morphology, etc.), especially when we can find parallels across a group of different word histories. Additionally, it is often crucial that questions of (non-linguistic) cultural and intellectual history are considered in tandem with questions of linguistic history.[1]

As well as using the word *etymology* as an abstract noun, we can also talk about *an etymology*, that is to say an account of a word's history. In the next section, we will look at two representative etymologies in some detail, as a practical way of introducing some basic concepts and at the same time some questions and issues which will concern us in much more detail later. The first example involves some very well-documented periods of linguistic history, while the second (which is rather more complex) will offer a first foray into historical reconstruction at a very considerable time depth. Concepts that we will explore include:

- tracing the linear history of a word
- change in word form
- change in word meaning
- borrowing
- genetic relationships between languages
- cognates
- comparative reconstruction
- sound change

1.2 Some basic concepts: two example etymologies

1.2.1 Example one: *friar*

The etymology of the English word *friar* can be sketched very crudely as follows:

> Latin *frāter* 'brother'
> > *develops into*
> Old French *frere* (modern French *frère*) 'brother', also 'member of a religious order of "brothers"'
> > *which is borrowed as*
> Middle English *frere* 'friar'
> > *which develops into*
> modern English *friar*

---

[1] For a short survey of previous definitions of the term 'etymology', accompanied by an adventurous attempt to formulate a fully adequate formal definition, see Alinei (1995).

The symbol '>' is frequently used to stand for both 'develops into' and 'is borrowed as', and so we can represent the same development in a more 'shorthand' way as:

> Latin *frāter* brother > Old French *frere* brother, also member of a religious order of 'brothers' > Middle English *frere* friar > modern English *friar*

Or we can reverse the arrows, and trace backwards from the modern English word. In fact, this is the style most frequently encountered in dictionaries and in most other scholarship:

> modern English *friar* < Middle English *frere* friar < Old French *frere* brother, also member of a religious order of 'brothers' < Latin *frāter* brother[2]

The etymology of the Latin word could also be traced back a lot further than this, and can be linked ultimately with English *brother*, but this requires an acquaintance with some topics which we will investigate in section 1.2.4.

Obviously, this is a summary of a series of events in linguistic history. We will now examine each of those events in turn, and to do so we will require a little background at each stage. The Latin language is the direct antecedent of French. That is to say, French, like the other Romance languages (Portuguese, Spanish, Italian, Romanian, etc.), developed from Latin, albeit probably from a form of the language rather different from that reflected by the majority of our literary records. French also shows many borrowings and some structural influences from other languages, especially the Germanic language spoken by the Franks, but its basic line of descent is indisputably from Latin. In the vulgar Latin and proto-Romance varieties which eventually developed into French, the Latin word for 'brother', *frāter* (or more accurately its oblique case forms, such as the accusative singular *frātrem*) underwent a number of (perfectly regular) changes in word form, resulting in Old French *frere*. Old French is the term used to denote the earliest recorded stage of the French language, up to the early fourteenth century.[3] Thus we have our first step:

> Latin *frāter* > Old French *frere*

[2] Some scholars use the symbols '<' and '>' only to link forms related by direct phonetic descent, and use different symbols for processes such as borrowing or derivation, but in this book I will use them to link any two consecutive stages in an etymology.

[3] Unusually, in this particular case, an intermediate step in the formal development of the Old French word is recorded in the very early Old French form *fradre* preserved in the *Strasbourg Oaths*, a unique (and very short) document from the year 842 which records (partly in Latin, partly in French, and partly in German) the oaths taken by Louis the German, Charles the Bald, and their followers during a time of conflict.

frere remained the basic word in French for 'brother', but it also acquired a secondary meaning denoting the (metaphorical) 'brothers' who belonged to various religious orders. This usage in French followed similar use of *frater* in medieval Latin.[4] The word was then borrowed into English from French. This happened in the Middle English period, the stage of the English language from roughly 1150 to 1500. More accurately, the word was borrowed from the Anglo-French variety of Old French which was used in England in the centuries after the Norman Conquest.[5] The usual form in Middle English, *frere*, matches the French form exactly, and the pronunciation is likely to have been almost identical in Anglo-French and in Middle English. However, in Middle English the meaning is much narrower, showing only the religious sense and occasionally one or two other metaphorical uses. Thus we have our second step:

> Old French *frere* brother, also member of a religious order of 'brothers' >
> Middle English *frere* friar

It is very common for a borrowed word to show only a very restricted and possibly rather peripheral portion of its meaning when it is borrowed into another language. In this particular instance, it is easy to see why (Anglo-)French *frere* was not borrowed into English with the much more basic meaning 'brother': the word *brother* (inherited from the Old English period, and from the Germanic antecedent of English before that) already had that meaning and was in common use, and even in the Middle English period, when very many words were borrowed from French into English, it is relatively uncommon for words with quite such basic meanings as this to be borrowed in place of native words. We will look at this issue in more detail in chapters 5 and 6. In fact English *brother* also had the meaning

---

[4] The macrons which indicate vowel length in forms like classical Latin *frāter* are not normally given when citing Latin forms from later than the classical period, although this does not necessarily indicate any change in the vowel length in particular words.

[5] In this book I use the term 'Anglo-French' to denote French as used in England (and elsewhere in Britain) in the centuries following the Norman Conquest. Scholarly practice is divided in this area: 'Anglo-Norman' is often used to denote this variety (as in the title of the *Anglo-Norman Dictionary*), but increasingly the broader term 'Anglo-French' is used instead, in order to reflect better the varied inputs from different varieties of Continental French which occurred both immediately after the Norman Conquest and in the subsequent centuries: for a useful discussion and further references see Rothwell (2005). For convenience, where a form or meaning belonged to both Insular and Continental French I use the style (Anglo-)French.

'(fellow) member of a religious order' in the Old English period on the model of use in Latin, and this meaning continued in the Middle English period (as it does today), reinforced by the similar use in both Latin and French. When *frere* is first found in Middle English it duplicates this meaning, as well as showing the more specialized meaning 'member of one of the mendicant orders (chiefly the Franciscans, Augustinians, Dominicans, and Carmelites, as opposed to the non-mendicant Benedictines, etc.)'. By the end of the Middle English period a process of semantic specialization took place, with *brother* used in the general sense 'member of a religious order' and *friar* in the narrower sense 'member of one of the mendicant orders'. Thus we might say that the borrowing filled a lexical gap in the vocabulary of English, providing a word specifically for 'a member of one of the mendicant orders', although we should perhaps be slightly cautious about such assumptions, since the same gap remained unfilled by any single word in French, even though the two languages were being used in very similar societies. Indeed, Anglo-French and Middle English were being used in precisely the same society. (See section 5.6 for discussion of the different functions of each language.) As we will see later, we can often run into problems of this sort when we attempt to explain word histories in functional terms, although this does not necessarily mean that the attempt is not worthwhile.

In its development from Middle English to modern English the word did not show any further change in meaning, but it did show an unusual change in form. The usually expected modern (British standard) pronunciation of a word which had the Middle English form *frere* would be /fri:ə/ (compare *here*, *deer*) but instead we find /fraɪə/. The same development is found in a small number of other words such as *briar* and *choir*. It probably shows a sporadic phenomenon of vowel raising before a following /r/.

Summary so far   We can trace the history of a word's sound and form. In doing so we are looking for regularity, i.e. developments which are the same as those which happened to the same sounds or combinations of sounds in other words. Where something unexpected or irregular has happened, as with the development of /fraɪə/ rather than /fri:ə/, we will want to find parallels, such as *briar*, etc. Ideally we will want to find an explanation for this as well.

The meaning of the word can also be traced historically. We can see how the meaning broadened in Latin and French, but how the English borrowing showed only a very narrow component of the donor word's meaning. We can also see how this borrowing fitted into a set of meaning relations with existing words in English (specifically *brother*). The meaning history of this word also shows the importance of factors from non-linguistic history: if we did not know something about the history of the religious orders in medieval Europe we would have considerable difficulty in explaining the historical development in the meaning of this word.

1.2.2 Example two: *sad* from modern English to proto-Germanic

For our next example we will start with the present day and work backwards. Modern English and Middle English *sad* show the reflex or linear historical development of Old English *sæd*. The symbol æ which occurs in the written form of this word and of many other Old English words (and some early Middle English ones) represents a front vowel phoneme /a/ (perhaps in fact [æ] rather than [a]) which in Old English was distinct from the back vowel /ɑ/, represented by *a*. (Its italic form *æ* is unfortunately very similar to that of the ligature œ, which can sometimes lead to confusion for the unwary.) We could represent this word history as Old English *sæd* > Middle English *sad* > modern English *sad*, but this would be rather artificial, since what we in fact have is a continuous history across all periods in the history of the language.

If we turn to the word's semantic history, a basic dictionary definition of the word *sad* as typically used in modern English is:

Of a person, or his or her feelings, disposition, etc.: feeling sorrow; sorrowful, mournful.

This meaning is first recorded *a*1300 (which stands for 'ante 1300', that is '1300 or a little earlier').[6] A similar basic dictionary definition for the word's earlier meanings would be:

[6] Some scholars use 'ante' in the more literal sense 'before', but most, including most dictionaries, use it in the generally more useful sense 'this date or a little earlier'. In this book the dates given for English words, forms, and senses are normally those provided by the *OED*. For words from other languages the data I give is generally drawn from the standard historical or etymological dictionaries of each language. Glosses and definitions of English words are normally based on those in either the *OED* or *The Oxford Dictionary of English* except where otherwise noted, although I have frequently shortened or otherwise adjusted them.

Having had one's fill; satisfied, sated; weary or tired (of something).

If we consider the likely historical development of these meanings, we can hypothesize that the meaning 'weary or tired (of something)' developed from 'satisfied, having had one's fill (of something)', hence showing a metaphorical, narrowed, negative meaning; compare the modern English idioms *to have had enough of something* or *to be fed up with something* for similar developments. Subsequently the sense 'weary or tired (of something)' broadened again (but still with an exclusively negative sense) to 'sorrowful, mournful' in general. Hence we can hypothesize that a meaning development occurred with two main steps:

satisfied, having had one's fill (of something)

[metaphorized and narrowed] > weary or tired (of something)

[broadened] > sorrowful, mournful

We get some further support for the last stage in this hypothesized development when we look at the meanings of the closest relatives of the Old English word, its cognates in the other Germanic languages. The next step back in the history of *sad* can be expressed as follows:

Old English *sæd* is cognate with Old Dutch *sat*, Old Saxon *sad*, Old High German *sat*, Old Icelandic *saðr*, Gothic *saþs*, all of which have meanings broadly corresponding to the Old English one, 'having had one's fill; satisfied, sated; weary or tired (of something)'

However, the concept expressed by 'cognate with' needs some unpacking, and we will now look at this in more detail.

1.2.3 Cognates and language families

What does it mean to say that Old English *sæd* (English *sad*) is 'cognate with' the words from Old Dutch, Old Saxon, etc. listed at the end of the previous section? Just as the Romance languages all developed from (some form of) Latin (see section 1.2.2), so English and a number of other languages, which linguists call the Germanic languages, developed from a common antecedent called proto-Germanic. Unlike Latin, we have no historical records for proto-Germanic, but we can reconstruct a good deal of information about it from the evidence of the languages that developed

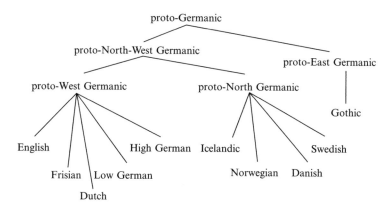

Fig 1.1 The major Germanic languages

from it. The other Germanic languages include Dutch (and hence Afrikaans), German (and hence Yiddish), Danish, Norwegian, Swedish, and Icelandic, as well as others such as Frisian (the closest relative of English, but with very few speakers today) and the extinct language Gothic (which is the Germanic language for which we have the earliest extensive documentary records, in the form of a bible translation dating from the fourth century AD). The cognates of an English word are the words in these other Germanic languages which can be explained as having developed from the same (unrecorded) antecedent word in proto-Germanic.

In fact, we can also identify subdivisions within the larger group of Germanic languages, on the basis of shared innovations that allow us to group the Scandinavian languages together as descendants of a common North Germanic sub-branch and likewise (albeit with rather more rough edges) English, Frisian, Dutch, Saxon/Low German, and High German as descendants of a West Germanic sub-branch. In turn, many scholars would now group together West Germanic and North Germanic as being descended from a shared North-West Germanic sub-branch with shared differences from East Germanic.[7] Thus the relationships between the major Germanic languages can be represented schematically as in figure 1.1. We can reconstruct a similar tree structure for the major Romance languages, with the difference that in this instance the common ancestor, Latin, is of course attested (figure 1.2).

---

[7] See for example Ringe (2006) 213. For a useful introduction to the early Germanic languages, see Robinson (1992).

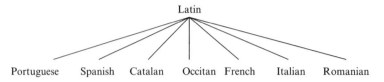

Fig 1.2 The major Romance languages

It is as well to pause for a moment and consider in a little more detail what this concept of a reconstructed antecedent language implies, because it will be crucial to many arguments later in this book. From present-day English to Old English (back as far as the eighth century, or even earlier in runic inscriptions) we have a chain of documents which enable us to trace the history of the English language in reasonable detail. In fact, these documents reflect many different local varieties of the language, showing many divergent developments. Some of these are reflected in different varieties of English today, such as the English of Chicago, or London, or Cape Town. We may analyse these as forming part of larger varieties, such as US English (or perhaps North American English), British English, or South African English. Alternatively we may subdivide them further, by looking for instance at different geographical or administrative areas of London, or at the language of different social classes within the city, or of different age groups, etc. Such variation must have been present throughout the history of English, although in earlier periods the nature and amount of the surviving evidence mean that we can only reconstruct a very limited picture. Modern US English and British English have developed as distinct varieties in different geographical locations from roughly the same antecedent, English as spoken in Britain in the early modern period (usually defined as approximately 1500–1750), but the historical record, as well as the evidence of modern US and British English, shows us that this common antecedent showed considerable internal variation. Similarly English and all of the other Germanic languages developed from a common antecedent (as did French, Spanish, etc. from Latin), but there is no reason to doubt, and every reason to suspect, that Germanic already showed internal variation. (Even though our surviving records for classical Latin are mostly literary and reflect a highly homogeneous literary language, there is indeed some variation in our surviving Latin evidence, and the later evidence of the Romance languages suggests the existence of a good deal of further variation in Latin which is not reflected in the surviving documentary evidence).[8] Over the course of time, groups of Germanic-speaking peoples developed distinct communities in different geographical locations (to some of which, like England, they had spread as part of the considerable movements of peoples which occurred in the later stages of the history of the Roman Empire and in the following centuries). As they did so, linguistic differences would have become more pronounced, as different variants from among the existing variation in Germanic came to predominate in different speech communities, and as new variation arose in each speech community.

At the time of our earliest substantial records for English, from several centuries after the Anglo-Saxons arrived in England, there are already important differences between English and its continental relatives, but these clearly took time to develop. We can also trace significant differences between different regional varieties of English in this early period, although the surviving documents leave very many questions unanswered.[9] The demarcation of the various national languages of modern Europe owes a great deal to geography and, especially, politics. In the sixteenth and seventeenth centuries Scots was well on the way to developing a standard, 'official' form, distinct from the English of England, but subsequent political developments led to the adoption in official functions of a highly anglicized variety now usually referred to as Scottish English (although in recent decades as a result of the political process of devolution there have been some interesting developments in the use of Scots once again as an officially recognized variety in some functions). Today Dutch and German are well-defined national languages, sufficiently different from one another that monolingual speakers of either standard language have only an extremely limited degree of mutual intelligibility, but the situation is different among speakers of traditional dialects on or near the geographical boundaries between the two countries: such speakers can with a little effort understand the speech of their neighbours on the other side of the national border, even though one person is speaking something that is classified as a dialect of Dutch and the other something that is classified as a dialect of German. We can say that there is a dialect continuum which crosses the Dutch–German border. Another crosses the French–Italian border, and

---

[8] On the degree of regional variation shown by surviving Latin documents from antiquity see Adams (2008).

[9] For an introduction to the various issues involved see Hogg (2006).

similar cases can be found in many other parts of the world, essentially wherever languages have developed from a common source in adjacent territories.[10]

Such dialect continua lead us fairly directly to some limitations in the tree diagrams for the Romance and Germanic languages which I offered above. Diagrams of this type are a good way of representing where the most important shared innovations are found among various dialects in a group, but they have the disadvantage of making linguistic history appear artificially simple and neat. When two speech communities diverge, as represented by the branching on a tree, each takes with it a particular selection of features from the parent language. When further divergences occur subsequently, we may find that a particular feature is retained, quite by chance, in two languages or dialects which the weight of evidence places on completely different sides of the tree. In other cases the same innovation may occur independently in two different places, giving a false indication of inherited similarity. Additionally, where languages or dialects remain in contact, especially when they are spoken in geographically contiguous or overlapping territories, we can find that some features spread by diffusion (i.e. contact) from one variety to another, hence muddling the apparently clean branching shown by a tree. A better metaphor for such diffusion of features through language contact may be the spreading of a wave from a point of origin, rather than the branching of a tree.[11]

1.2.4 Example two revisited: *sad* from proto-Germanic to proto-Indo-European

If we return to our example of *sad*, we can push this particular word history back further than just to proto-Germanic. The Germanic languages themselves form one branch of a much larger language family which historical linguists call Indo-European, which has numerous other branches, sub-branches, and isolate languages including for example:[12]

---

[10] For an introductory account of these issues see Chambers and Trudgill (1998) 3–12. On the concept of a traditional dialect see especially Wells (1982) 4–8.

[11] For discussions of this issue with reference to the Germanic languages see Trask (1996) 181–7 (also Millar (2007) 225–31) and, at a rather more advanced level, Lass (1997) 139–59. On more general issues to do with language trees see McMahon and McMahon (2005).

[12] For an overview of the Indo-European languages see Fortson (2004).

- the Celtic languages: Welsh, Irish, etc.
- the Italic languages: Latin (and hence the Romance languages), Oscan, Umbrian, etc.
- Greek
- the Balto-Slavonic languages, comprising the Slavonic languages (Russian, Polish, etc.) and the Baltic languages (Lithuanian, Latvian, etc.)
- Albanian
- Armenian
- the Indo-Iranian languages, comprising the Iranian languages (Persian, etc.) and the Indic languages (Sanskrit and hence modern Hindi, etc.)

All of these languages can be shown to have developed from a single parent, proto-Indo-European, although of course all of them show the effects of contact with other languages during their histories. The identification of a shared ancestor for all of these languages rests upon the evidence of regular correspondences of sounds between the various languages, which we will look at in more detail below, and also upon systematic grammatical similarities, which are largely outside the scope of this book.

Many people have attempted to link Indo-European with other language families, but all such attempts remain extremely controversial, and the general view is that no genetic relationship has been reliably established between Indo-European and any other language family.

Precisely when and where proto-Indo-European existed as a spoken language is the subject of a very great deal of debate. This is complicated by the fact that the earliest recorded Indo-European language, Hittite, the oldest documentation for which dates back approximately 4,000 years, belongs to a branch, Anatolian, which probably split from the rest of Indo-European very early. However, what is reasonably certain is that proto-Indo-European began to split into its various daughter languages very much earlier than the date of our earliest documentary records for those languages. It is therefore unsurprising that many of the cognate forms bear little if any superficial resemblance to one another, since we are working at such a great time depth, and centuries of linguistic change lie between proto-Indo-European and even our earliest documentary evidence.

In this section we will trace the history of the word *sad* from proto-Germanic back to proto-Indo-European, and we will examine some of the procedures by which etymologies can be established at this time depth.

In doing so, we will encounter some principles and procedures which are equally applicable to much more recent linguistic history, and which we will investigate mostly from the standpoint of rather more recent linguistic evidence in the remainder of this book. However, reconstruction of linguistic data at a very considerable time depth is one of the big attractions of etymological research for many people, and it is also true that many of the most important aspects of modern etymological research came to fruition in the context of research into proto-Indo-European in the second half of the nineteenth century. We will therefore begin our investigation of the relationship between sound change and etymology by taking a look at how the sound changes known as Grimm's Law and Verner's Law help explain the etymology of *sad*.

By comparing the forms found in the Germanic languages with one another and also with forms in other Indo-European languages, we can reconstruct the proto-Germanic ancestor of *sad* as **saða-*.[13] An asterisk conventionally marks reconstructed forms, i.e. forms which are not actually recorded. **saða-* ends with a hyphen because it is a reconstructed word stem, i.e. the morphological stem to which inflectional endings were then added. In this book I will usually give reconstructions using IPA symbols, but without using square brackets [] implying that they are hypothetical phonetic transcriptions, nor // slashes implying that they necessarily have phonemic status. This is a traditional philological practice, which is useful for three main reasons: (i) we cannot always be certain about the precise phonetic quality of reconstructed sounds; (ii) any past historical sound system almost certainly showed considerable variation in the realization of sounds, which we cannot recover in detail from our historical evidence; (iii) we cannot always be sure whether certain distributions of sounds were phonemic or allophonic in a given historical period.[14] We will look at issues

---

[13] The exact phonetic quality and phonemic status of the consonant I have represented here as **ð* is in fact very uncertain. Many scholars choose to use **d* in reconstructions of proto-Germanic forms to represent any sound which may have been either a voiced plosive /d/ or a voiced fricative /ð/. In many modern etymological dictionaries the proto-Germanic form of this particular word is hence represented as **sada-*. However, since the sound in this instance was almost certainly a voiced fricative at an early stage in proto-Germanic, I have used the reconstruction **saða-*, which has the advantage of making the changes from proto-Indo-European to proto-Germanic easier to follow.

[14] For a recent detailed argument for this position see Lass and Laing (2007) §§2.4.2, 8.3.2.

to do with variation and change in any linguistic system in more detail in chapters 3 and 7.

The reconstruction *saða- depends upon the evidence of the various Germanic languages, and also upon the evidence of forms in other Indo-European languages which can plausibly be referred to the same root form. Most crucially, it depends upon:

(a) regular sound correspondences between the various languages
(b) sound changes which can be posited to explain apparent irregularities

To get from proto-Germanic *saða- to the recorded words Old English sæd, Old Dutch sat, Old Saxon sad, Old High German sat, Old Icelandic saðr, Gothic saþs requires just a couple of small steps:

- In West Germanic, proto-Germanic *ð regularly became the voiced plosive /d/, as in our Old English form sæd /sad/ or Old Saxon sad. Old Dutch sat and Old High German sat show subsequent devoicing of this plosive (compare section 2.1.1.3).
- Old English sæd additionally shows Old English (and Old Frisian) fronting of West Germanic *a to /a/.

These are regular, predictable sound changes in a word of this phonological shape in these languages.

This reconstructed proto-Germanic form *saða- itself shows the reflex of an earlier Indo-European form *sǝto-. (The symbol *ǝ in this reconstruction represents a sound which was realized as a vowel when it occurred in this position, hence giving rise to vowels in the daughter languages, but which is now generally believed to have resulted from the vocalic realization of one of a series of so-called laryngeal sounds which are hypothesized for proto-Indo-European. They are called laryngeals for historical reasons, although no one in fact knows exactly what their phonetic quality was. This particular laryngeal is sometimes represented as $ǝ_2$ or as h_2 or as H_2, depending on which transcription conventions are being followed. We will return to this topic in sections 1.3.1 and 4.4.1.)

Related words in other Indo-European languages include:

classical Latin sat, satis 'enough', satur 'satisfied, full'
Lithuanian sotus 'filling, full, satisfied, substantial'
ancient Greek áatos 'insatiate' (showing a negative prefix)

We can see that the meanings of these words help support our hypothesis about the meaning development in the Germanic languages from 'satisfied, having had one's fill (of something)' to 'weary or tired (of something)'. It is difficult to be certain about the precise relationships between these words. They probably reflect two different variants, *sǝ- and *sā-, of a single Indo-European root for which the approximate meanings 'fill up, (make) replete' can be reconstructed. In our surviving cognates various different suffixes, *-to-, *-ti-, and *-tu-, have been added to this root. The cognates thus do not represent the reflexes of a single word form, but rather the survivors of an extended word family, derived in various different ways from a common root.[15] The Germanic words probably show what was originally a suffix which formed verbal adjectives, proto-Indo-European *-to-. The same suffix is probably found in *old* (< proto-Germanic *al-da-) and *cold* (< proto-Germanic *kal-da-; compare Latin *gelidus*), and in many Latin words ending in *-tus*. (On roots and their meanings see further sections 4.4.1 and 8.7.3.)

The assumption made in the last paragraph that proto-Germanic *saða- is likely to have developed from proto-Indo-European *sǝto- may seem rather startling to anyone who does not have a prior acquaintance with Indo-European linguistics. On the face of it only the initial consonant *s is common to both forms. However, the development of the vowels is easily dealt with, by the principle of regular sound correspondences. Proto-Indo-European *ǝ (with the caveats given above) and (short) *o both regularly develop to *a in proto-Germanic, thus *sǝto- > *saða-. A sound change of this sort is called a merger: the phonetic development of *ǝ, *o, and *a in proto-Germanic led to loss of the distinction between the three separate proto-Indo-European phonemes and merger as the single phoneme *a in proto-Germanic. Compare Latin *hostis* 'stranger, enemy' with its cognate Gothic *gasts* 'guest', or Latin *hortus* 'garden' with its cognate Gothic *gards* 'garden'. (Latin *h* and Gothic *g* in these words show the regular development in Latin and in proto-Germanic of proto-Indo-European *gʰ; we will look further at the Germanic side of this in the next paragraph. The modern English cognates of these words are respectively *guest* and *yard*, showing the result of a number of sound changes during the history of English.)

---

[15] For a specialist readership, the best recent detailed account of the Germanic component of this etymology is provided (in German) by Heidermanns (1993) 458–9; on the Indo-European component see especially Szemerényi (1979).

Probably, on the basis of the evidence of other Indo-European languages, in proto-Germanic the reflexes of proto-Indo-European *ə̯ and *a merged first as *a, with which *o then also merged. Conversely, the proto-Indo-European long vowels *ō and *ā merge as *ō in proto-Germanic.

The explanation for the medial consonant in proto-Germanic *saða- is a little more complicated, and involves two reconstructed sound changes. Comparison among the Indo-European languages excluding Germanic leads to the reconstruction of three sets of stop consonants: voiceless stops (*p, *t, *k, *kʷ), voiced stops (*b, *d, *g, *gʷ), and breathy-voiced stops (*bʰ, *dʰ, *gʰ, *gʰʷ). Comparison with the forms in the Germanic languages leads to the conclusion that a series of sound shifts occurred in proto-Germanic:

$$*p > *f$$
$$*t > \theta \text{ (represented in traditional philological notation as } *\text{þ})$$
$$*k > *h$$
$$*k^w > *hw$$
$$*b > *p$$
$$*d > *t$$
$$*g > *k$$
$$*g^w > *kw$$
$$*b^h > *\beta \text{ (in some environments} > *b)$$
$$*d^h > *\eth \text{ (in some environments} > *d)$$
$$*g^h > *\gamma \text{ (in some environments} > *g)$$
$$*g^{hw} > *\gamma w \text{ (in some environments} > *gw)$$

Thus the voiceless stops became voiceless fricatives, the voiced stops became voiceless stops, and the breathy-voiced stops lost their breathy-voice and probably became fricatives before becoming voiced stops in many environments. Experts in fact differ on many details of this process, especially as regards the proto-Indo-European breathy-voiced stops and also the proto-Indo-European voiced stop *b (which was very rare, and some argue did not exist at all), but this is not of importance for our present purposes.[16] This sound change (or series of changes) is known as Grimm's Law, after the German philologist Jakob Grimm (1785–1863), who compiled with his brother Wilhelm both the celebrated fairy tale collection and the early

[16] The literature on Grimm's Law, and Verner's Law, is vast. For a recent detailed account of the changes see Ringe (2006) 93–116; for particularly useful analyses see also Bynon (1977) 83–6, Collinge (1985) 63–76. See also the discussion in section 7.1 below.

fascicles of the major historical dictionary of the German language. Grimm produced an important early formulation of this sound change, although it had in fact been described earlier by other scholars. An alternative name for this sound change is the Germanic Consonant Shift.

We can illustrate the changes in the proto-Indo-European voiceless stops with the following examples:

*p > *f

I-E root *ped- 'foot': ancient Greek poús (stem pod-), Latin pēs (stem ped-); Gothic fōtus, English foot

*t > *θ

I-E *tū 'you (singular)': Latin tū, Old Irish tū; Gothic þū, English thou

*k > *h

I-E root *kerd- 'heart': ancient Greek kardía, Latin cor (stem cord-); Gothic hairtō, English heart

*kʷ > *hw

I-E *kʷós 'who': Sanskrit kás 'who', Lithuanian kàs 'who, what'; Gothic hwas 'who', English who

In the first example here, 'foot', Grimm's Law explains not only the shift of the initial consonant from *p to *f but also the shift of the final consonant of the stem from *d to *t. However, it will be obvious at a glance that there are other differences between the cognates apart from those explained by Grimm's Law, even though I have attempted to select forms which have an unusually close mutual resemblance (another of the cognates of English foot is in fact Armenian otn). In the case of 'foot', the Greek, Latin, and Germanic words all have different stem vowels. In this instance the difference is not due to sound changes which have occurred in the daughter languages, but to slightly different etymons in proto-Indo-European: the Greek stem form pod- is from proto-Indo-European *pod-, the Latin stem form ped- is from proto-Indo-European *ped-, and the Germanic forms are from proto-Indo-European *pōd-. These different etymons are all derived from the root *ped- by a process known as ablaut which we will look at in section 4.4.1. This also explains the variation between *sə- and *sā- which we encountered above in the etymology of sad.

The operation of Grimm's Law thus explains why proto-Germanic *saða- < proto-Indo-European *səto- does not show medial *t, but it does not explain why it shows *ð rather than the expected *θ. This is explained by another sound change known as Verner's Law, after the Danish philologist

Karl Verner (1846–96), by which the proto-Germanic voiceless fricatives became voiced whenever the accent did not fall on the immediately preceding syllable. (For an analogous situation in modern English, compare *ex'ert* /ɛg'zə:t/ with *'exercise* /'ɛksəsʌɪz/.) In the ancestor of *sad* the suffix, not the root, was stressed, and hence Verner's Law applied, giving voiced *ð. Later, the accent shifted to the first syllable in all words in proto-Germanic, thus giving the pattern which we find reflected in all of the recorded Germanic languages. Hence, finally, we can explain how proto-Indo-European *sə'to would give rise to proto-Germanic *'saða, via the following stages: *sə'to > *sa'ta > *sa'θa > *sa'ða > *'saða. We will not do so here, but pre-histories can similarly be reconstructed for classical Latin *sat, satis, satur*, Lithuanian *sotus*, and also ancient Greek *áatos*, and it is this (rather than vague resemblance in form and meaning) which gives substance to the hypothesis that all of these forms are ultimately cognate.

We will return to Grimm's Law and Verner's Law in a little more detail at the beginning of chapter 7, but for the time being there are one or two very important general observations which arise from this example. Note that in the preceding paragraph I said that proto-Indo-European *sə̥to- 'would give rise to' proto-Germanic *saða-, and not 'could give rise to'. The merger of *ə, *o, and *a as *a in proto-Germanic, and the Grimm's Law and Verner's Law changes, are all regular processes, which apply in all cases (where not excluded by specific phonetic environments, which simply involve more precise statement of what the sound change was and in which environments it applied). The standard methodology of comparative linguistics does not permit us to say 'perhaps in this particular instance the merger simply did not happen' or 'perhaps Grimm's Law did not apply to this word' or 'perhaps in this instance an entirely unparalleled change of *ð to *m occurred'. As I have formulated it here, this is an oversimplification, but not a huge one. In chapter 7 we will look at the reasoning behind this in much more detail, and at some important qualifications, but for present purposes it is sufficient to be aware that comparative reconstruction depends upon the regularity of the correspondences and sound changes which are posited: this (as well as general phonetic plausibility, and the existence of parallels in the documented history of languages) is what gives a solid foundation to comparative etymological research.

A useful illustration of this principle is shown by the histories of the words *mother*, *father*, and *brother*. All three words show a voiced fricative /ð/ in modern English. However, in Old English the situation was rather different: *brōðor* 'brother' showed a voiced fricative /ð/, but *mōdor* 'mother' and *fæder* 'father' both showed a voiced plosive /d/. In proto-Indo-European all three words in fact showed the same termination, *-tēr-* (in the nominative case), which seems typical of terms for family kinship: **mātēr* 'mother', **pəƫēr* 'father', and **bhrātēr* 'brother';[17] compare Latin *māter* 'mother', *pater* 'father', *frāter* 'brother' (proto-Indo-European **b^h* > *f* in word-initial position in Latin; compare also Sanskrit *bhrātar-*). The explanation for the different outcomes in Old English is the regular operation of Verner's Law. In the case of *mother* and *father* the stress in proto-Germanic fell on the second syllable, while in the case of *brother* it fell on the first syllable. Thus Verner's Law applied in the case of *mother* and *father*, but not in the case of *brother*, and so we find that proto-Germanic **brōþēr*, with voiceless fricative **θ*, corresponds to Latin *frāter*, but that proto-Germanic **mōðēr* and **faðēr*, with voiced fricative **ð*, correspond to Latin *māter* and *pater*. In *mother* and *father* the proto-Germanic voiced fricative subsequently became a plosive in West Germanic, just as in the case of *sad*, hence Old English *mōder* (or in fact more commonly *mōdor*, showing variation in the unstressed vowel of the second syllable) and *fæder*. In the case of *brother*, the medial voiceless fricative of proto-Germanic **brōþēr* became voiced in intervocalic position in Old English, hence Old English *brōðer* (again in fact more commonly *brōðor*). Subsequently, in late Middle English, by another sound change, the voiced plosive of *moder* and *fader* developed into a fricative before either /ər/ or syllabic /r/, resulting from reduction or loss of the vowel in the endings *-or*, *-er*. Thus, *mother* and *father* came to have the same voiced fricative as *brother*. So we can see that *mother*, *father*, and *brother* provide a very rare example of how subsequent sound changes can, very occasionally and entirely fortuitously, restore a formal resemblance which had been obscured by a much earlier sound change (figure 1.3). We have also now seen how *brother* and *friar*, discussed in section 1.2.1, are in fact cognate, both being ultimately from proto-Indo-European **bhrātēr*. In the latter case the development was: *friar* < Old French *frere* < Latin *frāter* < proto-Indo-European **bhrātēr*.

---

[17] In the reconstructions **mātēr* and **bhrātēr* the **ā* in the first syllable shows what is now generally considered to have been the output of earlier **eh₂*, i.e. the vowel **e* followed by a laryngeal which caused colouring and lengthening of the vowel. For a fuller explanation of this see section 4.4.1.

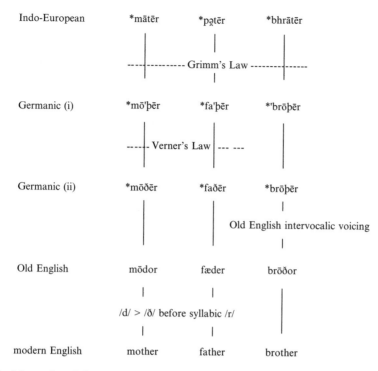

Fig 1.3 *mother, father,* and *brother* from proto-Indo-European to modern English

1.2.5 Summary

Our initial supposition about the meaning development of *sad* within English was supported by comparison with the meanings of its cognates in other Germanic languages, and ultimately also by the meanings of its cognates elsewhere in Indo-European.

In tracing the word's cognates at a great time depth we have seen the importance of regular sound correspondences and of regular sound changes in accounting for apparent discrepancies. We will return to this topic in more detail in chapter 7.

In the etymologies of both *friar* and *sad*, there is little or no connection between the processes of formal development and the processes of meaning development that we have examined. This is often the case, although there are also cases where form history and meaning history are very closely intertwined, and we will look closely at a number of such cases in chapters 7 and 8.

1.3 Why study etymology?

1.3.1 Etymology, historical and comparative grammars, and dictionaries

Etymology is an essential tool in reconstructing the history of a language, since a corpus of word histories provides a necessary basis for many other aspects of historical linguistic work. Conversely, each individual word history depends for its plausibility on the work that has been done in various subfields of historical linguistics. For instance, someone interested in historical semantics will want to look at the meaning histories of individual words which have been traced through the application of etymology, just as an etymologist will want to draw on the general observations about a whole body of meaning changes and their likely motivations which have been identified by specialists in historical semantics. Each activity informs and enriches the other in a mutually beneficial relationship.

Traditionally, etymology has been associated most closely with the construction of historical and comparative grammars. A historical grammar traces the developments in word forms which are found in the history of a language, often also extending into its pre-history. A comparative grammar relates the developments found in one language to those found in cognate languages, to explain the development of two or more languages from a common source using the technique of comparative reconstruction.

We have seen in the case of *friar* an example of how etymology interacts with the functions of a historical grammar:

- Etymological investigation suggests that *friar* shows the continuation of Middle English *frere*.
- A historical grammar identifies parallels such as *briar* and *choir* (themselves the result of other etymological investigations). Ideally, it will also supply an explanation for the unusual form history shown by such groups of words.

Our investigation of *sad* gave an insight into the world of comparative etymology and comparative reconstruction. The identification of regular sound correspondences depends at first upon the investigation of large numbers of potential etymological connections. This may make it possible to identify the regular processes of sound change. If so, our corpus of etymologies can be refined, and some at first apparently attractive connections can be discarded, at least until we can find a new explanation to account for them.

The best illustration of this may be to look at an example of how a sound method may enable us to identify a case of chance resemblance. If we start out, from an entirely uninformed perspective, by looking simply for words which are similar in form and meaning, English *care* and Latin *cūra* 'care' might seem attractive candidates for investigation: they overlap completely in their core meaning, and the consonants at least are the same. There is thus more resemblance in both form and meaning than there is between English *sad* and Latin *satis* 'enough' or Lithuanian *sotus* 'filling, full, satisfied, substantial'. However, English *care* is an inherited Germanic word, with a good set of cognates from all branches of Germanic which enable us to reconstruct a proto-Germanic form *karō-*. If we remember Grimm's Law, we will see that proto-Germanic /k/ is not going to correspond to Latin /k/, and in fact proto-Germanic *karō-* is usually referred to a proto-Indo-European root *gar-* with the meaning 'to call, cry'. This same root is probably reflected also by Latin *garrīre* 'to chatter' (ultimately the base of English *garrulous*). Latin *cūra* shows the regular development of an earlier form *koisā*, which can be reconstructed on the basis of forms in inscriptions and cognates from other Italic dialects; it has no generally accepted further etymology, but could not conceivably be connected with proto-Germanic *karō-*. In fact some doubts have been raised about the connection of proto-Germanic *karō-* with proto-Indo-European *gar-*.[18] Revised or contested hypotheses are very common in etymological work at this sort of time depth. However, the important point is that a connection with Latin *cūra* remains impossible, even if we have no viable etymology for *karō-*: we do not need to have an alternative explanation in order to reject an impossible etymology.

Latin *deus* 'god' and Greek *theós* 'god' are another pair of words which are synonymous and have a superficial resemblance in form, but which the methodology of comparative linguistics demonstrates have no etymological connection whatever: the first goes back to proto-Indo-European *deiwós* and the other probably to proto-Indo-European *dhesos*. We can thus make an important generalization: comparative reconstruction provides an essential tool for quickly eliminating very many cases of chance resemblance in form and meaning, just as it identifies many cognates which have little or no superficial resemblance in form or meaning.[19] It also leaves us with

---

[18]   See for instance (in German) Rix (2001) 161.

[19]   For an excellent and much more detailed account of these and related issues see Campbell (2003).

very many rather doubtful cases, some examples of which we will examine later.

Sometimes 'etymology' has been seen as almost synonymous with 'comparative reconstruction', or at least it has been assumed that everything else which an etymologist has to consider is of secondary importance in comparison with the reconstruction of antecedent word forms and the identification of historical sound changes. This will not be entirely the approach adopted in this book, although it should not be forgotten that form history, as reflected in historical and comparative grammars, provides the backbone for nearly all etymological research: we will examine in detail in chapters 7 and 8 how and why it is that arguments based on word form usually provide by far the strongest foundation for etymologies.

Comparative reconstruction has a sister methodology known as internal reconstruction, in which reconstruction is based purely on the data provided by a single language. This is generally much more limited, and also less reliable, than comparative reconstruction, and it will not be a major topic in this book, although it should be noted that methods of internal reconstruction have contributed some important advances in knowledge even in areas such as Indo-European linguistics where the comparative data is relatively rich and plentiful. It tends to be most effective in tracing the origins of morphophonemic relationships, as between English *mouse* and *mice* (see section 7.2.4) or the contrast between voiceless and voiced consonants in German *Rad* and *Rades* (section 2.1.1.3), although even here comparative data is often much more conclusive.[20] One very important and justly famous success of internal reconstruction was Ferdinand de Saussure's identification in the late nineteenth century of a series of hypothetical sounds in proto-Indo-European which he termed (in French) 'coefficients sonantiques'. These are now generally recognized as a series of so-called laryngeal sounds (although their exact quality is in fact unknown and the subject of much dispute). Hittite documents which began to be deciphered and studied in detail in the early twentieth century, long after Saussure's initial hypothesis based on internal reconstruction, provided crucial data which confirmed the reconstruction.[21] We will return to this topic, and to its implications for the sound represented by *ə in the proto-Indo-European reconstructed forms given here, in section 4.4.1.

[20] For thorough accounts of internal reconstruction see Fox (1995) or Ringe (2003).

[21] For short accounts of this see for example Fortson (2004) 75–6; also Hock (1991) 545–9, Clackson (2007) 53–61, or Millar (2007) 322–7.

Aside from historical and comparative grammars, etymology is also a crucial scholarly tool in historical lexicography. Historical dictionaries present in linear form the word histories which are treated thematically in grammars: in grammars we can see the connections between the developments shown by individual words, while in historical dictionaries we can see word histories whole and uninterrupted, together with the interplay between form history and meaning history, and at least some information on the influence of extralinguistic cultural and historical factors.

1.3.2 Historical relationships between words

A key function of etymology is that it illuminates the formal and semantic relationships between the words of a language. This is an area where a layman's interests may not be entirely dissimilar to those of a historical linguist, and thus it can be a very good entry point for people who are relatively new to the study of etymology. Indeed, this topic is of particular interest for speakers of a language like English which has seen a good deal of borrowing, and where the semantic relationship between for example *hand* and *manual* 'involving the hand, operated by hand, etc.' is obscured by the absence of any formal relationship between the two words. In this particular instance, the word *manual* is ultimately a derivative formation from a word meaning 'hand', but the word in question is Latin *manus* 'hand' (plus a Latin suffix - *ālis* which forms adjectives with the meaning 'connected with') rather than English *hand*. Latin *manuālis* was borrowed into English (via French) as *manual* in the fifteenth century. For a time it competed with a word with the same meaning which did have a transparent formal relationship with *hand*, namely *handy*. This word today only has the specialized meanings 'convenient to handle or use', 'ready to hand', 'skilful, good with his or her hands', but in early use it also had the meaning 'done by hand, manual'. It is formed from *hand* and the suffix -*y* (which has a function similar to Latin -*ālis*), although this is not the full story: *handy* probably originally arose as a result of reanalysis of the word *handiwork*, which was itself formed much earlier. *handiwork* is not (as we may at first assume) formed from *handy* and *work* but from *hand* and the obsolete noun *geweorc* 'work', which is a derivative of Old English *weorc* 'work' formed with a prefix *ge-* which had a collective meaning (thus 'work collectively') and which was pronounced with a palatal initial consonant /j/, thus /jeweərk/. In course of time phonetic reduction occurred in the unstressed medial syllable of *handgeweorc*, giving the form *handiwork*, which was then reanalysed as showing *hand*, *-y*, and *work*.

This small example illustrates some very important tendencies in word histories, which etymologists must always bear in mind. There will often be a formal relationship between words which have a semantic connection with one another. Thus, a word which means 'performed by hand' will very likely be related in form to a word meaning 'hand': in English we can imagine compound formations such as **hand-done* (compare *handmade*) or derivative formations such as **handish*, *handly*, or indeed *handy*. The asterisk here indicates entirely hypothetical word forms, rather than reconstructed word forms as we saw before with **saða-* in section 1.2.4. The word *handly* has no asterisk because it is in fact recorded several times in Middle English, and with precisely the meaning 'manual'. It was thus another synonym in competition with *manual* and *handy*.

This sort of relationship is called an iconic one: the word forms echo what seems to be the intuitive meaning relationship between the words. Such compound or derivative formations are called transparent when there is a clear form-and-meaning relationship between the complex word and its component parts. (We will look at transparency in more detail in chapter 2, and iconicity in chapter 4.)

Borrowing can disrupt these relationships, if, as typically happens, not all of the words in a related group are borrowed. In this particular instance so-called prestige borrowing of a relatively technical word has occurred, but the more basic word *hand* has not been replaced by a parallel borrowing of (Anglo-)French *main* or Latin *manus*. We will look at different sorts of borrowing situations, and their often unpredictable outcomes, in much more detail in chapters 5 and 6. For one example of the rather messy results of different borrowing processes compare the synonymous nouns *manual* and *handbook* in modern English. Both denote a book containing concise information readily to hand. *manual* shows borrowing from (Anglo-) French *manual*, which is itself from Latin *manuāle*. *handbook* was formed as a calque or loan translation (see section 5.1.2) on the model of Latin *manuāle*, although in modern use it owes its currency mostly to the influence of German *Handbuch* in the nineteenth century (which was also formed on the model of Latin *manuāle*).

handiwork shows another typical process, where the composition of a word has become obscured or opaque with the passage of time. Had Old English *geweorc* survived into Middle English it would have had the form *iwork (or more properly *iwerk), and so it would have paralleled the formal changes shown by handiwork, but it did not survive, and handiwork became as it were an 'orphan', open to reinterpretation as showing hand, -y, and work. This reanalysis leads to the appearance of the adjective handy, and probably also to the remodelling of the word handcraft as handicraft. Thus, loss of other words in the linguistic system can lead to what were originally transparent relationships becoming opaque. Opacity can also result from many other factors, such as sound change. The great counter-force is analogy, in this case leading to reanalysis of handiwork and the formation of new words on the same pattern, thus setting up a new set of correspondences between form and meaning, albeit ones quite different from those found earlier in the word's history. (We will look at the workings of analogy in detail in chapter 7.)

We see here that an example of how etymology can help us to understand oddities in the modern-day structure of the vocabulary of a language has also brought us back to the interconnection of etymology with many other aspects of historical linguistics. This is one of the most fascinating aspects of etymology: we can move quite swiftly from interesting information which helps inform our understanding of the historical relationships between words in everyday use, to data that helps us to understand processes of historical linguistic change. Indeed, very often the same information serves both functions at once.

1.3.3 The etymological fallacy

It may seem odd to spend part of this chapter discussing what etymology is not for, but the misconceptions are very widespread, and colour many popular ideas about word histories. Additionally, of course, in examining what etymology is not about, we will uncover a good deal of what it really is about, and we will also see some further illustrations of how words change in both form and meaning over time.

The etymological fallacy is the idea that knowing about a word's origin, and particularly its original meaning, gives us the key to understanding its present-day use. Very frequently, this is combined with an assertion about how a word ought to be used today: certain uses are privileged as 'etymological' and hence 'valid', while others are regarded as 'unetymological' and hence 'invalid' (or at least 'less valid'). This attitude certainly has a venerable history: the word etymology is itself ultimately from ancient

Greek *etumología*, which is formed from *étumos* 'true' and *lógos* 'word, speech', hence denoting 'the study of true meanings or forms'.[22]

Perhaps the easiest way to illustrate the assumptions lying behind the etymological fallacy is to look at some verbal controversies of the relatively recent past. Today use of the word *meticulous* in the sense 'painstakingly careful' is perfectly normal and does not invite any negative reaction, but in the late nineteenth and early twentieth centuries it attracted a good deal of comment. The central ground of the objection was etymological. The word comes ultimately from Latin *metus* 'fear', and it first occurs in English (as also in French) in the sixteenth and seventeenth centuries in the sense 'fearful', for instance in the Older Scots writer William Stewart's translation of Hector Boece's *Chronicle of Scotland*, 'Gif thow be...Meticulos, and dar nocht se blude drawin' ('if you are fearful, and do not dare see blood drawn').[23] The word resurfaces in French in the early nineteenth century in the sense 'overscrupulous', with the connotation 'fearful of making a mistake', and it swiftly enters English in this sense, being found in 1827 in *Blackwood's Magazine*: 'He does many things which we ourselves, and we do not hold ourselves peculiarly meticulous, will not venture upon.' However, the word subsequently developed more positive connotations in both French and English, as defined by the *OED*: 'Subsequently usually in more positive sense: careful, punctilious, scrupulous, precise'. As we will see in chapter 8, this is a very far from unusual process of semantic change: the word's meaning has first narrowed, and then it has developed more positive connotations or ameliorated – or in this particular instance, it would perhaps be more accurate to say that it has lost its negative connotations. But for many prescriptive commentators on English usage in the early twentieth century, this new sense was to be avoided, on the grounds that it was not sanctioned by the word's history, and specifically by the meaning of the Latin word from which it was ultimately borrowed. (For a useful summary of such comment see *Webster's Dictionary of English Usage* (1989) 634.)

---

[22] On the early history of the word and the concept see the short sketch in Lass (2007) §8.1.1 and further references there, and also the discussion in the four chronological volumes of Lepschy (1994a), (1994b), (1998), and Morpurgo Davies (1998). On the study of the etymology of English words up to 1882, when the first fascicle of the *OED* appeared, see Görlach (2002b) 71–136. On etymology in the twentieth century see especially Malkiel (1993).

[23] See *OED3* at *meticulous* adj., as also for the quotation from *Blackwood's Magazine* below.

Similarly, the word *obnoxious* comes ultimately from Latin *obnoxius*, which is formed from the preposition *ob* 'in front of, in view of' and the noun *noxa* 'hurt, injury' (compare modern English *noxious*, used frequently of harmful substances, especially gases). The Latin adjective had the meanings 'exposed to harm, liable, answerable, submissive, subject to punishment', and it is broadly these meanings which are commonest from the word's first occurrence in English in the sixteenth century down to the nineteenth century. As late as 1902 we find in William James *Varieties of Religious Experience*: 'The impulse…is…far too immediate and spontaneous an expression of self-despair and anxiety to be obnoxious to any such reproach.'[24] However, from the late seventeenth century onwards we find a sense which the *OED* defines as: 'Offensive, objectionable, odious, highly disagreeable. Now esp. (of a person): giving offence, acting objectionably; extremely unpleasant, highly dislikeable.' This results from association with *noxious*, and has become the usual sense in modern English (indeed it is the only one for which the *OED* records any examples later than 1902), but in the nineteenth century use in this sense was a matter of contention, and again the focus of debate was the word's etymology. (For a summary see again *Webster's Dictionary of English Usage* (1989) 676.)

These are both complex words, and their original meaning is to some extent guessable for people who know some Latin because the composition of each word is transparent. It is notable that in English attempts to determine usage by recourse to etymology very often involve words of Latin origin, and particularly words which remain reasonably close in form to their Latin etymons, so that the historical connection between the two is fairly obvious, as in the cases of *meticulous* or *obnoxious*. We can see an interesting cultural phenomenon in action here, where the authority of an ancient language is taken to be an effective arbiter of usage even in a quite different language some two thousand years later. However, so far as the scientific study of language is concerned, such assertions about the authority of 'etymological meanings' are quite irrelevant; or rather, if they are relevant to anyone, it is to people studying attitudes towards language use, rather than to etymologists. It is one of the linguistic facts of life that words change both in form and in meaning. Predicting exactly what those changes will be and when they will occur is normally impossible, although

---

[24] See *OED3* at *obnoxious* adj.

describing and explaining changes which have occurred in the past is a much more achievable goal, and forms the main focus of this book.

The changes in meaning shown by *meticulous* or *obnoxious* look very minor when compared with some much more dramatic changes in meaning which have occurred during the recorded history of English, but which tend to be noticed only by linguistic historians and by people reading texts from earlier periods.

To take a much cited example, the English word *deer* originally denoted any animal, as its cognates Dutch *dier* and German *Tier* still do today. However, in the course of the Middle English period the word came to be applied more and more often specifically to the deer, and in early modern English the broader sense 'animal' was lost completely, so that whenever the word occurred it had the narrowed sense 'deer'. Explaining why this happened is much more difficult, and in spite of the popularity of this example in the literature, there is no generally accepted explanation.[25]

To take another example, the word *treacle* originally (from the fourteenth century) denoted a kind of medicine, as it did also in its donor language French and in the other Romance languages; in an extended figurative meaning it could denote anything with healing effects. Its transferred use to denote a type of sugar product dates only from the end of the seventeenth century, but now is the only one which remains in current use (except when this sense is itself used figuratively, especially of compliments or praise).

We will look in more detail at the mechanisms of meaning change in chapter 8, but we should already be able to put the etymological fallacy to one side if we consider how foolish it would be to assert that English *deer* should be used in the sense 'animal' (and another word be used in the meaning 'deer') because of its history and the modern meanings of its cognates Dutch *dier* and German *Tier*, or that *treacle* should revert to the meaning 'medicine' because of its history (its ultimate etymon in Greek in fact means an antidote against a venomous bite). Earlier in this chapter we

---

[25] For one attempt see Samuels (1972) 73–4, who examines the relationships between the terms *beast*, *hart*, and *deer* in Middle English, and suggests that the homophony between *hart* and *heart* may have blocked adoption of *hart* as a general term for the deer, while partial homophony between *deer* and the adjective *dear* may have been a pressure against continued use of *deer* to denote more ferocious wild animals. Such arguments based on what is often termed 'dangerous homophony' are controversial, especially in cases where, as in this instance, genuine ambiguity must rarely if ever have occurred. See further discussion of arguments of this type in section 3.8.

saw a similarly dramatic semantic development in the word *sad*: it would be absurd to suggest today that *sad* should be used only in the sense 'satisfied' because of its etymology.

1.4 What an etymologist does

Our initial investigation of the comparative method has given a first illustration of the methodology of an etymologist. Various aspects of this methodology will take up most of the rest of this book. We will end this first chapter by considering some of the typical activities that characterize etymological research. In any (hypothetical) day of etymological research a lot of what happens will depend upon the particular circumstances of the language or period being studied, reflecting such factors as how much data is available, and what form that data takes. However, some things are almost certain to be true: there will be few, if any, blinding flashes of insight, and any that do occur will be the result of a good deal of painstaking work. Gathering data together (from important source texts, from corpora, from dictionaries, or from the work of previous researchers) is likely to figure largely, along with the careful analysis of this data. Frequently this analysis will involve approaching the same material time and again from different points of view, testing out one hypothesis after another, and probably discarding most of them as they run aground in insuperable difficulties. When real progress is made, it is most likely that it will emerge slowly, as the etymologist attempts to approach the same set of data with (yet) another hypothesis, to find that on this occasion the hypothesis does not collapse, but holds up against all of the challenges that one can think of to test it with. And then very probably one puts the hypothesis to one side for a little while and comes back to it another day, to see whether one had overlooked an obvious difficulty. Only then may one begin to feel that perhaps some real progress has been made.

Whenever we try to establish a link between two pieces of data, we must remember to check how plausible this link is from a variety of different perspectives. Is there any difficulty semantically? Can we find parallels for any changes in meaning that we assume? Is the connection acceptable phonologically? If phonological changes are posited, are they plausible, and do we have parallels for them? Are any morphological relationships which are posited plausible, and are they supported by parallels? Finally, is this hypothesis demonstrably preferable to any others which have been proposed or which we can formulate?

More often than not, the word history which emerges from this process will reflect the work of more than one researcher. A lot of etymological research involves taking up the threads of past investigations, carefully going through the work of previous researchers (who perhaps worked generations ago), and seeing whether new data or new insights help reinforce and confirm a hypothesis suggested by earlier research, or instead challenge this hypothesis, or even suggest a new one. Fortunately, a lot of etymological work ages rather well. Of course, we must always be very careful when revisiting older scholarship to take note of any places where it rests on outdated assumptions, and to investigate it rigorously by applying modern methodologies and procedures. But so long as due caution is exercised, a great deal of scholarship dating from at least as far back as the late nineteenth century is still an excellent foundation for further work. There is, of course, a good reason for this: as we have already noted in discussing Verner's Law, many of the most important advances in the development of linguistic reconstruction and the comparative method belong to the late nineteenth century, and although there have been very important methodological advances since then, much of the scholarship of that period still does not appear to be in a completely alien scholarly 'language'.

Finally, words form part of a system, the lexis of a language, with numerous links to its grammar also. Any change in our understanding of one part of that system may have echoes or repercussions in another, possibly quite distantly removed, part of the same large system, and we must always be alert to such implications in our own or others' work. Sometimes, one changed etymology can open the way to a whole set of new solutions to old problems. One should bear in mind the adage of the great French comparative linguist and etymologist Antoine Meillet that a language is 'un système . . . où tout se tient', 'a system where everything is connected' (Meillet (1921) 16; also cited in similar form at many other points in Meillet's work: see Koerner (1999)). Some linguists would reformulate this as 'a system where many things are connected', but still we should be alert to the implications that one etymology may have for many other word histories. Additionally, we must never forget that words and languages are spoken by real people, living in a particular society at a particular point in history, and it is in the usage of individual speakers that changes in word form and word meaning arise and develop. In order to understand the words of the past we must often immerse ourselves in its material and intellectual culture, in order to trace connections between words and concepts which may seem quite unrelated from a modern perspective. We should also give consideration to the many different registers and styles of language, and the specialist vocabularies of different groups and communities. When we take account of such issues, we are likely to produce much better etymologies, and we may also make some important discoveries about social and cultural history.

As we have seen, a lot of argumentation in etymology, whether it concerns form history or meaning history, works on the basis of establishing parallels, in order to identify regular patterns of language change which lend support to individual etymologies. However, if we also have a reasonable explanation for why a change may have occurred, this is inherently much more satisfying, and more productive for work in historical linguistics in general. Additionally, if we have a plausible explanation for why a change is likely to have happened in one case, we can assess whether similar circumstances are likely to have existed in a hypothetical parallel case.

The task of an etymologist is thus a very large one. It was described with characteristic boldness by one of the great etymologists of the twentieth century, Walther von Wartburg:

> Today the task of etymology is no longer solely to look for the root of a word or group of words. It must follow the group in question throughout the whole period during which it belongs to the language, in all its ramifications and all its relations to other groups, constantly asking the questions appropriate to etymology in the strict sense of the word.
>
> (von Wartburg, tr. Reid (1969) 121)[26]

We may not always be able to answer all of the questions that such an investigation poses, and sometimes there may be so little evidence that we can barely establish any trace even of a word's existence, but we should still not lose sight of this ultimate aim.

---

[26] Die Erforschung des Radix eines Wortes oder einer Wortgruppe ist heute nicht mehr die einzige Aufgabe der Etymologie. Sie hat die zu betrachtende Wortgruppe in ihrer Verästelung und mit all ihren Beziehungen zu anderen Gruppen während der ganzen Zeit, da sie einer Sprache angehört, zu verfolgen, ohne jemals die etymologisierende Fragestellung aufzugeben.

(von Wartburg (1962) 120–1)

2

What is a word? Which words need etymologies?

In chapter 1 we encountered some of the main characteristics of etymology, its aims, and some important features of its methodology. We considered some examples of change in word meaning and change in word form, and began to look at some of the mechanisms by which both of these occur. We will return to these topics in more detail later. In this chapter and the next we will take a closer look at the main objects of study in etymological research, words. In etymological dictionaries a 'word' stands at the head of each dictionary entry, and the status and selection of these words can seem to be a given. However, the identification of words as coherent entities for study raises a number of quite complex questions. Additionally, selection of which words to concentrate on is a far from trivial matter.

2.1 What are words?

2.1.1 Problems of definition

So far in this book I have taken the term 'word' rather for granted, as being a self-evident one which any reader will readily understand. The concept is very familiar to a non-specialist, and the term forms part of general vocabulary and so does not have to be learnt by beginners in linguistics, unlike phoneme, morpheme, etc. In literate societies lay conceptions of word boundaries (i.e. where one word ends and another begins) are often very much bound up with literacy and the rules of various writing systems, but there is also at least some evidence that non-literate speakers of languages with no written form also have intuitions about word boundaries, as do children who have not yet learned to read in literate societies.[1] However, it is also notoriously difficult to define a 'word' in a way which makes sense consistently at all levels of linguistic analysis. Specialists in morphology and also in phonology often grapple with this particular problem, and a full discussion would take up much more space than is available to us here. The discussion that follows will be brief, and will focus on those aspects which most affect etymological research.[2]

2.1.1.1 *Spelling*   A non-specialist from most modern literate societies who is asked what a word is will probably say that the words in a sentence are the things written with a space on either side. This definition is unsatisfactory for linguists for various reasons. Firstly, not all languages have a written form, and even when they do they do not necessarily separate words. Certainly, the way that many languages are written tells us something about writers' intuitions about what constitute words, but a definition on this basis runs the risk of circularity, and is also detached from any analysis of linguistic structure: by this criterion, words are the things that people write as separate words (i.e. with spaces between them) because they perceive them as separate words (whatever that may mean).

Written language also tends to be rather inconsistent in its treatment of certain kinds of units. Any survey even of published written English will show very considerable variation in whether some combinations of two nouns are written as a solid, or with a hyphen, or with a space between the two elements. Thus *lunchbox* can also appear as either *lunch box* or *lunch-box*, and even dictionaries do not agree on which to list as a preferred spelling. We would have to resort to some very odd reasoning to argue that *lunchbox* is one word but *lunch box* is two: both have the same meaning and behave the same way syntactically, as does *lunch-box*, and in the spoken language the pronunciation is the same for all three. This leads to the

---

[1] See further Bauer (2003) 57, Sapir (1921) 34–5.

[2] For detailed discussion of most of the points in this section see e.g. Bauer (2003), which I have largely followed here, or (with some slightly different perspectives) Adams (2001: 2–5), Booij (2007: 281–94), Plag (2003: 4–9).

fairly obvious conclusion that we are looking at three different spellings of precisely the same linguistic unit.

2.1.1.2 *Meaning*   One useful and conventional way of thinking about words as linguistic units is that a word is a linguistic sign which has both form and meaning. (We will come to the very important concept of the arbitrariness of this linguistic sign in chapter 4.) Linguistic meaning is expressed by the combination of units in a sentence. This might seem to give us a shortcut to a definition of a word: words are minimal units of meaning in a sentence. However, a little reflection will present us with some major problems. It is not always possible to infer the established, conventional or institutionalized meaning of phrases from their constituent words: consider idioms like *it's raining cats and dogs* (and see further section 2.1.5 below). There is also ample evidence that people often analyse the morphological composition of unfamiliar complex words as and when they hear them in order to interpret their meaning, and that they do this as part of their general competence as speakers of a language. For instance, if someone knows the word *vinaceous* 'of the colour of red wine' they are unlikely to have any more difficulty in understanding the derivative formations *vinaceousness* or *vinaceously* than the phrase *very vinaceous*, although they will probably never have encountered these particular derivative words before. (Both words are extremely rare, and even a Google search shows only a couple of examples of each.)

2.1.1.3 *Phonological criteria*   Phonological criteria can provide very useful evidence about word boundaries. In some languages, probably including proto-Germanic at one point in its history, stress regularly falls at the beginning of a word. (In proto-Germanic more accurately on the first syllable of a lexical root, rather than on prefixes.) In some other languages, such as modern English, each word has a particular syllable on which the main stress will normally fall if that word is stressed in a sentence (e.g. ˈkindness, inˈeptitude, inconˈsolable); but this is not true of all languages.

Some phonological processes apply only at particular positions in a word. In the history of German a sound change occurred by which obstruents were devoiced when they occurred word-finally, but not when they occurred medially or initially, giving rise to a situation in modern German where e.g. *Rat* 'counsel' and *Rad* 'wheel' are homophonous in the nominative singular (both /raːt/) but not in inflected case forms in which an inflectional ending follows the obstruent (e.g. genitive singular *Rates* /raːtəs/ 'of counsel' beside *Rades* /raːdəs/ 'of a wheel').[3] Some phonological processes, especially vowel harmony, typically operate across syllable boundaries within a word, but not across word boundaries. (See for example section 7.2.4 on *i*-mutation in the history of English.) However, other processes do apply across word boundaries, such as the assimilatory devoicing in English /haftuː/ as a realization of *have to*. This is usually called external sandhi, following the terminology of the ancient Sanskrit grammarians.

2.1.1.4 *Morphological criteria*   A commonly cited morphological criterion is that words are uninterruptible units, although there are exceptions, as for instance when expletives are inserted in the middle of a word in English, e.g. *absobloominglutely*.

2.1.2 Problems of analysis

In addition to there being no generally accepted and completely satisfactory definition of what constitutes a word, there is also considerable scholarly disagreement about whether some particular linguistic units should be regarded as words or as phrases, i.e. syntactic combinations of more than one word. In English it is notoriously difficult to define what constitutes a compound and what constitutes a phrase. To begin with an unproblematic example, it would normally be accepted that *blackbird* is a compound, and *a black bird* is a noun phrase. *blackbird* has reference to a particular variety of bird, and if someone calls a crow a *blackbird* they will be using the English language in an idiosyncratic way that is unlikely to be understood by anyone else. However, if someone refers to a crow as *a black bird*, then they will be making a simple factual statement, and in grammatical terms we will analyse their utterance as a noun phrase showing *bird* as a head modified by the adjective *black*. Conversely, female and younger male blackbirds are mostly brown. Even white blackbirds sometimes occur, and they are still *blackbirds*, albeit uncharacteristic ones, although they are not *black birds*. However, if we try to extrapolate from this unproblematic example precisely what it is that distinguishes a compound from a phrase, we start to encounter some real difficulties:

---

[3] For discussion of this particular phenomenon from a number of different theoretical standpoints see Lass (1984).

- *blackbird* has a meaning not predictable from its component parts, whereas *black bird* refers very predictably to any bird which is black. But many phrases and idioms also have unpredictable meanings.
- *blackbird* is written without any spaces, *black bird* is written with a space. But compare again *lunchbox*, *lunch-box*, *lunch box*.
- In some languages an adjective will show agreement with a noun in a phrase but will show a bare stem form in a compound, giving a clear morphological criterion for telling phrases from adjective-noun compounds, but this is not the case in other languages such as modern English.
- *blackbird* shows stress on the first element, while *black bird* shows stress on *bird*, the head of the phrase. But consider *blackcurrant*, in American English typically *'blackcurrant*, but in British English typically *black 'currant* (except sometimes as the first element in a compound, when the stress may be shifted, e.g. *'blackcurrant bush*). Consider also idiosyncratic cases, such as street names ending in *street* (e.g. *'Downing Street*, *Coro'nation Street*, *'Ship Street*) as opposed to those ending in *road*, *lane*, *avenue*, etc. (e.g. *Station 'Road*, *Cemetery 'Road*, *Park 'Lane*, *Shaftesbury 'Avenue*).[4]

This last point in particular is the subject of much debate, but it is sufficient for our purposes to know that there is as yet no clear consensus.[5] In the case of adjective-noun compounds, gradability of the adjective can be a safer test, at least if the adjective is gradable:

- We may talk about *a very black bird*, or indeed *a very black blackbird*, but not **a very blackbird*.

However, this criterion often conflicts with what we might predict from the position of the stress. *red admiral*, the name of a type of butterfly, has stress on the second element, suggesting phrasal status, but we cannot speak of *a very red admiral* or *the reddest admiral* (at least, not if we are speaking about the butterfly; either phrase would be perfectly plausible if referring to the left-wing politics or the flushed face of a naval officer).

---

[4] For a useful discussion of these see Plag (2005).

[5] For a recent summary see Bauer (2006a), and also Bauer (1998a); for a sample of rather different views see Booij (2007) or Giegerich (2004).

2.1.3 Why these are not major problems for etymology

I have introduced these issues largely to show that the use of 'word' and 'compound' is not always uncontroversial, and because it is important to realize that the simple statement 'etymologists study the origins of words' may not really be so simple as it at first sounds.

Whatever definition of the term 'word' we adopt, etymologists cannot avoid interesting themselves very closely in many units much larger than the word. Very many phrases have complex meanings and complex histories which require etymological explanation. Furthermore, many single words have their origin in what is sometimes termed the univerbation of what were originally phrasal units consisting of more than one word, e.g.:

- *upon* < *up* and *on*
- *goodbye* shows a contraction of *God be with you*, with remodelling of the first element after *good day*, *good night*, etc.
- the phrase *at one* > the adverb *atone*, on which the abstract noun *atonement* is formed, which in turn gives rise to the verb *to atone*

In some other languages, such as French, lexicalized phrases frequently occur in meanings which are typically realized by compounds in English, for instance French *sac à main* beside English *handbag*. We can also examine the etymologies of units smaller than the word, for example derivational affixes such as *pre-*, *un-*, *-ness*, etc., and even morphological inflections, although these do raise some rather different issues, which we will explore in chapter 4.

Conversely, if we are studying a contemporary language, or even a past stage which has a large corpus of surviving evidence, then we cannot possibly pay attention to the etymology of every word ever uttered, or even every word ever recorded, in that language, and nor would we want to. As we will see in section 2.2.4, the lexicon of every language is constantly open to new words, formed according to the productive word-forming patterns of that language. Nearly all such new words are immediately transparent in meaning (when heard in the appropriate context) to other speakers of that language. Additionally, nearly all such words fail to enter more extensive usage, and remain 'one-offs' or nonce formations (although the same word may well be formed again, quite separately, by other speakers on other occasions).

2.1.4 Word forms and word meanings

If we return to the expression of meaning by words, we can observe that some words, like *a* or *the*, have grammatical content but no other meaning content. Other words, like *haddock* or *ankle*, have clear meaning content. Many words have multiple established meanings, i.e. they are polysemous, and we can only tell which meaning is intended from the context of a particular utterance. For example, we can speak of someone working in an *office* (a physical place) or holding an elected *office* (an abstract social role), or we can say that a container is *full* (there is no room left in it) or that the moon is *full* (none of the side turned towards the earth is in shade). In fact, meanings are often stretched or extended in particular contexts. It is only when particular new or extended meanings of words in particular contexts become institutionalized, i.e. used fairly frequently by different speakers of a language, and perhaps extended to other contexts, that they begin to be recorded in dictionaries. We will return to this point and its importance for etymological research in chapter 8.

Additionally, we need to distinguish between different homonyms, i.e. quite separate words which happen to be identical in form. For instance, distinct homonyms are shown by *file* 'type of metal tool' (of Germanic origin) and *file* 'set of documents' (a borrowing from French). In this instance the words are distinct from a synchronic point of view, since there is no semantic common ground between the meanings which they realize, and also from a diachronic point of view, since they have different histories. However, these two criteria do not always coincide, as we will explore in detail in section 3.3.

Meaning is also expressed by the inflections of a word, e.g. in the singular/plural distinction between *giraffe/giraffes*, *board/boards*, *fish/fishes*, *man/men*, etc. Technically, these inflected forms are distinct word forms, which belong to a single unit called a lexeme. In order to identify the lexeme to which the word forms *giraffe* and *giraffes* both correspond, we normally use what is called the citation form, i.e. the form that we can look up in a dictionary. So *giraffe* is the citation form of the lexeme which has the word forms *giraffe* and *giraffes* (also *giraffe's*, *giraffes'*). Sometimes small capitals are used to identify lexemes, e.g. GIRAFFE, MAN. Note that in the case of *man/men* the morphological relationship is realized by variation in the stem vowel, rather than by an inflectional affix (see further section 4.4.1).

Sometimes we find the phenomenon known as suppletion, where word forms of different historical origins stand in the same sort of relationship, within a grammatical paradigm, as inflected forms like *giraffe* and *giraffes* do to one another. Thus, *was* and *is* are not inflected forms of *be* (they are of a quite different historical origin), but they stand in the same paradigmatic relationship to it as *opened* and *opens* do to *open*. Similarly, *worse* and *worst* stand in the same paradigmatic relationship to *bad* as *poorer* and *poorest* do to *poor*. We can say that *be*, *was*, and *is* (and also *are*) are word forms of the lexeme BE, and that *worse* and *worst* are word forms of the lexeme BAD (and also of the lexeme BADLY). Interestingly, in the case of *worse* and *worst* this pattern is relatively modern. Both forms go back to the Old English period (Old English *wyrsa* and *wyrst*), and they have been the antonyms of *better* and *best* (Old English *betra* and *betst*) throughout their history in English, but the adjective in the general sense 'bad' to which they correspond (again suppletively) as comparative and superlative in Old English is *yfel* (modern English *evil*). In early Middle English we find a new adjective *ill* in many of the same senses as *evil*, and *worse* and *worst* are also found as its comparative and superlative. Finally, *bad* becomes increasingly common in senses formerly expressed by *evil* and *ill*, and gradually *worse* and *worst* become established as its comparative and superlative forms. However, there is a long transitional period in which *worse* and *worst* are found in paradigmatic relationships with all of these three words, e.g. we find examples of *from evil to worse*, *from ill to worse*, and *from bad to worse*. Thus patterns of suppletion can vary over time, and can also vary in the usage of particular individuals or speech communities within a particular period.

Suppletion is quite different from the phenomenon where different variants realize the same grammatical form of a single lexical item. Modern standardized written languages do much to disguise this sort of variation, but consider the regional differences in pronunciation between for example /tʊθ/ *tooth* in the English West Midlands as against /tuːθ/ elsewhere, or the variation in the pronunciation of *either* as / iːðə/ or / aɪðə/ in the speech of different individuals in both Britain and the US. This is an issue that we will look at in much more detail in chapter 3.

In this book, I will normally use 'word' rather loosely in the sense 'lexeme', and I will refer to words by their citation forms. This is not normally a problem in etymological work, so long as we have a more sophisticated terminology available for instances where we need to tease the various distinctions apart more carefully, and so long as we remain aware of the bundle of different forms and meanings which a single word may show.

2.1.5 Idioms

As we have noted, units larger than a single word also often have conventional or institutionalized meaning which is not predictable from their component parts. Idioms are by their nature constructions which are stored in one's memory and form part of one's competence in speaking a particular language, even if this only involves selection of the correct preposition or adverb in verbal constructions such as *to sober up*, or selection between for example *to engage in* 'to participate in' and *to engage with* 'to establish a meaningful contact or connection with'. In these particular cases it might be possible to interpret the meaning of the expression correctly even if one has not encountered it before, i.e. to apprehend it passively even if it lies outside one's active competence, but it is questionable how far most speakers ever stop to analyse idiomatic expressions such as *to catch up on, to give (something) up, to leave off (doing something), on the one hand ... on the other hand, to run (someone) to ground.*

There is thus a very strong case for listing idiomatic expressions in dictionaries, so long as they are in sufficiently common use. They are often denoted technically by the broader term lexical item, as distinct from individual words or lexemes. However, not every lexical item that is listed in a dictionary automatically requires etymological investigation. We may feel that constructions such as *to engage in* and *to engage with* will normally be outside the scope of etymological research. However, some of the examples given above are less clear-cut. Understanding of the origin of the idiom *on the one hand ... on the other hand* is helped by knowing that *hand* in earlier use had the senses 'side of the body' and more generally 'side, direction' (e.g. in an example from 1548 'on the other hand or side of the gate'[6]). The origin of *to run (someone) to ground* is understandable only when one realizes it originated in the specialist language of fox-hunting, referring to hounds running a fox to its burrow or earth. Many other idioms similarly rely on conventional metaphors which may or may not become opaque as a result of technological or cultural change, e.g. *to run out of steam* 'to lose impetus or enthusiasm' (which originated in the age of the steam engine) or

[6] See *OED* at *hand* n.[1] sense B.4.

to have shot one's bolt 'to have done all that one could do' (which originated in the age of the crossbow), while others reflect otherwise obsolete or near-obsolete senses of words, e.g. *to cut a caper* 'to make a playful, skipping movement, to act ridiculously' (showing *cut* in the sense 'to perform or execute' and *caper* 'a frolicsome leap, especially in dancing'). Some originate in quotations, e.g. biblical quotations or paraphrase such as *to turn the other cheek* or *to take someone's name in vain*, or quotations from Shakespeare such as *the milk of human kindness* or *the world's your oyster*. (This last example becomes rather less opaque when the metaphor is heard in its original fuller context: *The Merry Wives of Windsor* II. ii. Falstaff: *I will not lend thee a penny*. Pistol: *Why then, the world's mine oyster Which I with sword will open.*) We will take up the difficult issues that such cases raise about the role of non-linguistic, encyclopedic knowledge in etymological research in chapters 8 and 9. Some idioms remain stubbornly resistant to all attempts to explain their origin, e.g. *Bob's your uncle* 'there you are' (said in a situation where a task becomes easy to complete) or *the full monty* 'everything which is necessary, appropriate, or possible, the works'.

Sometimes idioms arise from remodelling of earlier expressions. For instance, the rather opaque expression *to have another thing coming* (as in, *If you think you can get away with that, you have another thing coming*) becomes much more readily explicable when a little etymological research reveals that it is an alteration of earlier *to have another think coming*, in which *think* 'action of thinking' has been replaced by the commoner word *thing* (perhaps as a result of homophony in casual speech), even though the outcome is an idiom which is semantically much more opaque.

2.2 How new words arise

As well as looking at word forms and how they realize meaning, we can look at structure within the word, and in a book on etymology it makes most sense to do this primarily from the point of view of word origins, and thus to take a preliminary look at how new words enter a language.

2.2.1 Monomorphemic words and complex words

An important initial distinction is between monomorphemic words and complex words. As the name implies, monomorphemic words are composed of only a single morpheme or meaningful unit. Examples which we encountered in chapter 1 include *friar*, *sad*, and *deer*: at least in modern English, these words are unanalysable units, and if we understand them it must either be because they are stored as meaningful units in our memory or because a given context in which they appear makes their meaning obvious. Other words are clearly analysable, such as *happiness*, *steadiness*, *freshness*, or *closeness*, although compare *highness*, which is analysable but not transparent, at least not in its use as an honorific title. It is important to note that it is not necessarily the case that these words are not also stored in our memory; but we can analyse all of them from their component parts (*happy*, *steady*, *fresh*, *close*, *high*, and the suffix *-ness*), and all except *highness* are semantically transparent. Throughout this section we will return often to the following questions:

(i) Do words of this type need to be included in an etymological dictionary?

(ii) Are words of this type interesting to etymologists?

We can immediately conclude that any monomorphemic words in a language will need to be included in any etymological dictionary which claims to be at all comprehensive, and that they will be of obvious interest to etymologists: from the point of view of the contemporary language they are stand-alone items which must have an origin and history which we will want to trace. A good case can also be made for including all affixes which are found in analysable words. (We will return to the etymologies of affixes in chapter 4.) The situation is much less clear-cut with words which are analysable, and we will need to look at a number of issues before we will be in any position to address this question.

2.2.2 Borrowed words

Words which have been borrowed from another language are typically monomorphemic, such as *friar* in chapter 1. However, some are analysable, usually because each of the elements of which they are composed have also been borrowed. For instance, English *municipality* is a borrowing from French *municipalité*, but it is analysable, because *municipal* has also been borrowed, and the ending *-ity* is familiar as the ending of a great many abstract nouns borrowed from French nouns in *-ité* (and/or Latin nouns in *-itās*) and has also become productive within English. Often it is difficult to determine whether complex words of this type show borrowing at all:

LIBRARY, UNIVERSITY OF CHESTER

we will examine some of the issues concerned in sections 5.1 and 6.8. At a greater time depth, or where there is little data, borrowing generally becomes much more difficult to detect, and we will look at some of the implications of this in chapter 7.

Lexical borrowing is probably found to at least some extent in all languages, although the extent varies greatly (see chapter 5). We may fairly safely conclude that all words which have been borrowed will be of some interest to an etymologist, since we will want to find out how, when, and from which other language they have been borrowed. As we will see in chapters 5 and 6, these are very often difficult questions to answer, because of lack of evidence and/or difficulties of analysis. If we are even reasonably inquisitive about the ulterior histories of words, we will also want to delve further than this, and discover whether the word in the donor language is itself analysable and what its history is.

It may thus seem that all borrowed words will automatically need to be included in any etymological dictionary which attempts to be comprehensive. However, this presents some problems, both of a practical and of a theoretical nature. Fundamentally, words are borrowed, just as they are used, by individuals, not by 'languages', and we may find that very different selections of borrowed words belong to the vocabularies of particular social groups, geographical areas, etc., and even to the vocabularies of individuals within those groups, areas, etc.

Lexical borrowing is one of the many areas in which we can observe the open-ended nature of the lexicon of a language. Even if we restrict our focus to the usage of monolingual speakers, individuals have different interests or pursuits which will bring them into contact with different words from other languages. For example, very often people will have different enthusiasms for different cuisines, and accordingly they will have slightly different (active or passive) vocabularies of food terms. The Italian bread name *focaccia* has reasonable currency in contemporary British English, and also in many other varieties of English. The *OED* has an entry for this word as an English borrowing from Italian, with illustrative quotations dating back to 1881. However, the early quotations given in the *OED* present the word as an unusual item which authors feel the need to explain to their readers, and it is not until relatively recent years that we find examples reflecting more general currency of the word.

This particular example of a food term imported from another culture may seem an obvious symptom of modern cosmopolitanism and hence not applicable to earlier historical periods, but in fact we find that imported items (foodstuffs, items of manufacture, etc.) are a very frequent source of new borrowings in almost all cultures and almost all historical periods. Inevitably, whenever we have a reasonably large body of historical data, we can ask, but not necessarily answer, the same sorts of questions about precisely whose vocabulary particular borrowed words may or may not have belonged to in a given place and time.[7]

Additionally, we should remember that mobility of individuals or groups between different speech communities is hardly a modern innovation, and much recent work in linguistics has highlighted just how typical (and indeed normal) bilingualism and multilingualism are in many parts of the world today and have probably been at all times in the past. We will look in chapter 6 at the rather vexed question of whether switches between languages by bilingual speakers actually show borrowing at all, and if not how great the connection between the processes is. However, as soon as we are dealing with a situation where people speak more than one language, it is fairly certain that there will be some interchange of lexis between the two languages, even if this is restricted to technical or specialist registers.

We can thus see that in any language a core of well-established borrowings is likely to be surrounded by a periphery of much less well-established ones. Wherever there is a language contact situation, any large sample of actual usage is likely to include nonce, one-off, borrowings which do not show more general adoption (although the same word may well occur as a nonce borrowing on multiple separate occasions).

The open-ended nature of the lexicon of any language becomes yet more apparent if we now consider new words which are formed within a language rather than borrowed from another language.

2.2.3 New formations: aspects of affixation and compounding

One very common method of forming new words is by affixation (or derivation). Both prefixes (which involve addition of material at the beginning of a base, e.g. *un-*, *in-*, *pre-*) and suffixes (which involve addition of material at the end of a base, e.g. *-ness*, *-ment*, *-ly*) are common in very many languages. We will look at both in detail in chapter 4. Much more rarely infixes are found,

---

[7] For a detailed discussion of the general importance in etymological research of paying attention to how words can shift between specialist vocabularies and general usage see von Wartburg (1969) 107–14.

which interrupt a morphological base; in its inflectional morphology (rather than its derivational morphology) proto-Indo-European probably had an infix *-n- which formed present stems as part of its verbal system, reflected in for instance English *stand*.[8] We sometimes also find circumfixes, which involve addition simultaneously of material at the beginning and the end of a base; by some analyses a circumfix is shown by the *ge- -t* which is added to the stem of weak verbs in modern German to form the past participle, as e.g. *gefragt* 'asked', past participle of *fragen* 'to ask' (stem *frag-*), although again this belongs to inflectional rather than derivational morphology (unless we take the past participle to be an adjective formed on a verbal stem).[9] In section 4.4.1 we will look at ablaut, the systematic employment of variation in a stem vowel to mark different morphological or derivational categories.

Another very common process is, as we have seen, compounding. One important thing that compounding and affixation have in common is that the resulting word is 'bigger' than the elements from which it is formed. The word form thus enacts the semantic relationship between a base word and a compound or derivative. When we encounter a new compound or derivative, we recognize that it contains a base word plus something else (an affix or another base word). This suggests to us that the new word will have a meaning related to that of the base word but modified in some way. This sort of relationship between word form and word meaning is termed iconic. (See further section 4.5.)

2.2.4 Productivity

If an affix is productive, i.e. capable of forming new words, it can sometimes generate an enormous number of new word forms.[10] The process may be open-ended; this is particularly clearly illustrated by affixes which

---

[8] See Plag (2003) 101–4 for an argument that derivational infixation is shown in modern English in expletive insertion of the sort shown by *absobloominglutely* (see also section 2.1.1.4). On the distinction between derivation and inflection see Plag (2003) 14–16.

[9] Circumfixation should be distinguished from the simultaneous addition of both a prefix and a suffix in cases like *decaffeinate* < *de-* + *caffein* + *-ate*, where *de-* and *-ate* remain distinct affixes with distinct meaning and function. Such formations are normally called parasynthetic.

[10] For a detailed analysis of morphological productivity see Bauer (2001); a useful account, with further references, is also given by Plag (2006). Productivity is a difficult and somewhat disputed term, and is not used in exactly the same way by all scholars.

can attach to names to form new lexical items, like *-ism* in *Thatcherism*, *Stalinism*, etc. New derivational formations may be formed at almost any time within the context of a particular utterance, and be understood within the context of that utterance. An influential study in this area is Baayen and Renouf (1996), in which the authors looked at frequencies of word forms with the affixes *-ly*, *-ness*, *-ity*, *un-*, and *in-* in the British newspaper *The Times* over a period between 1989 and 1993. They found very large numbers of forms which occurred only once in this corpus, and which were not recorded in any dictionaries.[11] Their findings point strongly to very many of these formations being genuinely one-off nonce uses (examples include *archdukely*, *composerly*, *conductorly*), which readers of the newspaper process effortlessly by means of their knowledge of the productive word-forming patterns of the language. These words are not stored in the reader's memory, and yet they pose no problems for interpretation. Baayen and Renouf concentrated on words formed with derivational suffixes, but we can find just as great if not greater facility in the production of new compounds in English, which will be readily interpreted and understood by a hearer even if they are being encountered for the first time. (Of course, as noted in section 2.1.2, some scholars would anyway interpret at least some of these as showing phrases rather than compounds.)

Many words can be processed as they are encountered in context, drawing on the hearer's or reader's knowledge of the word-forming rules of the language. We can compare this to the way that any of an almost infinite number of different possible sentences can be interpreted (normally quite unconsciously) through the hearer/reader's knowledge of the syntactic patterns of a language. Other words are stored in our memory, including some which are perfectly transparent and analysable. Some people will encounter and/or use some words regularly which some other people never encounter: Baayen and Renouf's *composerly*, *conductorly*, and even *archdukely* may be part of everyday discourse for some people. Many linguists invoke the concept of a mental lexicon, which will probably differ at least slightly for each individual speaker of a language.[12]

If we take the view that an etymologist's task is to account for the origin and development of the lexicon of a language, then this begins to appear

---

[11] Additionally, they found that formations with the native, non-borrowed affixes *-ly*, *-ness*, and *un-* appeared to be much more frequent than would be suggested if one worked simply from the wordlists of dictionaries.

[12] For an overview of this topic see Aitchison (2003).

an impossible endeavour if new words are continually arising in the speech or writing of different individual speakers and writers on a daily basis, and if different individuals will have different lexical items stored in their memories. A more useful framework for defining the main focus of an etymologist's work is provided by the concepts of transparent and opaque (and also analysable and unanalysable) meanings and word forms which we have already encountered, and by the diachronic processes of institutionalization and lexicalization by which these commonly come about.

2.3 Lexicalization

A distinction is often made between nonce formations, institutionalized words, and lexicalized words. (More strictly, we should speak of lexical items here, so as to allow phrases to be included in the same framework.) Some scholars regard these as stages in a process which words may (but need not) undergo:[13]

nonce formation > institutionalization > lexicalization

Nonce formations are ad hoc coinages by individuals in particular circumstances, the majority of which will never gain any wider currency, such as the words encountered in the Baayen and Renouf study which we looked at in the preceding section. Institutionalized words, while they remain (at least relatively) transparent, are used conventionally within a certain speech community in a given context or with a fairly specific meaning. Lexicalized words are opaque – in meaning, or composition, or both.

lunchbox is, compositionally, a transparent compound of *lunch* and *box*, and we are not surprised to find that it denotes a box for transporting one's lunch. However, the definition in the *OED* suggests that it has some more conventional meaning characteristics than this:

A container designed to carry a packed lunch (or other meal). Formerly, any of various types and sizes of receptacle, sometimes also carrying crockery, etc., but now usually a small lidded box for food.

From the accompanying illustrative quotations in the *OED* we see that the modern use is most often specifically to denote such a box used for

---

[13] See for example Bauer (1983) 45–50. For a thorough overview of this field see Brinton and Traugott (2005).

transporting lunch to a workplace or, especially, to school. This suggests that it is an institutionalized word for this item. If someone called the same thing a *foodbox or a *lunchcarrier we might understand from context what was meant, but it would strike us as not being the right word: in fact, it would be a nonce formation which we would interpret from the context in which it occurred, and we would soon conclude that it was intended as a synonym of the institutionalized word *lunchbox*. To take another example from the same semantic field, not many decades ago many British workers, particularly miners, carried their lunch in a metal container, usually called a *snap-tin*. *Snap* was a word for a light meal, and hence the compound was transparent, if institutionalized. However, today snap-tins (i.e. the physical objects) tend to be encountered only as collectables or museum pieces, and the word itself is encountered either as the name associated with these artefacts or in recollections of a bygone world. Internet discussions sometimes speculate on the meaning of *snap* in the compound, or feel the need to explain the word's origin. In fact it shows *snap* 'light or packed lunch', itself a metaphorical use of *snap* 'quick or sudden closing of the jaws or teeth in biting' (compare *a bite to eat*), which is in turn related to the verb *snap*. We could imagine an alternative scenario in which *snap-tin* was formed directly from the verb *snap*, perhaps because of its lid snapping shut when closing, and in which *snap* 'light or packed lunch' was so called because it was carried in a *snap-tin*; it is the historical record that shows us otherwise, rather than anything that we can intuit from the modern use of the word. Hence we see that for some speakers at least the term is not just institutionalized but lexicalized: they call this sort of box a *snap-tin*, but at least some of them are not sure why.

Lexicalization is an important process in any study of etymology, because it is key to explaining many word histories. In the case of *snap-tin* it is both the meaning and the composition of the word that have become not just institutionalized but opaque: someone encountering the word *lunchbox* for the first time will have a good idea of what a *lunchbox* is simply from the composition of the word (even though they may miss some of the nuances of the institutionalized meaning), but someone encountering the word *snap-tin* for the first time is going to need to make careful use of information from the context of the wider utterance in order to work out what the word denotes, and will have little idea which out of numerous possible meanings *snap* shows in this word.

There are various different processes by which a word may become lexicalized. The most typical are:

(1) Semantic change occurs, either in the lexicalized word or in one or more of its constituent elements (i.e. the words, affixes, etc. from which it is composed)
(2) The word may become 'orphaned' as a result of one or more of its constituent elements becoming obsolete
(3) Changes in word form (typically through the operation of sound change) may obscure the relationship between the word and its constituent elements

Often, more than one of these processes is found in a single word history, and it is sometimes hard to tell in what order they occurred. It is also often difficult to tell when a word became opaque, and a word may well remain transparent for some speakers when it is already opaque for others. Any change which results in the original morphological composition of a word becoming opaque is sometimes referred to as demorphemization or demorphologization (see e.g. Brinton and Traugott (2005) 52–4): for instance, in the case of *handiwork* which we encountered in section 1.3.2, the prefix *ge-* in the medial syllable has become opaque, as a result of loss of *i-* (< *ge-*) where it occurred word initially. (For further discussion of the prefix *ge-* see section 4.1.2.)

2.4 Examples of lexicalization

So far we have looked at *lunchbox*, a word which has an institutionalized meaning but is of transparent composition, and *snap-tin*, which is opaque for some speakers, but is also now a rather rare word. However, very many perfectly common words have shown a historical development from being analysable and transparent to being completely unanalysable and opaque.

husband is a word with something of a 'disguised' history. As a modern English word it is unanalysable and indisputably monomorphemic, but this is not true at all points in its history. It occurs in its modern sense 'a man joined to a woman by marriage' from the thirteenth century. The word first appears, as late Old English *hūsbonda*, in the eleventh century, in the sense 'the master of a house, the male head of a household'. It is a borrowing from Old Norse *hūsbōndi* (with assimilation to the class of weak masculine nouns, hence the ending -*a* in the nominative case in Old English). However, the composition of *hūsbonda* would have been transparent to speakers of Old English, since the first element *hūs* is identical in form and meaning to its Old English cognate *hūs* 'house', and the second element *bōndi* 'peasant owning his own house and land, freeholder, franklin, yeoman' was also borrowed into late Old English as *bonda* (i.e. again with assimilation to the class of weak nouns). Indeed, as with many borrowed compounds, it could alternatively be argued that *hūsbonda* was formed in Old English from *hūs* and *bonda* on the model of Old Norse *hūsbōndi* (see section 5.1 for discussion of this topic, and also 5.2 for terminological complications to do with the term 'Old Norse'). In the Middle English period the vowel in the first syllable of the English word was shortened as part of a regular process of shortening before consonant clusters. Consequently it did not participate in the Great Vowel Shift affecting long vowels, as *house* did, with the result that the first element of the word became opaque, since *hus*- /hʊz/ (later /hʌz/ or /həz/) showed no obvious relation to *house* /haʊs/. (We will return to the Great Vowel Shift in section 7.2.3.) Old English *bonda* is continued by Middle English and early modern English *bonde*, *bond*, but the word is now obsolete. *husband* has thus become opaque as a result of:

- semantic specialization
- formal change in its first syllable (and different formal change in the parent word *house*)
- obsolescence of the word which forms its second element

As is typical in such cases, it would be very difficult to identify exactly when the word ceased to be transparent. If we consider that a language is something spoken by large numbers of individuals, we can see that it will be impossible ever to pin down a precise moment when change occurred, because the relevant changes in word form and word meaning will not have occurred for all speakers at the same time. In fact, the evidence of spelling forms and recorded meanings in the *OED* suggests considerable overlap both between different meanings and between different forms in the history of this word, just as we find in a great many other cases as well. Additionally, if we are trying to assess whether people in the past perceived a word as a transparent compound, we will always be engaging in guesswork to some degree: we can show that in such and such a period the language contained relevant word forms, so that someone so minded could make the connection between simplex word and compound word, but we cannot demonstrate that this actually happened. Thus we may in some cases be able to show when a word ceased to be analysable, but we cannot show when it ceased to be analysed. (It can be difficult to gauge whether a word is perceived as a transparent compound even by contemporary speakers.)

To take another example, English *lord* was also originally a compound, even though in modern English it is both monomorphemic and monosyllabic. It is recorded in Old English most commonly in the form *hlāford*, but also once in the form *hlāfweard*. It has a range of meanings in Old English, including 'master', 'prince', 'chief', 'sovereign', 'feudal superior', and even 'husband', but probably its original meaning was 'the male head of a household'. Although poorly attested, *hlāfweard* is almost certainly the earlier form of the word, showing a compound of *hlāf* (modern English *loaf*) and *weard* 'keeper' (modern English *ward*); the original meaning was thus metaphorical, referring to the role of the head of a household as owner and provider of the food eaten by his servants and dependants. In the more usual Old English form *hlāford* with reduced second syllable the connection with *weard* is already obscured, and very possibly no connection with *hlāf* was felt either. Certainly, all formal connection with *loaf* is lost in the reduced monosyllabic form *lord* which becomes the usual form from the middle of the Middle English period. *lady* (Old English *hlǣfdige*) probably shows a similar origin, < *hlāf* + an otherwise unrecorded word with the meaning 'kneader' ultimately related to *dough*. (In this instance *hlǣf* in the Old English word form shows the sound change known as *i*-mutation: see section 7.2.4.)

In each of these cases changes in word form have played a major part in making the etymologies and early meanings of the words opaque, i.e. demorphologization has occurred. In other cases change in meaning is much more important than change in word form. The word *handsome* is formed from *hand* and the suffix -*some*. This suffix seldom produces new words in modern English: it has become unproductive and now only occurs in occasional analogous nonce formations. The words in which it survives are a rather complex set of lexicalized words in which the suffix shows a number of different relationships with the base word, e.g. *quarrelsome*, *bothersome*, *loathsome*, *fearsome*, *wholesome*, *cumbersome*. However, in all of these cases it remains clear that e.g. *quarrelsome* has some connection with *quarrels* or *quarrelling*, and *bothersome* with *bother* or *bothering*, even if a particular speaker is unfamiliar with the lexicalized meanings 'given to or characterized by quarrelling', 'annoying, causing bother', etc. In some other cases the parent word has simply become obsolete, as in the case of *winsome* (from Old English *wynn* 'joy'); viewed synchronically, it has become unanalysable and so a unique morph (more commonly called a cranberry morph, for reasons we will see in section 2.6). In the case of *handsome* the situation is rather different. The first element is *hand*, and this is still very clear from the written form of the word. There is often no /d/ in the spoken form, but careful listening shows that the same applies to *handshake*, *handsaw*, *hands-off*, *hands-on*, *handstand*, and other words with a similar sequence of sounds, as pronouncing dictionaries will confirm, and yet in all of these cases the relationship with *hand* remains perfectly obvious. The crucial difference in the case of *handsome* is the development in meaning that the word has shown. When first found in the fifteenth century the word meant 'easy to handle or manipulate, or to wield, deal with, or use in any way', and in the early sixteenth century also 'handy, ready at hand, convenient, suitable' (we may compare the semantic history of *handy* already investigated in chapter 1). But these senses are now obsolete in most varieties of English, and the word has passed via the senses 'apt', 'proper', 'fitting' to the core modern senses '(especially of a man) good-looking', '(of a number, sum of money, etc.) substantial'. In consequence all semantic connection with *hand* has been lost, and the word has become opaque.

penknife presents an interesting case of a word which is perhaps rather less far down the route of lexicalization. It obviously and transparently denotes a type of knife. However, to the vast majority of modern speakers, it does not have any obvious or transparent connection with pens. The *Oxford Dictionary of English* (revised edition, 2005), a dictionary which takes a synchronic (i.e. non-historical) approach based on a corpus of contemporary usage, boldly defines *penknife* as 'a small knife with a blade which folds into the handle'. It also offers no etymology for the word, and in my view this could conceivably leave some readers confused about its origin; they might guess wrongly at some connection with *pen* 'small enclosure for animals' (reasoning that penknives have some sort of basic out-of-doors function), or they might assume that this kind of folding pocket knife was invented by someone with the surname *Pen* or *Penn*. Or perhaps they will alight on the right *pen*, but with the wrong reasoning, assuming that a *penknife* is a knife which is taken to resemble a pen when folded away. This is perhaps a little unlikely, but most people will probably need to engage in a little lateral historical thinking to arrive at the right answer. It is much more likely that in the ordinary course of events they will give the matter no thought at all, and regard *penknife* as the specific but inherently uninformative name of a type of knife. The historically based definition in the *OED* (third edition, entry published 2005) informs anyone about the history of the word *penknife* immediately: 'Originally: a small knife for use in making and mending quill pens (now rare). Now usu.: a pocket knife with one or more blades (and occas. other tools) designed to fold back into the handle when not in use.' And to avoid any lingering confusion, a brief formal etymology is provided, identifying that the word is indeed a compound of *pen* 'writing implement' and *knife*; hence *pen* has in formal terms an objective relation to *knife*, denoting the thing which the knife is (or rather was) used to sharpen. In this case it is the changing use of the denotatum, i.e. technological change in the non-linguistic world, which has been the driving force leading to lexicalization.

A final example will introduce some further themes which we will explore more fully later in this book. The word *acorn* is clearly monomorphemic and unanalysable in modern English. Furthermore it has a satisfying meaning relationship with an easily identified and very tangible entity in the real world. If someone asks us what the word *acorn* means (or more likely, what an acorn is) we can point to an acorn and say 'it means one of these'. (Although a botanist may note that different types of oak tree in fact have different types of acorns.) However, etymologically the word *acorn* is almost certainly related ultimately to the word *acre*, the modern reflex of Old English *æcer* 'field'. It probably originally had the meaning 'fruit of the unenclosed land, natural produce of the forest', although by the date of its earliest recorded appearance in English (in the form *æceren*) its sense has become restricted to 'acorn', the fruit of the oak tree, to which the authoritative *Dictionary of Old English* adds 'perhaps other fruit of similar form, mast' (that is to say, the fruit of woodland trees, such as acorns, beech mast, etc.). The meaning development, and the relationship between *acorn* and *acre*, become clearer when we look at some of *acorn*'s cognates in other Germanic languages: Dutch *aker* 'acorn', Old Norse *akarn* 'acorn', Old High German *ackeran* 'oak or beech mast', Gothic *akran* 'fruit'. We have no real way of knowing for certain whether the Anglo-Saxons connected the word with *acre*, but the restricted meaning, and the lack of any metalinguistic comments to the contrary, would suggest quite strongly that they did not. In modern English both the word's meaning and its form disguise the etymological connection with *acre*, and etymological investigation is required to establish the connection and to trace how the two words subsequently diverged. Interestingly, the word has been subject to various folk-etymological alterations during its history in English, indicating a desire on the part of language users to establish iconic relationships with other words in the language. (See further section 7.4.5, and also 4.5 on iconicity.) In the seventeenth century we find the form *oke-corn*, in which the word has been remodelled after *oke*, a variant of *oak*, and *corn*. Thus the word's form has been altered in such a way as to make transparent a perceived basic meaning 'corn (or fruit) of the oak', which certainly reflects what an acorn is, but this does not coincide with the word's historical composition. The modern form *acorn* (rather than **akern*) results from this same folk-etymological association with *corn*.

2.5 Apparent reversals of the process

Very occasionally the interaction between the written language and the spoken language may lead to apparent reversal of the lexicalization process. This typically happens in languages which have a standard and long-settled written form. The written language may therefore not reflect changes in word form which have occurred since. Thus *breakfast*, *blackguard*, or *boatswain* all reflect their composition transparently in the written form, but not in the spoken form (/brɛkfəst/, /blagəd/, /bəʊsən/), although since *blackguard* and *boatswain* are both now relatively rare words 'spelling pro-nunciations' are sometimes heard for each of these, hence /blakga:d/ or /bəʊtsweɪn/ (but /bəʊtsweɪn/ would never occur as the spoken realization of the adapted spelling *bosun*). Such spelling pronunciations can sometimes completely oust an older pronunciation which shows demorphologization, hence /weɪstkəʊt/ rather than /wɛskɪt/ is now usual for *waistcoat*, and /fɔːhɛd/ is becoming more common than /fɔrɪd/ for *forehead*. We will look in section 7.4 at various other processes such as folk etymology which run counter to lexicalization, since they lead to an increase in compositionality and analysability, and which are therefore sometimes described as showing anti-lexicalization.[14]

2.6 Cranberry morphs

If compounds and derivatives are common in a language (as they cer-tainly are in English), this can lead to a certain degree of tolerance of words which have the appearance of being compounds or derivatives but

---

[14] See for example Brinton and Traugott (2005) 102–3.

in which one of the elements is not analysable. The first element of the word *cranberry* is totally opaque to a speaker of modern English who does not know something about the history of the word, and morphologists often refer to unanalysable morphemes of this kind as cranberry morphs (or alternatively, and less colourfully, as unique morphs).[15] In fact, the word *cranberry* has been opaque for all of its history in English. It shows a seventeenth-century North American English borrowing from another Germanic language, probably Low German, in which the word ultimately shows a cognate of the bird name *crane* and a cognate of *berry*; compare the forms Low German *kranebere*, High German *Kranbeere*. In English, the second element of the word has been remodelled after, or perhaps assimilated to, the English cognate *berry*. As a result the word belongs to a family of words denoting types of (relatively) soft fruit, which also includes such transparent formations as *blackberry* and *blueberry* which both have fairly clear reference to the characteristic appearance of the fruit, although both are clearly institutionalized names. (Someone might hypothetically perceive blueberries as being more black than blue in colour, but that person could not then reasonably expect to be understood if she began to refer to blueberries as *blackberries* without making it very clear that she was making a deliberate departure from conventional linguistic usage.) Various shrubs of the genus *Symphoricarpus* (most of them originally native to North America) are normally called *snowberry* in English. Many of these have white berries, and this might seem the obvious reason for the name, but some others have red berries. The name may simply have been transferred from the white-berried type to the red-berried type, and indeed the white-berried type do appear to have been the first to be given this name. However, most snowberries, regardless of colour, bear their berries in winter, and this might suggest a quite different motivation for the name, or alternatively explain how the name could easily be transferred from the white-berried to the red-berried type, if reanalysed as referring to the season when the plants bear their berries. The reason for the *strawberry* being so called is far from obvious; it is normally considered by etymologists that it shows the word *straw* 'stem(s) or stalk(s) of various cereal plants', but various explanations have been suggested to account for this, such as the appearance of the plant's runners, or the appearance of the small seeds on the surface of the fruit, or perhaps the name reflects the cultivation of strawberries

---

[15] See e.g. Bauer (2003) 48, 50; Booij (2007) 30–1.

on beds of straw to keep the berries off the ground. *Raspberry* is almost certainly a compound of the earlier word *rasp* denoting a raspberry, but without a knowledge of linguistic history we may just as well think that *rasp* is a clipping (or shortening; see section 4.4.3) of *raspberry*; compare some fruiterers' use of *straws* for *strawberries*. Thus we see that within this group of words we have a cline of different degrees of analysability: *blackberry* and *blueberry* are obvious descriptive names; *snowberry* may be a less certain case; *strawberry* may be analysable if we stop to think about it, but is hardly likely to be apprehended as a descriptive name in everyday use; *raspberry* may be a longer alternative name for *rasp*, but in synchronic terms the two words are merely synonyms and *rasp* is of no aid in explaining *raspberry* since we do not know the origin of *rasp*; *cranberry*, so far as its existence in English is concerned, is evidently a type of berry, but has a first element with no connections elsewhere in the language, unless we happen to know its further etymology in Low German and work backwards from that to the English cognate *crane*, but that is purely extralinguistic knowledge. If we consider the different types of fruit which these various plants have, it also becomes clear that the concept denoted by *berry* in these formations is not a very precise one; we will return to this point when we consider prototype semantics in section 8.2. Nonetheless, the group of words ending in *-berry* has acquired new members through folk etymology: *naseberry* denoting the sapodilla (a type of fruit which grows on a tree) in fact shows a borrowing from either Spanish *néspera* or Portuguese *nêspera*, with the ending remodelled by folk-etymological association with words ending in *-berry*. (On this etymology compare sections 7.4.5 and 8.8.1. For some further *berry* names see section 9.7. A further interesting example to pursue is *gooseberry*.)

2.7 Which words need etymologies?

We have seen that the lexicon of any language will be extended by speakers in an ad hoc way, as new words are formed by productive word-forming processes such as derivation or compounding. These will normally be understood very easily by other users of the language from their transparent composition and from clues in the context of the utterance which help to explain the meaning. Only a tiny percentage of such introductions are likely to be adopted more widely. If we are working on a dead language or an earlier historical stage of a living language which has a relatively small corpus of surviving material, then we may decide nonetheless to include all of the surviving words in any etymological dictionary or corpus of etymologies, on the not unreasonable assumption that not enough evidence survives to enable us to see which formations are completely trivial and transparent and which are not, and it is therefore much better to be safe than to be sorry. If we are working on a contemporary language, we will certainly not have this luxury. Since the lexicon is almost infinitely extendible, it will be impossible for us to compile a comprehensive list of all of its words, let alone etymologize all of them. But this poses a problem for etymologists: as we will see in subsequent chapters, investigating almost any word history involves either implicitly or explicitly drawing parallels with other word histories, and we will not want to run the risk of neglecting words which may provide crucial information in explaining another etymology.

A useful framework for deciding which words to concentrate our energies on is provided by the concepts of transparency, opacity, and analysability, and by the insights provided by observing the diachronic processes of institutionalization and lexicalization. We might decide that our ideal etymological coverage of a language will include:

- any monomorphemic words (although we may need to reconsider this in the case of languages where variation of the stem vowel is a productive method of realizing derivational relationships: see section 4.4.1)
- any word containing a cranberry morph
- any word which has a form which is not explicable by the productive word-formation processes of the language
- any word which is formally analysable but semantically opaque, e.g. *handsome*, *handy*, or for some speakers *penknife*; also idioms such as *to cut a caper*

The last category is particularly difficult to define, since what is opaque for one speaker may not be for another. In each of these categories, our etymological investigations will in many cases show that the current status of a word results from earlier lexicalization, as e.g. *lord*, *lady*, *acorn*, *strawberry*.

We may also decide to add:

- all remaining words with a non-predictable, institutionalized meaning
- all phrases and constructions with institutionalized meanings not readily predictable from the meanings of the words of which they consist

These last two categories pose some difficulties, since it is not always easy to determine which meanings are readily predictable (or to put it another way, which meanings are institutionalized or even lexicalized). However, ideally we will want to ensure that problematic cases such as *snowberry* do not escape our notice. We will always have to assess our resources very carefully: if limited time is available, we may want to concentrate on just the monomorphemic words, or even just on monomorphemic words which have a certain level of currency. But if we do so, there will be losses. If we are working with a system where everything is connected, or even just a system where many things are connected, any unexamined word history may have contained vital clues to help explain other word histories. Limitations on our resources may force a pragmatic approach, but we should be alert to what may be lost as a result.

3

Are words coherent entities?

In this chapter we will look more closely at the variation in form and meaning shown by individual words. Variation may be found within a single time period and locality, and between different historical periods (diachronic variation) or different geographical areas (diatopic variation). We will take up the crucial issue of how words change with time, and we will examine critically whether we can always take it for granted that a word has continuity as a coherent unit from one historical period to another. We will look at the importance of tracing the process by which a word has developed. In comparison with this, the actual point of origin may be a relatively trivial matter, although we will also look at some cases where it is very difficult to pin down exactly when a particular word originated. We will examine cases where two originally separate words have merged, and conversely cases where one individual word has split into two or more separate words. In doing so, we will gain a better understanding of the data which forms the basis of etymological research, and will be better prepared for a more detailed investigation of the major issues in etymological research.

3.1 Variety in form and meaning: *poke* 'bag, sack'

The noun *poke* 'bag, small sack' is probably familiar to most speakers of modern English only as part of the idiom *a pig in a poke* 'something bought or accepted without prior inspection'. This is a good example of the kind of idiom we considered in section 2.1.5, where one of the words (*poke*) is either obsolete or near-obsolete except for its use in this idiom. At least, this word is obsolete or near-obsolete in modern standard varieties, but it retains much more currency in many regional varieties. Because of its obsoleteness or obsolescence in standard varieties, it provides a fairly unusual example in modern English of the sort of divergence in form and meaning in different regional varieties of a language which is typical when comparison with a supra-regional standard variety does not act as a brake on variation and change. (By contrast, if we looked for instance at the history of northern English and Scots *mickle* and southern English *much* (< *muchel*), a large part of the modern history of the form *mickle* would concern its relationship with the modern standard form *much*.)

The *Oxford Dictionary of English Etymology* summarizes the current meaning, history, and ulterior etymology of *poke* as follows (with my silent expansions of its abbreviations):

poke . . . bag, small sack (now dialectal except in 'to buy a pig in a poke'). 13th century. – Old Northern French *poque*, *poke* (compare Anglo-Latin *poca*), variant of (Old) French *poche* (compare POUCH).

The *ODEE* is a fairly typical example of a single-volume etymological dictionary of a major modern language, and is based principally upon the documentation of the much fuller historical dictionary, the *OED*. The word *poke* has recently been revised for the new edition of the *OED*, and some aspects of the ulterior etymology of *poke* have been reconsidered, but the analysis remains very similar. The English word is first recorded in the Middle English period, at the beginning of the fourteenth century, or perhaps a little earlier in Latin documents, which could show either the Middle English or the Anglo-French word, and also in some surnames which probably originated as nicknames, e.g. *haripoke* 'hairy poke'. It probably shows a borrowing from Anglo-French or northern French variants of Old French *poche* 'bag, sack'. This French word is itself ultimately a borrowing from a form in a Germanic language, cognate with Middle Dutch *pōke* and Old Icelandic *poki*, which both mean 'bag'. In Anglo-French and some northern varieties of French, a sound change common to other varieties of French did not take place. This resulted in a dialectal distinction between Anglo-French and northern Old French *poke*, *poque* as opposed to *poche* elsewhere. Middle English *poke* is most likely to have been borrowed from this source. Another, less likely, possibility is that it was borrowed from the unrecorded Old Dutch antecedent of Middle Dutch *pōke* (which, rather confusingly, would have shown a short vowel, since the long vowel in Middle Dutch results from later lengthening of short vowels in open syllables). Additionally, in Scandinavian-settled areas of northern and eastern England, the word could have been either borrowed from Old Norse *poki* or reinforced by association with this word (compare section 6.5 on this process).

All of these input forms would have given the same result, early Middle English *poke* /pokə/, with a short vowel. Beyond this initial input, no further foreign-language influence is found in the history of English *poke*, nor is there any important influence discernible from other English words. To that extent, the very simple, short presentation in *ODEE* serves us well. However, it does very little to get us from a Middle English borrowing *poke* (with a short vowel) to the modern English word *poke* (with a diphthong): the orthography may be the same, but we need to explain the phonological development. To do this we need to know a little about a couple of major English sound changes. To work from the present day backwards, the diphthong /əʊ/ in modern English *poke* is a relatively recent (nineteenth-century) development from the close mid long vowel /o:/, which itself developed from the open mid long vowel /ɔ:/ as a result of the early modern English Great Vowel Shift (see 7.2.3). This open mid long vowel /ɔ:/ itself resulted from another earlier sound change, early Middle English lengthening in open syllables in disyllabic words. In the case of a word like *poke*, the first syllable was open, i.e. the word had only one medial consonant, and the vowel lowered and lengthened as a result of the operation of this sound change. Subsequently, as a result of another Middle English sound change, the final vowel was lost, and the *-e* which was preserved in the written form served merely as a spelling convention indicating a preceding long vowel. (This is a traditional account of how this sound change operated. We will look at a different analysis in section 7.2.2.) We can thus put together the main sequence of events explaining the form history of the word from its first appearance in Middle English to its present-day form in standard English:

Middle English *poke* /pokə/ > *pōke* /pɔːkə/ (by open syllable lengthening)
> *pōke* /pɔːk/ (with loss of the final -*e*, which remains in spelling)
> early modern English /poːk/ (with vowel raising as a result of the Great
Vowel Shift)
> modern English *poke* /pəʊk/

Etymological dictionaries normally leave out this sort of information, as the developments are regular ones which are documented in historical grammars, but it is all actually a part of the etymology of the modern English word form *poke*.

If we look now at the documentation on spelling history provided by the *OED*, we see a large number of different forms in different varieties of English, all of which developed from Middle English forms with a long vowel as a result of open syllable lengthening:[1]

ME pook, ME-16 (17 *Irish English* (*Wexford*)) pooke, ME- poke, 15 poeck, 15-16 (18 *Irish English* (*Wexford*)) poake, 16 poak, 19- polk (*U.S. regional*); *Eng. regional* (*chiefly north.*) 17- poak, 17- poake, 18- pooak, 18- pook, 18- pwoak, 18- pwok, 18- pwoke; *Sc.* pre-17 poike, pre-17 poilk, pre-17 pook, pre-17 pooke, pre-17 poolke, pre-17 poyk, pre-17 poyke, pre-17 17- poke, pre-17 18 poak, pre-17 18 poik, 18 puock (*south.*), 18- pyock (*north-east.*), 18- pyoke (*north-east.*), 19- peock (*north-east.*); *N.E.D.* (1907) also records a form 18 puok (*regional*).

(*OED3* at *poke* n.[1])

Of course, what we are in fact looking at here is a collection of spelling forms, which represent spoken forms with varying degrees of faithfulness, within the constraints and conventions of a number of different spelling systems. In spite of this limitation on our data, we can trace a number of divergent histories, which we can piece together by looking at what is known of both the historical phonology and the spelling conventions of each variety of English. We will not do this here, but theoretically we could trace a different formal etymology for each of these word forms; indeed, in some cases the same spelling form in different documents might represent different spoken forms, or might represent the same spoken form but with a slightly different history. This approach of offering a distinct etymology for each distinct word form is currently being adopted on a large scale for the

---

[1] 'ME' here stands for 'Middle English', and the numbers represent the first two digits of each century, hence '17-' means 'found from the eighteenth century onwards'. Early Scots forms are all dated 'pre-17' because of the difficulties of assigning precise dates to many of the early Scots sources.

historical atlas project *A Linguistic Atlas of Early Middle English*: see Laing and Lass (2008).

What we have seen so far is not the full form history of *poke*. The *OED* entry for this word also presents a further set of forms which indicate the existence of a variant with a short vowel:

ME poc, ME pok, ME puc, 15 pokke, 15-16 pocke, 15- pock, 19- pok (*Canad. regional*); *Sc.* pre-17 pocke, pre-17 17- pock, pre-17 (19- *Shetland*) pok; *N.E.D.* (1907) also records a form ME pokke.

These forms seem to show failure of Middle English open syllable lengthening, and hence a Middle English form *pok* with preserved short vowel. Most of the evidence for these forms is from northern sources, and when we check the historical grammars we find that there are some parallels in Older Scots and northern Middle English also showing failure of open syllable lengthening in disyllabic words which historically had final /ə/, especially when the intervening consonant was a velar (see Macafee (2002) §6.6.1). We will look at some possible explanations for this in section 7.2.2. In fact, some of the examples of spellings of the type *pok* could reflect a spoken form with a long vowel, and likewise some examples of spellings of the type *poke* could reflect a spoken form with a short vowel, but overall the evidence is sufficiently clear that both forms with a long vowel and forms with a short vowel have existed in the past, and still do in at least some varieties of English today.

The *OED* has a third group of spellings for *poke*, also originating from the forms with a short vowel. These reflect a further sound change in Scots which caused diphthongization before a velar plosive:

Sc. pre-17 polk, pre-17 18 pouk, 18 powk.

In the case of the form *polk* we see what is called an inverse spelling, a spelling convention resulting from earlier vocalization of /l/ in words like *folk* which thus came to rhyme with *pouk*. Interestingly, among the first group of forms we also had US regional *polk*, showing a similar generalization of the spelling conventions for rhyming words such as *folk* or *yolk*.

We need not concern ourselves further with the origin of all of these variant spellings and the pronunciations which they represent, but we can already see that the development from Middle English *poke* to modern English *poke* via Middle English open syllable lengthening and the Great Vowel Shift is paralleled by a number of other historical pathways in different varieties of English. Most of the variation displayed by *poke* is regionally based, showing different formal developments of the same input form in different regional varieties. However, we also find formal variation that is not regionally based in origin. Open syllable lengthening often produced differences in vowel quantity in different parts of the paradigm of a single word, for instance in nouns which were monosyllabic in uninflected forms but disyllabic in inflected forms (e.g. uninflected *staf* 'staff' beside plural *stāves*), or which were disyllabic in uninflected forms but trisyllabic in inflected forms (e.g. *hēven* 'heaven' beside *hevenes*). We typically find that one form or the other is generalized (or levelled) to all parts of the paradigm by a process of analogy, but sometimes traces of the earlier variation are preserved. For instance, the modern spelling of *heaven* with *-ea-* probably reflects the disyllabic form with lengthening (*hēven*), while the pronunciation reflects the trisyllabic form without lengthening. In some cases forms with and without lengthening have survived, for example *staff* (< *staf*), showing absence of lengthening in uninflected monosyllabic forms, beside *stave*, a new form arising by levelling from the inflected disyllabic forms (*stāves*, etc.). In this case the two forms are now largely differentiated in meaning: *staff* 'stick used as a support, group of employees, etc.' beside *stave* 'length of wood forming part of a structure, set of lines on which musical lines are written, stanza, etc.'

When there is so much formal variation, we must consider whether all of this data can be said to show a single word, common to modern standard varieties of English, different varieties of modern Scots (as well as Scottish standard English), northern English regional varieties, English as spoken in Wexford in Ireland, etc. The problems become yet more complex when we look at the senses of *poke*, as recorded by the *OED*. I give here the *OED*'s definitions, omitting the illustrative quotations, but giving the year of the first quotation for each sense, and also of the last quotation for senses marked obsolete:[2]

> **1. a.** A bag, now esp. a paper bag; a small sack; (*Sc.*) †a beggar's bundle (*obs.*). Also: a bagful. Now *regional* exc[ept] in *pig in a poke* (see PIG n.[1] Phrases 4). *c*1300
> Formerly used as a measure of quantity, varying according to the quality and nature of the commodity. Pokes seem to have been used particularly for the conveyance of raw wool.

---

[2] We will look in chapter 8 at some of the processes of semantic change which are involved here.

    b. Originally: † a small bag or pouch worn on the person (*obs.*). Later: a pocket in a person's clothing (now *rare*). *a*1616

    c. *N. Amer. Criminals' slang.* A purse, a wallet; a pocketbook. 1859

    d. *slang.* A roll of banknotes; money; a supply or stash of money. 1926

2. † **a.** The funnel-shaped opening of a fish-trap. *Obs. a*1325 – *c*1350

    b. Chiefly *Sc.* A bag-shaped fishing net, a purse-net. Cf. *poke-net* n. at Compounds. 1579

3. A long full sleeve. Cf. *poke sleeve* n. at Compounds. Now *hist.* 1402

4. The stomach, esp. of a fish; (also) the swim bladder of a fish. Now *regional. c*1450

5. † **a.** More fully *Bavarian poke*. A goitre. *Obs.* 1621 – 1819

    b. *Sc.* and *Eng. regional* (*north.*). An oedematous swelling on the neck of a sheep, caused by infection with liver flukes (fascioliasis); the disease fascioliasis. Now *rare.* 1793

6. *N. Amer.* Chiefly *Whaling.* A bag or bladder filled with air, used as a buoy or float. Now *hist.* 1883

We can discover a great deal from looking at the labelling of each of these senses. For instance, sense 6 is labelled *N. Amer.* 'North American', and is not recorded outside North American use (except perhaps for occasional references to usage in North America); additionally, it belongs chiefly to the specialist discourse of whaling, and hence will only ever have been in common use among those in North America involved with the whaling industry. It is also labelled 'now *hist.*', i.e. today it is found only with reference to the past. Sense 1c is also North American, but in this case is restricted to the slang used by criminals. Sense 5b has only ever been recorded in Scotland and in northern English regional varieties, and is now rare even there. Sense 4 appears early on to have been in fairly general use, but is now restricted to a number of different varieties of regional English. Senses 2a and 5a, and parts of the senses defined at 1a and 1b, are now obsolete everywhere.

Summary   This discussion of the word *poke* has highlighted some important issues in tracing any word history:

- A simplified account which identifies a modern standard English word form with its earliest precursor in English, and then provides an ulterior etymology, may well be all that there is space for in most standard single-volume etymological dictionaries, but such an account tends to leave out a great deal of information about form and meaning history.

- Form and meaning history can be very different in different varieties of English.

- If we are attempting to etymologize any word it is a practical necessity to gather as much information as we can about form and meaning in different locations and historical periods, and not make rash assumptions about forms and meanings being identical in different places and at different times.

In the case of *poke*, we do not see any differentiation of forms in particular senses (except that senses found only in North America do not show specifically Scottish forms, etc.). However, in many word histories we find that such differentiation does occur, and can lead eventually to a split into two separate words, distinct in both form and meaning. We will look at examples of this (and of merger of distinct words) later in this chapter.

3.2 Do we know precisely when a word's history begins? Can we assume continuity of use?

We saw in chapter 2 that words are typically formed according to the productive word-forming patterns of a language, or else borrowed from another language. When the relevant processes of word formation remain productive it is possible for an identical word to be formed again. Similarly, in the case of a borrowing, if the contacts with the source language still exist it is possible for the same word to be borrowed again. If the original word has shown no subsequent change in form or meaning, then the original word and the re-formation or re-borrowing will be indistinguishable, and will merge. It is very likely (although rarely demonstrable) that most words show some degree of polygenesis of this sort: they are not coined once and for all, but enter a language on numerous separate occasions. A similar process probably also lies behind the development of most new senses, as we will explore in section 8.3.[3] Those words which enter dictionaries belong to the minority which gain some general currency. However, it is not always clear that even the entries in historical dictionaries reflect actual continuity of use, rather than a series of separate episodes of use.

The following are some examples of discontinuity in the historical record drawn from entries recently revised for the new edition of the *OED* (this is a small sample from a much larger number of cases):

> *air kiss* – attested once in 1887, then from 1986
> *appled* 'resembling apples, bearing apples' – gap between OE and *a*1729

---

[3] The term polygenesis was in fact introduced in this context by Dirk Geeraerts to refer to the emergence of the same meaning on two separate occasions: see section 8.3.

appley 'resembling apples' – attested once in ?*a*1425, then from 1854
applicatively – gap between 1792 and 1966
appliedly – attested in the 17th century, then from 1901
artificiously – gap between 1710 and 1938
ballading – gap between 1630 and 1959
boyly 'boyish' – gap between 1615 and 1902
carcinogen – attested once in 1853, then from 1936
caringly – attested in 1606, 1797, then from 1961
effectable – attested in the 17th century, then from 1897 (but rare)
effectivate – attested in 1717, then from 1935 (but rare)
heavenish – gap between 1577 and 1884
ladied – apparently isolated examples from 1628 and 1999
ladyly (adjective) – gap between *a*1500 and 1840 (now rare)
ladyly (adverb) – gap between *a*1450 and 1829 (now rare)
lovesomeness – gap between *a*1568 and 1869
masterfulness – attested once in *a*1586, then from 1880
monumentary – attested once in 1592, then from 1810
nonsensicalness – attested once in 1674, then from 1882
openness – gap between Old English and 1530
piquantness – gap between 1733 and 1918
planetography – attested in 1735 and 1736, then from 1936
prototypically – attested once in 1642, then from 1860
reabridge – attested once in *a*1631, then from 1950
sextuplication – attested once in *a*1690, then from 1935
streetlet – attested once in *a*1552, then from 1885
table-boarder – attested once in 1647, then from 1845 (but rare)
thingliness – attested twice in 1662, then from 1913
thingly – attested once in ?*a*1450, then from 1860

In all of these cases we find gaps in the historical record in periods for which English more commonly presents a reasonably continuous documentary record. (I have excluded examples where revival of words as historical terms denoting things or concepts from the past seems clear, such as *ballistier* 'person who operates a ballista, a type of military engine' or *apple-moyse* 'any of various dishes made from stewed apples'.) Some words are rare even in the periods for which we do have examples (e.g. *effectable, effectivate, ladyly, table-boarder* above), perhaps leading us to suspect that the gaps in the documentation may be purely accidental. However, independent formation in different periods probably cannot be ruled out in any of these cases. For instance, *OED* records *reabridge* 'to abridge again' once in the seventeenth century in the sermons of John Donne, and then examples can be found again from the mid twentieth century onwards. Prefixation in *re-* is productive in both periods, and there is no reason to assume any continuity between the seventeenth century and the twentieth, although there is also no linguistic argument against continuity, except for the failure of any documentary record. In other cases there are further complex factors at play: for instance, the contexts of the later uses of *boyly* suggest that it is being newly formed as a humorous formation on the model of *manly* and *womanly*.

Some words are of imitative origin, echoing natural (non-linguistic) utterances such as groans, or sounds in the natural world. (We will examine these also in much more depth in the next chapter.) These are particularly likely to be formed anew in different times and places. The *OED* has an entry for an exclamation *ou* /u:/ expressing surprise, excitement, or some similar emotion, and has examples showing three distinct pockets of use, in the Middle English period, in the seventeenth to mid eighteenth centuries, and in Scots from the nineteenth century onwards. The exclamation is probably imitative in origin (representing a shocked or surprised expelling of air through the mouth), and very likely the three periods of use have no connection with one another, although we cannot prove this.

Borrowed words can also show historical discontinuities, which may indicate that the word has been borrowed independently on two or more separate occasions.

- *operable*, a borrowing from post-classical Latin *operabilis*, occurs in the seventeenth century, and then again in the early twentieth century, when it may be influenced also by French *opérable*, which interestingly also occurs in two distinct periods, in the fifteenth century, and then again from the mid nineteenth century. (Alternatively, the modern word could show a new formation from *operate* or *operation* on the model of other words in *-able*: compare sections 4.1, 7.4. This could have happened in either English or French, or separately in both.)
- *Parasceve* 'the day of preparation for the Jewish Sabbath', is another borrowing from post-classical Latin (and in turn from ancient Greek *paraskeuê*). It occurs in the Old English period, and then from the

fifteenth to the seventeenth centuries, and then again (in the usage of Roman Catholics) from the twentieth century onwards, although it is rare in modern use. In fact, since the word occurred in the English Bible used by Catholics in the eighteenth and nineteenth centuries it was still arguably current in this period, even though no new uses of the word are recorded.

- *obol* 'a silver coin of ancient Greece' (< classical Latin *obolus*, itself < Greek) occurs in Old English and then again from the late seventeenth century onwards.

In these cases neither form nor meaning offer any particular clues as to whether there has been continuity of use for which we simply have no documentation, or whether a word has been formed or borrowed more than once. However, sometimes there is helpful evidence of this kind. *ordeal* (which in early use refers only to trial by ordeal, rather than in its modern metaphorical use) occurs in the Old English period as *ordēl*, *ordāl*, and *ordōl*, and has cognates in the other West Germanic languages. It is barely found at all between the Old English period and the early fifteenth century: there is only one recorded example, in the thirteenth century, and in that single example the word's meaning is completely misunderstood. In the late Middle English and early modern periods we find, beside the expected forms *ordel* and *ordele*, the forms *ordal* and *ordale* in parts of the country where these forms are extremely unlikely as developments of the Old English word, suggesting quite strongly that the word has been at least partly borrowed back into English from post-classical Latin, in which it appears as *ordalium* (and also *ordela*, *ordelum*) as a borrowing from Old English. Thus one explanation of this part of this word history would be as follows:

Old English *ordāl* > post-classical Latin *ordalium* (showing the Latin abstract-noun-forming suffix -*ium*) > Middle English or early modern English *ordal*, *ordale*

In chapter 6 we will look in some detail at cases where a borrowed word reflects borrowing from more than one language (6.5) and also at cases where differences in form or meaning indicate the existence of etymological doublets, showing borrowing from the same source in different historical periods (6.7). The frequency of both types of phenomena suggests rather strongly that many apparently simple borrowings probably also reflect the coalescence of a series of separate borrowings by different individuals, rather than a single occasion of borrowing.

It is often difficult to tell whether we have a case of a single or multiple word histories when a morphologically identical word occurs in several cognate languages. For instance, Old English *frēodom* (modern English *freedom*) is paralleled by Old Frisian *frīdōm*, Middle Dutch *vrīdom*, Middle Low German *vrīdōm*, and Old High German *frītuom*. These words could all show reflexes of a proto-West Germanic derivative formation; or they could all be independent derivative formations in each of the separate languages, since the suffix is productive at an early stage in each of them; or, theoretically, some of the forms could be from a common origin, others not. There is really no way of being certain in such cases. In this instance many of the languages also show a parallel formation with a different suffix: Old Frisian *frīhēd*, Middle Dutch *vrīheid*, Middle Low German *vrīhēt*, *vrīheit*, Old High German *frīheit*. We could thus assume that proto-West Germanic possessed two abstract nouns with the sense 'freedom' formed with different suffixes, or we could assume that these words have been formed independently in the different languages, or some combination of the two scenarios. In either case, there is apparently redundancy in the existence of synonyms, but this is commonplace among groups of derivatives. (See further discussion of synonymy in section 4.2.)

However, there are other words where there are good grounds for assuming that a gap in the dictionary record is purely a matter of accident, and does not reflect any actual discontinuity of use. *pretty* is recorded in the Old English period (as *prættig*) with the meaning 'cunning, crafty' and then from the mid fifteenth century in a wide variety of senses, including: clever, skilful, able, cleverly or elegantly made or done, ingenious, artful, well-conceived, attractive and pleasing in appearance, pleasing to the senses, aesthetically pleasing, attractive or charming, considerable, sizeable. There are some probable uses in surnames in the fourteenth century, but no earlier Middle English evidence. The form history and the meaning development of the word present some difficulties, but these would become yet more difficult to explain if we did not assume that Old English *prættig* was the starting point, even though there is a major discontinuity in our evidence.

The adjective *rash* is not recorded at all in English until the late Middle English period, but it has clear cognates in other Germanic languages, and it seems likeliest that it did in fact exist in Old English and early Middle

English but happens not to be attested in the documentary record. (The only other possibility is that it was borrowed into English from either Middle Dutch *rasch* or Middle Low German *rasch*. Borrowing from Scandinavian languages can be ruled out on phonological grounds, since the forms in these languages show a velar plosive – compare Old Icelandic *rǫskr* – and hence would give English **rask*.)

3.2.1 Coinages

It may seem that we are on much surer ground when we have evidence for the coinage of a word. For instance, we know that the blend words *mimsy* and *slithy* were coined by Lewis Carroll in his poem *Jabberwocky*, first published in 1855. Similarly, we often have documentary evidence for a specialist introducing a new term in a particular technical or specialist register, especially in the scientific world, although sometimes such claims can prove to be incorrect, either because the word has already been in independent use by someone else unbeknown to the claimant, or, very rarely, because the person claiming the coinage deliberately ignores someone else's prior claim. More frequently, earliest examples which look like coinages can be misleading. *electromobile* 'a motor vehicle powered by an electric motor rather than an internal-combustion engine; an electric car' has an earliest example in the *OED* from 1899, from the *Twin-City News* (Uhrichsville and Dennison, Ohio), 27 July:

An electrical journal has opened its columns to a competition for a good word to describe electric carriages, and 'electromobile' has been selected, but it is doubtful if it will 'stick'.

From this we may perhaps imagine that *electromobile* was one of a number of coinages suggested by people entering this competition, and was subsequently chosen as the winner. Thus we would have a satisfying and rather entertaining account of the origin of the word. However, if we stop to investigate our assumptions here a little more closely, maybe this is not the only possible explanation. Could the word *electromobile* not already have been in circulation, and been picked up on by entrants to the competition? It may even have been known to the organizers of the competition, but not been felt by them to have become institutionalized as the obvious word to denote such a vehicle. This hypothesis seems more plausible when we check the lexicographical record for French in the same period, and find that *électromobile* is recorded one year earlier, in 1898, and in an example where there is no indication that it is a newly coined word:

Pour la première fois les électromobiles occupent une large place dans l'Exposition.
  'For the first time electromobiles occupy a large space in the Exhibition'

(*La Nature* II.55; see *Datations et documents lexicographiques: Matériaux pour l'histoire du vocabulaire français* 10 (1976) 74)

3.3 Homonymy and polysemy

In section 2.1.4 we touched briefly on the topic of homonymy, with the example of *file* 'type of metal tool' and *file* 'set of documents'. We established that these two words are of separate origin (the first being an inherited Germanic word, and the second a borrowing from French), and also that there is no semantic common ground. These two observations each have a very different basis: the first is based on the historical record, and is thus empirical, and as long as we have lots of data we will normally not have too much difficulty in tracing the historical development. (We will look in chapter 8 at the difficulties which can arise when we do not have very much historical data.) The second observation, that there is no semantic common ground between *file* 'type of metal tool' and *file* 'set of documents', concerns the connections which contemporary speakers perceive between words, and is much more difficult to be certain of, and brings us to an area of some controversy. It is fairly uncontroversial that the kinds of meanings we find in dictionaries are typical or core meanings, which will reflect average usage, but which will not come close to capturing all of the nuances of usage in actual speech or writing. It is also fairly generally accepted that some words have several interconnected core meanings, at the level described by a dictionary. Such words are polysemous.

For instance, among the conventional meanings of the word *extension* are:

- an increase in length of time (to hold office, complete a project, etc.)
- an application of an existing idea in a new area
- a new part added to a building

We can group all three of these meanings under a broader meaning such as 'part that is added to something', and hence some scholars would regard this as not a case of true polysemy at all but simply of contextually determined conventional uses of a single main sense, but nonetheless we will expect any good dictionary to list them all as established meanings of this word. Even a simple case like this raises some further questions: perhaps it is reasonable to assume that no one who knows all of these senses will doubt that they are all meanings of a single word, but it is very possible that some speakers will know some but not all of these senses. Many speakers will be unfamiliar with the further conventional meaning 'extramural instruction by a university or college' (as in *an extension course*), and others will be unfamiliar with the meaning in computing: 'an optional suffix to a file name'. For different people the word will thus have a different range of meanings, according to their interests, experiences, membership of different professional or leisure groups, etc. Perhaps this will not worry us unduly, since all of these senses can reasonably easily be related to a simple meaning 'part that is added to something', although we might observe that, from a diachronic perspective, the potential for quite a radical divergence is certainly in place if the simple meaning 'part that is added to something' should come in the future to be realized by a different word. (For an extended example of just such a word history see *board* in section 8.5.1.)

The difficulties will become much more apparent if we now look at a case where, historically, we have two separate homonyms. From a diachronic perspective English has two homonyms with the form *bank*: the one is a borrowing from Old Norse, and has 'land at the side of a river' among its meanings; the other is a borrowing from French, and has 'place where money is deposited' among its meanings. The Norse and French words may perhaps ultimately be connected etymologically, but this is irrelevant to the history of the two words within English. The word *bank* 'land at the side of a river' shows other meanings which have developed historically from the same source, including:

- elevation in the seabed or a river bed (as in *mudbank* or *sandbank*)
- set or series of similar things (as in *banks of lights*)
- the cushion of a pool table

It is very debatable how far individual speakers will feel a connection between these rather specialized meanings, still less how confident they will feel that these meanings all constitute aspects of the meaning of a single word which is quite distinct from *bank* 'place where money is deposited'. From a synchronic point of view polysemy is thus a rather difficult concept: very close meanings may simply show different conventional contextual uses of a single core meaning, while it is difficult to be sure that more distant meanings are perceived by speakers as having anything more in common than the meanings of unrelated homonyms.[4]

We will consider some further aspects of how new meanings develop, and how they interact with other meanings of a word, in chapter 8. In the rest of this chapter we will explore further the divergence that can occur between the conventional meanings of a word, and the implications that this has for the coherence of that word as a single unit over a long period of time. Additionally, we will look at how historically unrelated words can become associated in meaning, and the further effects that this can have on both word meaning and word form.

3.4 How polysemy–homonymy relations can change

However much uncertainty there may be about how we identify homonymy and polysemy in the synchronic meaning relations between words, relationships of homonymy and polysemy certainly change over the course of time. To take a simpler example than *bank*, *crane* 'a type of tall, long-legged, long-necked bird' and *crane* 'machine for raising and lowering heavy weights' show developments of what is historically a single word: the machine was originally so called (by metaphor) on account of its resemblance to the bird in shape. However, it is debatable whether any connection is felt between the bird and the machine by contemporary speakers of English, and these are treated as distinct words by many dictionaries which have a synchronic perspective (such as the *Oxford Dictionary of English*). Nonetheless, it is difficult to prove that no connection is felt between the words, at least without elaborate fieldwork, although in this particular instance it might be easier to prove that a good many speakers know what a building-site *crane* is but have no knowledge at all of what sort of bird a *crane* is, hence demonstrating at least that a building-site *crane* is for these speakers a self-sufficient lexeme, and not a metaphorical extension of *crane* 'type of bird'.[5]

The dissociation between earlier and newer meanings is often particularly great when a word has acquired a more grammatical meaning (i.e. it has moved along the cline of grammaticalization) in addition to retaining

---

[4] For a useful discussion of polysemy from the perspective of cognitive linguistics see Croft and Cruse (2004) 109–40. For a discussion of some of the types of tests for polysemy which are commonly applied, and their limitations, see Lewandowska-Tomaszczyk (2007).

[5] For discussion of this issue compare Traugott and Dasher (2005) 15.

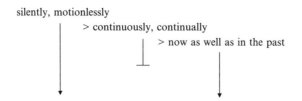

silently, motionlessly

> continuously, continually

> now as well as in the past

Fig 3.1 The meaning development of *still*

an earlier, more transparent meaning. The adverb *still* originally had the meanings 'silently', 'motionlessly'; it is derived from the adjective *still*. In the Middle English period it developed additionally the meaning (now obsolete) 'continuously, continually', and from this in the early modern period it developed the meaning 'now as well as in the past'. Today the meaning 'motionlessly' survives in such expressions as *to sit still* (which could alternatively be analysed syntactically as showing a predicative adjective, although the historical evidence favours analysis as an adverb), but very few speakers will feel that this is the same word as occurs in such sentences as 'he is still there', 'there is still time to make a difference' (although in this instance the two are placed under a single headword by the *Oxford Dictionary of English*). We can represent this as in figure 3.1.

In neither of these cases, *crane* or *still*, has divergence in meaning been accompanied by divergence in word form, which usually gives the clearest evidence that a language now has two separate words where formerly it had only one. We will look at some examples of this phenomenon in section 3.6, but first we will consider the even more difficult area of semantic convergence of originally unrelated words.

ear 'organ of hearing' has the Old English form *ēare*, and a set of cognates which correspond in meaning and are fully explicable in form, e.g. Old Frisian *āre*, Middle Dutch *ōre*, *oore* (Dutch *ore*), Old Saxon *ōre*, *ōra*, Old High German *ōra* (German *Ohr*), Old Norse *eyra*, Gothic *ausō*, and (in other branches of Indo-European) Latin *auris*, Old Irish *ó*, etc. The modern English homonym *ear* 'spike or head of corn' has the Old English form *ēar* (that is to say, it belongs to a different declensional class from *ēare* 'organ of hearing'), and it has a quite different set of cognates, which again correspond in meaning and are fully explicable in form, e.g. Old Frisian *ār*, Middle Dutch *aar*, *aer* (Dutch *aar*), Old Saxon *ahar* (Middle Low German *ār*), Old High German *ehir*, *ahir* (German *Ähre*), Old Norse *ax*, Gothic *ahs*, and (outside Germanic) Latin *acus*. The two words thus have completely different origins, but as a result of perfectly regular phonological and morphological processes they have come to be homonyms.

Similarly, *corn* 'small, painful area of thickened skin on the foot' is a borrowing from Middle French *corn*, which shows this sense as a metaphorical development of the sense 'horn', and is itself derived from Latin *cornū* 'horn' (the English word *horn* is ultimately a cognate of the Latin word, showing the regular operation of Grimm's Law). *corn* 'cereal crop' is of quite different origin, being an inherited English word of Germanic descent (it is ultimately cognate with Latin *grānum* > English *grain*). There is thus no historical connection, although the two words have always been homonyms in English.

Rather more controversially, Bloomfield (1933: 436) suggested that each of these pairs of words is identified by speakers of modern English as showing a semantic connection. According to Bloomfield, *ear* 'spike or head of corn' is perceived as a metaphorical application of *ear* 'organ of hearing', on account of a perceived similarity of shape (in Bloomfield's words, 'since the meanings have some resemblance, *ear* of grain has become a marginal (transferred) meaning of *ear* of an animal'). Likewise *corn* 'small, painful area of thickened skin on the foot' is perceived as a metaphorical application of *corn* 'cereal crop' (presumably on the basis that the thickened area of skin is likened to a grain of corn). Bloomfield acknowledges the difficulty of proving this assumption concerning speakers' perceptions about the meaning relationships between these words, although it is clear that he believes that this analysis is correct:

> Of course, the degree of nearness of the meanings is not subject to precise measurement; the lexicographer or historian who knows the origins will insist on describing such forms as pairs of homonyms. Nevertheless, for many speakers, doubtless, a corn on the foot represents merely a marginal meaning of 'corn' grain.
>
> (Bloomfield (1933) 436)

This discussion was taken up also by Ullmann (1962: 104, 164), and treatment in two such distinguished works has led to frequent occurrence of the same examples elsewhere. As both writers acknowledge, this perception of a relationship between the two words is difficult to prove; some fieldwork might perhaps be framed, but to the best of my knowledge, no such fieldwork has been carried out on these examples.[6] Personally, I do not find these particular examples entirely convincing, but they do illustrate well

---

[6] On the types of tests which are commonly applied in such cases, and their limitations, see footnote 4 above.

that the actual history of words may be totally obscure to speakers of a language, and certainly it is very feasible that new, historically unjustified, links in meaning may become established between etymologically unrelated homonyms.

We can have much more certainty that merger has occurred when there comes to be complete overlap in one or more of the senses of two homophonous words, as we will investigate in the following section.[7]

3.5 Merger (or near-merger) in form and meaning

The modern English verb *melt* is the reflex of two different Old English verbs. One was a strong verb, *meltan*, and was intransitive, with the meaning 'to melt, become liquid' (e.g. 'the butter melted'). In what are called strong verbs in Germanic, different parts of the verbal paradigm show different stem vowels (on the origins of this variation see section 4.4.1). Thus *meltan* had, beside the present stem *melt-*, the forms: past tense (first and third person singular) *mealt*, past tense (plural) *multon*, and past participle *gemolten*. The other verb was a weak verb, also with the infinitive *meltan* (or in the West Saxon dialect *mieltan*), and it was transitive, with the meaning 'to melt (something), to make (something) liquid' (e.g. 'the heat of the sun melted the butter'). Germanic weak verbs form the past tense by means of a dental suffix, usually represented by *-ed* in modern English, although in the case of *meltan* this is somewhat obscured by regular syncope of the vowel in the second syllable and simplification of the consonant cluster, giving (in the West Saxon dialect, in which Old English forms are normally cited) past tense (first and third person singular) *mielte* and past participle *mielt* (compare the non-West Saxon form *gemælted*, without syncope). Germanic weak verbs are mostly derivative formations from other stems. The weak verb *meltan* was originally a derivative formation, Germanic **maltjan*, from the base **malt-* of the past tense of the strong verb *meltan* plus a causative suffix, hence 'to cause to melt' (see further section 4.4.1).

---

[7] Occasionally there can be different sorts of evidence for speakers assuming that words which have become homophonous show a single word. Compare for example von Wartburg (1969) on the homophony in some southern French dialects of *aze* 'blackberry' (< Latin *acinus*) and *aze* 'donkey' (< Latin *asinus*) leading to use also of *saumo* 'donkey' in the sense 'blackberry'. We can present this as a proportional analogy, *aze* 'donkey': *aze* 'blackberry' = *saumo* 'donkey': *saumo* 'blackberry'

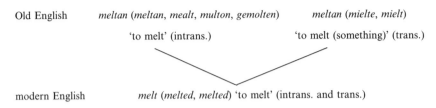

Old English   *meltan (meltan, mealt, multon, gemolten)*   *meltan (mielte, mielt)*

'to melt' (intrans.)   'to melt (something)' (trans.)

modern English   *melt (melted, melted)* 'to melt' (intrans. and trans.)

Fig 3.2 Merger of Old English *meltan* (strong verb) and *meltan, mieltan* (weak verb)

Gradually in the course of the Middle English period (if not earlier) the strong verb *melten* (Old English *meltan*) 'to become liquid' began instead to show weak inflections. This is a pattern shown by many originally strong verbs which gradually moved over to the numerically much larger class of weak verbs. The (originally) strong verb *melten* thus became formally indistinguishable from the weak verb *melten* 'to make liquid', which in Middle English normally shows past tense *melted*, past participle *melted*. Alternatively, we could interpret the same data as showing the weak verb displaying a change in meaning, from transitive 'to melt (something)' to intransitive 'to melt', a development that again would have many parallels among originally causative verbs in this period. Either way, the result in modern English was a single verb *melt*, with both intransitive and transitive meanings, and with regular, weak inflections (see figure 3.2), although the originally participial adjective *molten* is still found in specialized semantic use designating liquefied metal or glass.

Some other cases of merger or near-merger are harder to pin down because the semantics are less clear-cut. Such is the case with English *mystery*. In classical Latin there are two distinct words of quite different origins, *mystērium* 'secret' (in the plural, 'secret rites'; this word is a borrowing from Greek) and *ministerium* 'office, service, agency, instrumentality' (a derivative of *minister* 'servant, subordinate', which is itself ultimately < *minus* 'less'). As a learned loanword, Latin *ministerium* gives English *ministry*, quite unproblematically. However, in their application to the Christian faith in the early medieval period, the Latin words *mysterium* and *ministerium* became more closely associated in sense, and both came to be used in the sense 'ecclesiastical service'. This in turn led to confusion in word form, and a variant *misterium* emerged for the word *ministerium*. The form *misterium* gave, by regular development, (Anglo-)French *mester, mister* (modern French *métier*), and, as a borrowing of this, English *mister* 'occupation' (not the same word as the title *mister* or *Mr.*). *misterium* was also borrowed into English directly as *mystery* (in early use also *mistery*), with the meanings 'ministry, office; service, occupation' and (probably partly by association with *mastery*) 'craft, trade, profession, skill' and 'trade guild or company'. Meanwhile, Latin *mysterium* was also borrowed into English as *mystery* (in early use also *mistery*); this has a wide range of senses including 'mystical presence or nature', 'religious truth known or understood only by divine revelation', 'incident in the life of Christ', 'ordinance, rite, or sacrament of the Christian Church', 'hidden or secret thing', 'mystery play', 'an action or practice about which there is or is reputed to be some secrecy', 'a highly skilful or technical operation in a trade or art' – or at least, all of these senses are normally attributed to this word, but it is at least possible that some of them developed instead as senses of *mystery* 'ministry, office; service, occupation'. If we start out from the modern English word forms, the formal development of each can be summarized as follows:

A. English *ministry* < classical (and post-classical) Latin *ministerium*
B. English *mister* < (Anglo-)French *mester*, *mister* < post-classical Latin *misterium*, variant (by association with *mysterium*) of *ministerium*
C. English *mystery*, †*mistery* < post-classical Latin *misterium*, variant (by association with *mysterium*) of *ministerium*
D. English *mystery*, †*mistery* < classical (and post-classical) Latin *mysterium*

C and D are formally identical in English, and the assignment of particular senses to one word or the other is at best somewhat tentative. Historical or etymological dictionaries will endeavour to trace the development of each word, looking closely at the order of the examples of each sense, and also at the senses in the donor language, but it may prove impossible to be certain which development belongs to which word. So far as the speaker of contemporary English is concerned, it is surely the case that the word form *mystery* corresponds to a whole variety of meanings, some very familiar and some rather abstruse, some of which may strike some speakers as transparently related to one another, but on the whole rather disparate, and certainly not identifiable as showing two clearly differentiated words.

A very interesting case of partial semantic merger is shown by English *mean*. In the meaning 'common', English *mean* is the reflex of Old English *mǣne*, a variant of Old English *gemǣne* (Middle English *i-mene*), which is cognate with German *gemein* and is ultimately from the same

Indo-European base as Latin *commūnis* 'common'. The *OED* distinguishes three separate main branches of sense development in this word (*OED mean* adj.[1]):

    I. Held commonly or jointly

    II. Inferior in rank or quality; unpleasant

    III. With approbative connotation

In the meaning 'intermediate', English *mean* shows a quite different origin, as a borrowing from (Anglo-)French *mene, meen* (modern French *moyen*; ultimately < Latin *mediānus* 'that is in the middle'). The *OED* distinguishes two main branches of sense development for this word (*OED mean* adj.[2]):

    I. Intermediate, intermediary

    II. Moderate, middling; average

Semantic overlap between the two words occurs when the senses 'moderate, middling, average' of the second (Romance-derived) adjective are used depreciatively, i.e. 'only middling', hence 'not good'. The *OED* describes this convergence in sense as follows, in the entry for *mean* adj.[1] (Old English *gemǣne*):

In Old English (and in the earlier stages of other Germanic languages) substantially the only sense of I-MENE adj. and its cognates was 'possessed jointly', 'belonging equally to a number of persons'; however, already in Old English there existed a spec[ific] sense 'of ecclesiastical orders: minor, inferior in degree', which, although it did not survive into Middle English, may have informed the development of *mean*.

    The semantic development shown by the Old English spec[ific] sense of I-MENE adj. was carried further with Middle English *mene, mean* (as with Dutch *gemeen* and German *gemein*; cf. COMMON adj.), so that the word acquired the general senses of 'ordinary', 'not exceptionally good', 'inferior'. In English this development was aided by the fact that the native word coincided in form with MEAN adj.[2], which was often used in a disparaging or reproachful sense. The uses in branch II might be referred almost equally well to the native or to the foreign adjective; the truth is probably that the meanings of two originally quite distinct words have merged.

It is relatively easy to explain what has happened here in historical terms. Two words which are etymologically quite unrelated happen to have the same form in Middle English and modern English. Both words are semantically complex, and they show areas of convergence and overlap, with the result that in some particular instances it is impossible to say whether we have a use that has developed ultimately from Old English *gemǣne* or from (Anglo-)French *mene*. In synchronic terms, it is more difficult to explain the situation here in terms of either homonymy or polysemy. If there are meanings which overlap, perhaps we have a case of polysemy. However, although we can establish a plausible link between 'mediocre' and the other senses of either word, it is less clear that all of the senses of both words could be construed as constituting polysemous senses of a single word.

3.6 Splits in word form

In section 3.4 we saw the difficulty of determining whether divergence in meaning results in polysemy or homonymy in cases such as *crane*. We can be more certain that the synchronic result is two separate words when divergence in meaning is accompanied by a split in word form. We will look presently at some cases where a split occurs in the spoken language, and the result is indisputably two separate words with different word forms. In some other cases a split occurs only in the written language. Such cases are particularly interesting because they show homophones being distinguished by different spellings in the written language, even though historically they were senses of a single word. They thus provide us with clear evidence of polysemy leading eventually to homonymy.

mantle 'loose sleeveless cloak' and *mantel* 'ornamental structure of wood, marble, etc., above and around a fireplace' are in origin a single word. In the Old English period Latin *mantellum* was borrowed in the sense 'long sleeveless cloak'. In the Middle English period this was reinforced by borrowing of Anglo-French *mantel*, itself from the Latin word. In the medieval period the Latin word also developed the (originally metaphorical) meaning 'piece of timber or stone supporting the masonry above a fireplace', and this is reflected also in English. In Middle English *mantel* and *mantle* are both expected word forms for a word of this etymology, and both are found, as indeed they are also in Anglo-French. However, in the subsequent centuries we find a gradual process of differentiation of the two word forms in different meanings. *mantle* shows the meaning 'long sleeveless cloak' (and subsequent metaphorical developments from this, such as 'the region of the earth's interior between the crust and the core', which is in fact modelled on earlier use of the equivalent word *Mantel* in German at the end of the nineteenth century). *mantel* shows only the senses connected with fireplaces, 'piece of timber or stone supporting the masonry above a fireplace' (now obsolete), 'ornamental structure of wood, marble, etc., above and around a fireplace', 'manteltree of a fireplace together with its supports', 'shelf formed by the projecting surface of a mantelpiece' (figure 3.3). Both

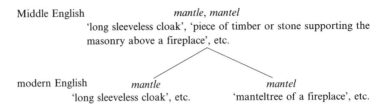

Fig 3.3 Split of *mantle* and *mantel*

word forms thus show semantic specialization, although the process is very gradual, and occasional instances of the 'incorrect' spelling are still found for each word. In this instance, a split has occurred, but only affecting the written form, since the pronunciation of each is the same, /'mantl/.[8]

Similarly, *flour* is in origin the same word as *flower*. *flower* was borrowed from Anglo-French *flur*, *flour*, *flor* in the thirteenth century. Among its early spellings in English are *flure*, *floure*, *flowre*, *flowur*, *flower*. The meaning 'flour' is found from the thirteenth century onwards, originally being a metaphorical use, denoting the 'flower' or finer portion of flour meal. The graphic split does not occur until much later than this: in the early modern period, *flour* or *floure* are just spelling variants of the word *flower*. In Johnson's great Dictionary of 1755 only the form *flower* is found and both senses are listed under the same entry. However, seventeen years earlier in Cruden's Bible concordance of 1738 the modern distinction in form and meaning is made between *flower* and *flour*, and this usage, not Johnson's, was rapidly becoming the standard one during the eighteenth century, with the result that (at least in print) *flour* is very rarely found as a spelling of *flower* and vice versa after the beginning of the nineteenth century. Today very few people without some knowledge of the linguistic history of the two words are likely to have any inkling that they are of the same origin. (On the pronunciation of the two words see further section 3.8.) Some other similar examples are *canvas* and *canvass*, *metal* and *mettle*, and (showing split into three different spelling forms) *coin*, *coign*, and *quoin*.

The splits that we have encountered so far are purely graphic. They are thus an oddity of the languages of modern highly literate societies where each word has a settled orthographic form. They are also very unlikely to arise in languages such as Dutch or Italian where spelling reflects pronunciation much more closely. Nonetheless, in a language like modern English

---

[8] For the somewhat mixed evidence of pronouncing dictionaries, and for a detailed account of how this material is treated in the new edition of the *OED*, see Durkin (2006c).

they may come to be regarded by speakers as signalling very fundamental distinctions in word form. The basic mechanism which they show is much more universal: existing variation is exploited in order to distinguish between particular meanings.

The same mechanism can be seen at work in cases where the spoken form as well as the written form is affected. *ordinance* and *ordnance* were originally variants of a single word, Middle English *ordenance, ordinance, ordnance*, etc., which was a borrowing of (Anglo-)French *ordenance, ordinance*, etc. This showed a wide variety of senses such as 'decision made by a superior', 'ruling', 'arrangement in a certain order', 'provisions', 'legislative decree', 'machinery, engine', 'disposition of troops in battle'. It is a derivative formation from the verb *ordener*, from which English *ordain* is borrowed. Over a period of centuries the form without the medial vowel, *ordnance*, became more and more common in English in the 'military' senses 'military materials', 'artillery for discharging missiles', 'the government department responsible for military materials and artillery', etc., and it became progressively less and less common in the other senses of the word, until in contemporary English near-complete differentiation has occurred, with the form *ordinance* very rarely occurring in the military senses, and the form *ordnance* only occurring in these senses. In this case it seems clear that the differentiation occurred because of selection of the disyllabic variant in a particular group language, that of the military.

ballad and *ballade* show differentiation of respectively more and less naturalized borrowings of French *ballade*, in the less specific sense 'light, simple song of any kind' (*ballad* /ˈbaləd/) and the more specific sense 'poem or song written in any of several similar metres typically consisting of stanzas of seven or eight lines of equal length' (*ballade* /baˈlad/ or /bəˈlɑːd/). The documentary record shows that in this case we do have differentiation rather than reborrowing of the French word in a more specific meaning, although in many similar cases the data is rather finely balanced.

We will see further examples of formal variation being exploited to distinguish between meanings with *pattern* and *patron*, and with Dutch *pertig* and *prettig*, in section 7.3.

Some splits affect only the spoken form of a word, and thus the result is two words which are homographs but not homophones. The verb *recollect* shows a sixteenth-century borrowing from Latin *recollect-*, the past participial stem of *recolligere* 'to gather together (again), to recall, remember'. In early use all senses of the English word were pronounced alike, with

/ɛ/ in the first syllable, as is usual in borrowings from Latin showing the prefix *re-* (e.g. *reconcile, recognize*). However, from the nineteenth century onwards we find evidence for the modern pattern, with a pronunciation with /iː/ in the first syllable in the sense 'to gather together (again)' and /ɛ/ in 'to recall, remember' and related senses. Interestingly, the mechanism in this split is almost certainly different from that in a number of the other examples we have looked at. In this instance the pronunciations with /iː/ result from reanalysis (see section 7.4.3) of the existing word as showing a native formation from *re-* and *collect*, and hence a pronunciation in accord with the usual pattern for English formations in *re-*. The senses relating to mental activity show a less transparent semantic relationship with the elements *re-* and *collect*, and thus retain the pronunciation typical of Latin borrowings. In such cases it can be hard to be certain that we are dealing with a split, rather than a new formation from *re-* and *collect* which happens to be a homograph of the earlier word. In this particular instance the identification of a split is supported by the evidence of eighteenth-century pronouncing dictionaries, which record the pronunciation with /ɛ/ for both groups of senses.

3.7 A case of merger followed by a split

council and *counsel* show a rather complicated and entwined history as far back as classical antiquity. The ultimate origin of these two English words lies in two distinct Latin words, *concilium* and *consilium*. Latin *concilium* (< the prefix *con-* 'together' + the verb *calere* 'to call') has the senses 'a convocation, assembly, meeting, union, connection, close conjunction'. A convocation or assembly might specifically be one called for the purposes of consultation, and in this sense the word overlapped in meaning with *consilium* 'consultation, plan decided on as the result of consultation, advice, counsel, advising faculty, prudence; a deliberating body, a council of state, war, etc.; a counsellor' (< the verb *consulere* 'to consult, deliberate' < the same prefix *con-* + an element of uncertain origin). The two words were perhaps confused in antiquity; they certainly are in medieval manuscript copies of classical texts. In French *consilium* gave rise by regular phonological development to *conseil*, which has roughly the same range of senses as in Latin, while *concilium* gave as a learned borrowing French *concile*, denoting only a type of ecclesiastical assembly. (See further section 6.7 on learned

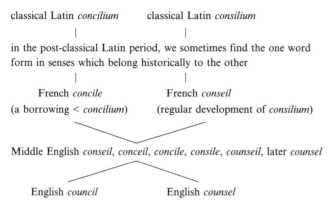

Fig 3.4 Merger followed by split: *council* and *counsel*

borrowings of this type.) Both French words were borrowed into English in the Middle English period. The *OED* provides a succinct summary of the subsequent developments:

In English, the two words were, from the beginning, completely confused: *conseil* was frequently spelt *conceil*; *concile* was spelt *consile* and *conceil*; and the two words were treated as one, under a variety of forms, of which *counseil*, later *counsel*, was the central type. In the 16th c[entury] differentiation again began: *councel*, later *council*, was established for the ecclesiastical *concilium*, F[rench] *concile*; and this spelling has been extended to all cases in which the word means a deliberative assembly or advisory body (where L[atin] has *consilium*, Fr[ench] *conseil*), leaving *counsel* to the action of counselling and kindred senses. The practical distinction thus established between *council* and *counsel* does not correspond to Latin or French usage.

We can summarize this history graphically as in figure 3.4.

As we can see, we do not have two separate word histories, the one linking English *council* with Latin *concilium* and the other linking English *counsel* with Latin *consilium*. Crucially, the distinction between two distinct French words was lost in Middle English. The *Middle English Dictionary* treats all of this material in a single entry, *counseil* n. Subsequently, in early modern English the available word forms were exploited to realize differentiations of meaning, partly under the influence of the original etymons, especially as a result of classicizing influence in the early modern period, but with a result which is ultimately different from that in either the donor language (French) or its donor (Latin): English *council* shows senses which belonged originally to Latin *consilium* rather than to *concilium*, while English *counsel* realizes only a subset of the senses realized by Latin *consilium*. In formal terms we appear to have a merger of the two words in the Middle English period, followed by a fresh split which is informed by knowledge of the classical Latin words but which does not restore the earlier semantic distinction precisely.

3.8 Homonymic clash

As already exemplified, I take both homonymy and polysemy to be very widespread phenomena and part of the natural state of languages. This point is in itself fairly uncontroversial, although a lot hinges on the word 'natural', and on the extent to which various mechanisms may work to eliminate homonymy.

It is sometimes observed that the high degree of homonymy in modern English results in part from very large-scale borrowing from a language which is not very closely related, French. However, homonymy is also quite common in Old English, and also in Icelandic, which has shown relatively little borrowing from other languages over the past millennium and also very little of the kind of reductive change in word shape that often produces homonymy. (On the degree of homonymy in what can be reconstructed of the lexicon of proto-Indo-European see Mallory and Adams (2006) 115–6.)

If we accept that homonymy is a common phenomenon in the languages of the world today, this gives us a good typologically based reason for assuming that it was also common in languages in earlier times. This has important implications for some arguments that we will look at in detail in chapters 7 and 8: put very simply, just because we reconstruct formally identical etymons for two words this does not mean that the two words must be cognate; if there is no plausible semantic link, it is usually much safer to assume that we have two unrelated homonyms. Defining semantic plausibility is the real challenge here, and will form a major topic of chapter 8.

However, running counter to my assumption that homonymy and polysemy are common and natural phenomena is the assumption often made that the most desirable state for languages, as systems of communication, is one where there is a state of 'one meaning one form', or isomorphism. If such an assumption is valid, one consequence might be that homonymy is undesirable, since it involves the same form realizing two meanings, which brings no communicational advantage, and could conceivably lead to ambiguity. Some scholars would conclude from this that homonymy is therefore likely to be eliminated over time.

It is less clearly the case that polysemy brings no communicational advantage, since it can be argued that some types of polysemy enable links to be made simply and effectively between contiguous senses without any semantic ambiguity. An extreme case is the regular polysemy in such cases as *a beer* (as in *he drank a beer*) by metonymy from the mass noun *beer* (as in *he drank some beer*).

Many scholars have identified a mechanism tending to eliminate homonyms, under a variety of names such as homonymic clash (or homophonic clash), harmful homonymy (or harmful homophony), homonymiphobia, etc.[9] Pioneering work was done in this area by Gilliéron in the early twentieth century (see Gilliéron and Roques (1912)). In one now famous example, Gilliéron looked at the words for 'cat' and 'cockerel' in Gascon, a Romance variety of south-western France. The Latin names *cattus* and *gallus* would have been expected, by normal phonological development, both to show the same reflex in Gascon, /gat/. However, while this is the form found for 'cat', for 'cockerel' we find instead substitution of alternative names such as *faisan*, which normally has the meaning 'pheasant', or *vicaire*, normally 'curate'. The homonymic clash thus appears to have led to replacement of the inherited word for 'cockerel'. In this instance the two words belong to the same semantic field, and it is easy to imagine actual ambiguity arising, for example if someone were stating that one animal or the other was standing in the farmyard.

A rather interesting example of avoidance of a homonymic clash within a particular semantic field is provided by the French term for a sequence of four consecutive cards of the same suit in various card games. In the seventeenth century this is *quarte*, literally 'fourth', forming part of a group of terms with *tierce*, literally 'third', *quinte* 'fifth', etc., but subsequently the synonym *quatrième* 'fourth' replaced it in this use. This was probably because of the homophony with *carte* 'card', a supposition which is supported by the fact that *tierce* and *quinte* do not show similar replacement, and also by the fact that in English the borrowing *quart*, which is not homophonous with English *card*, remained in use much longer, and still is used with reference to historic card games such as piquet. In this particular

---

[9] For important accounts see Ullmann (1962), Samuels (1972), Malkiel (1979), Geeraerts (1997).

instance there thus appears to be a good deal of (albeit circumstantial) evidence that avoidance of homonymic clash has motivated the change.[10]

A particular pressure restricting use of words, at least in some social contexts, appears to arise from homonymy, or in some cases possibly polysemy, with taboo or other disfavoured words. This is often identified in the literature as a specific category, embarrassing homonymy. For instance, *cock* 'male hen' is rarely heard in many varieties of American English, being replaced by *rooster* or another synonym because of the homonymy with *cock* 'penis'. The same motivation probably explains use of the derivative *cockerel* in place of *cock* 'male hen'. Historically, *cock* 'penis' shows a metaphorical use of the bird name, perhaps originally as a euphemism.[11] However, cases of words becoming obsolete for such reasons, rather than just restricted to coarse slang registers, etc., are less common, and counterexamples, where such homonymy has not motivated avoidance or replacement, are also not hard to find.[12]

Within the literature on homonymic clash, four different types of responses to homonymy are often distinguished (see especially Malkiel (1979)):

(i) both homonyms are tolerated (often because they can be shown to belong to different word classes, or to different semantic fields, or to different registers or stylistic levels);

(ii) one of the homonyms becomes obsolete, or shows restriction in use to reduce overlap;

(iii) the two homonyms merge;

(iv) the two homonyms diverge in form (often in unusual or unpredictable ways).

However, it is possible to take a rather sceptical approach to the claim that these phenomena have anything to do with homonymy. Group (i) are basically exceptions, and the criteria for possible exception are extremely

---

[10] For the details see *Französisches etymologisches Wörterbuch* (*FEW*) II. 1423/1. Assumptions of homonphonic clash are frequent in von Wartburg's work, in *FEW* and elsewhere. Compare e.g. von Wartburg (1969) 119 on near-homophony between inflected forms of *edere* 'to eat' and *esse* 'to be' in post-classical Latin leading to adoption in place of *edere* of the originally more emphatic or expressive formations *comedere*, *manducare*, or *pappare*.

[11] See Cooper (2008).   [12] See Lass (1997: 355 note 25) for some examples.

broad. A particular difficulty is that many of the examples typically given for processes (ii), (iii), and (iv) present no more convincing evidence of actual homonymic clash than many of the exceptions under (i), since the words do not demonstrably belong to the same semantic field without any differentiation in register or stylistic level.

Process (ii) is open to the objection that very many non-homonymous words also become obsolete or come to be used only in a restricted range of contexts, and very often no causal explanation for this can be established.[13] As Malkiel (1979: 4) notes, in standard English the homonymy of *lie* 'to be in a reclining position' and *lie* 'to tell an untruth' has long been tolerated, although the phrasal verb *lie down* is also common in the sense 'to be in a reclining position', and in colloquial and regional varieties of English the originally transitive verb *lay* is often found in intransitive uses, as in *he was laying on the ground*. Malkiel suggests that adoption of both *lie down* and intransitive *lay* possibly results from avoidance of the homonymy of *lie* with *lie* 'to tell an untruth'.[14] However, there are many parallel cases of originally transitive verbs which have developed intransitive uses where there is no suggestion of avoidance of homonymy. Similarly, Malkiel suggests that *cleave* 'to hew asunder, split' (< Old English *clēofan*) has reduced *cleave* 'to stick fast, adhere' (< Old English *clifian, cleofian*) 'to a precarious status' (1979: 5). However, perhaps the more surprising fact here is that the two words ever became homophonous, since the more expected reflex of the second verb would have been **clive*. This word history therefore seems actually to show that a variant form can become generalized even when this results in the creation of homonymy.

Process (iii) may simply be a result of contiguity of sense, and not the result of any pressures resulting from homonymy. Process (iv) hinges on the assumptions firstly that some changes in form can be shown to be particularly unusual or unexpected, and secondly that unusual or unexpected changes can be shown to be particularly common in cases of avoidance of homonymy, but the case here is far from proven.

---

[13] Anttila (1989: 332) suggests, in the context of linguistic reconstruction, that it should be a principle of etymological research that an explanation is always sought for non-survival of a word: 'If it seems that a word is guaranteed for the protolanguage, its (alleged) absence in any of the daughter languages requires an explanation.' However, in practice explanations for lexical non-survival are often elusive, even when we are looking at very well documented periods of linguistic history.

[14] Compare also Samuels (1972: 67–8) on *lie*, and criticism of this in Lass (1980: 78).

Splits which affect only the written form of a word, as with *mantle* and *mantel*, *flower* and *flour* (see section 3.6), pose a further problem from a functionalist point of view, since any ambiguity obviously remains in the spoken form. In the case of *flower*, there was considerable variation in pronunciation in the early modern period (compare Dobson (1969) §§165, 218), and it is hard to see why a semantic differentiation was not established between the available pronunciation variants /flu:r/ (without diphthongization) and /flʌur/ (with diphthongization; ultimately > /flauə/).[15] The conclusion seems inescapable that the exploitation of variation to reduce (synchronic) homophony can only be a very sporadic process.

In some cases where a distinction in form does arise, it can be shown to be determined by factors other than the avoidance of homonymy. The English indefinite article *a, an* arose historically from the numeral *one*, but the differentiation in form in this instance can be attributed to the occurrence of the article in a position of low stress before the noun which it modifies, in contrast to the fuller stress of the numeral in most functions. In many other classic cases of grammaticalization, such as the development of the French negator *pas* from the noun *pas* 'pace', no such differentiation in form has occurred.[16]

One response to these difficulties would be to reject the concept of homonymic clash as an explanation for historical linguistic change in almost any circumstances. For an extended argument which comes close to this position, see Lass (1980) 75–80, and also Lass (1997) 355, note 25. See also Lass (1997) for rejection of the idea of 'one meaning one form' being a target towards which languages move. The evidence suggests that avoidance of homonymic clash is at most a minor tendency in language change, which may provide a plausible explanation for some word histories, where the selection of one variant over another avoids genuine ambiguity or homonymy with a taboo word. Certainly, examples such as *quarte/quatrième* offer very tempting explanations for what would otherwise seem random events of lexical replacement. However, there are far more exceptions than positive examples, and this leads to a very important conclusion for etymological research: there are no grounds for thinking that the existence of homonyms was not tolerated in earlier language states just

---

[15] There is no difference in pronunciation between *flour* and *flower* in modern British English, but most US pronouncing dictionaries record at least an optional distinction between *flour* /flau(ə)r/ and *flower* /flauər/.

[16] For much more detail on both of these examples see Hopper and Traugott (2003).

as it is today, and we can very confidently reject any assertion that a particular etymology is impossible simply because it assumes the existence of homonymy. Whether or not the existence of certain types of homonymy can sometimes lead to a pressure for the selection of one variant over another, or the use of a synonym or another avoidance strategy, is a more debatable question, but we can be certain that such pressures will not inevitably lead to the elimination of homonymy.

4

Word formation

In the first three chapters of this book, and particularly in chapter 2, we have considered a number of topics to do with word formation. An understanding of word-formation processes is crucial to etymological research. Let us imagine for a moment a future age where only a few scraps of modern English survive. If an etymologist in this future age encounters the word *bitterness* in a scrap of surviving writing, and the word *bitter* is not attested in the surviving records, but *dark*, *darkness*, and *hardness* all are, then comparison among these words will provide just enough evidence to show that *bitterness* should be analysed as *bitter-ness* (not **bit-terness*), that *-ness* is a derivative suffix, and that *bitter* is an adjective. In any given period of the history of any particular language, the word-formation processes which are found will have their own characteristic patterns and peculiarities. In this chapter we will look in more detail at affixation and compounding, two very major sources of new words in English and in many other languages, and then we will look more briefly at some other typical methods of word formation. I will concentrate particularly on those processes which are found in modern English, because I assume that they will provide common ground for most readers of this book. Throughout, the focus will be on the implications of such processes for etymological research, and on how knowledge of the word-formation processes operative in a particular language in a particular historical period can shape and inform etymological judgements. The final part of this chapter is devoted to the difficult and often controversial area of onomatopoeic, expressive, and sound-symbolic formations, some acquaintance with which is essential for etymological research.

4.1 Issues concerning affixation

4.1.1 Development of new affixes; borrowing of affixes

As we saw in section 2.2.3, affixation normally forms new words which, at least at first, have a transparent semantic relationship with the bases on which they are formed. Frequently they also cause a change in word class, e.g. an affix may form abstract nouns from adjectives, or verbs from nouns, etc. Thus, in English, *-ness* is normally added to an adjective to form an abstract noun denoting the state or condition designated by the adjective: *hardness, darkness, bitterness*, etc. Many other affixes do not cause a change in word class, e.g. the negative prefix *un-* in *unkind, unreasonable*, etc.

Affixes present two areas of interest for an etymologist: (a) the word-forming patterns which they show, and how these change over time; and (b) their own origins, or in other words the etymologies of affixes. A brief investigation of *-ness* will illustrate both. In most of the recorded history of English, *-ness* is generally added to adjectival bases, although there are exceptions, e.g. the rare words *belongingness* or *whatness*. In the early history of the West Germanic languages the suffix is found with a much wider variety of bases, and in East Germanic (i.e. in Gothic) it is found mostly with verbal bases. Perhaps somewhat surprisingly, it is not found at all in North Germanic. This suffix originated from reanalysis of formations in an earlier suffix, proto-Germanic *-assu-* (also *-issu-*, *-ussu-*), shown by for instance Gothic *ufarassus* 'abundance'. Old English *-nes* (modern English *-ness*) has /e/ rather than /a/ because of a sound change (*i*-mutation: see section 7.2.4, and compare 4.4.1) caused by further suffixation in a stem-forming suffix *-jō-* which was subsequently lost. The /n/ is of rather more interesting origin. If we compare Old English *wōdnes* 'madness' with Old English *efnes* 'equality', it is obvious that both words end in *-nes*. The word *wōdnes* shows suffixation of *wōd* 'mad' (archaic modern English *wood*) with the suffix -nes. However, in the case of efnes the /n/ is actually part of the word stem; the word is related to emnettan 'to make even' and efn 'even', and has a parallel in Gothic ibnassus 'equality' (formed on ibns 'even'). Stems ending in *-n- were very frequent in proto-Germanic and in the early Germanic languages: the large class of weak nouns all had stems ending with *-n-, as did the past participles of strong verbs. The frequency with which *-assu- was found suffixed to a stem with final *-n- led to reanalysis of such words as instead showing an ending *-nassu-. This in turn led to analogical use of *-nassu- as a suffix on stems without a final *-n-. (On reanalysis and analogy see further section 7.4.) Forms from Gothic illustrate this particularly well, although in Gothic the suffix usually has the rather different form -inassus.[1] In fact, it is possible that Gothic shows a separate development, parallel to the one found in West Germanic languages. We can divide the forms found in Gothic into three groups:

- Forms without /n/, e.g. ufarassus 'abundance'.
- Forms in which /n/ is part of the stem, e.g. fraujinassus 'mastery' or ibnassus 'equality' (fraujinassus is formed on the verb fraujinon 'to rule over', which is in turn formed on the noun frauja 'lord').
- Forms in which /n/ is part of the suffix, e.g. waninassus 'shortage' < wans 'lacking' (in which -inassus is by reanalysis of formations such as fraujinassus).

The first and second groups of forms show the same suffix, -assus, but reanalysis of the second group leads by analogy to new formations where /n/ has become part of the suffix.

Aside from reanalysis, affixes often result from grammaticalization of adverbs or prepositions. For instance, the adverb-forming suffix -ment in French (and likewise Spanish -mente, Italian -mente, etc.) originates in uses of Latin mēns, ment- in the ablative case in collocations such as clārā mente 'with a clear mind'. Such collocations showed semantic broadening, e.g. 'clear manner of being or behaving' rather than simply 'with a clear mind', and the pattern became extended to adjectival bases which had no connection with mental activity, ultimately giving rise to a very productive adverb-forming suffix (compare modern French formations such as occasionellement 'occasionally', synthétiquement 'synthetically', géologiquement

---

[1] For more detail, and a number of complexities which I have omitted here, see (in German) Krahe (1969) 159–62.

'geologically', etc.).[2] Similarly, affixes often result from grammaticalization of adverbs or prepositions, as in the case of *over-* or *out-*, or the borrowed prefixes *per-* and *pro-* (< Latin formations in *per-* and *prō-*, which are ultimately < *per* 'through, by means of' and *prō* 'in front of, on behalf of, on account of' respectively, as e.g. in *perambulāre* 'to walk through', *perficere* 'to do thoroughly, complete', *prōclāmāre* 'to cry out, declare', *prōtrūdere* 'to thrust or push forward or forth'). In fact, there is some hesitation about whether English formations with *over-* and *out-*, such as *overcome*, *overeat*, *overwinter*, *outdo*, *outbreak*, *outgrowth* (or indeed with *-over* and *-out*, such as *voiceover*, *sleepover*, *breakout*, *shootout*) should be regarded as showing prefixation (or suffixation) at all, or as compounds, or as a separate class of formations with particles.[3] In such debated areas the most essential thing for etymological research is that we have as good a knowledge as possible of the patterns typically found in the relevant language in the period in question, to provide a sound basis for assessing etymological hypotheses.

If we are looking at the earliest recorded stage of a language, we may find that we are able to establish quite a lot about which affixes are found in what appear to have been analysable formations, but relatively little about how old those formations are. In some cases there may be information on dating from datable sound changes which would have affected an affixed form differently from the unaffixed base, or we may be able to identify a base borrowed from a foreign language during a particular historical period. By and large, we will not be able to judge the age of formations, and so we will be unable to establish very clearly which affixes were productive in a particular period. Thus, we can establish quite a good picture of the range of affixes found in Old English, but often we have no real way of telling whether the words containing those affixes were formed in Old English or in proto-Germanic. (Compare the example of *freedom* discussed in section 3.2.)

We can sometimes trace the development of new affixes in historical times. To take a simple example, *-scape* has become a (very minor) productive suffix in modern English. It originates from the second element of the noun *landscape*, which is a seventeenth-century borrowing from Dutch *landschap*. The Dutch word is a derivative of the noun *land* 'land' with the suffix *-schap*, which is related ultimately to English *-ship* in e.g. *hardship*,

---

[2] For further discussion see Hopper and Traugott (2003) 140–1.
[3] For the latter view see Adams (2001) 71–7.

lordship, *township*, etc. In English the ending of the word *landscape* was opaque, but the meaning of the word made it clear that the first element was *land*, and by analogy we find the new formations *seascape* and *prisonscape* at the end of the eighteenth century, denoting a sea view and, somewhat idiosyncratically, a view dominated by prisons. Subsequently we find *cityscape*, *treescape*, *riverscape*, *moonscape*, *nightscape*, *manscape*, *marinescape*, *roofscape*, *mindscape*, *slumscape*, etc., which begin to suggest that we are no longer encountering analogous formations on the model of *landscape*, but instead a productive suffix *-scape* which forms nouns denoting panoramic or comprehensive views, including figurative ones such as *mindscape*. (Since there is usually secondary stress on the final syllable of words in *-scape*, which is not normally a characteristic of suffixed words in English, we could alternatively argue that *-scape* is a bound element in compounds, rather than a true suffix.) It is very hard to draw any dividing line between analogous formations and formations in a productive affix, and indeed in some theoretical models even the most productive affixes are regarded as functioning largely by analogy, while in other models productive affixes are regarded as part of the grammar of a language, not of its lexis.[4] The crucial thing for etymological research is to establish as far as possible whether analysable models were available for a particular hypothesized formation.

Very similar considerations arise with the borrowing of affixes from one language to another. Indeed, it is a rather loose use of terminology to say that an affix is 'borrowed' at all. For example, in the Middle English period English borrowed many words from (Anglo-)French and Latin which showed the endings *-ment* and *-mentum* respectively. In Latin *-mentum* forms nouns from verbs, denoting either the result or product of the action of the verb, e.g. *fragmentum* 'fragment' < *frangere* 'to break', or the means or instrument of the action, e.g. *ōrnāmentum* 'ornament' < *ōrnāre* 'to adorn'. It also forms nouns from adjectives, e.g. *ātrāmentum* < *āter* 'black'. The same patterns are continued in French, as in *garnement* (< *garner* 'to fit out, equip') or *accomplissement* (< *accomplir* 'to accomplish'). (This *-ment* is thus different in origin and function from the French adverb-forming *-ment* discussed above. The two are simply homonymous suffixes.) All of these words were borrowed into English, as *fragment*, *ornament*, *garment*, *accomplishment*, (rare) *atrament*, along with many others. On the model of these borrowings, analogous formations began to appear in English from

---

[4] For a very useful introductory discussion of these issues see Adams (2001) 7–10.

bases of native (i.e. non-Latin, non-Romance) origin, e.g. *acknowledgement,
amazement, wonderment, atonement* (see section 2.1.3), and from the seventeenth century onwards the suffix *-ment* is very productive in English. However, it is rather artificial, although a useful shorthand, to say that *-ment* was
borrowed into English: more accurately, a large number of words of fairly
transparent formation containing the Latin or French suffix were borrowed
into English, and on the model of these a new suffix developed in English.[5]

The rather complex way in which new affixes become established in a
language can often result in uncertainty about whether a particular affix
is borrowed from a foreign-language source, or is simply cognate with it.
For instance, there is little doubt that there is an etymological relationship
between the English agent-noun suffix *-er* and the Latin agent-noun suffix
-ārius. However, there is some doubt and dispute as to whether the two
are cognate, or whether the English suffix ultimately results from early
Germanic borrowing of Latin words ending in *-ārius*, e.g. *monetārius* 'person who makes coins' (which ultimately gives English *minter*).[6] The etymological situation with the suffix *-er* in English becomes yet more complicated
in the Middle English period, when many Anglo-French words were borrowed showing an agent-noun suffix *-er* (which is definitely developed from
Latin *-ārius*); thus, beside very many English formations in *-er* (e.g. *singer,
leader*), English also shows a fairly large number of Romance borrowings
in *-er* (e.g. *mariner, officer*), which are distinguishable only by their etymology. It is likely that earlier linguistic history contains many similar cases
which we lack sufficient evidence to retrace, and which may have been more
complex than they appear to be from our available data.

4.1.2 Affixes with a variety of meanings and functions

Some affixes show a range of different senses and uses, which can be difficult
to piece together in detail. Analysis of Old English words showing the prefix
ge- reveals a wide variety of different meanings and uses:

- 'with', 'together' (probably the earliest meaning in the Germanic
  languages), reflected in a relatively small number of Old English words,

---

[5] Compare Adams (2001) 134. Borrowing of inflectional affixes also sometimes
occurs: see for example Weinreich (1953) 2.32.

[6] For the argument in favour of borrowing see e.g. Bammesberger (1984) 71–2.

e.g. *geþēodan* 'to join together, connect' or *gedræg* 'band, multitude' (<
the same base as *draw*, hence literally 'people drawn together')

- association, as in:

  - words for people holding a particular relationship with others, e.g.
    gebedda 'bedfellow, consort' (< *bedd* 'bed'), or *gefēra* and *gesīþ*, both
    'companion' (the first related to *faran* to go, and the second < *sīþ*
    journey)
  - adjectives and nouns expressing appropriateness, convenience, or
    similarity, e.g. *gemet* 'measure, proper measure, proportion, modera-
    tion', *gemǣte* 'of suitable measure, fit, proper' (modern English *meet*,
    adjective), both ultimately related to *metan* 'to measure' (modern
    English *to mete out*)

- mutual relationship, e.g. *gesweostor* 'sisters', *gebrōðor* 'brothers', or
  gefrīend 'friends'
- collective formations, e.g. *gewǣde* 'clothing' (related to archaic modern
  English *weeds*), *gebæcu* 'back parts', or *geweorc* 'work' (see section
  1.3.2)
- use in forming generalizing or indefinite pronouns, as *gehwā* or *gehwilc*,
  both (roughly) 'each or every one'
- perfective or intensive meaning, as e.g. in *gemōt* 'meeting' (> modern
  English *moot*) or *gemynd* 'memory, remembrance' (> modern English
  mind) and numerous verbs such as *geetan* 'to eat up, consume', *geærnan*
  'to gain by running' (beside unprefixed *ærnan* 'to run')

  - Related to this last category is the use in forming the past par-
    ticiple of verbs, which will be familiar to anyone who has some
    knowledge of modern German (although the use in modern German
    itself represents the outcome of a number of complex historical
    developments).

Not all of the uses of the prefix in Old English are fully understood, and
some aspects of the summary above touch on areas of controversy. It is a
safe assumption that if we had only the data of early Middle English to go
on, in which some words preserve the prefix (as *i*- or *y*-), some do not, and
many others show substitution of other prefixes (see Stanley (1982)), then
we would have little idea of the complexity of the picture in Old English (and
in proto-Germanic). This prefix is by far the most productive one found in
Old English, but has left relatively little trace in modern English, except

in occasional archaizing past participle forms such as *yclept* or in further reduced and obscured form as the first syllable of *aware* (Old English *gewær*) or *afford* (Old English *geforðian*).

4.1.3 Cases which could show either affixation or compounding

Apparently simple, readily analysable compound and derivative formations can often present interesting questions of linguistic analysis. Indeed, it can sometimes be difficult to determine whether we have a case of compounding or derivation. For example, *palaeogeographical* 'relating to (the study of) the geographical features of an area at some point in the past' stands in a transparent semantic relationship with *palaeogeography*, but we may hesitate in deciding whether it shows a compound or a derivative formation. There are certainly English formations in the suffix *-ical*. The stages in the development of this suffix can be traced as follows:

- In Latin the adjective-forming suffix *-ālis* is suffixed to formations, probably originally nouns, in the suffix *-icus*, which forms both nouns and adjectives; hence post-classical Latin *clericalis* 'clerical' < *clericus* 'clergyman, cleric' (occasionally also as adjective, 'clerical').
- On the model of such words, borrowed Latin adjectives ending in *-icus* are often suffixed with *-al* in English, e.g. *historical* < Latin *historicus* + *-al*, beside *historic* < Latin *historicus*; in this case, as in some others, the two words *historic* and *historical* have come to be distinguished in meaning more or less consistently over the course of time, while in many other cases one of the two words has become much more frequent and the other appears only as a rare variant.[7]
- By analogy with such formations, noun bases, most but not all ultimately of Latin origin, are suffixed with *-ical* within English, often giving rise to further pairs of adjectives in *-ic* and *-ical*, e.g. *artistical* and *artistic* (< *artist*), *atomical* and *atomic* (< *atom*), *ecological* and *ecologic* (< *ecology*), *pedantical* and *pedantic* (< *pedant*).

In the case of *palaeogeography* and *palaeogeographical*, suffixation in *-ical* would be explained very easily by analogy with the pair *geography*, *geographical*. We could present this as a case of proportional analogy (see section 7.4.1):

geography : *geographical* = *palaeogeography* : *palaeogeographical*

---

[7] On this question see Kaunisto (2007).

However, we could alternatively interpret *palaeogeographical* as not show-ing derivation at all, but instead compounding. *palaeo-* is a (marginally) productive neo-classical combining form in English (see section 4.3.1), and we could take *palaeogeographical* to be simply a compound formation < *palaeo-* + *geographical*, on the model of *palaeogeography*. There is really no very easy way of deciding which analysis is preferable in such cases, particularly since there are apparently parallel cases in favour of each analysis.

In some cases both semantic and morphological arguments point strongly towards analysis as a derivative. For instance, a *microfilmer* is someone who microfilms things. Analysis as a formation < *microfilm* + the agent-noun suffix *-er* is supported strongly both by the fact that *-er* is overwhelmingly the commonest agent-noun-forming suffix in English, and also by the fact that analysis as a compound < *micro-* + *filmer* would be awkward semantically: *microfilmer* does not mean 'a very small maker of films'. Similar considerations apply in some cases which it is probably best to regard as nonce-formations in an unproductive or barely productive affix on the model of an existing word. Thus, although the adjective-forming suffix *-ly* is found only very rarely in new formations in modern English, in the nineteenth century we find a new formation *big brotherly* 'characteristic of a big brother' (i.e. an elder brother, although in more recent use also someone who behaves in a way reminiscent of Big Brother in Orwell's novel *1984*). The semantic relationship with *big brother* suggests an analysis as a derivative of this compound, and compounding from *big* and *brotherly* would make little sense semantically. However, the selection of the suffix *-ly* (rather than say *-ish*) is clearly motivated by the prior existence of the adjective *brotherly*, which was formed in the sixteenth century, when formations in *-ly* were fairly common. (The equivalent form *brōðorlic* is in fact also recorded in Old English, but not in Middle English, and the sixteenth-century word probably shows a new formation, independent of the Old English use. Compare section 3.2.) A rather similar example is presented by *Middle Eastern*, showing the suffix *-ern* that is only found in the adjectives *northern*, *eastern*, etc., which designate points of the compass.

Sometimes semantic analysis and morphological analysis seem to point in different directions. A *particle physicist* is a person who studies *particle physics*. This would suggest an explanation as a derivative of *particle physics*, but that would involve an awkward morphological process of truncation and remodelling of the stem by analogy with the relationship between *physics* and *physicist* (and other word groups such as *aerodynamic, aerodynamics, aerodynamicist,* etc.). The much simpler and more economical morphological explanation would be compounding of *particle* and *physicist,* but this is much less satisfactory semantically. Morphologists often describe such difficult cases as showing a bracketing paradox.[8]

The more theoretical aspects of such questions are fundamentally matters for specialists in morphology, who, inevitably, will not all agree on the approach that should be taken. However, if we are attempting to establish the etymological connections among a group of words, an awareness of different possible analyses of derivational relationships can often lead to a new and more satisfactory solution to an etymological problem.

4.2 Synonyms, nonce formations, and blocking

This section will deal with two rather different topics, because each appears to raise some rather similar issues for etymology work, and I believe that in each case the solution to the apparent problem is very similar.

It is a much-debated question whether the lexis of any particular variety of a language, within a particular period, shows true synonymy, that is to say pairs of words with precisely the same meaning. If we took the view that true synonyms do not occur, this might seem to have important implications for the practice of etymologists: if we have clear evidence that one word existed with a particular meaning in a particular place and time, and we believe that true synonyms will not occur, should we not reject any hypothesis which involves assuming the existence of another word with the same meaning?

We can easily demonstrate empirically that this is an incorrect inference. Dictionaries abound with words or senses which are defined in the same way as one another, and which can be shown to exist in the same historical period, and which dictionaries do not mark as belonging to different registers or stylistic levels from one another. To take some examples fairly randomly from the *OED*, we can find (in etymologically unrelated or only very distantly related word groups) *myoneural* and *neuromuscular*, or (in related word groups) *pediculate* and *pediculated, purification* and *purifaction, aerify* and *aerate* (or compare the pairs of words in *-ic* and *-ical* in section 4.1.3).

---

[8] See for example Bauer (2003) 325, from which I have taken this example.

These examples all belong to more or less technical registers, and it is in such registers that synonyms with no differentiation at all in stylistic level are commonly found. However, if we disregard the constraint that there should be no differentiation in stylistic level, we can add pairs of much commoner words which show at least one meaning which overlaps, such as *mariner* and *sailor*, *marry* and *wed*, or (historically related) *oldest* and *eldest*. It would be easy (if tedious) to produce extremely long lists illustrating each category. It may be the case that none of these words were ever full synonyms within the usage of any particular individual, and that any individual who has used both words has always done so with some distinction in meaning, or a difference of connotation, or of register or stylistic level. However, we should bear in mind that our information about the meanings of words in past stages of language history is always rather limited, the more so the fewer documents we have surviving from a given period. The situation is much worse when we come to register or stylistic level: we may sometimes be able to recover some information about these in past language states, but our information will always be very limited, and often we will have none at all. We should therefore not be at all surprised if we find that we very often encounter words which appear to be full synonyms in the historical record: there may have been very obvious differences for contemporary speakers in meaning, or register, or stylistic level, but this information is not necessarily recoverable by us today. Alternatively, two words may have had a different geographical localization, or they may not have overlapped in meaning in precisely the same period, but we cannot always recover this information. Thus, regardless of whether we think that full synonyms are possible, or likely, or adopt any intermediate theoretical position, we will often have to accept that the available historical data presents us with two or more words which we simply cannot distinguish in meaning or use.

This becomes a very important factor if we now consider the phenomenon known as blocking (or pre-emption), by which new formations are blocked (or pre-empted) by the prior existence of a synonym. There are good reasons for thinking that blocking is an important factor in restricting word formation. Thus we expect that the prior existence of *difficulty* will block *difficultness* from being formed, and similarly that *coolness* will block *coolth*. (The reasons why I have not marked *difficultness* or *coolth* with asterisks will become clear from the following paragraphs.) But, as we have seen in the preceding paragraph, we do find *pediculate* beside *pediculated*, *purification* beside *purifaction*, *aerify* beside *aerate*, and so on, even though theoretically the existence of the one formation should have blocked the coining of the other. We can easily see how such a situation can arise in practice: in a developing area of discourse, field of study, etc., one group of people may begin using the one formation, and another group may begin using the other, before either has become institutionalized even within the linguistic usage of a particular technical register. Additionally, as we have seen in chapter 3, many words show a rather tenuous historical record, and we cannot be certain whether we are seeing a history of continuous use, or a series of re-coinings of the same word form in the same (or very similar) meaning. Or to follow another possibility, *pediculated* could reflect simply a faulty recollection of *pediculate*, or an alteration on the model of other words ending in -*ated*, and hence we could have a case not of separate coining of synonyms but of formal remodelling of an existing word, where there is not a large body of existing language use to 'correct' the alteration in word form. Thus it is unsurprising that blocking often seems a rather weak force in parts of the lexicon which belong only to technical discourse, where a particular word is likely to be known and used by only a small number of people.[9]

A slightly different sort of example is shown by *coolth*. The usual abstract noun corresponding to the adjective *cool* is *coolness*, and we would expect this to block the formation of *coolth*: that is to say, since *coolness* already exists as an institutionalized word, in common use by large numbers of speakers, *coolth* would be a redundant synonym, and even if one speaker coined it (perhaps as a verbal slip for *coolness*) we would not expect it to be widely adopted by other speakers. But there is a rather strong proportional analogy in favour of the coining of *coolth* by analogy with *cool*'s antonym *warm* and its corresponding abstract noun *warmth*. We can represent this as follows:

$$warm : warmth = cool : coolth$$

(On analogy see further section 7.4.) The *OED* shows a rather patchy record for *coolth* from the mid sixteenth century to the present day. A number of the recorded uses are self-consciously humorous, especially from the late nineteenth century onwards, but others are not. There is probably not a continuous history of use, but rather a succession of separate formations of the word. The existence of *coolth* beside *coolness* appears on at least two separate occasions to have been exploited to realize a semantic distinction:

---

[9] For a detailed exploration of issues of this type see Bauer (2006b).

in regional dialect use in the eighteenth and nineteenth centuries we find *coolth* in the specialized sense 'a common cold', and from the 1960s onwards in US English we find some evidence for semantic specialization in the sense 'quality of being relaxed, assured, or sophisticated' (thus corresponding to *cool* in its use as a key term in youth culture).

Similarly, because of the prior existence of *difficulty*, a Middle English borrowing from Latin and/or (Anglo-)French, we do not expect also to find *difficultness*, even though the derivational morphology of modern English would suggest *difficultness* as by far the likeliest abstract noun to be formed from the adjective *difficult*. However, *difficultness* is indeed recorded in the *OED*, with examples from 1560 to the present day. The historical record for this word is patchy, and it is likely that the word has not shown a continuous existence in English. The presence of examples in the *OED* from 1560, 1580, and 1644 suggests that there was some continuity of use in the early modern period, and indeed searching the *Early English Books Online* database of early modern English texts provides a cluster of further examples, although there are many, many more examples of *difficulty* in this same period.[10] The later picture is rather different, since the *OED* records no examples of *difficultness* from the eighteenth or nineteenth centuries, and its two twentieth-century examples seem to show a clear semantic nuance, with reference specifically to *difficult*, i.e. socially challenging or unacceptable, behaviour by an individual.[11]

When we are considering the remoter linguistic past, we often have little or no information about the relative frequency of particular words. We thus cannot tell whether two parallel formations from the same base with different affixes may have coexisted, perhaps with a difference of meaning, or register, or stylistic level which is now unrecoverable; or perhaps one word of a pair was institutionalized, and the other existed only as an occasional variant, perhaps as a remodelling of the institutionalized word on the model of a more productive word-forming pattern. As a point of methodology, we can almost never rule out the existence of one word in the past simply because we have very strong indications that another existed.

---

[10] On the frequency with which parallel formations from the same base are found in early modern English see e.g. Nevalainen (1999) 358, and evaluation in Bauer (2001) 183–4.

[11] See Adams (2001) 13 on this particular observation.

4.3 Issues concerning compounding

In etymological research we also often need to establish as much as we can about the patterns of compounding found in a particular language in a particular historical period. Armed with such knowledge, if an etymological hypothesis involves assuming the existence of a certain compound then we will be in a much better position to judge how likely that compound is to have existed in that language in that period. For instance, we occasionally find compounds in English where the first element is a verb and the second element is its object, such as *pickpocket*, denoting a person who performs this action. In technical terms, this is a type of exocentric compound, denoting something which is not a sub-class of either of the elements of the compound, unlike endocentric compounds such as *blackbird* or *paperclip*. This type of compound probably arose in English as a result of (Anglo-) French influence in the centuries after the Norman Conquest. *pickpocket* belongs to a small family of similar formations with *pick*, and we can trace the historical development of this word family:

- In later Middle English (or slightly earlier as surnames) we find *pick-purse*, *pickthank* 'person who curries favour with another', *pickharness* 'person who strips the slain of their armour', and *pickpenny*.
- In the early modern period we find *pickpocket* itself and a few other formations.
- We find occasional later (rather self-conscious) formations, e.g. *pick-brain* in the early twentieth century.

Similarly, a number of formations with *make* are found in the sixteenth and seventeenth centuries, such as *makepeace*. In both cases, the compounds are frequently paralleled by (and were probably modelled on) verbal phrases, *to make peace*, *to pick someone's purse*, etc. Thus, if we have formulated an etymological hypothesis which involves assuming the existence of an exocentric compound of this type at a certain point in the history of English, we can quickly draw up a check-list of things that we will want to know which might either strengthen or weaken our hypothesis:

- Since such formations often appear in small clusters, can we find other similar formations from the same verb?
- Is there a similar phrasal construction with the same verb in the same period?

- Are there many other compounds of the same type found in the same period, geographical area, register, etc.?

If we are very fortunate, a reference work will provide a catalogue of such formations. In the case of English, this exists in the form of Marchand (1969), in which section 5.8 catalogues and discusses formations of just this type.

4.3.1 Neo-classical combining forms, and other compounding patterns

Sometimes extensive borrowing can lead to new patterns of compounding becoming established in a language. In Latin and in Greek the first element of a compound typically shows what is called a thematic vowel, determined by the morphology of that word. Thus in Greek the adjective *mikrós* 'small' occurs as *mikro-* as the first element in compounds, e.g. *mikropsuchía* 'littleness of soul'. In Latin, where an internal *-o-* was replaced by *-i-* in certain environments, *pēs* (stem *ped-*) appears as *pedi-* in compounds, e.g. *pedisequus* 'attendant'. In English, as in many other European languages, new formations are found on the same pattern, with the result that we find elements, usually called (neo-classical) combining forms, which exist only as bound forms in compounds but which are productive in forming new compounds:

- in combination with other bound forms ultimately of classical origin, e.g. *micrography* < *micro-* + *-graphy*
- with English nouns ultimately of classical origin, e.g. *microbiology* < *micro-* + *biology*
- (sometimes) with English nouns not ultimately of classical origin, e.g. *microskirt* < *micro-* + *skirt*

It is the formations with other bound forms, such as *micrography*, which serve as the main criterion for distinguishing combining forms from affixes in the analysis I have followed here, although this is something that not all scholars would agree with.

Additionally, new combining forms of this type are formed within English (and in other modern languages) from elements ultimately of Latin or Greek origin plus a connecting vowel *-o-*, since this is the thematic vowel most commonly found in formations borrowed ultimately from Greek and in very many post-classical Latin formations modelled on these.

Thus for example we find English *radio-* (< Latin *radius* + *-o-*), which is found in English forming compounds to do with radiation and radio communications from the late nineteenth century onwards, as it is also in French and German.

Very occasionally similar formations are found on bases not ultimately of Latin or Greek origin, as for instance *sado-* (in *sadomasochism*, etc.), formed on the name of the Marquis de Sade, albeit on the model of earlier formations with derivative suffixes such as *sadism*, *sadistic*, etc. (There would perhaps be a case for saying that, in spite of its having the connecting vowel *-o-*, *sado-* is actually a prefix, not a true combining form, since it is found only in formations with an independent word as second element, not another bound form, although this would conflict with the fact that it clearly has lexical content in formations such as *sadomasochism*.)

The status of *micro-* etc. as bound forms is not affected by use of the same word form as an adjective or noun. Thus when *micro* occurs as an adjective, e.g. in *strictly micro*, *something so very micro*, or *of a more micro nature* (all recorded in *OED*), it shows conversion (see section 4.4.2) to a different word class. The same is true of uses as a noun in senses such as 'micro dress or skirt', 'microcomputer', 'microwave oven', unless we take these simply to show clipped forms (see section 4.4.3) of the nouns *microdress*, *microskirt*, *microcomputer*, *microwave oven*, etc.

Somewhat more problematic are the cases we sometimes find where a neo-classical combining form appears to be combined with a derivational affix. The theoretical model usually adopted tells us that neo-classical combining forms can be found forming compounds either with other neo-classical combining forms or with independent words (e.g. *micrography* or *microbiology*, as above), but that, as bound forms, they should not be found as bases for derivational suffixation.[12] Thus we should not expect to find **micral* (< *micro-* + *-al*, adjective-forming suffix) or **microness* (< *micro-* + *-ness*). We do in fact very occasionally find formations such as *orthic* (which has various technical meanings in mineralogy, geometry, and soil sciences), which has the appearance of being a derivative formation from the combining form *ortho-* (< ancient Greek *orthós* 'straight') with the adjective-forming suffix *-ic*. Here there is the alternative analysis of regarding the English word as a formation directly from the ancient Greek adjective plus the English derivative suffix (i.e. < ancient Greek *orthós* + English *-ic*), a pattern which

---

[12] See e.g. Bauer (1983) 213–16.

would certainly not be without parallels among modern vocabulary in technical registers, even in cases where there is no corresponding combining form in English use. In other cases an analysis as a blend (see section 4.4.4) or as a formation on a clipping (see section 4.4.3) may resolve the difficulty. However, Bauer (1998b: 409) sounds an important note of caution: 'Rather than having a clearly defined set of neoclassical compounds, it seems that neoclassical compounding acts as some kind of prototype, from which actual formations may diverge in unpredictable ways'. This sort of case illustrates well the importance of interaction between detailed analysis of individual word histories (i.e. etymology) and more general theoretical approaches.

Formations with neo-classical combining forms are mostly restricted to scientific and other technical registers, and they may seem a rather marginal part of the lexis of English, French, German, etc., although they are certainly extremely numerous. It might be tempting to dismiss the unusual compounding patterns shown by neo-classical combining forms as something of a historical accident resulting from the unusual status of Latin- and Greek-derived elements as part of the 'international language' of science in the modern world. However, there are parallels elsewhere, both for the introduction of a large number of productive bound forms as a result of very substantial borrowing from another language, and for such bound forms showing patterns of word formation different from the usual ones in the borrowing language. For instance, during the last two millennia Japanese has borrowed huge numbers of words from Chinese, totalling over 50 per cent of the vocabulary in a modern Japanese dictionary. These are mostly compounds, showing Chinese words which do not occur in Japanese except in compounds, and which have the status of bound forms in Japanese. In addition to the compound words borrowed from Chinese, compounds have also been formed in Japanese from these originally Chinese bound forms, as have hybrid words showing one element ultimately of Japanese origin and one ultimately of Chinese origin. Collectively all of these types are usually referred to as Sino-Japanese compounds. Such compounds tend, like neo-classical formations in European languages, to belong to technical registers, and to be of less frequent occurrence than words of native Japanese origin, although in certain text types they can make up more than half of the total words uttered (i.e. of the tokens) as well as of the distinct word forms (i.e. of the types). Most interestingly for our present purposes, the formation of new Sino-Japanese compounds also shows some differences from regular word formation in Japanese: compounds consisting of a verb and its object reflect Japanese word order when they are formed from elements of Japanese origin, but generally reflect Chinese word order when they are formed from borrowed Chinese elements.[13]

4.4 Some other important processes

4.4.1 Root allomorphy and ablaut

As noted in section 2.2.3, one thing that affixation and compounding have in common is that the result of the word-forming process is a longer word form. However, morphological relationships can also be indicated by variation in the root vowel in a word or group of words, and such variation can form the basis for productive word-forming processes.

In the inflectional morphology of modern English, the plural of *man* is indicated not by the regular plural inflection -*s*, but by a change in the root vowel: *men*. Synchronically this can be described as a case of root allomorphy. Historically, in this particular instance it results from a sound change called *i*-mutation (or sometimes *i*-umlaut) which involved raising and/or fronting of vowels when an *$*i$* or *$*j$* followed in the next syllable. In this instance, the *$*i$* belonged to an inflection which has since been lost, thus /mani/ > [mɛni] > /mɛn/; we will look at the details of this in section 7.2.4. The German name umlaut is sometimes used as a cover term for any such sound change caused by a vowel in a following syllable, and hence for any vowel variation which has its origin in such a process. However, the terms metaphony or vowel harmony are more commonly used today (and also refer to influence of a vowel in a preceding syllable, as found for instance in Finnish or Turkish).

Root allomorphy is also found in many irregular verbs in modern English, e.g. present stem *sing*, past tense *sang*, past participle *sung*. In this instance the variation results from a process in proto-Indo-European morphology called ablaut, by which morphological relationships are indicated by vowel alternation (also called apophony). Indo-European ablaut very

---

[13] For the data drawn on here see Shibatani (1990) 145–7, 237–41; compare also e.g. Backhouse (1993) 75–6; Cannon and Warren (1996) 82–3.

possibly had its origin in variation in the position of the accent, although this is a very uncertain matter, involving assumptions about a prior stage in the history of a reconstructed proto-language which is already at a considerable remove from our oldest linguistic evidence. By the stage in the history of proto-Indo-European which we are able to reconstruct with any degree of confidence, ablaut was a very widespread and undoubtedly productive process, in both the inflectional morphology and the derivational morphology of the language. Most proto-Indo-European roots which can be reconstructed show the pattern *CeC*, showing a consonant (or consonant cluster), the vowel *e*, and another consonant (or consonant cluster). In many cases a resonant (*l*, *r*, *m*, *n* or the glides *i* or *j*) was found either before or after the vowel, thus we also have roots of the shape *CeRC*, *CReC*, or *CReRC*, where *R* represents a resonant sound (for examples of roots of this type see ancient Greek *peíthomen* or English *sing* below). The initial or final consonant could also be a resonant, hence *ReC* and *CeR* are included when we write *CeC*.

The form of a root with the vowel *e* (i.e. *CeC*, *CReC*, etc.) is called the full ablaut grade. The full grade of the reconstructed root **kel-* 'to conceal' is reflected by Old Irish *celim* 'to conceal' and Old English *helan* 'to conceal' (showing **k* > **h* by Grimm's Law). This root also shows an *o*-grade, in which *o* takes the place of *e*. This is reflected by Gothic *halja* 'to conceal' (with **k* > **h* by Grimm's Law again, and with the Germanic change of short **o* to **a*; English *hell* is ultimately from the same base, with *i*-mutation). There is also a zero grade, in which no vowel appears between the two consonants. This is reflected for instance by the initial consonant cluster of Latin *clam* 'secretly' (in which *-am* shows an adverbial termination also shown by *cōram* 'face to face' and *palam* 'openly, publicy'). Finally, a long grade with long *ē* is reflected by Latin *cēlāre* 'to conceal'. Some roots also show a long *ō* grade in the same series.

In traditional accounts of proto-Indo-European other ablaut series have also been identified, although today interpretations of these differ. In 1.2.4 we encountered ablaut variation between **sə-* and **sā-*, and we noted that **ə* represents the realization as a vowel of one of a series of hypothesized so-called laryngeal sounds (the phonetic quality of which is in fact unknown). In this analysis, **sə-* shows the zero grade of a root **seH-* of the standard shape *CeC* (or *CeR*), in which the final sound was a laryngeal which shows a vocal realization when it occurs in zero-grade forms or before a consonant.

*sā- shows the full grade, with the laryngeal consonant having a lengthening and colouring effect on the full-grade vowel *e.[14]

The morphological functions of ablaut in proto-Indo-European are not perfectly understood, but certainly there are some regularities that can be observed in various of the Indo-European languages. Thus verbal roots in the full grade often have corresponding nominal formations in the o grade, e.g. Latin *toga* 'garment' (literally 'a covering') beside *tegĕre* 'to cover'; Old English *þæc* 'roof', modern English *thatch*, is also from the o grade of the same root, showing the subsequent effects of Grimm's Law and the change of short *o to *a in proto-Germanic, followed by fronting of *a* to *æ* in Old English. On the typical morphological structure of words in proto-Indo-European see further section 8.7.3.

In a number of ancient Greek verbs which reflect Indo-European patterns the present shows the full grade with *e*, the perfect shows the o grade, and the verbal adjective and the aorist show the zero grade: e.g. *peíthomen* 'we persuade', *pepoíthamen* 'we are persuaded, we have been persuaded', *epíthomen* 'we persuaded', showing the full grade, o grade, and zero grade of a root which has the gradation pattern *ei, oi, i*, that is to say *CeiC* in the full grade, *CoiC* in the o grade, *CiC* in the zero grade. In the inflectional morphology of the Germanic languages, ablaut is most obviously present in the morphology of the strong verbs. In the case of *sing, sang, sung*:

- the present stem *sing* shows the full grade with *e* (with raising of *e to *i before a nasal in proto-Germanic)
- the past tense *sang* shows the o grade (with the proto-Germanic change of short *o to *a), as also does the noun *song* (with *o* resulting from another sound change in English)
- the past participle *sung* shows the zero grade (showing a syllabic *n in Indo-European, giving *un in proto-Germanic)

This root thus shows the gradation pattern *CenC, ConC, CnC*. However, the reflexes of many historically strong verbs in modern English do not in fact show the expected vowel alternations, because the paradigms of many verbs have shown considerable alteration as a result of analogy, as we will explore in section 7.4.1.

---

[14] For a fuller introduction to these issues from the viewpoint particularly of the history and pre-history of English, see Lass (1994) 105–19. For an overview of the history of this question see also Szemerényi (1996) §§4.1.11, 5.3.4, 6.4.1.

Another pattern frequently found in Germanic is that (weak) causative derivative verbs are formed from suffixation of the *o* grade of strong verbal roots. For example, in section 3.5 we encountered the Old English weak verb *meltan* 'to melt (something)' (< Germanic *maltjan), formed from the *o* grade (Germanic **malt-*) of the root of the strong verb *meltan* 'to melt' plus a suffix. The change in vowel from Germanic *maltjan to Old English *meltan* results from *i*-mutation, caused by the *-*j*- in the Germanic suffix.

The term ablaut is sometimes used of similar realization of morphological distinctions through variation of the stem vowel in other languages (as for instance in Arabic, in which such variation plays a major role). However, it is important to realize that this does not imply that the historical origin of the variation has anything in common in each case.

4.4.2 Conversion

One word-formation process which causes no change at all in word form is conversion, the process by which a word in one class gives rise to an identical word form in another word class, e.g.:

- *to knife* < the noun *knife*
- *a look* < the verb *to look*

Depending on the theoretical position adopted, this is sometimes called instead either zero-derivation or functional shift. The linguistic analysis of this process is the topic of much debate, but this debate need not concern etymologists greatly. The important thing is that we are aware of the likelihood and frequency of conversion in the language and historical period that we are considering. Conversion has been very common in English from the Old English period onwards, greatly helped by (i) the loss of many distinctive derivative suffixes as a result of the reduction or loss of unstressed vowels in late Old English and early Middle English, and (ii) the increasing frequency of the weak conjugation of verbs, in which the stem vowel remains the same in all tenses.[15]

---

[15] For discussion of the early period see Kastovsky (1992: 382–3, 392–6); for some useful statistics see Algeo (1998: 67–8). For an analysis of the types found in contemporary English see Hickey (2006).

4.4.3 Ellipsis and clipping

Some processes typically give rise to new dictionary words, i.e. forms which stand at the head of dictionary entries, but they are arguably not word-formation processes.

A type of change which sits uneasily between word formation, change in word form, and semantic change is ellipsis. This is the shortening of an existing compound or phrase so that one element comes to take on the previous meaning of the whole compound or phrase. It is probably shown by the names of many military ranks in English, e.g. *major* which arose from *sergeant-major* in the same meaning (even though the two terms are distinguished in meaning in present-day English: see further section 8.6.3). This could be explained as a change in word form, with the longer form *sergeant-major* being clipped at the boundary between its two constituent elements to give *major*. Alternatively, we could explain it as semantic change, with *major* (which existed earlier in other uses as a noun) taking on the meaning denoting a military officer as a result of association with *sergeant-major*. Compare similarly *private* or *general*. In other cases there is no antecedent use in the same word class, and thus analysis as a change in word form seems more certain, e.g.:

- *porky* (1985; < *porky pie*, itself rhyming slang for 'lie')
- *rarebit* (1848; < *Welsh rarebit*, itself a folk-etymological alteration of *Welsh rabbit*)

Similarly in Latin one finds:

- *persicum* 'peach' (< *persicum mālum*, literally 'Persian apple')
- *magica* 'magic' (< *ars magica* 'magical art')
- *mīlle* 'mile' (< *mīlle passuum*, literally 'thousand paces')

In the case of *mīlle* we could perhaps analyse this as showing a specific sense development of *mīlle* 'thousand' on the model of the longer phrase, but this seems less likely with *magica* (formally the feminine of the adjective *magicus*) or *persicum* (formally the neuter of the adjective *persicus*). When we are examining past stages in a language's history, we will often have no direct evidence for the longer compound or phrase which has been subject to ellipsis, and we will have to reconstruct on the basis of known patterns in the language concerned: for instance, in the case of *magica*, if we had no evidence for *ars magica* we would have to work backwards from the fact that we have what is formally a feminine adjective used as a noun, and try to work out whether this could reasonably be explained as an ellipsis for some longer phrase.

Clipping is a process of shortening of a word form without change of meaning or word class, usually leaving a form which is morphologically incomplete or unanalysable. The point at which a clipping may occur in a word is generally quite unpredictable, although there may be observable patterns in some languages in some periods. Since the result of clipping has the same meaning and word class as the longer form which has been clipped, we could describe clipping as a change in word form rather than a process of word formation. Against this analysis is the fact that there is often a difference of stylistic level, since clipped forms are often familiar or slang formations. Clipping is common in contemporary English, usually forming colloquial synonyms of the clipped word, but it is not at all common in most earlier periods of the language's history.[16] Some recent examples include:

- *prole* (< *proletarian*; first recorded in 1887)
- *prefab* (< *prefabricated*; 1937)
- *mayo* (< *mayonnaise*; 1940)
- *narco* (< *narcotic*; 1954)
- *decaf* (< *decaffeinated*; 1956)
- *blog* (< *weblog*; 1999)

Earlier examples include:

- *coz* (1559; < *cousin*)
- *wig* (1675; < *periwig*)
- *canter* '(of a horse) to move at a moderate gallop' (1706; < *canterbury* 'to canter' < *Canterbury* 'an easy galloping pace', elliptical for *Canterbury pace, Canterbury gallop*, etc. < the place name *Canterbury*, with allusion to the pace taken to be characteristic of Canterbury pilgrims on horseback)

Some early examples, such as *gent* < *gentleman*, *miss* < *mistress*, or *ma* < *master*, may have originated as graphic abbreviations in the written language, at first read as the full word and only later coming to be realized by a clipped spoken form, but we can seldom be sure of this.

---

[16] See for instance the discussion in Marchand (1969) 441–50. For some examples from the early modern period see also Nevalainen (1999) 432–3. For eighteenth-century comment on clipping see Baugh and Cable (2002) 259–60.

In English clipping is often accompanied by some remodelling of the ending of the clipped form: e.g. *nappy < napkin, barbie < barbecue*, in both of which the ending is probably modelled after words with the diminutive suffix *-iel-y*. Similarly *heinie* 'the buttocks' *< behind* with remodelling after *-iel-y*, but probably also with some influence from *Heine*, a slang term for a German soldier; or *jammies < pyjamas*, where the clipped form has also retained the plural ending. The same phenomenon is frequent in personal names, e.g. *Andy (< Andrew), Charlie (< Charles), Patty (< Patricia)*.[17]

Clipping is also common in several other modern European languages, as for instance French *météo < météorologique* 'meteorological', or German *Uni < Universität* 'university'. In Japanese clipping is often found in borrowed words from English and other Western languages, which often have a large number of syllables as a result of accommodation to the sound system of Japanese, for example *hoomu* 'platform' *< purattohoomu <* English *platform*. Clipping is also common in Japanese in the dimorphemic compounds borrowed from or modelled on Chinese words which we encountered in section 4.3.1, and in these both parts of the compound may be clipped, for instance *tokkyuu* 'special express (train)' *< tokubetukyuukoo*.[18] Clipping has much less frequently been identified in ancient or medieval languages, although this may to some extent be a result of the type of vocabulary which is recorded in our surviving documentation. The exception to this is personal names, where clipping is quite common in earlier periods, especially when accompanied by morphological remodelling or suffixation (as in *Andy* etc. above): see discussion in section 9.2.3.

There are also phonetic processes involving loss of one or more sounds from a word, which are not normally regarded as part of word formation, although the resulting word forms are often listed separately in dictionaries if they gain some currency, and particularly if they come to realize a different nuance of meaning or belong to a different register or stylistic level. These include:

- aphaeresis, loss of an unstressed initial syllable, e.g. *monish < admonish*. When only an unstressed initial vowel is lost, this is sometimes distinguished as aphesis, e.g. *gainst < against*.

---

[17] For a detailed discussion see Plag (2003) 116–21.
[18] For the Japanese examples see Backhouse (1993) 85-6.

- apocope, loss of a single sound at the end of a word, for example in processes of assimilation and loss such as /θaʊzən/ for *thousand*, or in the characteristic loss of unstressed final vowels in Middle English.
- syncope, loss of a sound or sounds medially, e.g. *kerchief* < *keverchief* or *coverchief*, *curtsy* < *courtesy*, *fancy* < *fantasy*, in the last two cases with subsequent differentiation in meaning.

In well-documented periods of linguistic history we may have the luxury of observing a period in which the parent form and the variant coexist in the same meaning, followed by a period in which differentiation occurs. In less well-documented periods all that we may have is evidence for forms which are already differentiated in meaning, and we may have to hypothesize that the one originated as a variant of the other, in a process similar to that seen with *ordnance* and *ordinance* in section 3.6.

4.4.4 Blends

There is a very familiar type of formation in modern English known as a blend, in which two truncated word stems combine to form a new word, e.g. *smog* < *smoke* and *fog*. Several categories of such formations can be distinguished.[19] In one common type, the two truncated word stems are combined at a point in each word where the same sound occurs, or where there is at least some similarity of sound, as in *smog* or the following examples:

- *mockumentary* (< *mock* and *documentary*)
- *motel* (< *motor* and *hotel*)
- *banjolin* (< *banjo* and *mandolin*)
- *threequel* (< *three* and *sequel*, denoting a second sequel)
- *hacktivist* (< *hack* and *activist*, denoting a politically motivated computer hacker)
- *faction* (< *fact* and *fiction*)

Often the formations denote things which are themselves hybrid, or else which are regarded as being hybrid (as *mockumentary*, *banjolin*, *faction*), and thus the formations are at least partly iconic, embodying hybridity in

---

[19] For a more detailed analysis of blends in modern English based on prosodic morphology see Plag (2003) 121–6.

their own hybrid form. Another formal characteristic shown by all of these examples is that the resulting blend word has the same number of syllables as one of the parent words, and the same stressed syllable. However, some other blends do not show this characteristic, e.g.:

- *penultimatum* (< *penultimate* and *ultimatum*; although this could instead be explained as an analogous formation, *ultimate* : *ultimatum* = *penultimate* : *penultimatum*)

In other examples there is shared phonetic material, but not at precisely the point where the blend occurs, although the criteria of having the same number of syllables as one of the parent words, and the same stressed syllable, are met:

- *chunnel* (< *channel* and *tunnel*)
- *stagflation* (< *stagnation* and *inflation*)

Some linguists would group these together with a wider class of words which are formed from non-meaningful segments of other words, such as:

- *docudrama* (< *documentary* and *drama*, denoting a type of hybrid television programme)
- *edutainment* (< *education* and *entertainment*)
- *infotainment* (< *information* and *entertainment*)

These formations clearly also convey hybridity iconically, and do not show meaningful segments of the words from which they are formed. However, *-tainment* could also be analysed as a new affix with very low-level productivity within a particular specialist register; interestingly, *docutainment* is also found. Perhaps it is in fact an affix which has developed from blend formations. Such a development is probably shown by *-istor*, found in *transistor* (a blend of *transfer* and *resistor*) and then subsequently in *neuristor*, *spacistor*, *thermistor*, *thyristor*, *varistor*, etc.

A slightly more complex case is presented by *-burger*. English *hamburger* originally showed a borrowing from German *Hamburger* 'person from Hamburg', which was also its earliest meaning in English. In the late nineteenth century *Hamburger steak* is found denoting a beef patty, and shortly afterwards *hamburger* is found in the same meaning, and also denoting a type of sandwich containing such a patty. This last meaning gave rise to blend formations which we can divide into two groups semantically:

(1) *cheeseburger*, a hamburger sandwich with the addition of cheese, *egg-burger*, a hamburger sandwich with the addition of egg, etc.
(2) *chickenburger*, a hamburger sandwich with chicken substituted for the beef patty, *crab burger*, a hamburger sandwich with crab substituted for the beef patty, etc.

In British English (but not generally in North American English) *hamburger* and the clipped form *burger* also remained in frequent use denoting the beef patty, rather than the sandwich as a whole, giving rise to the new formation *beefburger* in the same meaning, which we could analyse as showing either a compound of *beef* and *burger* or a blend of *beef* and *hamburger*. In British English we similarly find *chickenburger*, *porkburger*, *nutburger*, etc., denoting patties made out of chicken, pork, nuts, etc. (This *chickenburger* is hence distinct semantically from the *chickenburger* noted above.) On semantic grounds, it seems more reasonable to analyse these as showing either blends or formations in a suffix *-burger*, rather than compounds in the clipped form *burger*, although this is complicated by the fact that *burger* is itself sometimes found in the broader sense 'patty (made out of a foodstuff identified contextually)' in British English.

Blends of the type shown by *smog* or *mockumentary* are found in English with some frequency from the late nineteenth century onwards. This is thus a process which anyone looking at the etymologies of contemporary English words needs to be aware of, as a typical word-forming process, with its own characteristic patterns as regards position of stress, shared phonetic material, etc. This type is not common in the earlier history of English, nor in other languages. The type shown by *docudrama*, *edutainment*, etc. (and by *transistor*, *cheeseburger*, etc.) is found sporadically in many other periods, and in many other languages. Blending of this sort shows a good deal of overlap with the processes of contamination and reanalysis, which we will look at in detail in section 7.4.4. It is also typically found among groups of expressive words, and we will look at some examples in section 4.5.3.

4.4.5 Back formation

Back formation is a process in which reanalysis of an existing word as showing a particular affix leads to the creation of a new word which is taken to be its morphological base. The verb *peddle* (first recorded in the seventeenth century) is probably a back formation from *pedlar, peddler* (fourteenth century), which is in turn probably an alteration of *pedder* (twelfth century) by analogy with the variation found between *tinkler* and *tinker*. However, since *pedder* has no secure further etymology, all of the suppositions in this instance rest on the relative dates of first occurrence in the historical record. Likewise, *burgle* (nineteenth century) is probably from *burglar* (sixteenth century), which probably reflects a post-classical Latin alteration of *burgator*.

To take an example where the further etymology is known with more certainty, *mase* 'to function or act as a maser' (1962) has been formed as a result of reanalysis of *maser* (1955), which is in fact in origin an acronym from the initial letters of *m*icrowave *a*mplification by *s*timulated *e*mission of *r*adiation, although it could be argued here that the acronym *maser* is itself partially motivated by its resemblance to an agent noun in *-er*, hence with an analysis as 'something which mases' always potentially available. (See section 4.4.6 on the related word *laser*.)

marl (1617), a nautical term meaning 'to fasten with marline or small line', was formed by reanalysis of *marling* 'marline', as though it showed a verb stem *marl* and the noun-forming suffix *-ing*. Historically, both *marling* and *marline* are borrowings from Dutch *marlinc*, in the case of *marling* showing assimilation to the *-ing* ending of verbal nouns, and in the case of *marline* showing folk-etymological alteration as a result of semantic association with *line*. An unfamiliar, monomorphemic borrowed word has thus been reanalysed in two different ways, resulting in at least partially analysable forms, and in the case of *marling* this has led to further reanalysis of the first syllable of the word as a verb stem, and hence the back formation *marl*. In fact, in this instance the same process probably also occurred in Dutch, which also has a verb *marlen* which is probably based on *marling*, a similarly motivated variant of *marlinc*. Alternatively, the English verb could show a borrowing from Dutch, in which case the back formation occurred only in Dutch. We will return to the wider question of reanalysis and associated processes in section 7.4.

In some cases the arguments in support of an analysis as a back formation are rather more complex. *word processor* (1968) considerably antedates the verb *word process* (1982), and in the well-documented world of office activity in the late twentieth century there are no reasonable grounds for suspecting that *word process* in fact existed for fourteen years without leaving any trace in documents available to lexicographers. It therefore seems certain that *word processor* must have preceded *word process* chronologically, and *word processor* is easily explicable as a compound in which *word* stands in an objective relationship to *processor* (i.e. this is a device which processes words). However, we are then faced with a difficulty: does *word process* show a back formation < *word processor*, or does it show a verb-headed compound < *word* and *process*, on the model of *word processor*? To answer this question, we need to know something about the frequency of verb-headed compounds of this type in modern English. As it turns out, such formations are rare, except in cases like *word process* (or *typewrite*) which can alternatively be explained as back formations, or cases like *litmus-test*, which can alternatively be explained as showing conversion from a noun compound.[20] On this basis, many scholars identify cases such as *word process* as back formations.[21]

4.4.6 Acronyms and initialisms

Some types of formation belong very characteristically to the languages of modern literate societies, because they are based upon the (regular, standardized) spellings of longer phrases. Both acronyms and initialisms are formed from the initial letters of phrases, although there is often some licence regarding which letters are actually included in the formation, particularly in the case of acronyms. Acronyms are pronounced as the 'word' spelt by the resulting string of letters, such as *maser* in the preceding section, or the slightly later formation *laser* (1960) which was modelled on it (< the initial letters of *l*ight *a*mplification by the *s*timulated *e*mission of *r*adiation, although with the express intention of providing a name for an 'optical maser'). Initialisms are pronounced simply as a series of letter names, such as *DVD* < the initial letters of *d*igital *v*ideo *d*isk (although a group of companies later agreed to reinterpret the initialism as in fact standing for *d*igital *v*ersatile *d*isk, to better reflect the uses of the disks so denoted for e.g. storage of computer data as well as for storing video).

Both acronyms and initialisms are far removed from more natural modes of word formation, whose products can emerge for the first time with little or no introspection from speakers in the context of natural language

---

[20] Compare discussion in Adams (2001) 100–9, Plag (2003) 154–5.

[21] For discussion of some other types which present difficulties of analysis see Barnhart (1989), Adams (2001) 136–8.

use. Acronyms and initialisms are by their nature thought-out, conscious coinages, and sometimes are indeed decided on by committees, selecting names for new products, organizations, etc. from a variety of possibilities. However, this is also true of many particular examples of other types of word formation, and there is only a cline separating entirely natural formations from entirely contrived ones.

Rather oddly, acronyms are very frequently invoked as explanations of the etymologies of slang words in popular, non-scientifically based attempts at etymology: see section 7.4.5.1.

4.5 Arbitrary and non-arbitrary linguistic signs

The types of word formation which we have so far encountered all draw on the internal resources of language. Everything that is involved is contained entirely within the sphere of language. The same is true of borrowing, where words or other units are taken from one language into another. However, some words have a more direct connection with the external, non-linguistic world in their origin, for instance through onomatopoeia, and we will look at these in this final section.

The default state of affairs in linguistics was characterized by the great Swiss linguist Ferdinand de Saussure as reflecting the 'arbitrariness of the linguistic sign'.[22] To take a very simple illustration from the world of etymology, the connection between the word form *apple* and the thing it denotes is entirely arbitrary. From the standpoint of an etymologist, if we want to trace the origin of the word *apple*, we certainly want to know what an apple is, and what the main qualities are that people have in mind when they call something an apple. However, we can contemplate an orchard full of apples for as long as we like without gaining any insight into why an apple is called by the name *apple*, since the relationship between the real-world object and its name is arbitrary. Knowledge about what an apple is, and knowledge about what people think of as being characteristic of an apple, may help us in the task of establishing relationships between the word

---

[22] 'The linguistic sign is arbitrary. There is no internal connexion, for example, between the idea "sister" and the French sequence of sounds s-ö-r which acts as its signal.' (de Saussure, translated Harris (1983) 67): 'Le signe linguistique est arbitraire. Ainsi l'idée de "sœur" n'est liée par aucun rapport intérieur avec la suite des sons *s-ö-r* qui lui sert de signifiant.' (de Saussure (1972) 100).

apple and other words which denote related things or concepts. However, this will be essentially a language-internal investigation, in which real-world knowledge has simply enabled us to identify a set of potentially related words within the linguistic system of arbitrary signs. To put things the other way around, if we were to encounter an apple for the first time but did not know what it was called, there is nothing about its physical properties that could give us any clue that *apple* was the name for this object.

We have encountered many words which are analysable, such as *blackbird*. As we noted in section 2.1.2, *blackbird* is clearly a lexicalized name for a particular type of black bird: thus, within the linguistic system, it is a non-arbitrary word. However, there is no more connection between the name *blackbird* and its real-world referent than there is between a monomorphemic word like *apple* and its referent. If the word *black* meant 'green' and *bird* meant 'largish round hard fruit', then *blackbird* would be a perfectly good analysable name for an apple, rather than for a blackbird. There is no non-arbitrary connection between the word *black* and blackness, or between the word *bird* and the type of animal, any more than there is between *apple* and a real-world apple. The word *blackbird* is analysable only within the world of language, and at no point is the connection with the real-world referent anything other than completely arbitrary. In French the words for 'apple' and 'blackbird' are respectively *pomme* and *merle*, both of which have equally arbitrary relationships with their real-world referents. (The situation would become rapidly much more complex if we were to look at some abstract words, and at how the ranges of senses realized by a particular word form differ in different languages, but that is outside the scope of the present discussion.)

A very small minority of words in most languages are apprehended by speakers as having a more direct connection with the real world, in that they are taken to express some facet of the real world onomatopoeically or expressively. Without doubt such factors do actually play a part in the formation of some words. However, beyond this almost everything is very much disputed. Certainly there are some true cases of onomatopoeia, i.e. words which through their sound represent some non-linguistic sound iconically, albeit often only very approximately. However, there are also certainly cases which many speakers perceive as onomatopoeic which in fact belong entirely to the conventions of the language-internal realm. We can also term such relationships iconic, but if so we must make an important distinction in our use of the term. Truly onomatopoeic words make a connection between linguistic form and the external, non-linguistic world. We can term this sort of iconicity imagic iconicity. Most other types of iconicity which we have encountered so far in this book involve associations and connections entirely within the world of linguistic signs. We can term this sort of iconicity diagrammatic iconicity.[23] It is this sort of iconicity that is shown by expressive formations which depend for their expressive quality on sounds which they have in common with other words of similar meaning, such as for instance the /sl/ of words such as *slip*, *slide*, or *slime*. Expressive formations, and what are called phonaesthemes, open up some very difficult theoretical areas, but we must give them some consideration here, because they are often invoked in etymological arguments, and are almost as often extremely controversial.

4.5.1 Words representing sounds in the natural world, and related phenomena

Some cases of onomatopoeia are fairly uncontroversial, such as words which represent certain sounds in the natural world, e.g. *bang*, *pop*, *whoosh*. In sentences such as *It went bang* the onomatopoeic aspect can be emphasized in the pronunciation of the onomatopoeic word, for instance *bang* might be pronounced more loudly and/or rapidly than the other words in the utterance, although it need not be, and all onomatopoeic words are to a large extent conventionalized iconic representations of sounds in the real world. A similar group of words comprises interjections such as *pah*, *pish*, *phew*, *pooh*, showing verbal realizations of various non-verbal means of expressing one's feelings by blowing, expressing air through pursed lips, with or without puffed-out cheeks, etc. This is an area where the boundaries between the verbal and the non-verbal can be very indistinct.

Slightly further removed from the natural world are many verbs denoting manners of speaking which have some expressive component, iconically representing the mode of speech denoted, e.g. Latin *murmurāre* (> English *murmur*) or English *mumble* or *mamble*. However, in the case of the latter two words we also appear to have some more familiar derivational morphology in the shape of the frequentative suffix *-le*. A little comparative work also brings to light *mum*, *mammer*, *mammock* in related meanings, and

---

[23] For an introduction to these concepts see Fischer and Nänny (1999) or Van Langendonck (2007).

forms in other Germanic languages such as German *mammeln, memmeln, mummeln, mummen* or Dutch *mommelen, mummelen, mommen.* This brings us immediately face to face with a very common problem in exploring words which have any sort of expressive or sound-symbolic component: they tend to come in rather extended 'families' of similar formations, which may or may not be related to one another historically. We can sometimes analyse such word groups in terms of regular word-formation processes from a common base, but they often defy such analysis. Very often within such groups we find full or partial blends of existing words, contamination of word forms, or fresh remodelling on a sound-symbolic basis, e.g. substitution of a different stem vowel because it better satisfies some speakers' perceptions of the sound denoted. We will look at some more extreme examples of this type in section 4.5.3.

4.5.2 Animal sounds and animal names

We find onomatopoeia in many of the names of different animals' distinctive cries, such as the *miaow* of a cat, the *bow-wow* or *woof-woof* of a dog, the *baa* of a sheep, and so on. However, these are not necessarily the same in all languages, and even within a language we can find variation, as between *bow-wow* and *woof-woof* in modern English. The *miaow* of a cat has plenty of parallels elsewhere. We may be slightly suspicious of French *miaou*, Italian *miao*, or German *miau*, since these could perhaps result from borrowing in one direction or another, but we can be fairly confident that this is not the case with Japanese *nyaa* or Chinese *miao miao*. In other words, there is no reason to suspect that this particular word shows widespread early borrowing which is reflected by an odd collection of historically unrelated languages in different corners of the world, when we can much more plausibly hypothesize that a similar onomatopoeic formation has arisen independently in different languages. However, if we turn to the dog's cry, alongside English *bow-wow* (or *woof-woof*) we find French *ouah ouah*, Italian *bau bau*, German *wau wau* (or *wuff wuff*), Japanese *wanwan* (or *kyankyan*), and Chinese *wang wang*. For sheep, beside English *baa* we find French *beee*, Italian *beeee*, German *bähh*, but Japanese *mee* and Chinese *mieh mieh.* (Some of these forms show very approximate orthographic transcriptions of words which are commonly perceived as having only an unofficial or casual status.) It seems clear that each of these words was formed with the plain intention of representing the animal's cry transparently, and yet the results are different, and not just in ways that we might be able to predict from the range of possible sounds permitted by the phonology of each language. Additionally, a spectrogram of a speaker saying one of these words and a spectrogram of an animal actually making its sound are, unsurprisingly, quite different from one another. Humans are only imitating the sounds of animals in a very loose sense, and can often make much better imitations when not operating within the constraints of language. However, we can see that the onomatopoeic quality of such words is definitely felt by speakers when, as frequently happens, onomatopoeic words are excluded from the operation of otherwise regular sound changes. Thus, in an often cited example, in Middle English there is a verb *pīpen* /piːpən/ denoting the sound made by a small bird (and also the sound made by a piper, etc.), which should give /paɪp/ in modern English as a result of the Great Vowel Shift, yet from the early modern English period onwards we find *peep* /piːp/ denoting the sound made by a small bird, thus apparently showing the reflex of the Middle English verb with failure of the Great Vowel Shift diphthongization. However, there is a little complexity to this story, since at least in literature we also find that small birds continue to *pipe* with the expected (eventual) Great Vowel Shift output /paɪp/. We could explain this situation in various different ways, but it is clear that there are competing pressures at work here, which may result either in the iconic, onomatopoeic relationship with the sound in the real world being preserved, or in the conventionalized nature even of an originally onomatopoeic linguistic sign becoming increased through the operation of regular sound change.[24]

In addition to words which denote the sound made by an animal, we also find numerous names of animals, especially birds, which originate in more or less close conventionalized representations of the animals' cries, for instance bird names such as *chiff-chaff, petchary, peewee, peesweep, peetweet, peewit, morepork, poorwill, potrack, purl, whippoorwill*, etc. But even names of this kind are to some extent conventionalized, conforming to the phonological and phonotactic rules of the language in question, rather than realistic representations of the bird's cry. Several of these examples almost certainly also show some degree of folk-etymological association with other words: hence an iconic pressure for relationships between linguistic signs can be seen to be competing with the iconic motivation of a link between the linguistic sign and a sound in the real world. Additionally, some of these names are applied to more than one different type of bird, each with a rather different cry, and in the *peewee, peesweep, peetweet, peewit* group

---

[24] Compare on this example also Hock (1991) 50.

we also find some cases of a single bird being denoted by more than one different name.

In time the conventional nature of such names tends to gain at the expense of the onomatopoeic element. A frequently cited example is French *pigeon* (> English *pigeon*) which is separated by a number of regular sound changes from its etymon Latin *pīpio, pīpion-*, hence losing its original onomatopoeic connection with the call of a young bird; an indirect effect of the increasing conventionalization of this word can be seen in the semantic shift from 'nestling, young bird' to 'pigeon (irrespective of age)', even though adult pigeons coo rather than peep.

4.5.3 Phonaesthesia and expressive formations

Some other words which are often identified as onomatopoeic in everyday speech or in literary criticism do not in fact show any explicit imitative component, but are instead identified popularly as 'sounding like' the thing or action they express because of the common semantic associations that a sound or sound combination has in a group of different words. (They thus show diagrammatic iconicity, not imagic iconicity.) For instance, since the Old English period English has had (earlier forms of) the nouns *slime* and *slough* and the verbs *slide* (plus a related word *slidder*, which in turn gave rise to *slither*) and *slip* (or at least the related adjective *slipper* which gave rise to later *slippery*). These words have no historical relationship with one another, but all have the initial consonant cluster /sl/, and some semantic common ground. It is very debatable whether the /sl/ of these words has any intrinsic connection with slime or slipperiness for someone who is not a speaker of English, but what is not in any doubt is that English has since accrued a number of further words for mud or slimy stuff all of which begin with the same consonant cluster: (in very roughly chronological order) *slike, slitch, sleech, sludge, slutch, slush*, and *slosh*. Of these, *slike* and *slitch* probably show reflexes of an unrecorded Old English word, since there are likely cognates such as Frisian *slyk*, Middle Dutch *slijc*, and Middle Low German *slīk*. The other words have no firmly established formal etymology. They probably show alterations or remodellings of *slitch*, probably with an expressive motivation. The /sl/ element can perhaps be identified as a phonaestheme, a constant element which speakers identify as reflecting the perceived semantic similarity between these words, even though the original members of the group have no historical relationship with one another. We should perhaps also draw into this word group *slaver* and *slobber* (both first recorded in Middle English), and regional *slabber* and *slubber*, which have probable connections with similar words in Dutch and Low German. If /sl/ does have any sort of coherent identity across this group of words, it must be at a submorphemic level, since the words are clearly all monomorphemic (except for the frequentative derivative formations *slidder* and *slither*).[25] In the later members of this group of words with initial /sl/, such as *sludge*, *slush*, or *slosh*, the initial phonaestheme appears to be a constant, followed by a variety of different expressive word endings. Of course, if we do think that /sl/ has any coherent identity across this group of words, we must acknowledge that there are many other English words with initial /sl/ which have no semantic connection with mud, slime, slipperiness, etc., e.g. *slender*, *slight*, *slake*, *sloe*, *slay*, *slaughter*, *slat*, *slit*, etc.

Quite often words for which we may suspect an expressive or ono-matopoeic origin are encountered in groups of apparently related items for which no coherent formal etymology can easily be constructed. For instance, we can compare *piddle, paddle, pittle, tiddle, widdle, twiddle, diddle, niddle, fiddle, quiddle, toddle, doddle, tottle*, all with meanings denoting repeated movement, often of an ineffectual or desultory sort. Much of this may be attributed to the shared suffix *-le*, which forms verbs with a frequentative meaning (i.e. describing repeated actions), often also with diminutive meaning or connotation. However, the presence of a dental preceding the suffix, preceded in turn by a short vowel, in this large group of words may not be accidental. How this should be explained, whether as showing a phonaestheme, or as showing the result of analogy in the formation of this group of words, is a much more difficult question. Some of these words are formed from fairly reliably identified bases, but many are of quite unknown etymology. However, it should be noted that there are other similar formations with other frequentative suffixes, such as *totter*, *dodder*, etc., and we should hesitate to assert too confidently that English has a dental + syllabic /l/ phonaestheme. Blending could also explain some instances (compare section 4.4.4).[26]

---

[25] Following a distinction introduced in Bolinger (1950), such a proposed phonaes-thetic element at the beginning of a word is sometimes referred to as an assonance, and a similar element at the end of a word is referred to as a rime.

[26] For a useful discussion of the difficulties encountered in the analysis of such extended word groups see Hock (1991) 177–9. For overviews of phonaesthetic

quagmire occurs first in the sixteenth century. It has no established etymology, but does have a lot of synonyms or near-synonyms, which are all
first recorded in the sixteenth or seventeenth centuries, and which show a
striking similarity of form: *quallmire, quamire, quavemire, quawmire, quab-
mire, quadmire, quakemire,* and more remotely *bogmire* and *gogmire.* Of
these, *quakemire* appears transparently related to the verb *quake,* which is
recorded from the Old English period onwards, although it has no further
known etymology. *quavemire* can plausibly be connected with *quave* 'to
quake', which is first recorded in early Middle English, and again has no
further etymology. We could perhaps speculate that the other words all
show alterations of one or other of these words, perhaps as remodellings
of what was already felt to be an expressive word in order to achieve what
seemed to various speakers more expressive forms. However, this must
remain pure speculation, especially since neither *quake* nor *quave* has any
further etymology, except for the suggestion that both may be expressive
formations themselves. They are recorded much earlier than any of the
words of the *quagmire* type, but with expressive words chronology is often
no sure guide, since such words may be rare in the sorts of registers and stylistic levels reflected by the majority of our documentary evidence. However,
such doubt about the relationships among a group of word forms and their
ulterior etymology is hardly unique to the world of expressive formations
(we will look at a number of examples in chapters 7 and 8), and were it not
for the semantics of this word group we could classify this as just another
example of a word cluster of unascertained etymology.

There is perhaps less doubt that there is some imitative motivation for the
sorts of reduplicated formations we find in English expressing some sort of
repeated or alternating action or sound, such as *trip-trap, chit-chat, tittle-
tattle,* etc.[27], although it is less clear that the characteristic patterns of vowel
variation found in such formations owe anything to sound symbolism.[28]

formations in English see Adams (2001) 121–32, Marchand (1969) 397–428, and see
also the analysis in Wales (1990). For an attempt to link *paddle* with a different group of
possibly expressively motivated words see Smithers (1954) 88–91. Smithers in this paper
proposes a detailed scheme for analysis of patterns of consonant and vowel variation
in groups of apparently related words of an expressive or imitative nature. On various
different methodological and terminological approaches to material of this nature see
also Meier (1999).

[27] For further examples see Marchand (1969: 429–39).

[28] See Minkova (2002) for an important account which explains the vowel variation
without invoking sound symbolism or phonaesthesia.

The similarity to the patterns of alternation seen in the present and past stems of English strong verbs (see section 4.4.1) is striking and is open to a range of interpretations.

It is very debatable whether there are sounds which have iconic value across a range of languages without being directly onomatopoeic. A fairly uncontroversial example is the occurrence of consonant doubling in expressive derivative formations in many languages, such as Latin *garrīre* 'to chatter' (probably < Indo-European **gar-*; see section 1.3.1).[29] A rather more controversial but very frequently cited example is the tendency for words with diminutive meanings to have high front vowels, e.g. *wee*, *teeny*, *little*, and for words denoting large size to have low back vowels, e.g. *vast*, *large*,[30] although there are obvious exceptions, e.g. English *big* and *small*. This example is discussed in detail in Wescott (1971), where many other possible examples of iconic features of this sort are collected together. However, it is perhaps not unfair to observe that (i) few of the other examples listed by Wescott have been taken up so widely as this one, (ii) many of these are regarded by a great many scholars as being quite untenable, and (iii) few additions to Wescott's list have been made by other scholars, even those sympathetic to this approach.

This book is not the place for more extensive treatment of this topic, but it is one that no etymologist can completely ignore. We may conclude for present purposes that it is important for etymologists to be aware of work of this kind, but also to be aware of how controversial it is, and to be wary of setting too much store by arguments based on phonaesthesia or iconicity without investigating all other possibilities very carefully.

[29] On such consonant gemination in English and in other Germanic languages compare Martinet (1937), and also Smithers (1954), Hogg (1982).

[30] Compare also Smith (2006) on proximal *these* and distal *those*. See also Fischer (1999) 126–9, and further references given there.

5

Lexical borrowing

5.1 Basic concepts and terminology

Borrowing is the usual term for the process by which a language (or variety) takes new linguistic material from another language (or variety), usually called the donor. In keeping with the focus of this book, I will look mostly at borrowed words, but it is important to note that other units such as morphemes or phonemes, or even syntactic features, may also be borrowed. Borrowing occurs in situations of language contact, and is indeed an almost inevitable consequence of it, although the levels and the types of borrowing which are found differ greatly in different types of contact situation.

The term *borrowing* is conventional and is in almost universal use, but it is no new observation that the metaphor of 'borrowing' is not entirely apposite. The relevant item is not taken away from the 'donor' language as a result of the 'borrowing'; rather, it spreads from one language to another, with the result that it is subsequently found in both. Furthermore, there is no assumption that anything will be 'given back' to the 'donor', precisely because nothing has been given away in the first place. Crucially, a word which has been borrowed will very likely change and develop in different ways in the donor language and in the borrowing language, or it may very possibly die out in either or both.

Perhaps the easiest way to illustrate this is by looking at some of the relatively rare instances when a word or phrase which has been borrowed from one language into another is either borrowed back subsequently into the original donor language, or affects the meaning of the donor:

- French *prêt-à-porter* 'designer clothing sold ready to wear' (1951) is formed < *prêt* 'ready' + *à* 'for, to' + *porter* 'to carry, to wear' on the model of (or as a loan translation of) English *ready-to-wear*. The French expression is then borrowed into English (in unnaturalized or semi-naturalized form) as *prêt-à-porter* (in 1957), hence as a synonym or near-synonym of the existing expression *ready-to-wear*, but with the advantage of the perceived prestige of French terminology in the world of fashion.
- English *milord* 'an English nobleman in Europe, an Englishman travelling in Europe in aristocratic style' (1607) is a borrowing < French *milord* (earlier *milourt*), but this is itself a borrowing (with conversion from form of address to noun, and narrowing of meaning) < English *my lord*. In this instance, English speakers adopting French *milord* in its restricted sense were probably aware of its origin, and were making something of an ironic joke.
- English *panchway* 'light rowing boat used on rivers in Bengal' (1737) is < Bengali *pānsui*, variant of *pānsi* 'pinnace' < English *pinnace* + Bengali *-i*, suffix forming adjectives. (The form of the word in Bengali is perhaps influenced by various words in local vernaculars with meanings connected with water and sailing which have initial *pān-*.)
- English *mama-san* (1904) is < Japanese *mama-san* 'honoured mother, madam, proprietress, manageress of a bar, etc.', which is itself < *mama* 'mother' (an early-twentieth-century borrowing < English *mama*) + *-san*, an honorific title. (We might perhaps wonder how far such a word, which is used only when referring to Japanese cultural contexts, can be said to have been borrowed into English at all: this is a topic which we will turn to in detail in chapter 6.)
- *phase* was borrowed into English from French in the seventeenth century. In English, it developed specific senses in the fields of physics and chemistry, which were then borrowed back into French as semantic loans. In other words, the French word retained the same word

form, including its distinct pronunciation, but adopted new senses from English.

- English *pioneer* is < Middle French *pionnier* (French *pionnier*) 'labourer employed in digging' (*a*1230; earlier in senses 'foot soldier', 'pedestrian'), 'soldier employed to dig trenches and mines' (*c*1380); but subsequently in the nineteenth century the French word shows the senses 'an early colonist', 'an innovator' as semantic loans from English.
- English *plumber* is < Anglo-French *plummer*, *plomner* and Middle French *plommier*, *plombier*. In the 1970s, English *plumber* comes to have a specific metaphorical meaning (originally in the context of the Watergate scandal) 'a person employed to investigate or prevent "leaks" of information from a government office, department, etc.', and (in spite of the divergence in word form) this specific sense is borrowed by French *plombier* as early as 1973.

In these examples we have already seen several different types of lexical borrowing, and it is clear that we need some sort of typology and terminology to distinguish between them. A typology which is often employed makes the following main divisions:[1]

- Loanwords
- Loan translations
- Semantic loans
- Loan blends

5.1.1 Loanwords

Loanwords show borrowing of a word form and its associated word meaning, or a component of its meaning. Usually there is some degree of accommodation to the sound system of the borrowing language, e.g. English *phase* /feɪz/ (or when borrowed in the late seventeenth century /feːz/ or /fɛːz/) < French *phase* /faz/. Loanwords may show adaptation to the inflectional morphology of the borrowing language; for instance, many nouns borrowed into English show a regular plural in -*s* or -*es* in place of whatever plural morpheme is found in the donor language. However, many scholars draw a distinction between loanwords and words which show complete

---

[1] For an important, and more detailed, analysis see Haugen (1950). See also Fischer (2003) for an overview of different approaches.

replacement of a morph in the stem of the borrowed word with a morph from the borrowing language: for such cases see below on loan blends.

5.1.2 Loan translations

Loan translations (or calques) show replication of the structure of a foreign-language word or expression by use of synonymous word forms in the borrowing language, e.g. French *prêt-à-porter* is a calque on English *ready-to-wear*. We might be tempted to define loan translation as the use of 'the corresponding word forms' in the borrowing language, but this begs many questions, as there is seldom a precise one-to-one correspondence between any part of the lexicon of two languages. Even in the example of *prêt-à-porter* it is not completely certain that the French expression is modelled on English *ready-to-wear* rather than being a less exact loan translation of the synonymous *ready-for-wear*.

We cannot always be sure whether a particular formation is a loan translation, or simply a coincidental parallel in another language. For instance, English *Middle Europe* 'a loosely defined region of central northern Europe, extending roughly from Germany in the west to Poland and Hungary in the east' is probably formed on the model of German *Mitteleuropa*. The German term is recorded earlier with the same meaning, and in the culturally dominant language in the relevant geographical area, but we lack any evidence to prove that a loan translation has occurred. Clearer cases occur when we encounter a highly lexicalized (possibly encyclopedic) meaning which is very unlikely to be coincidental, such as English *New Christian* '(in medieval and early modern Spain) a Christianized Jew or (less frequently) Moor, especially one who converted only nominally in order to escape persecution or expulsion'. This is clearly modelled on Spanish *cristiano nuevo* in the same meaning and attested considerably earlier. Sometimes the historical record indicates the existence of a parallel in another language which is unlikely, on grounds of semantic probability, to be the result of coincidence, but one may have no clear way of telling which direction the influence has taken. However, if both languages have a well-documented historical record for the period in question, then dates of first attestation alone may sometimes be sufficient to create reasonable certainty about the direction of borrowing. For instance, *Nile green* 'a pale bluish green colour supposedly resembling that of the Nile' probably shows a calque on French *vert du Nile*. There is nothing in the contexts of the earliest examples in English or French which would preclude the reverse being the case, but the relative dates of first attestation, 1871 in English, 1830 in French, are probably enough for reasonable certainty that the French usage came first. In such cases, exhaustive searching in documentary sources might provide convincing support for a French origin of the term (or the reverse), but any definite proof on purely linguistic grounds is impossible.

5.1.3 Semantic loans

These show extension of the meaning of a word as a result of association with the meaning of a partly synonymous word in another language. The two words may be ultimately related, as in the cases above of French *phase* and English *phase* or French *plombier* and English *plumber*. They may have a formal resemblance to one another, but in fact not be related at all historically: for instance English *manage* and *management* were influenced semantically by French (unrelated but similar-sounding) *ménager* and *ménagement*. In other cases, the words involved may be unrelated and also bear no significant formal resemblance to one another: for instance, English *manner* shows considerable semantic influence from both Latin *modus* and Latin *mōs*; it occurs as a conventional translation equivalent of both of these from an early date. Similarly, classical Latin *ratiō* probably meant originally 'count, account', but acquired numerous other senses (such as 'reason') by association with ancient Greek *lógos*, which also had the meanings 'count, account'.

As with loan translations, it can often be difficult to differentiate cases of semantic borrowing from coincidental semantic development in two languages.[2] An additional concern is that it may sometimes be hard to tell apart (a) cases where the meaning of a word has been influenced directly by association with the range of meanings of a foreign-language word with which it shows some semantic overlap, and (b) cases of (not specifically linguistic) cultural influence in the development of concepts. For instance, the meanings of words denoting such concepts as 'god', 'heaven', 'hell' in English and other Germanic languages are profoundly influenced by contact both with Christian culture and with the paganism of Roman and

---

[2] For discussion and exemplification of this issue see Hoad (1993).

Greek antiquity, but it is often difficult to tell whether this shows a linguistic process of influence of Latin and Greek words on the meaning development of partial synonyms in English, or whether the influence is an extralinguistic one on the development of the concepts which these words denote. The development of the meaning of the word *hell* in Old English and Middle English was greatly influenced by both Christian and pagan Roman and Greek conceptions of the afterlife, but in lexical terms English *hell* corresponds to at least two different, semantically non-overlapping, groups of words in Latin, Greek, and Hebrew: in Latin, *Orcus*, *īnferī*, and *īnferna* all denote the abode of the dead (or *Hades* in the Greek tradition, in biblical use corresponding to Hebrew *šě'ōl*, literally 'grave'), while hell as a place or condition of punishment for sin is denoted by *gehenna* (a word ultimately of Hebrew origin via Greek). Is the influence that we have in this instance primarily lexical, or cultural? And how viable is it to make a distinction between the two?

In some cases we may wonder whether there is any continuity at all with the existing word, or whether we do not in fact have an independent borrowing, hence a new loanword, which happens to be homonymous with an existing word. English *milord* presents just such a difficult case: is it a borrowing of French *milord* (with a naturalized pronunciation, with final /d/ based either on the spelling or on association with *lord*), or does it show the existing reduced form of the form of address *my lord* (as in *You rang, milord?*), in (semantically narrowed) use as a noun on the model of the French word?

In cases of semantic loan, and perhaps also in cases of loan translation, we may prefer to say that we do not have borrowings at all but (in the case of semantic loan) semantic change or (in the case of loan translation) new words or phrases occurring as a result of influence from another language. We might indeed choose to explain the process in terms of analogy (see section 7.4), and say that what all three categories have in common is that they show the influence of one language on the lexis of another.

5.1.4 Loan blends

The three categories already described provide a useful framework for considering different types of lexical borrowing, but, as already noted, the dividing line between them is often unclear. We may have difficulty in assigning a particular example to a particular category: some examples may seem to sit rather awkwardly between categories. Many scholars in fact identify an intermediate category between loanwords and loan translations: loan blends. These show borrowing of a complex word with substitution of one or more native morphs for morphs in the borrowed word. English *neurotize* 'to provide with new nerve fibres or nerves' shows a borrowing of French *neurotiser* with substitution of English *-ize* or *-ise* for (ultimately related) French *-iser*. I have chosen a very rare word, because it has the advantage of being a very clear example of this phenomenon: *neurotiser* is a coinage by the French scientist Vanlair from 1882; its *-t-* is unexplained (it is perhaps after French *névrotique* 'neurotic') and is carried over faithfully into the English word. Another fairly clear case is shown by the example of *pioneer* which we encountered in section 5.1. The recorded French forms all show the ending *-ier*, and the English forms all show morphological substitution of either *-eer* or (in early forms such as *pioner*) *-er*. The French word is a derivative of *pion* 'foot soldier', which did not exist in English in this form at the date when *pioneer* was borrowed. (*pawn* does show borrowing of a variant of the same French word, and *pion* was itself later borrowed into English in some specialist uses.)

In very many other possible instances of loan blends (in English, certainly the majority) there are other available analyses. For instance, *martyrize*, *moralize*, *naturalize*, *neutralize*, *organize* all certainly show at least some degree of French influence. However, we cannot confidently eliminate the possibility that they may not be loan blends but loan translations, from a previously borrowed or otherwise related root word with the English suffix *-ize* added, on the model of the French word. Thus we could analyse *martyrize* as showing borrowing of French *martyriser* with remodelling of the ending after *-ize*, or we could analyse it as a formation < *martyr* + *-ize* on the model of French *martyriser*. In particular instances etymological dictionaries may make decisions in favour of, or have a policy of opting for, one possibility or the other, but this is a different matter from demonstrating without doubt that a particular word shows either a loan blend or a loan translation.

To take a couple of further examples, English *nosology* 'treatise dealing with diseases, classification of diseases' (1721) could readily be interpreted either as a formation from the neo-classical combining forms *noso-* and *-logy* (both of which are productive in English at this date) on the model of Latin *nosologia* (i.e. as a loan translation), or as a borrowing of the Latin word with substitution of *-y* for final *-ia* (i.e. as a loan blend). Similarly,

South African English *moderature* 'the executive council of a synod of the Dutch Reformed Church in South Africa' clearly shows some sort of influence from Afrikaans *moderatuur* in the same sense, but it is less clear whether the English word shows a loan blend with substitution of *-ure* for Afrikaans *-uur*, or a formation < *moderate* (verb) + *-ure*, on the model of the Afrikaans word (i.e. a loan translation).

5.1.5 Lehnwörter and Fremdwörter

An important and influential tradition in linguistics in the German-speaking world makes a further distinction within the category of loanword, distinguishing *Lehnwörter* 'loanwords' from *Fremdwörter* 'foreign words'. In this tradition, a *Lehnwort* shows accommodation (where appropriate) to native phonology and morphology and may give rise to new derivatives within the borrowing language, while a *Fremdwort* retains (broadly) its foreign-language pronunciation and may show non-native morphology (especially plural inflections which are not found in native words), and does not give rise to new derivatives within the borrowing language. This distinction has been very influential in many aspects of linguistic work in the German-speaking world, including lexicography: all but the most clearly assimilated and frequently used loanwords are often excluded from historical or etymological dictionaries of German, and find their place instead in separate dictionaries of *Fremdwörter*. However, in practice the distinction is hard to maintain consistently. Where different variants of a particular borrowed word show differing degrees of naturalization in pronunciation, or where the plural morphology shown by a word differs between naturalized and non-naturalized patterns, the distinction between *Lehnwörter* and *Fremdwörter* cannot easily be used as a criterion for determining how words will be treated lexicographically. For instance, in English the plural of *appendix* is sometimes *appendixes*, following the usual pattern of English plurals, and sometimes *appendices*, as in Latin (although with different pronunciation from in Latin). It would be very difficult to distinguish on that basis between a Lehnwort *appendix* with a plural *appendixes* and a Fremdwort *appendix* with a plural *appendices*, and if *appendix* was encountered in the singular, how could one tell which of the two it was? The distinction between *Lehnwörter* and *Fremdwörter* will not be used in this book, although it is interesting to note that it has some points of connection with current debates about code-switching which we will consider at the end of chapter 6.[3]

5.2 What constitutes a borrowing from language X into language Y?

In this book whenever I say that a word (or phrase etc.) was borrowed from one language to another, this means that, so far as we are able to ascertain, the borrowing was direct, unless it is specified that it was via the intermediary of another language. In the latter case, strictly speaking we have two separate acts of borrowing, from the first language into the intermediary, and thence into the destination language. However, if there has been no change in word form or meaning in the intermediary language, it may be difficult to demonstrate that this intermediate stage has actually occurred. Furthermore, we may suspect that perhaps the borrowing has been partly via an intermediary and partly direct from the original language (see section 6.5).

Some studies attempt to identify that component in the lexis of a language which shows a distinctive trace of origin in a certain other language. Terms ending in -ism such as Anglicism and Gallicism are frequently used to denote such lexis. The large collaborative project headed by Manfred Görlach which gave rise to the Dictionary of European Anglicisms and the accompanying set of studies English in Europe (Görlach 2001, 2002a) is a good illustration of this approach. Görlach and his collaborators looked at words ultimately of English origin in sixteen different contemporary European languages. They did not pay particular attention to the immediate mode of transmission. In many cases suitable information would anyway not have been available for them to identify this, at least not for a large and consistent wordlist across a wide range of languages. All words which were 'Latinate or neo-Greek' in composition were omitted from the study, unless 'an English pronunciation was attested in at least one language, making the word an Anglicism and forcing its inclusion' (Görlach (2001) xix). Additionally, 'words not known to the general educated reader' were omitted. (We will return to this problematic area at several points in this

---

[3] Chambers and Wilkie (1970: 70–1) make the point that these terms Lehnwort and Fremdwort are to a large extent artificial constructs of the debate about borrowing in German cultural history, which we will touch on again in sections 5.4 and 5.6.

and the following chapter.) Words formed from names were also omitted on the grounds that 'the process by which names become words is very different in individual languages and it was impossible to make clear-cut decisions'. The resulting study offers the reader an interesting perspective on the relative spread across a range of European languages of words found in general use which an Anglophone might spot as being ultimately of English origin. What it does not do, and would not purport to do, is to give an accurate impression of the extent of borrowing directly from English into each of these sixteen languages.[4] The two research questions concerned are different, and each demands a different approach.

To take another perspective, Dance (2003) makes a detailed study of lexis of Norse origin occurring in early Middle English texts from the south-west Midlands. This is an area which saw little or no Scandinavian settlement, so most lexis ultimately of Norse origin in texts from this region is likely to be the result of at least two stages of borrowing: initial borrowing from Norse into English in areas where speakers of the two languages were in direct contact, and subsequent internal borrowing into the dialect of the south-west Midlands. This is a point that Dance is careful to observe, describing such lexis as 'Norse-derived'.[5] (There is a further terminological problem whenever we speak about borrowing into English from 'Norse', since the forms commonly cited as 'Old Norse' are in fact predominantly Old Icelandic, because that is the earliest Scandinavian variety to have extensive written records, but these records are later than the period of greatest influence of Scandinavian languages on English, and also show significant dialectal differences from the varieties which were in contact with English. For a useful recent discussion of some of the main issues see Coates (2006a).)

Thus it is crucially important in etymologies involving borrowing to be clear what sort of event we think we are describing, or more often, what range of possible events we think our etymology might describe. The fact that a word ultimately appears to originate in a particular language need not mean that it was borrowed immediately from that language. Similarly, borrowing is not a simple, once-and-for-all process. We will look in detail at some more complex cases later on, but it is as well to be aware that

---

[4] An interesting methodological comparison is provided by Brown (1999), an investigation of the names found for European cultural importations in native American languages, in a context where there are very few early linguistic records on which to base an analysis.

[5] We will return to this study in section 6.3.

any model is naive which assumes that we can pick out a point at which borrowing into 'a language' occurs: the process of adoption and spread shown by borrowings tends to be just as gradual and incremental as that shown by any other new lexis.

5.3 Motivation for borrowing: traditional explanations

The commonest motivations for lexical borrowing have traditionally been identified as need and prestige. Typically, borrowing because of need is said to occur when a new thing or concept is encountered which already has a name in the donor language but not in the borrowing language, or at least not one known to the borrower. Borrowing because of prestige is sometimes said to occur when a speaker perceives that there is greater social cachet attached to a word from another language. (In the previous sentence *cachet* is a good example of a prestige borrowing from French; it is a near-synonym of the earlier French loan *prestige*.) Another way of putting the same distinction would be to say that borrowing for need is necessary borrowing, because there is a lexical gap, and borrowing for prestige is unnecessary borrowing, because an adequate means of expressing the same concept already exists.[6] Unnecessary borrowing is often an important source of stylistic variants in a language.

There are some difficulties with both concepts. Need is probably the less problematic of the two. As we will see, newly imported traded items, newly encountered products or features of the natural world, new scientific discoveries or intellectual concepts, will all have an effect on the lexis of a language: put simply, they all require names. When a new thing is first encountered through the agency of speakers of another language, or in or near an area in which they live, they will very likely already have a name for it, and this name is likely to have an influence on the name adopted in the language of the people encountering this thing for the first time. The foreign-language name is likely either to be borrowed as a loanword, or to form the basis for a loan translation or a semantic loan. (However, as we will see in the next section, this is far from inevitable.)

Borrowing for prestige is a more difficult concept, and can sometimes lead to oversimplification of complex sociolinguistic situations. Typically

[6] See for example Mahootian (2006) 513. For some further perspectives on this issue see also Ross and Durie (1996) 21.

the term is used to describe borrowings which occur in a context where the donor language has a particular status in any of various social or cultural situations: for instance, as a language of learning or science, as the language of a politically or socially dominant class, or as the language associated with a particular social activity. In some cases, dominance of one language in a particular function, field of discourse, etc. may seem a more apposite conception than prestige. Additionally, it is often necessary to distinguish between the processes responsible for the initial occurrence of a word in utterances in another language, and its subsequent adoption by increasing numbers of speakers and in an increasing range of contexts. (Compare sections 6.3, 6.4.)

5.4 Examples of borrowing because of 'need'

A frequent type of borrowing for 'need' occurs in the language of science when a new entity, process, concept, etc. is named in one language and that name is transferred to other languages. In section 5.1.4 we encountered *neurotize* and *nosology*, which either entered English from or were modelled on words in French and Latin, although in both cases the elements from which the words are formed are ultimately of Greek origin. Scientific naming of new entities and concepts normally remains restricted to technical registers, and it is common to speak of such vocabulary as belonging to an international 'language' of science. Within this scientific register, the boundaries between individual languages as regards lexis may be particularly fluid, and the composition of new words is often transparent as the result of the use of a shared set of word-forming elements which are for the most part ultimately of Latin and Greek origin (see section 4.3.1). Some languages may show slightly more resistance to the adoption of such vocabulary, or may have done so in earlier historical periods: compare for instance *oxygen*, French *oxygène*, etc. (from elements ultimately of Greek origin) with the loan translations German *Sauerstoff* and Dutch *zuurstof* (the names all ultimately reflect Lavoisier's conception of the nature of the substance). However, in a relatively small alphabetical sample of English words we can find *ommatin, ommatophore, ommin, ommochrome, omphacite, oncosine, onofrite, onomasiology, onomatopoesis, ontogenesis, ooblast, ooid, ombrophilous, ombrophily,* all of which are either borrowed from or modelled on German words (*Ommatin, Ommatophor, Ommin,*

Ommochrom, etc.), which in turn were formed from elements ultimately of Latin or Greek origin which are common to the technical vocabularies of many modern languages.[7] Such items would almost certainly be omitted from a study of 'Germanisms' in English of the sort we looked at in section 5.2, but they all first appear as German words in German sentences, and have entered English from German.

Occasionally a newly named scientific category comes to be part of a fairly basic level of vocabulary. The word *petal* is first recorded in English in 1712, denoting what the *OED* defines as 'each of the modified leaves, typically distinctly coloured, which form the segments of the corolla of a flower'. Its prior history can be summarized as follows:

> Greek *pétalon* 'leaf'
> > post-classical Latin *petalum* (mid 17th cent.), in various technical
> > senses (alongside the usual Latin word for a leaf, *folium*)
> > English *petalum* (1687), *petal* (1712)

Before the word *petal* was borrowed into English, petals were not distinguished from other kinds of leaf by any special name. Even the specifying compound *flower-leaf* is only recorded from the early eighteenth century, although it is evident that some particular collocations with *leaf* referred conventionally to the petals of particular plants: e.g. *rose leaf* (first recorded in the Middle English period) refers most frequently to the brightly-coloured leaves of the rose's flowers and not to the green waxy leaves of its stems. Today *petal* seems to be a name for an obvious category in the natural world, and few children will have difficulty in identifying the petals of at least those plants, such as a rose or a daisy, which have brightly-coloured flowers with well-defined individual petals, even though in some cases what is identified by the child or layman as a *petal* will be differently classified by a botanist. (In section 8.2 we will look at prototype semantics, a framework which explains this sort of situation very well.) Yet both the word and (it seems) the concept were borrowed into English from Latin as used by early scientists, and then within English we might say that a further borrowing occurred, from the language of science to the more general language. From the perspective of the meaning relations found in modern English, we might say that this borrowing of the word *petal* helped

---

[7] See Durkin (2006a) for full details of this sample, and for discussion of why an English historical dictionary can sometimes be the easiest place to find information about such words even when they do not originate in English.

fill a lexical gap, in providing a word for this distinctive part of a flower, but we might also note that speakers up to this point seem not to have perceived this as an important distinctive category. Hence it might be better to say that the borrowing led to the creation of a new semantic category rather than filling a gap in the lexicon.

5.5 Borrowing of a new word when a new product of the natural world is encountered

The word *tomato* shows a relatively simple case of borrowing a new word to denote a newly encountered thing. The Spanish word *tomate* is first recorded in 1532, soon after the Spanish conquest of the Aztec empire. The word is a borrowing of Nahuatl *tomatl* denoting the same plant. Nahuatl was the language of the Aztecs, as well as other peoples of the region, and is still spoken in parts of Mexico today; the word *tomatl* may ultimately be a derivative from *tomau* 'to grow'. The English word *tomato* first appears in the form *tomate* in 1604, and is a borrowing from Spanish *tomate*. Similarly, French *tomate* occurs in the late sixteenth century in an isolated early example in a translation from Spanish, although it does not become frequent until the eighteenth century; German *Tomate* is first recorded in the seventeenth century, and Portuguese *tomate* in the early eighteenth century. We so far have a very simple picture: Spanish has borrowed the word from Nahuatl, almost certainly close to the time when Spanish speakers first encountered the plant. The Spanish word shows minimal formal adaptation of the Nahuatl word in order to replace the final consonant cluster /tl/, not found in native Spanish words, with the much more familiar combination of consonant plus vowel /te/. English, French, German, and Portuguese all borrow the Spanish word, either directly or via one another, although in some instances with loss of the final vowel in the spoken form. The modern English form *tomato*, first recorded in the middle of the eighteenth century, poses the only slight difficulty in the story presented so far: it probably arose as an alteration of earlier *tomate* by association with the name of a different plant which also happened to have originated in the Americas, *potato*.

However, this pattern of borrowing was far from inevitable, as becomes clear when we consider for a moment the modern Italian word for the tomato, *pomodoro*, a (rather fanciful) descriptive name compounded from Italian elements, and meaning literally 'apple of gold' (1544). Likewise

French earlier had *pomme dorée* and *pomme d'or*, and also *pomme d'amour*, literally 'apple of love' (1549; still found in the south of France), which gave rise to English *love-apple* as a loan translation of the French word. English *love-apple* is recorded as a name of the tomato in 1578, a quarter of a century before the occurrence of any form of the word *tomato* in English. Similarly *apple of love* is found from 1597. However, the evidence of corpora of historical texts suggests that neither term was ever very common in English. In modern-day Austrian German the usual name is *Paradeiser*, reflecting earlier *Paradiesapfel*, literally 'apple of paradise', a word found in the fourteenth century denoting the pomegranate and alluding to the fruit in the biblical story of the Garden of Eden, subsequently transferred in meaning after the arrival of tomatoes from the Americas. Thus even in a small selection of the major languages of western Europe we have several different strategies for naming the tomato, and a variety of different outputs.

  A. Nahuatl *tomatl* > Spanish *tomate* (1532) > French *tomate* (late 16th cent.), German *Tomate* (17th cent.), Portuguese *tomate* (18th cent.), English *tomate* (1604), later (with remodelling after *potato*) *tomato* (18th cent.)
  B. Italian *pomodoro* (1544), French *pomme dorée* (16th cent.), *pomme d'or* (17th cent.)
  C. French *pomme d'amour* (16th cent.), model for English *love apple* (1578), *apple of love* (1597)
  D. Austrian German *Paradeiser*, earlier †*Paradiesapfel*

We have already touched on the word *potato*. This shows some similarities to the history of *tomato*, but also some further complexities, involving the word's meaning as well as its form. The word is first recorded in English in 1565, denoting the edible root of the plant *Ipomoea batatas*, a plant of tropical American origin (in fact the product of cultivation by the peoples of the Americas) which is now usually referred to as the *sweet potato*. This plant was brought back to Spain from the Americas by Columbus after his voyage of 1492, and became widely cultivated in Europe, especially southern Europe. In Spanish this plant is called *batata*. This is a borrowing from an American Indian language, probably Taino. Borrowing of *batata* from Spanish is shown by Dutch *bataat* and German *Batate*, and also by obsolete English †*batata*. In the early sixteenth century a variant *patata* occurs in Spanish, probably arising from association with the name of a quite different plant *papa*, which we will discuss further in a moment. The Spanish word was borrowed into French as *patate* and Italian as *patata*, in both cases denoting the sweet potato. The word was also borrowed into English, appearing in the sixteenth century as *patata* but also in a variety of other forms, including *potato*, which gradually became the form in general use. The *o* in the first syllable of this form probably arose from confusion over the value of an unstressed vowel in an unfamiliar borrowed word; the final *-o* in English *potato* lacks any obvious explanation.[8] (For simplicity of presentation, I have not mentioned early variation in word form in Dutch, German, French, Italian, or related forms in other languages.) Thus:

'sweet potato' (*Ipomoea batatas*)

Spanish *batata* (< Taino?), later (probably after *papa* 'potato') *patata*
> Dutch *bataat*, German *Batate*, French *patate*, Italian *patata*, English
†*batata*, †*patata*, *potato*

In English the word *potato* was also used to denote many other edible tubers, especially those originally imported from the Americas. In particular, it was used from the end of the sixteenth century as the name of the plant *Solanum tuberosum* and its edible tubers. This was another cultivated plant species, this time of South American origin, which was first encountered by Europeans during Spanish exploration of the Andes in the 1530s. In Spanish this plant was called *papa*, a borrowing from Quechua, and that remains its usual name in the Spanish-speaking Americas. In Britain, as elsewhere in temperate parts of Europe, it became a major food source. As such it came to seem the obvious referent of the word *potato* in its broadened meaning 'plant (from the Americas) with edible tubers', with the result that the 'original' *potato*, *Ipomoea batatas*, came to be distinguished as the *sweet potato* or sometimes as *yam* (more usually the name of yet another plant from the Americas with edible tubers, *Dioscorea*). However, there was nothing inevitable about the transfer of the name from the one

---

[8] One possibility is perhaps that the word was identified with words of the type *meadow*, *pillow*, which had variants with both reduced and unreduced final syllable, and hence the form *potato* arose by analogy with these, although if so it is surprising that spellings with *-ow* or *-ou* are not more common. On the small number of (mostly learned) words in English in this period with final /ə/ see Britton (2007) 527. Another possibility is that final *-o* was perceived as typically Spanish, which would be supported by the frequent alteration of the ending of words in *-ade* or *-ada* as *-ado* in this period (see *OED* at *-ado* suffix).

plant to the other. In other parts of Europe where potatoes were much grown, such as the Netherlands and the German-speaking countries, different names were adopted. The usual word in modern Dutch is *aardappel*, and similarly in Austria and parts of Germany it is *Erdapfel*, in both cases a compound from the words for 'earth' and 'apple', found much earlier denoting various other edible products of plants which are found either on or in the earth, and transferred in meaning to denote the newly encountered South American plant. French *pomme de terre*, literally 'apple of the earth', is again found denoting other plants from an early date, long before the period of European contact with the Americas, although its use denoting *Solanum tuberosum* is probably modelled on either Dutch *aardappel* or German *Erdapfel*, since the cultivation of this plant in France probably spread from Holland or Germany. The standard German term is *Kartoffel*, a word of complex history borrowed originally from Italian *tartufolo*, itself from an unattested Latin **territūberum*, literally 'earth tuber', originally denoting a truffle. Meanwhile, in Spain, perhaps under the influence of English, *patata* has in fact been found in the sense *Solanum tuberosum* from the beginning of the nineteenth century or earlier. Thus:

'potato' (*Solanum tuberosum*)

A. Quechua *papa* > Spanish *papa*

B. Dutch *aardappel*, Austrian German *Erdapfel*, models for French *pomme de terre*

C. German *Kartoffel*, originally < Italian *tartufolo* (< an unattested Latin **territūberum*, literally 'earth tuber', originally denoting a truffle)

D. English *potato*, a transferred use of the name of the sweet potato; hence also Spanish *patata*

In several other major European languages the plant has names which were current as the names of different plants before the advent of the potato (ultimately) from the Americas. If we were to extend our survey to include names for this plant in non-standard and regional varieties of these languages, we would find a yet more varied and complex picture. An even more complex set of ultimately related vegetable names can be traced by pursuing *aubergine* and *brinjal* in a good etymological dictionary. For a very complex example, and a classic etymological tour de force, see Ross (1952) and (1958) 146–8 on *ginger*.

5.6 Patterns of borrowing in the history of a language

We have touched on cultural considerations already, and have seen that the study of lexical borrowing is often closely interconnected with cultural history and external, extralinguistic factors. A good example is provided by the history of borrowing from French into English.

Although communication is known to have occurred across the English Channel between the Anglo-Saxons and the French, there are barely any borrowings from French into English which can be dated reliably to before the Norman Conquest in 1066.[9] *proud* is one of the very few secure examples: phonology and semantics both point clearly to borrowing from Old French rather than Latin, and the phonology points more precisely to borrowing from a western variety of Old French, and to a date of borrowing probably not earlier than the ninth century. Its recorded meanings in English show pejoration (see section 8.6.3) of the Old French meanings 'courageous, valiant, good, noble, just, prudent, wise, profitable, advantageous'. We must be cautious here, since the Old French word is in fact not recorded until considerably later than the earliest records of the word in Old English, but the French word's Latin etymon *prode* 'profitable, advantageous, useful' supports the originally positive meaning. (We will return to *proud* and its derivative *pride* in section 7.2.4.)

In the post-Conquest period, large numbers of borrowings are found, including some items of basic vocabulary (on this difficult concept see further section 6.2). It has been argued that some of these words entered English as a result of members of the Norman governing class switching from French to English as their language of everyday use, but this is very uncertain.[10] What is more certain is that in the later medieval period French was the first language of very few people in England, but it remained in daily use in many branches of professional and intellectual life, including the law and parliamentary business, alongside Latin, which had enormous importance, especially as the language of the church and much secular

---

[9] On early borrowing from French compare Kastovsky (1992) 337–8, Burnley (1992) 429, von Mengden (1999), Dietz (2003); for a view of *proud* slightly different from the one from *OED3* presented here, see von Mengden (2001).

[10] Compare for example Thomason and Kaufman (1988) 68, but see further section 6.2 below.

administration, from the Old English period onwards. Crucially, Latin and French were both much more developed as instruments of literate activity than was English, which only begins to develop any sort of (post-Conquest) supra-regional literary status in the second half of the Middle English period. English was clearly the dominant vernacular in everyday use, at least if we ignore for the moment areas where there may have been competition from Celtic languages or in the early Middle English period from Scandinavian languages, but both French and Latin had well-established roles in the life of society, particularly in written use and in the performance of various official, technical, and economic functions. The variety of French in question was Anglo-French, the lexis of which showed numerous formal and semantic differences from the French of the continent. The situation is well summarized by William Rothwell, editor of the *Anglo-Norman Dictionary*:

> Anglo-French...was for centuries one of the two languages of record as used in government, the law, commerce and education in medieval England as well as of a wide-ranging literature. Insular French evolved in parallel and in constant contact with Middle English on the soil of England; it was not some sort of foreign decoration lightly superimposed on the native idiom. The officials of all ranks and their clerks who drafted and copied records all day in Latin and French were in large measure English and moved freely from one language to another according to the nature of their work and the company in which they found themselves.
>
> (Rothwell (1998) 159–60)

In the late Middle English period, and especially in the early fifteenth century, the use of (Anglo-)French in these technical and economic functions within England showed considerable decline,[11] but in this same period French culture was gaining in importance and dominance throughout the rest of Europe. French first became the principal language through which the Renaissance, and hence that part of the inherited classical learning which was in Latin and so most accessible to Western scholars, was conveyed to northern parts of Europe. The considerable borrowing of French lexis in Older Scots also reflects this. Then in the early modern period French began to outshine Italian as the leading vernacular language of culture and learning even in more southerly parts of Europe as well. Consequently, the level of borrowing from French remains high throughout the

---

[11] See the detailed sketch in Rothwell (2005). Compare also Machan (2003).

late Middle English and early modern English periods, although its relative importance declines in comparison with increasing numbers of new words of all origins, and particularly borrowings directly from Latin.[12] The actual numbers of borrowings from French do not show a significant decline until the eighteenth century, with a further steep drop in the twentieth century.[13] Much of the vocabulary borrowed from French in this period belongs to learned or literary discourse or to other specialist registers, or shows a notably high stylistic level.[14]

The influences of Latin and French on the lexis of English work largely in tandem: a large proportion of the borrowed French words are not only ultimately of Latin origin, but show a transparent correspondence in word form with their Latin etymons. Indeed, very many of these French words are not the regular reflexes of Latin words via proto-Romance, but are instead learned borrowings from Latin into French from the Old French period onwards. The impact on the lexis of English is enormous, as witnessed by the fact that ultimately many originally French or Latin affixes became productive in English (compare section 4.1.1), although there is scant evidence that this had happened before the end of the Middle English period.[15]

This process of borrowing of affixes ultimately facilitated further borrowing of more French and Latin lexis, since in many cases the composition of a newly encountered French or Latin word would be transparent to an

---

[12] For numerical analysis see Durkin (2008), and references to further literature given there; see also Dekeyser (1986), based on data from the *Middle English Dictionary*.

[13] For a preliminary discussion see Durkin (2006b); see also Mair (2006) 54, and further references given there.

[14] For a classic account of some of the results of this process in the lexis of modern English, where (near) synonyms of native and French/Latin origin often coexist (e.g. *brotherly* and *fraternal*, *heavenly* and *celestial*), and where a noun of native origin often has a corresponding adjective of Latin/Romance origin (e.g. *oral* beside *mouth*, *urban* beside *town*) see Ullmann (1962) 106–10, 145–51, who also offers a stimulating comparison with German and French. For an examination of the use of vocabulary of different origins in different literary styles in the early modern period see Adamson (1999).

[15] Dalton-Puffer (1996) finds very little evidence within the Middle English period for hybrid formations with native bases and Romance suffixes; there is also very little evidence for English formations from Romance elements which are not paralleled in French. Prefixes, which are excluded from Dalton-Puffer's study, might add a few further examples of hybrids, such as *renew*.

English speaker. In the subsequent centuries we find countless instances where it is almost impossible to judge whether an English word shows the result of word formation within English and just happens to have parallels in French and Latin, or whether it is modelled on French and/or Latin words, or whether it is in fact a borrowing from French and/or Latin. (See examples in section 5.1.4, and see further section 6.5 on words borrowed partly from French and partly from Latin.)

Many questions remain unanswered about even such a relatively well-investigated area as French borrowing in Middle English. Rothwell has done an enormous amount to demonstrate the continuing uses of Anglo-French in later medieval England, and to illustrate Middle English borrowing of distinctively Anglo-French lexis (compare *poke* in section 3.1 < Anglo-French *poke* as opposed to continental French *poche*). What we lack is any detailed study of just how frequently Middle English borrowing from French shows forms or meanings which are unique to either Anglo-French or continental French. Such a study would need to be backed up by an analysis of such factors as date of first occurrence, linguistic register, subject field, etc., in order to determine whether we can identify trends in borrowing from either Anglo-French or continental French in particular sub-periods or areas of social or intellectual activity. The new edition of the *Anglo-Norman Dictionary* now in preparation will make this much easier, although it may be that ultimately our surviving records of Anglo-French are not sufficient to allow us to gain a reliable picture of which words and senses may never have belonged to Anglo-French, and may instead have entered Middle English through direct contact with continental French, e.g. through literary contact.

Leaving aside the specific issue of borrowing from either Anglo-French or continental French, we can begin to sketch out some of the main factors which would need to be taken into account in any ideal, detailed analysis of borrowing from French into English:

- frequency (rather than just absolute dates of first attestation)
- later borrowing of specific senses (compare section 6.6)
- geographical variation and spread within English (compare section 6.4)
- linguistic register of the items borrowed
- how far we can estimate whether borrowings belonged to the 'general' vocabulary or only to more specialist vocabularies

Questions of the register and degree of currency of borrowings are crucial. As noted in Smithers's short essay 'Early Middle English' in Bennett and Smithers (1968) lii:

It was probably not only an author's audience, but also his own background, endowments, and tastes that determined the number of adoptions from O[ld] F[rench] that he used. This is one of the reasons why the first record of a French word in M[iddle] E[nglish] should not necessarily be assumed (as is commonly done) to imply that it was, or even soon became, generally current in the 'language'. In fact, so long as we are dealing with any one M[iddle] E[nglish] work, the influence of French vocabulary on the 'language' is an abstraction: such a notion applies only to words which are found, on analysis of many works, to recur in several of them.

The resulting receptivity of English to French (and Latin) borrowings is also a subtle matter. The extent of borrowing provoked some negative comment in the early modern period, although the overall picture is somewhat mixed.[16] There were also calls for linguistic purism in early modern Germany, but there they much more frequently had an actual impact on the shape and composition of the lexis of German. We might speculate that this was because there had been comparatively little integration of Latinate and Romance lexis into German up until this date, and also because language had a crucial role in defining identity before the unification of Germany in the late nineteenth century. To take two simple examples from the world of languages and linguistics:

- *Wörterbuch* (1631; in early use also *Wortbuch*) 'dictionary' (literally 'book of words') was adopted by linguistic purists as an alternative to borrowed *Lexicon* or *Nomenclator*[17]
- *Mundart* (1641) 'dialect' (< *Mund* 'mouth' and *Art* 'manner, type') was adopted as an alternative to borrowed *Dialect* (1634; now *Dialekt*)

Both *Wörterbuch* and *Mundart* have become the usual words in modern German, largely replacing the earlier borrowed terms. When assessing borrowing into a language it can be very important to examine the subsequent frequency of use of borrowed terms, and in particular how they compete

---

[16] Compare Nevalainen (1999) 358–60, Görlach (1999) 479–80.

[17] German *Wörterbuch* is in fact itself a calque of a word in another language, albeit in this instance a closely related language in which both parts of the compound are cognate with (and easily recognizable as being equivalent to) those in the German word: Dutch *woordboek* (1599; now *woordenboek* (1648)).

with synonyms of different origin: the difference in the receptivity of various languages to loans of various origins may often be a question of avoidance of the institutionalization of loans rather than avoidance of initial, nonce borrowing.[18]

[18] A very interesting comparison could be made with the complex history of the reception of English loanwords in Japanese, particularly the massive borrowing of English words since the end of the Second World War. For a very useful recent account of this topic (albeit largely from the standpoint of second language learning) see Daulton (2008), and compare also Shibatani (1990).

6

The mechanisms of borrowing

6.1 Perspectives from contact linguistics

In the preceding chapter we looked at some of the circumstances and causes of lexical borrowing. We saw that a satisfactory account of a borrowing will not simply assert that a borrowing has occurred, but will also provide some plausible context for it to have occurred in. We also saw that close investigation of such etymologies can reveal a great deal about linguistic and cultural history. Our focus has been largely on how individual speakers of languages adopt new lexical items. This reflects a major focus in the field of contact linguistics, well characterized by the Middle English dialectologist Angus McIntosh (1994: 137):

Fundamentally, what we mean by 'languages in contact' is 'users of language in contact' and to insist upon this is much more than a terminological quibble and has far from trivial consequences.

In the past several decades, work on contact linguistics has brought a certain amount of attention to bear on lexical borrowing. Sometimes, admittedly, the focus has been on borrowing of grammatical or phonological features, and lexical borrowing has been investigated more for the light it can throw on such phenomena than for its own sake. A good deal of attention has rightly been given to bilingualism. Only extremely limited borrowing is possible in a contact situation if neither the speaker of the donor language nor the speaker of the borrowing language knows anything of the other's language: someone pointing at an object and speaking a word is possibly giving its name, but the potential for confusion is enormous. Only a little more borrowing is possible if the speaker of the donor language knows something of the borrowing language, but the speaker of the borrowing language knows nothing of the donor language: the speaker of the borrowing language may ask 'what do you call this?' and receive in reply a word from the donor language, but again confusion may very easily result.[1] For any more extensive borrowing to occur we must have either a situation in which two dialects or languages are at least in part mutually intelligible, or one in which at least one speaker of one language has at least enough knowledge of another language to apprehend a word in that language and adopt it in her/his own language. To this limited extent, most borrowing will involve some degree of either mutual intelligibility or bilingualism. (In linguistic use the term 'bilingual' is often used in a very much broader sense than its everyday meaning 'having fluency approaching that of a native speaker in more than one language'.) A distinction is often made between basic and non-basic vocabulary, basic vocabulary being taken to be much

---

[1] For an example of confusion which probably arose in such a situation see the etymology in *OED* or in Coromines and Pascual (1981) 690–1 of the Spanish word *pulque*, the name of a kind of drink made from the fermented sap of the agave or maguey. This is probably borrowed from a Nahuatl word *puliuhki* which in fact means 'decomposed, spoiled'. The drink is called *octli* in Nahuatl, and the Spanish name probably results from misapprehension of the phrase *octli puliuhki* 'spoiled pulque', which would have been heard frequently since pulque spoils easily if not drunk within twenty-four to thirty-six hours.

more resistant to borrowing in normal borrowing situations than non-basic vocabulary.[2]

6.2 What is basic vocabulary?

Any assessment of borrowing on the basis of a distinction between basic and non-basic vocabulary begs the question of how these terms are defined. Here there is a good deal of opacity in much of the scholarly literature. A useful sketch of what is usually meant by basic vocabulary is provided by Trask:

> There is clear evidence that certain semantic classes of words are much less likely to be borrowed than other words. These are chiefly the items of very high frequency which we would expect to find in every language: pronouns, lower numerals, kinship terms, names of body parts, simple verbs like *go, be, have, want, see, eat,* and *die,* widespread colour terms like *black, white,* and *red,* simple adjectives like *big, small, good, bad,* and *old,* names of natural phenomena like *sun, moon, star, fire, rain, river, snow, day,* and *night,* grammatical words like *when, here, and, if,* and *this,* and a few others.
>
> (Trask (1996) 23; reprinted Millar (2007) 27)

The classic codification of this approach is in the lists of basic items devised by the linguist Morris Swadesh in the 1950s, especially a short list consisting of 100 items and a longer one with 200 items. A full listing with supporting discussion is given in McMahon and McMahon (2005) 33–9 (which provides an excellent introduction to this field), and also in Millar (2007) 483–4. To give an indication of the sorts of items that are included, the first ten items in alphabetical order in the 100-meaning list are 'all', 'ashes', 'bark', 'belly', 'big', 'bird', 'bite', 'black', 'blood', 'bone'; in the 200-meaning list 'and', 'animal', 'at', 'back', 'bad', 'because', 'blow' are added in the same section of the alphabet. I have given these items in quotation marks, because as items on the list they represent meanings, not words. However, if the language that we are considering is modern (standard) English, then the words

---

[2] A very influential set of generalizations about what happens when one language is in contact with another in a maintenance situation (i.e. where language A shows borrowing from language B, but where neither language is being abandoned by its speakers) is found in Thomason and Kaufman (1988: 74–6) in the form of a 'borrowing scale', which is revised considerably in Thomason (2001). On language maintenance and language shift see further section 6.3.

which denote these meanings are the same as those that occur in the list.[3] We can therefore use the Swadesh lists to tell us at least a little about the numbers of words ultimately borrowed from various sources that can be found in the most basic levels of the vocabulary of modern English. If we consider the origins of the words in just the sample that I have already given, then *animal* stands out as the only word which is a borrowing from French and/or Latin, and in the rest of the 200-meaning list we find additionally only *count, flower, fruit, mountain, person, push, river, round, turn* (originally an Old English borrowing from Latin), *vomit*, and (debatably) *lake*, plus *because* as a probable loan translation.[4] Out of these only *mountain, person*, and *round* occur in the shorter 100-meaning list. Interestingly, the first dates recorded for these words in English (excluding *turn*) range between the early thirteenth and late fourteenth centuries, with the largest concentration being in the fourteenth century.[5] The vast majority of the words in both lists are part of the lexical inheritance of Old English, although not all have secure Germanic etymologies, an extreme instance being *bird*, which has no known cognates outside English. One item in the 100-meaning list, *dog*, stands out as an English word of quite unknown and much disputed origin which is first recorded in the eleventh century; the usual word for a dog in Old English is *hund*, modern English *hound*. There are a number of words of Norse origin in the 100-meaning list, *bark* (of a tree), *egg, root, skin*, (partly) *give*, (perhaps) *big, die*, and additionally in the 200-meaning list *dirty, hit, husband, leg, near, rotten, sky, they, wing*, (perhaps) *fog*.[6] There are also a

---

[3] Although see McMahon and McMahon (2005) 41 on the problems that can arise where more than one lexical item could fill the same slot in the list: such as *little* or *small* in English, for example.

[4] For convenience I use here simply the etymologies offered in the *Oxford Dictionary of English Etymology*. Among these basic vocabulary items there are many words of uncertain etymology, and some of very hotly disputed etymology, and any more detailed analysis would need to take account of some of the major areas of uncertainty.

[5] The first edition of the *OED* lists unambiguous evidence for *animal* only from the sixteenth century onwards, but the *Middle English Dictionary* offers convincing evidence from the end of the fourteenth century.

[6] Thomason and Kaufman (1988: 365 note 22) also use the Swadesh 200-item list to assess borrowing of basic vocabulary from Norse and French, but with slightly different resulting totals from mine. As they do not list the items taken to be of Norse or French origin, it is impossible to see whether this results from using slightly different modern English words in the semantic slots of the Swadesh list, or from assuming different etymologies, or from some other cause.

few words probably borrowed from Middle Dutch or Middle Low German: *dull*, *split*, and (perhaps) *rub*. (For a slightly different approach based not on Swadesh lists but on lists of the highest-frequency items in corpora of contemporary English see Minkova and Stockwell (2006).)

What this very sketchy survey does not tell us is some very crucial information about each of these borrowings:

- When did the initial borrowing occur?
- How long did each item compete with an earlier synonym, and what estimates can we arrive at for the frequency levels of each?
- When did each item become the usual term for this meaning in everyday use?
- What factors, if any, can be identified which favoured its adoption?
- Is it the usual term in all stylistic levels, registers, and regional varieties even today?

Such questions are not all readily answered even for such common words as these in such a comparatively well-documented and thoroughly studied language as English.[7]

In the list I gave of English borrowings from Old Norse, the third person plural personal pronoun *they* is of particular interest. Even among the Swadesh list items, some items are more susceptible to borrowing than others, and it is generally held that personal pronouns are among those grammatical closed-class items which are least likely to be borrowed. Thomason (2001: 83–4, quoting work by Christopher Court posted on an electronic list) draws an interesting comparison with some languages of Southeast Asia, where borrowing of pronouns is fairly common, but where pronouns constitute less of a closed-class group, with numerous alternative forms occurring which can be exploited in marking different social relationships; compare the use of distinct second person pronoun forms for intimacy/informality and distance/respect/formality in many European languages from the Middle Ages onwards, as English *thou* and *you*, French *tu* and *vous*, etc. The English adoption of *they* from Norse is interesting in that the native form is simply replaced by a borrowed form. (Although it has been suggested that the native forms of the demonstrative pronoun may also have had some input.) Additionally, the borrowed form spread (gradually)

---

[7] For an interesting recent discussion of frequency of occurrence as a factor influencing rates of lexical replacement see Pagel, Atkinson, and Meade (2007).

from areas in which there was direct contact between speakers of Norse and English to areas in which there would have been little or no direct contact with Norse speakers; indeed, the spread to many areas occurred after the end of the period in which Norse was likely to have been in use in any part of mainland Britain. It has long since been shown that in fact language-internal factors played a crucial role in this process: borrowed *they* provided a much clearer contrast with the singular form *he* than did the inherited forms *hi*, *heo*, *he*, etc. This is sometimes referred to as a 'therapeutic' process, restoring important contrasts in the grammatical system which had become obscured as a result of phonetic change.[8]

Prestige is often offered as the explanation for the borrowing of basic vocabulary, but in some cases one may suspect that this is simply because it is clear that need will not work as an explanation, and prestige is the most readily available alternative. Lass (1997: 186–8) offers some very interesting examples of borrowing of fairly basic vocabulary items, such as names of parts of the body and of common foods, into Yiddish both from Hebrew and from Slavonic languages, in a sociolinguistic situation where Yiddish speakers in Eastern Europe would have been very unlikely to have regarded the language of neighbouring Slavonic speakers as particularly prestigious. He also provides a useful selection from among the many early borrowings into Finnish (a non-Indo-European, Uralic language) from Germanic languages and from other branches of Indo-European, including some numerals, names of body parts, and days of the week. These certainly show us that contact occurred between speakers of Finnish and speakers of various Indo-European languages (and incidentally, they often provide very useful evidence for earlier stages in the histories of these languages), but it is probably unwise to try to reconstruct any scenario for the type of contact which may have taken place.

Additionally, it must be recognized that the Swadesh lists cover only a tiny slice of the very most basic vocabulary, compiled explicitly in order to focus on those words thought least likely to be replaced as a result of borrowing over time. Even if we extend the list to include for instance larger numbers of names of body parts or of foodstuffs which are basic in a particular area, we will still only be looking at a fragment of the lexis

---

[8] See Samuels (1972) 71–2 for a daring but controversial account of the subsequent competition between the borrowed pronoun *thei* and *thei*, the southern reflex of Old English *þēah* 'although'.

of any language. If we are interested in the impact of borrowing on the whole of the lexis of a language, we may feel that there are distinctions just as significant to be drawn between much larger slices of the vocabulary. For instance, McMahon and McMahon (2005: 7) speak about borrowing from 'prestigious neighbours' being likely to include 'religious, cultural, or technological vocabulary'. In such contexts, we might suspect that there is an important distinction between the vocabulary which is at least in the passive competence of almost all adult speakers, and vocabulary which is largely confined to the competence of certain groups within society. We may also suspect that very many words which now form part of the passive competence of most speakers appeared first in one of the specialist vocabularies within a speech community, and only gradually spread more widely, although there has been surprisingly little research on this topic.

In the following section we will look at a rather different process which may also have a major impact on basic vocabulary, and which often cannot easily be distinguished from cases of borrowing.

6.3 Language shift

The situations that we have looked at so far all involve language maintenance, where the speakers of the borrowing language continue to speak the same language. However, lexis (as well as other features) can also enter a language through the distinct process of language shift. Here, the speakers of one language (let us call it language A) abandon that language in favour of another (B), but in the course of this process some features from language A are transferred into or imposed on language B. The process is typically inter-generational, when a bilingual generation is succeeded by one which retains only one of the languages, but with some transfer of vocabulary from the other. Townend, in the course of a wide-ranging investigation of the degree of mutual intelligibility likely to have existed between English and Old Norse in England, examines the possibility that at least some of the words of Norse origin which we encountered in the previous section could in fact show the result of shift-induced imposition (or lexical transfer) rather than borrowing in a situation of language maintenance:

Traditionally, it is a linguistic commonplace that, generally speaking, words are borrowed from one language to another on account of either need or prestige...The

Norse loans in English have posed problems for linguists, as it is not clear which of these two causations is operative, or whether there are diachronic and diatopic variations in causation . . . The Norse loans in Old English tend to be need-based borrowings, denoting new objects (particularly nautical and legal terminology), whereas many of the Norse loans in Middle English can in no way be regarded as need-based borrowings as they constitute so-called core vocabulary. Normally, this would imply that Norse enjoyed greater prestige in the Middle English period than it did in the Old English, but this seems impossible, since it was in the Viking Age (if ever, and only in certain areas) that the Norse-speaking population was in authority over the English-speaking. To regard the Norse core vocabulary items appearing in Middle English as the result of imposition through shift rather than of borrowing would appear to remove this problem.

(Townend (2002) 203–4)

Such ideas present a powerful challenge to traditional notions of the causation of borrowing in terms of need and prestige. However, it can be difficult to identify transfer of lexis resulting from language shift with any certainty. As already noted in section 5.6, it is sometimes assumed that language shift from Anglo-French to Middle English was a major cause in the borrowing (or importation) of French lexis into English, and further that Anglo-French constituted a superstratum (rather than an adstratum or substratum) on the basis of the large amount of vocabulary which entered English, particularly in specialist fields such as legal language.[9] (A superstratum is a language of a dominant group which influences that of a subordinate group. An adstratum is a language which influences that of a neighbouring group without any such relationship of social dominance. A substratum is either a language of a subordinate group which influences that of a dominant group, or a language formerly spoken by a group which influences their subsequent acquisition of another language through grammatical, lexical, or phonological features.) Such a claim would be greatly reinforced if one could first pinpoint the likely period in which French speakers shifted to English, then identify words which entered English from French in this same period, and finally demonstrate why they are less likely to show the results of general processes of borrowing. At the very least, one would want to demonstrate some difference between this period and those preceding and following it, e.g. in total numbers of words entering English from French, or in the registers to which they belong. It is not clear how well this has been demonstrated in the case of English and

[9] See especially Thomason and Kaufman (1988) 116.

French, although there is rather better evidence in the case of English and Norse, as set out by Townend. As already noted in section 6.2, even the basic vocabulary items which entered English from French (or Latin) span a considerable historical period, which in itself rather argues against the hypothesis that transfer rather than borrowing played a significant part in this process.

Additionally, while language shift may account for words entering a language, it does not explain their subsequent spread into more general usage, particularly when, as in the case of Anglo-French speakers in medieval England, the language-shifting population made up only a small proportion of the total population, or when, as in the case of Norse speakers, they were largely confined to particular geographical areas of settlement. Whether lexis initially entered a language through contact-induced borrowing or shift-induced transfer, we must still account for its subsequent spread and competition with any pre-existing native synonyms. In the case of the Norse-derived element in Middle English, this issue has been addressed very carefully by Dance (2003) 311, 313:[10]

Full acceptance of a lexical item as the dominant expression within its field can take centuries to occur, if it ever does. Some lexical redundancy, or variant ways of expressing the same concept within the same lexical field, is natural within a system...just as is variation in terms of pronunciation and morphology. And, while it is proper in historical terms to describe such variation as contributing towards the process of change, nevertheless from a synchronic perspective it need not be seen as having such an 'effect' at all: the variation merely exists, and is available to be conditioned by factors such as social/stylistic level, perceived dialectal flavour, or, put more generally, simply according to the contexts and uses with which the different forms in question happen to have become associated by a particular speaker...

Lexical borrowing can be seen simply as adding to variation in the first instance, a predictable consequence of the increase in weak social ties that results from a contact situation, and not as a drastic imposition on the core of a language's vocabulary that needs to be accounted for by tremendous pressures of 'prestige' attaching to the source tongue.

Ideally, etymologies of borrowed items will account for such factors, explaining not only the initial adoption of a word, but its subsequent spread within the lexical system. In many cases we may lack sufficient evidence to trace this process, and even where the evidence is available such an investigation will be outside the scope of all but the most adventurous

[10] See also in this connection the important discussion in McIntosh (1978) and the essays on Middle English word geography in Laing and Williamson (1994).

etymological projects. However, the example of research such as Dance's should at least caution us against drawing over-hasty conclusions about the causation of borrowing in any particular instance, and whether this applies to initial adoption or subsequent spread, or to both.

6.4 Borrowing within and between languages

There is an intimate connection between borrowing of vocabulary from one language to another and the spread of words from one person's vocabulary (or idiolect or personal linguistic system) to another's. The latter process is sometimes called internal borrowing. There are certainly similarities between the two processes, but there are also important distinctions to be made. Differences between the grammatical systems of any two languages may well have a significant impact on borrowing, or even prevent it from happening at all. If we consider also borrowing between different dialects of a language, as well as borrowing between closely related languages, especially those with at least some degree of mutual intelligibility, we can place different types of borrowing on a rough cline, indicating difficulty of borrowing:

Less difficulty

- Between individuals who speak the same dialect of the same language, and have similar social status, profession, interests, etc.
- Between different specialist registers
- Between dialects, especially where there are significant differences in the phonology and/or grammar of the two dialects
- Between languages with some degree of mutual intelligibility
- Between languages with a long history of contact
- Between closely related languages
- Between unrelated languages

More difficulty

As Samuels points out, in both interlinguistic and intralinguistic borrowing the communicative needs are the same (1972: 97):

In theory, the processes of spread could be regarded as the same, irrespective of whether the contact is between dialects of the same language or between different languages. This is because the dispositions and attitudes of those who have something to communicate are parallel; in both, there is a common tendency for speakers to adjust their speech to bring it nearer to that of their interlocutors.

Additionally, as we have seen, the two processes of interlinguistic and intra-linguistic borrowing very often work in succession to one another, with the initial adoption of a word from another language being followed by intralinguistic spread. Furthermore, what have traditionally been offered as causal explanations for interlinguistic borrowing may in a good many cases apply more properly to subsequent intralinguistic spread. There are also cases where a word history shows successive waves of interlinguistic borrowing, either through subsequent direct contact with the original donor (or a related word), or through intralinguistic merging of words of distinct origins, as we will investigate further in the next section. In doing so we will turn again to English borrowing from French and Latin, since the relatively rich documentation available for all three languages enables us to build up an especially detailed picture of various borrowing phenomena.

6.5 Borrowings from more than one language

Borrowing may play a part in the type of composite word origin that we encountered in chapter 3. For instance, English *mien* 'the look, bearing, or manner of a person' (first recorded in the sixteenth century) has normally been explained as showing a clipped form of the word *demean* (ultimately of French origin, but long established in English by this date) merged with a loan from the totally unrelated French word *mine* 'appearance'. The second word was borrowed during the course of the Great Vowel Shift (see section 7.2.3), and evidently its vowel was identified with a variety of different English sounds, as is reflected by sixteenth- and seventeenth-century spellings such as *mine, meine, miene*; it would appear that identification with *meane* (from *demean*) was crucial in blocking development to /maɪn/, although the modern spelling *mien* reflects consciousness of the (partial) origin from French *mine*.[11]

A distinct phenomenon is shown by words which appear to have been borrowed partly from a word in one language and partly from a cognate word (which is usually either identical or very similar in form) in another language. A good test case is provided by words borrowed into English originally from Latin before the Norman Conquest, and subsequently either

---

[11] For some very interesting similar examples from Jamaican Creole see Cassidy (1966).

reborrowed from or reinforced by the corresponding (Anglo-)French words in the centuries after the Norman Conquest:

- *hellebore* was borrowed in the Old English period from Latin *elleborus*, but Middle English forms of the type *ellebre* point very strongly to secondary borrowing from (Anglo-)French forms of the type *ellebre*.
- *purpure* was borrowed in the Old English period from Latin *purpura*; disyllabic forms partly result from Old English inflected forms with syncope of the medial vowel, but it is likely that their later frequency owes a good deal to the variation in (Anglo-)French between forms of the type *purpure* and forms of the type *porpre, pourpre*.
- *pease* (of which modern *pea* is an inferred singular form) shows Old English borrowing from post-classical Latin *pisa* (variant of *pisum*), but (Anglo-)French influence in the Middle English period is demonstrated by forms with a diphthong (e.g. *peise*).

In other cases such as *passion* there is no very conclusive formal or semantic evidence pointing to reborrowing, although the frequency of Middle English forms such as *passioun* or *passiun* would be most easily explained as resulting from direct Anglo-French influence. *pelican* shows no distinctive formal or semantic influence from French in the Middle English period, but the survival of what was originally an Old English borrowing from Latin was probably reinforced by the formally and semantically corresponding French word, and in the early modern period we find the Middle French word used in metaphorical senses denoting an alembic and a type of device for extracting teeth earlier than we find the corresponding senses in English, suggesting secondary semantic borrowing.[12] *turn* is another similar example which we encountered among the Latin and/or French items in the Swadesh lists in section 6.2.

In the period immediately after the Norman Conquest, and beyond into the early modern period, we can find examples where clear evidence of word form, or meaning, or date of first attestation points to borrowing from French and others where it points to borrowing from Latin. But we also find many other examples where we cannot be certain: *manifest* (first attested

---

[12] In fact Old English *pellican* only occurs in glosses to Latin *pellicanus* in Psalm 101 in the Vulgate, where (as also in many later examples in English) it refers to some sort of bird of uncertain identity found in the wilderness. For a very instructive account of the difficulties encountered by Old English glossators in glossing this line, and of the difficulties posed for modern philologists attempting to interpret this material, see Lass (1997: 83–8).

in English in the fourteenth century) could equally well be from either French *manifeste* or Latin *manifestus*; similar cases are presented by for instance *negotiation, opposition, opulent,* or *pedagogy*.[13] These are mostly words which appear in French either as learned or semi-learned borrowings from Latin, or as remodellings of words which had earlier undergone phonological or morphological change during the transition from Latin to French (see examples in section 6.7). In either case the result is a French word which shows an exact formal correspondence with its Latin etymon, making it impossible to tell which is the etymon of the corresponding English word. Should such words be regarded as borrowings from French, or from Latin, or from both? Close attention to the particular circumstances of many such examples, and to parallel cases where a word shows formal or semantic influence from each language, suggests that the best course is generally to assume borrowing partly from the one language and partly from the other. This accords well with a linguistic environment where many speakers of English had a good knowledge of both French and Latin and made use of both languages (either actively or passively) at one time or another for various different technical functions. It is hardly surprising that words which were identical or near-identical in form and meaning in both Latin and French should have affected English partly through the one route of transmission and partly through the other. It is likely that we are seeing the results of multiple acts of interlinguistic borrowing, some from French, some from Latin. In some cases even the initial adopter may have had little notion which of the two languages she or he was accessing. What subsequently becomes generalized in the lexis of English is a composite of these various acts of borrowing, open to further ongoing influence (in form or meaning) from either or both of the donors.

6.6 Continuing semantic influence and semantic interference

A borrowed word may continue to show semantic influence from its donor for centuries after the date of the original borrowing. For instance:

- English *presence* is a Middle English borrowing from French and Latin, but its use with reference to the external appearance or the impressive or handsome bearing of a person (from 1570) appears to follow slightly earlier use in this sense in French in the sixteenth century.

[13] See Durkin (2002a, 2002b, 2006a, 2008) for more detail on these and similar words.

- *present* in the sense 'to stage or put on (a play)' appears to follow French use in the sixteenth century, although the word was borrowed in a number of other senses over the preceding three centuries.

We may also find semantic influence from a related word in another language. English *popular* is on morphological grounds clearly to be identified as a borrowing of Latin *populāris* 'of or belonging to the people as a whole, belonging to or used by ordinary people, available to the whole community, of the common people, supporting or professing to support the interests of the common people, liked or admired by many people', and it largely corresponds to the Latin word in its earliest meanings in English. However, it also seems to show semantic influence from the morphologically distinct but transparently related French word *populaire* 'of, relating to, or consisting of ordinary people, current among the general public, seeking the favour of the populace, known and liked among the people, vulgar, coarse, democratic, (of a disease) epidemic'.[14]

If we were to classify these cases in terms of our typology in section 5.1, we might postulate a particular kind of semantic loan, where the foreign-language model happens to be either identical to the original donor form or related to it. We cannot assume that all of the senses shown by a borrowed word and shared with its donor were borrowed at the time of the original borrowing.

It is also interesting to consider such cases in the light of the phenomenon of code-alternation identified in research on contact linguistics, where interference from a source language on a target language has been identified as a result of speakers alternating between the use of one language and another. Thomason (2001: 138–9) summarizes several such instances, including that of a native speaker of Italian who spent the majority of her education in the United States and found subsequently that there were interference features from English in her use of Italian, such as using Italian *libreria* 'bookshop' in the sense 'library' (Italian *biblioteca*) as a result of association with English *library*. In the case of *library* and *libreria* there are no senses actually in common, just equivalent word forms with meanings which both have to do with books. We can see how much more readily interference phenomena may come into play with a word like *popular*, where English already shared many senses with the French word.

---

[14] For fuller discussion of all of these examples see Durkin (2008).

6.7 Multiple borrowings from the same source

Sometimes we find what are commonly referred to as etymological doublets, where two borrowings occur which are ultimately from the same source. For instance, the English verb *affect* shows a late Middle English borrowing from French *affecter*, but earlier in Middle English we find (now obsolete) *afaite* < French *afaiter*. Both French verbs, *affecter* and *afaiter*, have the same etymon, Latin *affectāre*: *afaiter* shows regular development of the Latin word, while *affecter* shows a later learned borrowing from Latin. In English we see a similar phenomenon with the verbs *provide* and *purvey*: the first of these is borrowed directly from Latin *prōvidēre*, while *purvey* is from French *purveier*, which shows the French development of the Latin word. In cases like these the distinct forms of the donor words lead in the borrowing language to formally distinct words which show partial synonymy. We also find cases where the identical donor form is borrowed in two different periods, giving rise to two distinct words in the borrowing language. For instance, French *artiste* is borrowed into English in the sixteenth century, giving rise to modern English *artist*. However, in the late eighteenth century the same French word was borrowed again, this time giving English *artiste*, a word form distinct from *artist* in both spelling and pronunciation, and at least sometimes employed with a semantic distinction: an *artist* typically being someone practising the fine arts, especially painting, whereas an *artiste* is typically a performing artist.

The occurrence of such repeated borrowings from the same ultimate source should alert us to the likelihood of multiple inputs also having existed in cases like those discussed in sections 6.5 and 6.6, where there is no significant change in word form in the donor language(s).[15]

6.8 How can we tell that borrowing has occurred?

If we are to be sure that a borrowing has occurred, ideally we will find an exact correspondence in word form, meaning, and date. Our supposed donor form will precisely explain the word form of the supposed borrowing, it will be recorded in a meaning or meanings which give

[15] For further examples compare: *attack* and *attach*, *cadence* and *chance*, *marchpane* and *marzipan*, *master* and *magister*, *maugre* and *malgré*, *minion* and *mignon*, *peasant* and *paysan*, *ransom* and *redemption*.

an adequate explanation of the meaning or meanings of the supposed borrowing, and it will be attested at an earlier date. Obviously, if our supposed donor also has a well-established further etymology, that will help eliminate the possibility that the relationships between the donor and borrower might in fact have been the other way around. Similarly, if one language shows only a figurative or narrowed sense development from what is demonstrably a more basic sense in another language, as in the case of English borrowing of *friar* in chapter 1, we may feel confident about the direction of borrowing, although many cases are much less clear-cut than this one, and it is often advisable to take a cautious approach to assumptions about the direction of semantic change.

However, very often we will be working in situations where we have less data, or where there is more uncertainty of other kinds. For instance, when we are looking at two closely related languages, it can often be hard to tell which language a word may have originated in. Norse borrowings into English present such a problem, and here the method usually applied is to look for either formal or semantic innovations in either language: if a word shows a sound change found in Norse but not in English, it is a near certainty that it shows Norse influence of some sort; if it shows a semantic innovation known to occur in Norse but not known to occur in Old English, it is also probable (although much less certain) that we have a borrowing.[16]

Sometimes the intralinguistic and extralinguistic data simply are not conclusive: *pack* 'bundle, package' is first recorded in English in an occupational surname *Pakbyndere* 'packbinder' at the end of the twelfth century. It first occurs only eight years later in Middle Dutch, a difference so slight as to be entirely trivial in this period. It subsequently occurs in Middle Low German, and thence in a number of other Germanic languages and in several of the Romance languages. The word has no further etymology, and its origin is a mystery. Similar mystery surrounds a number of words in Germanic languages with initial /p/, since it is normally thought that initial /b/, which would give /p/ by Grimm's Law, was either very rare or perhaps did not occur at all in proto-Indo-European.[17] The connection of *pack* with trade doubtless explains its almost simultaneous appearance on both sides of the English Channel. It has normally been assumed that the word was

[16] See Björkman (1900) and Dance (2003) for discussion of the methodology; compare also Lass (1997) 203–5.

[17] Compare also discussion of *plough* in section 8.10. Other notoriously difficult etymologies involving words with initial p- in Germanic languages include *park*, *pot*, and *path*.

borrowed into English from Dutch, which is not unreasonable given that there are very few Dutch documentary records earlier than this date, but it is also perhaps possible that Dutch borrowed the word from English, or both languages from a third source.

In some cases it can be very hard to tell whether a borrowing has occurred at all, particularly with words which are not the base word in a morphologically related group. English *ravine* is recorded from the seventeenth century onwards, and is a borrowing from French *ravine*. From the mid nineteenth century we also find in English a verb *ravine* 'to score (earth etc.) with ravines', earliest in 1858. This could easily be a conversion from the English noun *ravine*, and the existence of a verb *raviner* in the same meaning in French could be purely coincidental. Alternatively, particularly since the earliest example of the English verb is in a book about the geology of central France, we might think that a borrowing from French is likely: either the English word is a loanword from French *raviner*, or it is a conversion of the English noun but on the model of the French verb. However, the earlier existence of *ravined* and *ravinement* in English, which could both be explained as formations from the noun *ravine* but which could alternatively be analysed as formations from the verb, might help shift the balance back towards a derivation within English. Certainty is likely to continue to elude us. Such doubtful cases are very common, and can probably be found in any family of words in which the base word has originally been borrowed from a foreign language and there has been a subsequent history of contact with that language.

We may see just how finely balanced decisions can be in this area from an example where new information has led to a change in assumptions about whether a loan has occurred. I will take an example from the new edition of the *OED*. Modern English *ravenous* 'very hungry' shows a broadened use of the (still current) sense '(of an animal) given to seizing other animals as prey'. In early modern English it also shows a sense 'given to plundering', and is part of a small family of words together with the verb *raven* (also in the forms *ravin*, *ravine*, etc.) and the noun *ravin* (also in the forms *raven*, *ravine*, etc.) in similar senses. In the first edition of the *OED* (in a fascicle first issued in 1903) all three were given as borrowings from (Old) French, thus:

ravin, noun < French *ravine* (ultimately < Latin *rapīna* 'rapine')
raven, verb < French *raviner*
ravenous, adjective < French *ravineux*

These etymologies were based largely on information from the main source of information on Old and Middle French then available, Godefroy's *Dictionnaire de l'ancienne langue française* (1880–1902). However, of these three etymologies, only that given for the noun *ravin* seems entirely satisfactory today. So far as the verb *raven* is concerned, an Old French verb *raviner* is indeed recorded in the sense 'to take off by force', but only in the twelfth century, several hundred years before the first appearance of the English word. In later use the French verb has only the meanings 'to stream, rush' and 'to furrow (the earth etc.) with gullies or ravines', ultimately giving rise to the English noun *ravine* 'deep narrow gorge or cleft' encountered in the previous paragraph. The adjective *ravenous* is first recorded in English in the late fourteenth century in the sense '(of an animal) given to seizing other animals as prey'. There is a corresponding Old French adjective *ravineux*, *ravinos*, *rabinos*, recorded from the twelfth to the fourteenth centuries, but with the meanings 'rapid, impetuous' (although the related word *rapineux* is recorded with a meaning much closer to that of the English word). Thus in the case of the verb and the adjective the supposed French etymons do not provide a very good fit with regard to date or meaning, and it is advisable to look for another etymology if possible. One is ready to hand, since both words can be explained as formations within English from the noun *ravin*. Thus instead of the picture given above we now have:

ravin, noun < French *ravine* (ultimately < Latin *rapīna* 'rapine')
raven (also *ravin*, *ravine*, etc.), verb < *ravin* (also *raven*, *ravine*, etc.), noun
ravenous, adjective < *ravin* (also *raven*, *ravine*, etc.), noun + -*ous*

It is important to note that this picture could change again if new information on usage in French comes to light: it is very possible that this might emerge from the new edition of the *Anglo-Norman Dictionary* currently in preparation. Such etymologies are highly dependent on the nature and quality of the available data. The assumptions made in the first edition of the *OED* seemed sensible on the basis of the much sketchier information on Old French and Middle French lexis then available, and it is possible that some new lexicographical finds might come to light in the future that challenge our assumptions once again – although obviously the better and fuller our lexicographical resources become, the less likely it is that we will have quite so many such surprises.

The importance of cultural and historical background was shown earlier by the example of *tomato* in section 5.5. We know that the Nahuatl word was probably borrowed first into Spanish, because Spanish speakers were the first speakers of a European language to be in contact with speakers of Nahuatl. Hence it is very satisfactory to find Spanish is the first European language in which the word is recorded, and that the forms in other European languages also support the hypothesis of transmission originally via Spanish.

6.9 Lexical borrowing and code-switching

In section 2.2.2 we looked at nonce borrowing of foreign-language words, and at how the early history of a borrowing may be like that of *focaccia* in English, showing a number of separate introductions of the word, followed eventually by more general adoption. We have also seen that this sort of more general adoption will not happen for all words, and that most will not progress beyond the stage of nonce borrowing. In section 5.1.5 we looked at the difficulty of trying to distinguish between *Fremdwörter* and *Lehnwörter*. Morphological and phonological adaptation are only tendencies. Phonological adaptation in particular operates on a cline which makes it very difficult to say that adaptation has or has not occurred in a particular instance. If phonological adaptation consists of no more than pronouncing a foreign word with an accent, then this sort of adaptation will surely be shown also by many instances of the nonce use of a foreign word. If an early user of the word *focaccia* in an English sentence pronounces it with final /ə/ rather than /a/, this certainly reflects adaptation to the usual phonological structure of English words, but it does not necessarily show a naturalized borrowing: the speaker may simply be accommodating to the speech of interlocutors (perhaps in order to appear less pretentious), or may have a poor knowledge of Italian phonology.[18] It is perfectly possible for such a pronunciation to occur in a sentence of the type 'In Italian they call this type of bread *focaccia*', where the word is explicitly identified as belonging to Italian rather than English. We may find a similar situation with morphology, e.g. 'In Poland they eat stuffed dumplings resembling ravioli, which they call *pierogis*', where the Polish plural form *pierogi* is suffixed with the English plural ending -*s*, but where the established Italian borrowing *ravioli* retains the Italian plural form. It is likely that there is a

---

[18] See Haugen (1950) 215–17 for some further discussion and examples.

cline here, from explicit identification of a word as belonging to a foreign language, e.g.:

> (i) 'I had some of a type of bread which they call in Italian *focaccia*' (even though the form in such a sentence may show intentional or unintentional phonological or morphological adaptation)

to use of a word with reference to a foreign culture but without explicit identification of its foreign-language identity:

> (ii) 'On our holidays we had sandwiches made with focaccia every day' (where italics may well be used in print)

to uses where there is no flagging of foreign status:

> (iii) 'I always think that focaccia is the best type of bread to have with salad'

We may decide on a pragmatic basis that the first type of sentence does not show borrowing, even if the quoted foreign-language word may show some phonological or morphological adaptation, whereas the other two types of sentence do show borrowing. Many historical dictionaries adopt this approach. However, any systematic distinction between more and less naturalized borrowings is very difficult to apply with any consistency. Also, if we are working solely from the evidence of historical spelling forms, many of the finer details are likely to be irrecoverable.

A rather difficult complication is found in determining the relationship between lexical borrowing and the phenomenon known as code-switching, where bilingual speakers switch between use of one language and use of another, in the knowledge that they are addressing others who also have some knowledge of each language, and who are hence to at least a very limited extent bilingual. Code-switching may occur at sentence boundaries, i.e. intersententially, or at the level of the word, phrase, or clause, i.e. intrasententially. (In fact, some linguists reserve the term code-switching for switches which occur intersententially, and refer to those which occur intrasententially as code-mixing, but I will not adopt this distinction here.) The relationship between code-switching and lexical borrowing is much disputed, but it seems a reasonable assumption that code-switching within a bilingual community at least sometimes results in lexical borrowing.[19]

[19] For a useful overview and references to the relevant literature see Thomason (2001) 131–6, and compare also Mahootian (2006). For accounts broadly in favour of the

For instance, a word from language A may be used within sentences of language B by bilingual speakers as a code-switch. This may happen for any of various reasons, such as cultural associations, group identity, or because it expresses a concept not so easily expressed within the existing resources of language B. Subsequently this word may become adopted into the wider speech community of monolingual speakers of language B.

Such issues can often lead to practical difficulties in assessing written evidence from the past. As we noted in section 5.6, in the multilingual culture of later medieval England, English was the language of everyday life for all or nearly all speakers, but Latin and Anglo-French had important roles in many areas of professional and cultural life. In this context we often encounter situations where it is very difficult to tell whether a word ultimately of foreign origin occurring in a given document shows a borrowing or a code-switch. Many documents have a basic grammatical framework which is Latin, or at least they show Latin grammatical endings and concord, but they also contain many words of vernacular (English or Anglo-French) origin. Some of these vernacular words show Latin grammatical endings, and hence could be regarded as loanwords into Latin. Others do not, and hence we could argue that they show code-switches, from Latin to one of the vernacular languages. In other documents the basic framing language may be English or Anglo-French, but we find many words which belonged originally to the other vernacular language. In this situation the general similarity of inflectional endings, especially in nouns, often makes it impossible to identify words as belonging on morphological grounds to either Middle English or Anglo-French. In such a case, do we have a text which shows an extremely high incidence of lexical borrowing, or do we have a text which shows a great deal of code-switching? Some of the implications of this sort of text (of which my sketch represents only the crudest summary) are picked out by Hunt, a scholar who has done a great deal to draw attention to material of this kind:[20]

If language acquisition...takes place in a context of competing codes in a multilingual situation in which individuals accommodate their linguistic behaviour to that of groups with which they wish to be identified, or contrariwise, then the situation

proposition that single-word code-switching often leads to lexical borrowing see Myers-Scotton (2002) or Thomason (2003). For the alternative view that most singly occurring foreign-language words should be regarded not as code-switches but as borrowings, see Poplack, Sankoff, and Miller (1988), Poplack and Meechan (1998), Poplack (2004).

[20] For a summary of other recent work in this area see Pahta and Nurmi (2006).

is inevitably one of great complexity, which will not surprise anyone familiar with contact linguistics and the world of bi-dialectalism, bilingualism, diglossia, borrowing, transfers, interference, shift, relexicalisation, pidginisation, and creolisation. Linguists have frequently sought to identify borrowings in the languages of medieval Britain, but in the context of multilingual societies it can be unrealistic to attempt to distinguish code-switching from borrowing.

(Hunt (2000) 131)

Such issues as these pose problems for anyone who wishes to establish what the earliest example is of a particular borrowing. Historical dictionaries tend generally to take a pragmatic approach: if a word subsequently becomes frequent enough to merit inclusion, early examples found within the context of an utterance in the borrowing language will generally be taken as showing the borrowing, rather than an independent code-switch. More problematic can be cases where the word is found in a foreign-language or multilingual context. For instance, *plane* meaning either a bricklayer's or a carpenter's tool, is a Middle English borrowing from (Anglo-)French. In the evidence presented for this word in the new edition of the *OED*, a first example in an English context is found from a little before 1425 in a Latin–English glossary:

*a*1425 *Medulla Gram.* (Stonyhurst) f. 37v, Leuiga: a leuor or a plane.

An example from 1404 in a Latin context with the English plural morpheme -*ys* probably shows an earlier example of the English borrowing (on the grounds that -*ys* is not normally found as a plural morpheme in Anglo-French):

1404 in J. T. Fowler *Extracts Acct. Rolls Abbey of Durham* (1899) II. 397 In custodia Plumbarii, 2 planys.

Earlier still a vernacular word is found in other Latin documents, but in these cases there is nothing to tell us whether it is the English word or its French etymon:

1350 in J. T. Fowler *Extracts Acct. Rolls Abbey of Durham* (1899) II. 550 Uno Plane et aliis instrumentis pro officio plumbar', emptis, 2 s. 5 d. 1399 in J. Raine *Fabric Rolls York Minster* (1859) 18 Instrumenta carpentariorum . . . Item, j plane de ere.

Here the approach of different dictionaries in fact differs: the *OED* places these ambiguous examples in its etymology section, but the *Middle English Dictionary* places them in its main documentation for the Middle English word, without comment, in line with its general policy in dealing with vernacular words occurring in Latin documents. On a purely practical level, examples such as this remind us of the importance of looking closely at what the earliest examples presented in a dictionary are, and they should be a salutary reminder to any etymologist that dates alone, unsupported by a reference, are often not very helpful.[21]

Foreign-language phrases can also be ambiguous as to whether they are lexical borrowings or code-switches. They may show grammatical characteristics of the donor or source language which are alien to the borrowing or receiving language, such as agreement features or word order, although such features are not always reproduced faithfully, in which case we can probably safely assume that borrowing has occurred. This is typical of borrowing of French food terms in English. In French *moules marinières* the adjective *marinier* 'marine' is postposed after *moule* 'mussel', and shows feminine plural concord. The *OED*'s evidence suggests that the written form *moules marinière* is more common in modern use in English than *moules marinières*; this probably results simply from the final *-s* being silent, but it could also reflect influence from either French *moules à la marinière* 'mussels in the marine style' or the rare French blended form *moules marinière*. Substitution of one or more native elements is often found, as in *beef bourguignon* beside earlier *boeuf bourguignon*: we could say that the borrowed phrase has been remodelled with substitution of *beef* for French *boeuf*, or we could say that beside the original borrowing we have a subsequent loan blend. Extensive naturalization in form is often found in borrowed phrases, such as English *billy doo* 'love letter' < French *billet doux*. Such naturalization shows that we have a borrowing rather than a code-switch, but it does not tell us whether this was via an initial code-switch. Interestingly, *OED*'s first quotation for *billet-doux* suggests at the very least an imitation of code-switching: 'He sings and dances en François, and writes the billets doux to a miracle' (1673: John Dryden *Marriage à la Mode* II. i. 261).

6.10 Some conclusions from chapters 5 and 6

Some generalizations about etymologies which involve borrowing can be drawn from the topics we have examined in the last two chapters:

- Borrowed words are often subject to processes of accommodation to the phonology or morphology of the borrowing language, either at the

[21] On the source of the dates used in this book see chapter 1, footnote 6.

time of borrowing or subsequently. They may also form compounds or derivatives in the borrowing language.

- Not all components of the meaning of a word need be borrowed.
- Borrowed words are subject to change (semantically, phonologically, or morphologically), just like any other words.
- Borrowing between languages (interlinguistic borrowing) is not necessarily a once-and-for-all process, just as borrowing within languages (intralinguistic borrowing) is not either.
- Initial interlinguistic borrowing is typically followed by intralinguistic borrowing, as a word spreads to different registers or varieties of a language and to the usage of different speech communities.
- After the date of initial borrowing, borrowed items frequently show further influence from the donor language, through the borrowing of additional senses, or through formal remodelling after the donor form. Loanwords may in time become either less like the corresponding form in the donor language (through internal processes of change in either the borrowing language or the donor language), or more like it (through remodelling of a previously naturalized form after the form in the donor language).
- A good etymology which involves borrowing will have a working hypothesis as to how and why (as well as when and where) borrowing occurred, and also as to how and why the borrowed word, sense, etc. has subsequently spread within the borrowing language.

Of course, we will not always have sufficient data to address all of these issues, but we should not assume, simply because we have only limited data available to us, that the reality is likely to have been any less complex than in instances where we do have abundant data.

7

Change in word form

Nearly all etymological research involves analysis of change in word form. This analysis also raises some of the most theoretically complex areas which we will encounter in this book. In the first part of this chapter we will examine examples of:

- regular sound changes, both isolative ones, occurring irrespective of any particular phonetic environment, and conditioned ones, triggered by a particular conditioning environment
- sporadic sound changes
- analogy, folk etymology, and other types of associative change in word form

After this, we will turn to one of the key issues in historical linguistics, namely just how much regularity is in fact shown by what are called regular sound changes, and what the implications are for various different types of etymological research.

Finally, we will look at some detailed examples of etymologies in which changes in word form play a key role, including some successes of etymological research and some unresolved difficulties.

7.1 Two Germanic sound changes

7.1.1 Grimm's Law

As we saw in section 1.2.4, Grimm's Law describes a series of sound shifts by which the proto-Indo-European voiceless stops (*p, *t, *k, *k^w), voiced stops (*b, *d, *g, *g^w), and breathy-voiced stops (*b^h, *d^h, *g^h, *g^{hw}) became in proto-Germanic respectively voiceless fricatives (*f, *θ, *h, *hw), voiceless stops (*p, *t, *k, *kw), and voiced fricatives (*β, *$\eth$, *γ, *γw), with provisos as noted in chapter 1.

Why is it assumed that the operation of Grimm's Law was e.g. proto-Indo-European *p > proto-Germanic *f, rather than that Latin, Greek, etc. show a change *f > *p ? Firstly, it should be understood that the reasoning has nothing at all to do with the relative antiquity of the earliest documents in Latin, Greek, etc. in comparison with the Germanic languages. As discussed in chapter 1, the split of the various branches of Indo-European occurred much earlier than the date of our earliest documentary evidence for any of the Indo-European languages. So the relative antiquity of our documentary evidence gives no particular authority for determining what the direction of change was in a case like this.

In this particular instance, perhaps the most important piece of evidence is that we know from prior research on well-documented stages in the history of many languages that a change from *p > *f is typologically very common (i.e. it happens in lots of different languages) whereas *f > *p is not. It can also be observed that a change of this type, from stop to fricative, can be seen as part of a broader process of lenition of consonants observable in many languages of the world, which can be explained to some extent in terms of increasing ease of articulation for the speaker, since the degree of obstruction of airflow in the mouth is reduced.

Additionally, we can see that this set of regular correspondences distinguishes Germanic from all of the other branches of Indo-European. This would seem less significant if we were free to hypothesize that Germanic branched off particularly early from the rest of Indo-European, as it is generally held that Hittite and the other Anatolian languages probably did. Then we could be looking at a shared innovation in all of the other branches after Germanic had split off from them, but in fact other linguistic evidence suggests that Germanic did not branch off particularly early. Grimm's Law as a shared innovation among the Germanic languages is therefore a much more economical explanation. None of this of course offers any explanation at all for why the Grimm's Law changes occurred, but simply suggests why one direction of change seems much more likely than the other.[1]

7.1.2 Verner's Law

Grimm's Law describes a set of classic 'regular' sound changes of the type which form the main foundation of comparative linguistics. Each and every eligible consonant is assumed to have shifted in every word in which it occurred. Thus, if proto-Indo-European *t does not correspond to proto-Germanic *θ, we must find some way of accounting for this: our method does not permit us to say 'perhaps *t simply became a different sound in this word history' or 'perhaps the sound change simply did not occur in this word history'.

However, there were some environments in which the shifts did not occur. For instance, the voiceless stops inherited from proto-Indo-European did not shift if they were immediately preceded by another obstruent (often *s). Thus corresponding to Latin *spernere* we have Old English *spurnan* (English *spurn*), and corresponding to ancient Greek *astér* we have Old English *steorra* (English *star*). This does not indicate irregularity, but simply a need to define Grimm's Law more precisely: the voiceless stops shifted to voiceless fricatives except when immediately preceded by another obstruent.

In the etymology of English *sad* in section 1.2.4 we encountered a different sort of situation: the reflex of proto-Indo-European *sə̥to-* in proto-Germanic did indeed show the Grimm's Law shift *t > *θ (and hence a stage *sa'θa), but then the voiceless fricative *θ was voiced by the operation of Verner's Law, because the main stress did not fall on the immediately preceding syllable, giving *sa'ða.

Verner's paper explaining this voicing marked an epoch in the study of historical linguistics and in the development of etymological methodology (Verner 1875). It was entitled (in German) 'Eine Ausnahme der ersten Lautverschiebung' ('An exception to the first [Germanic] sound shift') and its importance was that it gave a rational explanation for what had

---

[1] For discussion of a daring but controversial explanation based on language contact see Smith (2007) 75–87. For detailed bibliography on many other suggested explanations see Collinge (1985) 63–76.

previously seemed the most troubling set of exceptions to Grimm's Law. It thus opened the way for the most important claim of the group of historical linguists known as the Junggrammatiker or Neogrammarians: sound changes operate without exceptions (or at least those of the systematic type illustrated by Gimm's Law and Verner's Law do: compare section 7.3). Where apparent exceptions were found, these could be shown to be susceptible to rational explanation by various means:

- Perhaps the conditioning environments in which the sound change did and did not operate had not been fully understood, and thus the resolution of the apparent exceptions might lie in a more precise definition of the sound change.
- Perhaps the sound change had occurred in one dialect but not in another, or perhaps it had occurred in both but in a slightly different set of conditioning environments. Subsequent mixing of forms from the different dialects may have occurred, giving the false appearance of irregularity of operation of the sound change.
- Perhaps apparent exceptions were caused by words entering a language or dialect by borrowing after the period in which the sound change operated.
- Perhaps the appearance of irregularity was created by the subsequent occurrence of another sound change.
- Perhaps apparent exceptions had been created by the subsequent operation of various analogical processes within grammatical paradigms or through association between words of similar form or meaning. (We saw examples of analogical levelling within a paradigm in the cases of *heaven* and *stave* in section 3.1, and we will look at many other types of analogical or associative processes in section 7.4.)

This framework provided the key to enormous advances in etymological research in the late nineteenth century and early twentieth century, especially on families of related languages. With certain qualifications (which we will consider in section 7.6), it remains key to a great deal of etymological work today.

7.2 Examples of English sound changes

The sets of sound changes described by Grimm's Law and Verner's Law both occurred considerably before the date of our earliest records for any of the Germanic languages. As we saw in section 1.2.4, another very important development which had an enormous impact on word forms in all of the Germanic languages, namely the shift of stress to the initial syllable of every word, occurred later than Verner's Law. Indeed, this projection back into a much earlier stage in the development of the Germanic languages was one of the most ingenious aspects of Verner's formulation. To a certain extent there is therefore a danger that our assertion of the regularity of Grimm's Law and Verner's Law could depend on some circular reasoning, and that we might be rejecting valid etymologies because they do not fit the hypothesis. We will look at this issue further in section 7.6, but much of the supporting evidence, and also many of the doubts and uncertainties, come from what we can observe about the operation of sound changes in documented linguistic history. We will therefore look in this section at several representative changes from the history of English, selected for the variety of different considerations relevant to etymological work which they raise, and because they figure in a number of the etymologies presented elsewhere in this book.

7.2.1 Early Middle English /ɑ:/ > /ɔ:/ in southern dialects

In early Middle English the long vowel /ɑ:/ (the reflex of Old English ā) rounded in southern dialects to /ɔ:/, but did not do so in northern dialects. Hence Old English *stān* gives Middle English (southern) *stōn* (modern standard English *stone*), (northern) *stān* (modern Scots or northern English *stane*). This is a classic example of an isolative (or spontaneous, or unconditioned) sound change, not determined by any particular phonetic context in the word. In this instance we have enough evidence to be able to observe something of the way that the sound change spread dialectally, as well as to be able to see that its results were ultimately regular:

Despite its variable implementation in different texts and different areas, we can date it as coming to fruition in the late twelfth to early thirteenth century, beginning in the south-east and spreading northwards – and constituting from that time on one of the major north/south isoglosses.

(Lass (1992) 46–7)

7.2.2 Early Middle English lengthening in open syllables in disyllabic words

A conditioned sound change which occurred slightly later in the early Middle English period was the lengthening (and in most cases lowering) of short vowels in open syllables in disyllabic words (or more precisely, in disyllabic words where there was only one medial consonant). We encountered this change in section 3.1 with the change *poke* /pokə/ > *pōke* /pɔːkə/, modern English *poke*. Similarly we find:

/makən/ > /maːkən/, modern English *make*
/metə/ > /mɛːtə/, modern English *meat*
/flotən/ > /flɔːtən/, modern English *float*
/wikə/ > /weːk/, modern English *week*
/wudə/ > /woːdə/, modern English *wood*

These examples (and many others like them) enable us to state the effects of the change more precisely: lengthening of each of these five vowels occurred, and in all cases except that of /a/ lowering also occurred.

The evidence of Middle English texts and of later dialect developments enables us to discern some more details: (1) the changes appear to have taken place earlier in northern varieties than in southern ones; (2) the lengthening (and lowering) of /i/ and /u/ generally occurred slightly later than that of the other vowels, and was more common in northern varieties than in southern ones. The very few examples of the results of lengthening of /i/ or /u/ which are reflected in forms in modern standard English include several very controversial and difficult examples. For a case-by-case discussion on etymological grounds see Smith (2007) 174–6. In my example *wood*, only the spelling of the modern word reflects the form with lengthening. The usual pronunciation /wʊd/ reflects either a form without lengthening (as argued by Dobson (1968) §36 note 2), or a form with lengthening to /woːdə/ which showed subsequent shortening in early modern English. For this shortening compare *good* /gʊd/ (Old English *gōd*) and *foot* /fʊt/ (Old English *fōt*), which both show the result of sporadic shortening of the Great Vowel Shift output of Middle English /oː/ (compare section 7.2.3).

Additionally, as we saw in section 3.1, levelling in grammatical paradigms has often obscured the results of the change, so that instead of *staff*/*staves* we find *staff*/*staffs* or *stave*/*staves*, and similarly the spoken form of *heaven* has the short vowel levelled from the (trisyllabic) inflected forms (although the written form still reflects the lengthened vowel). As noted in section 7.1.2, this is the sort of 'apparent exception' which is easily accounted for in the neogrammarian framework. The same would apply to modern English /wʊd/ if it shows late sporadic shortening, but not if it failed ever to show lengthening. Dialect mixing might just about be a plausible explanation within the neogrammarian framework for the uneven distribution of lengthening of /i/ and /u/ which we find in southern varieties. More troubling are cases like *poke* which we encountered in section 3.1, where the lengthening of /o/ appears sometimes to have failed in northern varieties (especially before velars), even though it is precisely in northern varieties that the change generally appears to have occurred earliest. We might be able to find a satisfactory neogrammarian explanation for this if we hypothesize that in some varieties loss of final /ə/ may have occurred earlier, hence removing the environment for open syllable lengthening; variants of *poke* with a short vowel could hence have resulted from dialect mixing from such varieties. However, recent research on Middle English open syllable lengthening has increased the impression that its results were patchy and unevenly distributed across the lexicon. Additionally, it has been suggested with some plausibility that the traditional account of how the change operated may not be correct. Lengthening seems generally to have been more likely to take place when the second syllable ended with /ə/, and there are numerous exceptions to the lengthening among words with a final consonant in the unstressed syllable, e.g. *ganot, ganet* 'gannet' or *otor, oter* 'otter'. Further, it has been suggested very plausibly that loss of final /ə/ may in some cases actually have preceded the lengthening, and that the lengthening was a compensatory process resulting from the loss of the unstressed vowel in the following syllable.[2] If this analysis is correct, then we cannot explain variants of *poke* with a short vowel as being the result of these sound changes occurring in a different order in some varieties, although a much more plausible explanation would be offered by the mechanism of lexical diffusion which we will look at in section 7.6.[3] However, this change is still the subject of much debate, as is its relationship with similar developments in other West Germanic languages which may or may not show the same process as in Middle English.[4] (We encountered an example of open syllable

---

[2] For summary of this proposal (advanced originally by Donka Minkova) see Lass (1992) 73–4, and compare also Smith (2007) 113–26.

[3] In the particular case of *poke* an alternative explanation might be borrowing from Anglo-French of a variant which already showed loss of the final vowel (compare Short (2007) §19.7–8 on such loss), but this is less likely in view of the early borrowing into English, and the same explanation would not hold for some of the other words which appear to show failure of open syllable lengthening.

[4] For a detailed defence of the traditional account, and for comparison with developments in Middle Dutch and Middle High German, see Lahiri and Dresher (1999).

lengthening in Middle Dutch with *pōke* in section 3.1.) For the time being we can take note of this change as an example of where close engagement with the actual historical data reveals a situation of some complexity, which is open to a variety of different interpretations.

7.2.3 The Great Vowel Shift

A very important series of isolative changes in the history of English generally go under the name of the Great Vowel Shift. This is the conventional name given to a very complex series of raisings and/or diphthongizations of the front and back long vowels which occurred in the late Middle English and early modern English periods. Crucially, slightly different developments occurred in different dialects (or in some cases, the same developments occurred but at different times). As this was a time of considerable social mobility, there was very considerable mixing of forms from different dialects. Many of the changes can be traced in considerable detail, especially because we possess large amounts of information from early modern writers on pronunciation, who are known as orthoepists. Other important evidence comes from the different outputs in different modern dialects, from contemporary spellings, and from rhymes and puns. Individual etymologies, i.e. what we can reconstruct of the earlier history of each lexical item, have a crucial role to play in the process.

As well as being very complex, many aspects of the Great Vowel Shift are extremely controversial, and have been so since the phenomenon first began to be examined closely by historians of English in the late nineteenth century. There is fairly widespread acceptance that the general shape of the changes as they affected southern English dialects can be represented as in figure 7.1, with the changes being divided into two phases. 'Phase I' extended from late Middle English (or possibly slightly earlier) to the beginning of the early modern period (being complete soon after 1500), but 'Phase II' was rather later, and was not complete until the middle of the seventeenth century. (This diagram follows Lass (1999a) 80, as does much of my discussion here.)

This book is not the place to do any sort of justice to the problems and complexities of the Great Vowel Shift, but if we look for a moment at some of the developments shown by the front vowels during the Great Vowel Shift and afterwards, we may be able to make some useful general

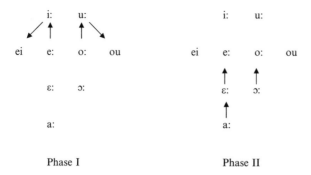

Fig 7.1 The Great Vowel Shift

observations about processes of phonological merger and their implications for etymological work.[5]

Middle English had distinct vowel phonemes in words such as *mile, meet, meat, mane,* and *main* ('strength'), respectively /i:/, /e:/, /ɛ:/, /a:/, and the diphthong /ai/. These sounds each had distinct etymological origins. In fact, each had multiple different origins, but these five example words illustrate perhaps the most typical origins of each:

- Middle English /i:/ in *mīle* (modern English *mile*) shows the reflex of Old English /i:/ (Old English *mīl*)
- Middle English /e:/ in *mēte* (modern English *meet*) shows the reflex of Old English /e:/ (Old English *mētan*)
- Middle English /ɛ:/ in *mēte* (modern English *meat*) developed from /e/ by early Middle English lengthening in open syllables (Old English *mete*)
- Middle English /a:/ in *māne* (modern English *mane*) developed from /a/ by early Middle English lengthening in open syllables (Old English *manu*)
- Middle English /ai/ in *main* ('strength'; modern English *main*) developed as a result of vocalization of the semi-vowel /j/, which itself

---

[5] For readers completely new to the Great Vowel Shift, a very useful and readable short summary is provided by Barber (1996), although this is dated in some respects, and should be followed up by more detailed accounts such as Lass (1999a). For an overview of controversies see McMahon (2006), and see also Smith (2007). The fullest account remains Dobson (1968), which also provides a useful guide to the principal works of the contemporary orthoepists.

resulted from palatalization of the reflex of Germanic */g/ (Old English *mægen*)

Of these five, Middle English /i:/ was diphthongized early in the Great Vowel Shift (Phase I), giving ultimately modern English *mile* /maɪl/. Middle English /e:/ was also raised early (Phase I), giving modern English *meet* /mi:t/, but its historical relationship with the other sounds is rather more complex. In modern standard English (but not in all modern dialects) *meet* and *meat* are homophones, and so are *mane* and *main*. Ultimately, we therefore have two sets of mergers: the reflexes of Middle English /e:/ and /ɛ:/ have merged (as /i:/), and so have the reflexes of Middle English /a:/ and /ai/ (as /eɪ/). However, the Great Vowel Shift maintained the contrasts between Middle English /e:/, /ɛ:/, and /a:/, as we saw in the figure above. The explanation for the modern system lies in some rather complex developments in the sixteenth, seventeenth, and eighteenth centuries, which illustrate some general issues to do with phonological mergers.

The Middle English diphthong /ai/ showed a complicated history in the sixteenth century, even if we look only at types of pronunciation current in London at the time. In some varieties it monophthongized to /ɛ:/, but in others it remained a diphthong /ai/. In some of those varieties in which /ai/ monophthongized to /ɛ:/, the reflex of Middle English /a:/ had already been raised to /ɛ:/, and hence these two sounds merged, and *main* would have been homophonous with *mane* just as it is today. In others the reflex of Middle English /ɛ:/ was still /ɛ:/ (and the reflex of Middle English /a:/ was perhaps /æ:/), and *main* hence showed the same sound as *meat* (and so *main* was homophonous with *mean*). We thus have three possible outcomes for Middle English /ai/ words like *main* in this period:

   (i) /ai/ monophthongized to /ɛ:/, and merged with the reflex of Middle English /a:/, hence *main* and *mane* are homophonous
   (ii) /ai/ monophthongized to /ɛ:/, and merged with the reflex of Middle English /ɛ:/, hence *main* and *mean* are homophonous
   (iii) /ai/ remained a diphthong, hence *main* is not homophonous with either *mane* or *mean*

If we turn now to the reflexes of Middle English /e:/ (in *meet*) and /ɛ:/ (in *meat*), in some varieties these had merged as /i:/ before the end of the sixteenth century, thus Shakespeare can rhyme *these* (Middle English /e:/) with *seas* (Middle English /ɛ:/). However, Shakespeare also rhymes *sea* with *play*

(Middle English /ai/), reflecting varieties in which /ai/ was monophthongized and merged with the reflex of Middle English /ɛ:/. In other varieties we also find merger of the reflexes of Middle English /ɛ:/ and /a:/, hence *mean* and *mane* are homophonous. Even in the eighteenth century we still find considerable variation where the reflex of Middle English /ɛ:/ is concerned: Pope has rhymes on the modern pattern with Middle English /e:/ words (as *flea/see, ease/these*), but also with Middle English /a:/ words (as *weak/take, eat/gate*), and with Middle English /ai/ words (as *tea/obey*).[6] In a very few Middle English /ɛ:/ words (e.g. *great, break*) the merger with the reflex of Middle English /i:/ did not occur in standard English, and instead merger with the reflexes of Middle English /a:/ and /ai/ is found.

Mergers are not particularly rare occurrences, and they invariably throw up problems for etymologists. In section 1.2.4 we encountered the proto-Germanic merger of *a* and *o* as *a*, reconstructed on the basis of the comparative evidence of other Indo-European languages. This means that whenever a Germanic word shows *a* and does not have secure cognates in other Germanic languages, we will have to consider the possibility that an Indo-European precursor may have shown *o* or *a*, or indeed *ə̥* (ultimately representing, as we saw in section 4.4.1, vocalic realization of a laryngeal consonant), although in many cases what we know of the morphophonology of Indo-European enables us to narrow down the possibilities. In section 7.7 we will look at some other etymologies where mergers create considerable uncertainty.

7.2.4 *i*-mutation

i-mutation (sometimes also called by the German name *i*-umlaut) is a process in the early history of Old English which caused raising and/or fronting of vowels when an /i/ or /j/ followed in the next syllable. It occurred slightly before the date of our earliest documentary records.[7] It was probably a vowel-harmony process: the vowel was raised and/or fronted in anticipation of the following high front sound. Since /i/ or /j/ occurred in a great many derivative suffixes and morphological inflections in Old English this sound change had an enormous effect on its word forms (as also in many

---

[6] For all of this data see Lass (1999a).

[7] On the possibility that some of the very earliest documents may still show the change in progress see e.g. Lass (1994) 62–3, although this is controversial.

of the other early Germanic languages in which parallel changes occurred). Often, the /i/ or /j/ which caused the change was subsequently lost (or in many other cases lowered to /e/).

We will look at this change as it affected the high back rounded vowel /u/, giving rise to the fronted sound /y/, which was a new sound in the sound system of Old English. The contrast that we see in modern English between singular *mouse* and plural *mice* results from exactly this process. Before the operation of *i*-mutation, the contrast would have been singular */muːs/, plural */muːsi/ (earlier */muːsiz/). *i*-mutation gave singular *[muːs], plural *[myːsi], with fronting of the vowel, although at this stage the variation between [uː] and [yː] was purely allophonic. Loss of the /i/ from the plural stem form gave singular /muːs/, plural /myːs/, which is the stage reflected by the recorded Old English forms *mūs*, plural *mȳs*.

> before *i*-mutation: singular */muːs/, plural */muːsi/
> after *i*-mutation: singular *[muːs], plural *[myːsi]
> after loss of /i/: singular /muːs/, plural /myːs/

At this last stage we have a new phonemic contrast between /uː/ and /yː/, which bears the functional load of distinguishing the singular from the plural after the final /i/ has been lost.

We can get from the Old English forms to the modern English ones by a few easy steps. The singular form /muːs/ shows diphthongization as a result of the Great Vowel Shift, eventually giving modern English /maʊs/. So far as the plural form is concerned, Old English /yː/ had different reflexes in different dialectal varieties of early Middle English. The one that is relevant to the modern English form of this word is the (originally northern and eastern) form /iː/, which again showed diphthongization as a result of the Great Vowel Shift, hence modern English /maɪs/. However, in many other cases plural contrasts based on variation in the stem vowel have subsequently been eliminated: see section 7.4.1 on *book*.

The presence or absence of *i*-mutation can give useful evidence in dating borrowings from Latin in Old English. *yntse* 'ounce' (< a variant of Latin *uncia*) shows *i*-mutation, whereas *tunece* 'tunic' (< Latin *tunica*) does not, presumably because it was borrowed later, after the change had ceased to be operative. However, there are some counterexamples. In section 5.6 we encountered English *proud* (late Old English *prūd*) < Old French. The derivative noun, Old English *prȳdo* (modern English *pride*), gives every appearance of showing *i*-mutation, but this surely cannot be the case. Not only is the word first recorded much later than the period of *i*-mutation, but the etymology of *prūd* also argues very strongly against the possibility that the word was borrowed much earlier, since the stem vowel of the Old French word reflects a sound change which probably did not take place before the ninth century. Probably what we have here is a case of analogy: Old English had pairs such as *full*, adjective (modern English *full*) and *fyllu*, noun (with *i*-mutation, resulting from a proto-Germanic stem-forming suffix *-īn-*; modern English *fill*); on the analogy of these we find *prūd*, adjective and *prȳdo*, noun. So:

$$full : fyllu = pr\bar{u}d : pr\bar{y}do$$

7.2.5 A sound change with messy results

In late Middle English, short /e/ shows lowering to /a/ before /r/ in final position in a word or before another consonant (*C*), hence *er(C)* > *ar(C)*. This change is recorded earliest in the north, and spreads only gradually to the south. In his classic account of English pronunciation in the early modern period, Dobson, before presenting his own much more detailed and nuanced analysis, reflects on earlier attempts to explain the observed data as the result of the operation of a classic neogrammarian exceptionless sound change within a single dialect:

Though this classical doctrine [that 'we are to regard all sound-changes as being without exceptions'] may be true of an individual dialect (provided it is rigidly enough defined), it is demonstrably untrue of modern St[andard] E[nglish], which is not a pure dialect but a mixed language and in consequence shows great variety of pronunciation in words which are clearly of the same class. It would be a fair guess in the present instance that the lowering was not at all typical of educated London English but was regular in more vulgar speech, and that the lowered forms made their way into edu-cated speech gradually and inconsistently from this dialect which had regular lowering. The lowered pronunciation is less freely accepted in words of Latin origin, obviously owing to the influence of Latin orthography and probably also pronunciation.

(Dobson (1968) II §64)

We thus appear to have a situation where both regional and social variation may be at play in determining whether or not we find this sound change in a particular word in a particular speaker's idiolect. We may decide to leave our analysis at this point, but it is possible to look in more detail at other determining factors which may be at play in particular instances. One factor is noted by nearly all writers on this subject: very often comparison with the Latin or French etymons of borrowed words led to either restoration of /e/ or the selection of variants without the lowering, as summarized for example by Lass (1999a: 109): 'The general tendency is to keep reflexes of /a/ in Germanic words (*heart*, *star*) and to reintroduce /e/ in loans (*mercy*, *serve*). Early sources show variation.' In a few cases, e.g. *clerk*, the pronunciation (at least in British English) reflects the lowering, but the spelling does not. Samuels (1972) attempts a much more elaborate analysis of the exceptions to this lowering, which is worth close examination as an example both of the role of etymology in this kind of work, and of the limits to what can be established even when we have a good deal of available historical data. Samuels categorizes the exceptions as follows:

(i) learned channels of transmission: the bulk of the examples with French and Latin counterparts, e.g. *universal, certain, service, concern...*;

(ii) avoidance of homonymy: *pert* (cf. *part*), *yearn* (cf. *yarn*), *herd, heard* (cf. *hard*); possibly *earth* (cf. *hearth*), *perch* (cf. *parch*);

(iii) avoidance of polysemy: *person* (cf. *parson*), *vermin* (cf. *varmint*);

(iv) phonaesthetic influence: *swerve* (cf. *swirl*);

(v) derivation: *dearth* (cf. *dear*);

(vi) prevalence of long variants in the spoken chain, especially when initial and/or preceding *n* or *l*: *earl, early, earn, earnest, earth* (cf. (ii) above), *learn, stern, fern, yearn* (cf. (ii) above), *kernel*.

(Samuels (1972) 143)

Samuels's category (i) is thus one with which nearly all scholars would agree. A very interesting case is presented by *merchant*. This word was borrowed into English in the early Middle English period from French, in which it shows forms of the types *merchant, merchand* and also *marchant, marchand*, in the latter case showing the parallel tendency to lowering of -*er*- > -*ar*- found in French (see Pope (1934) 187–8; Short (2007) 51). The French word is ultimately from classical Latin *mercārī* 'to buy, trade', via an unattested derivative formation. Its etymology can be presented as follows:

(Anglo-)French *merchant, marchant* < the present participial stem **mercatant-* of an unattested post-classical Latin (frequentative) derivative **mercatare* < classical Latin *mercārī* 'to buy, trade' < *merc-*, *merx* 'commodity'

The -*ar*- forms predominate in French and give rise to the modern French form *marchand*. In English, pronunciations with /a/ also predominate in our main sources of evidence for the early modern period (see Dobson (1968) II §66). However, the spelling history tells a rather different story: spellings with -er- become increasingly common during the sixteenth century and predominate in the seventeenth century (this story can now be traced in detail using the resources of *Early English Books Online*). At the end of the early modern period the pronunciation eventually follows suit (compare section 7.4.7 on spelling pronunciations). The spread of the -er- spellings seems to be due to learned association with Latin *mercārī* and its derivative *mercātōr*, even though these stand at some remove from either the English or the French word. In turn, the authority of the written form apparently led to a change also in the pronunciation of the word.

Samuels's categories (ii)–(iv) all involve functional pressures of one sort or another, and our approach to them will depend to some extent on how prepared we are to accept functionalist arguments.

We have already encountered category (ii) in section 3.8, where we saw that the effects of this sort of 'dangerous homonymy' are sporadic, unpredictable, and controversial, and certainly not all scholars would accept that the examples listed here are other than coincidental. As we see from Samuels's inclusion of *earth* and *yearn* also in category (vi), the interplay of more than one factor in a given example is not excluded in this sort of analysis.

As regards Samuels's category (iii), *person* and *parson* both show borrowings (partly via French) of Latin *persōna*, which in the classical period showed a variety of senses including 'mask used by a player, dramatic role, part played by a person in life, character, role, position, individual personality, human being in general, grammatical person'. Among the sense developments shown by the Latin word in the medieval period was 'ecclesiastical dignitary, curate', recorded earliest in the eleventh century. In French we find broadly the same range of senses, as also in Middle English. In Anglo-French we find forms with *par-* (e.g. *parson, parsone, parsoune*) as well as with *per-*, probably again reflecting the parallel tendency to lowering of -er- > -ar- found in French. In Middle English we find similar variation in form, probably partly reflecting the variation found in Anglo-French, and partly showing the lowering of -er- > -ar- in English. (In all medieval documents, whether in Latin, French, or English, there is an added complication, because in the heavily abbreviated writing used in many medieval manuscripts the abbreviations used for *per-* and *par-* were identical, hence the choice of *per-* or *par-* in modern edited texts will often reflect choices made by modern editors.) The general retention in French of the forms with *per-* in this word (French *personne*) probably results from the influence of

Latin *persōna* (as we saw in the case of English *merchant*, but not of French *marchand*). In early modern English we find a more complex development, with increasing specialization of forms, *parson* becoming usual in the ecclesiastical sense, normally 'holder of a parochial benefice', and *person* becoming usual in all other senses. After the end of the seventeenth century, at least in the standard language, the separation of two heteronyms with distinct forms and meanings is complete, although contemporary evidence suggests that the systematic distinction in the written form probably preceded that in the spoken form (see Dobson (1968) II §66). A similar process led to the differentiation of *arrant* in the pejorated sense 'notorious, downright' from *errant* 'travelling' (see also section 8.6.3). These splits are similar to those examined in chapter 3, and clearly show the differentiation of variants in distinct senses. The question here is whether, as suggested by Samuels, this was motivated by 'avoidance of polysemy', or whether (as I have assumed implicitly in chapter 3) the process could have been largely accidental, rather than the result of functional pressures.

The particular example of phonaesthetic influence offered by Samuels for category (iv) does not seem strong. The vowels in *swerve* and *swirl* may have become homophonous in some varieties of English in the course of the sixteenth century, but the semantic connection does not seem especially close, in comparison with for instance *sweep* (or the related *swope*) with different stem vowel. Additionally, the historical record indicates that *swirl* is only found in Scots until the eighteenth century.

Category (v) apparently shows the operation of analogy and iconicity, in maintaining or restoring the transparent relationship between the root word and derivative. However, it should be noted that in all varieties *dear* would have had a long vowel, and in many varieties this would not have been identical in quality to the short vowel in *dearth*. Interestingly, in the case of *darling*, another derivative of *dear*, the form with lowering did become the usual one in standard English, although *dereling*, *dearling* are still found sporadically until the eighteenth century.

The words listed in category (vi) all showed variants with either a long or a short vowel in Middle English and early modern English, as a result of the variable operation of various other sound changes in Old English and early Middle English. It is possible that the frequent occurrence of the forms with long vowels created an associative pressure in favour of variants with unlowered short vowel rather than the forms with lowered short vowel, although, as in the case of *dear* and *dearth*, this would generally have been a matter of greater phonetic similarity rather than exact identity.

I have offered this detailed example because of what it shows about the importance of close etymological examination of particular examples in cases where the results of a sound change appear irregular or inconsistent. It also brings to light how our theoretical assumptions, for instance about 'harmful homophony' or 'avoidance of polysemy', will have a major impact on our analysis of the data. Differences of opinion on such topics, and hence differences of approach, are inevitable and perfectly healthy in any discipline, so long as we are clear about which areas of research are controversial and what the arguments are for and against each type of approach.

7.3 Sporadic sound changes

We will look at some difficult and controversial issues concerning the regularity of sound changes in section 7.6. However, some sound changes occur as isolated events, affecting only a single lexical item at any one time, and typically only ever affecting a small proportion of the eligible word forms in a piecemeal manner over a very extended time period. These changes are usually known as sporadic sound changes (as opposed to regular sound changes, the regularity or otherwise of which we will return to later).

Precisely the same change in word form can occur as a regular sound change at one period in the history of one language, but in another language or in another period it can be sporadic (see for example below on assimilation and dissimilation). Additionally, most linguists would accept that there is no absolute division between sporadic sound changes and regular sound changes: the difference is one of degree (numbers of items affected, length of the period over which this occurs, etc.). Not all scholars accept that sporadic sound changes should be recognized as a distinct category (see for instance Hoenigswald (1978)). However, some types of change are very frequently sporadic in their incidence in the historical record. A particularly good example of this is metathesis, where a particular sound changes its position in the sequence of sounds in a word. Instances of metathesis involving a liquid consonant are very common:

- English *pattern* originated as a metathesized variant of *patron* (the two words subsequently becoming distinguished in sense)

- Dutch regional *pertig* 'cunning, quick, lively' originated as a variant of *prettig* 'pleasant, nice, agreeable, comfortable' (formed similarly to English *pretty*)
- *Neldare, Neldere* occur as variants of the medieval English surname *Needler* (< *needler* 'person who makes needles')
- Older Scots *pedral* occurs as a variant of *pedlar*

With non-liquids we can consider for example:

- French *moustique* 'mosquito' beside the earlier forms *mousquitte, mousquite* (< Spanish *mosquito*, as is also English *mosquito*), although in this instance there may also have been semantic association with *tique* 'tick' (probably < English *tick*)
- Old English *max* (where x represents /ks/) is a variant of *masc* 'mash'. This type of metathesis is relatively common in Old English, further examples being *fixas*, variant of *fiscas*, plural of *fisc* 'fish', or *āxian*, variant of *āscian* 'to ask'. It provides valuable evidence for the distribution of the sound change of /sk/ to /ʃ/ (see Campbell (1959) §440, Hogg (1992b) 7.96). However, it is still not a regular sound change, applying to all instances of /sk/ in all words.

In all of these instances the metathesized forms originated as variants, coexisting for a while with the original word form, even though some (such as French *moustique*) have eventually come to be the usual form of the word, and others (such as *pattern* or Dutch *pertig*) have come to be distinguished in meaning. *ask* provides a particularly interesting example: in southern Middle English the usual reflexes of Old English *āscian* were either *axen* (< the form *āxian* with metathesis) or *ashen* (< *āscian*, with the change /sk/ > /ʃ/), before the spread of the modern type *asken* (the northern development of *āscian*, with failure of the change /sk/ > /ʃ/) from the north.

Metathesis is often cited as an example of a sound change which has to be phonetically abrupt, not gradual, since it would be hard to imagine any intermediate step between for instance *mousquite* and *moustique*. However, its spread can be gradual, as a metathesized variant gains in currency or shows increasing semantic specialization.

Assimilation is a change by which two consonants become more similar or identical in articulation, while dissimilation is a change by which two consonants become less similar in articulation. We have encountered examples of assimilation already: Old English *emnes* 'equality' < *efnes* (see section 4.1.1.), or across word boundaries in /haftu:/ *have to* (see section 2.1.1.3). Dissimilation is shown by for instance *marble* < earlier *marbre* (< French *marbre*), or by *purple* < earlier *purpure*.

Assimilation is, typologically, much more frequent than dissimilation, and shows the benefit of ease of articulation for speakers. Conversely, dissimilation may produce forms which are more easily apprehended by the hearer. Both processes are normally sporadic in the recorded history of English, but certain assimilatory and dissimilatory processes are perfectly regular in some other languages. For instance, Grassmann's Law is the name usually given to the regular dissimilation in the first of a series of two aspirated stops which happened (independently) in both Sanskrit and Greek, hence ancient Greek *títhēmi* from earlier **thithēmi*.[8]

The term assimilation is also sometimes used for a quite different type of associative change in word form, which we will look at in section 7.4.4.

7.4 Associative change in word form

Sound change, of both the regular and the sporadic type, frequently obscures or erases previously transparent meaning relationships between words. However, various processes work in the opposite direction, creating fresh associations between words either on a semantic basis or within morphological paradigms, and thus increasing the degree of iconicity within the linguistic system. Sometimes these processes 'repair' relationships which have been obscured by sound change, although more frequently they establish new relationships which may in fact run counter to the historical relationships between words. Like sporadic sound changes, their operation is generally sporadic or piecemeal, although over the course of time all items in a particular class may be affected, and hence the ultimate result may be a new set of regular relationships among a group of words. They differ from all sound changes in that the processes involved are not phonetic but (in the broadest sense) grammatical, involving substitution, alteration, or creation on the basis of perceived parallels elsewhere in the linguistic system.

Some people group all such changes together under the very broad heading of analogy, but others reserve the name analogy for just a subset of such changes (especially proportional analogy), and distinguish other

---

[8] Compare Fortson (2004) 188, 227; Collinge (1985) 47–61.

types of changes under the names levelling, contamination (or assimilation), and folk etymology. In this book I will use the term associative change in word form as a general term for all of these processes, including also folk etymology. However, it is not my intention to present a detailed typology of the different types of associative change in word form, but just some illustrations of typical types of change. The analysis and identification of the mechanisms of associative change in word form is a complex and frequently controversial area, but these issues do not generally impinge very much on the separate question of establishing whether some sort of associative change in word form has occurred in a particular word history. Since this latter question is of much more central concern in practical etymological research, it will be my main focus in what follows.[9]

7.4.1 Proportional analogy

So far in this book I have presented various examples of analogical change in the form of proportions.[10] Thus in section 4.2 we saw that *coolth* is formed as an abstract noun corresponding to *cool* on the model of the relationship between *warm* and *warmth*:

$$warm : warmth = cool : coolth$$

Similarly in section 4.1.3 we saw that proportional analogy provides one possible explanation for the formation of *palaeogeographical* as the adjective corresponding to *palaeogeography*:

$$geography : geographical = palaeogeography : palaeogeographical$$

Some changes in inflectional patterns can also usefully be presented as proportional analogies. *strive* is a borrowing from French, and is therefore expected to be a weak verb, with past tense *strived* (which is in fact found in early use). Its strong past tense and past participle are probably by analogy with those of *drive*:

$$drive : drove = strive : strove$$
$$drive : driven = strive : striven$$

---

[9] For an overview of different approaches to analogy and other types of associative change in word form see for example Anttila (1989), Anttila (2003), Hock (2003), Kiparsky (2005).

[10] On the history of analogical proportions in linguistics see Morpurgo Davies (1978).

When a word's morphology is remodelled after a more common or dominant pattern, as for instance when originally strong verbs in English change to the weak inflection, we need to modify the proportional model, since there is less likely to be a single word acting as the model, but rather a large group. We can present the process as follows:

X : X*ed* = *bake* : *baked* (originally past singular *bōk*, past plural *baken*)

A similar situation applies in noun morphology when the plural morphology of a word is changed on the model of a more common or dominant pattern. *book* originally showed a mutation plural, just like *mice* beside *mouse*. The *i*-mutation of /o:/ was /e:/, and hence we find singular *bōc*, plural *bēc* (in this instance the final consonant was also affected by the original -*i* of the stem, hence the spoken forms were /bo:k/ and /be:tʃ/). In Middle English we find analogical alteration after the much more frequent type with unchanged stem and an inflection -*es*/-*s* in the plural, hence:

X : X*s* = *book* : *books*

It is important to note that in such cases of analogical change in a word's morphology the change takes the form of replacement of an earlier form. The plural form *books* is not the formal reflex of earlier *bēc*, it is a completely new plural form which replaces the earlier one. Analogy has thus eliminated some irregularity in the system by removing a plural formed on a pattern which was of dwindling frequency, and replacing it with one that conforms to the majority pattern. However, in doing so it has destroyed historical continuity: the old plural *bēc* has simply been lost.[11] This is true of analogical change, but not of analogical creation, as shown by *coolth* and (perhaps) *palaeogeographical* above.[12]

---

[11] It has long been held that *book* is ultimately cognate with the tree name *beech*, which may show a formation from the same base with a stem-forming suffix causing *i*-mutation (the connection being explained by the assumption that early runic inscriptions were made on beech tablets). However, this etymology has in recent decades been challenged by some, and in turn defended by others. For a summary of the controversy see Pierce (2006).

[12] On this distinction see Hoenigswald (1960) §4.6.4, Hoenigswald (1978).

7.4.2 Levelling

Associative remodelling of forms within a paradigm (rather than on the basis of comparison with the paradigms shown by other words) is generally referred to as levelling. We encountered examples in section 3.1, where the variation in vowel quantity in the paradigm of *heaven*, with lengthening in the disyllabic uninflected form *hēven* but absence of lengthening in trisyllabic inflected forms such as genitive *hevenes*, was undone by levelling of the form with short vowel to all parts of the paradigm. In the case of *staff* the alternation between uninflected *staf* and inflected *stāves* led to levelling in both directions, with subsequent semantic differentiation between *staff*, plural *staffs*, and *stave*, plural *staves*. Differentiation of this sort is possible because of the crucial intermediate period in which both the levelled and the non-levelled forms occur. Like many other types of linguistic change, changes of this sort generally follow the pattern:

$$A > A \sim B > B$$

where 'A' is one language state, 'B' is another state ultimately resulting from the change, and 'A $\sim$ B' is an intermediate state in which variation occurs.[13] Thus the singular of *heaven* has shown this trajectory:

hēven > *hēven* $\sim$ *heven* > *heaven* (with short vowel, although the spelling reflects the variant with long vowel)

In the case of *staff* and *stave*, semantic differentiation has occurred at the point at which the variation 'A $\sim$ B' was present in both the uninflected and the inflected forms, i.e. when levelling was proceeding for some speakers in the one direction, and for others in the opposite direction.

   (In modern Received Pronunciation *staff* shows a long vowel as a result of a relatively recent sound change. Because it occurred much later than the Great Vowel Shift, the sound is unshifted, hence the vowel in *staff* remains distinct from the diphthong in *stave* even for RP speakers.)

7.4.3 Reanalysis followed by analogous formations

Analogy frequently builds on the results of prior reanalysis. We saw in section 4.1.1 that this is frequently the mechanism at work in the formation of new affixes: *-ness* arises from reanalysis of earlier formations in which

---

[13] On the general implications of this pattern of variation in change see especially Lass (2007) §8.3.1.

-n- is historically part of the stem (e.g. *efnes*, related to *efn*), followed by analogous use of *-ness* as a suffix on other stems (e.g. *wōdnes* from *wōd*). Similarly in section 1.3.2 we saw that *handy* probably arose as a result of prior reanalysis of *handiwork* (historically from *hand* and *geweorc*) as showing *hand*, *-y*, and *work*. In such cases it is normally only through the subsequent emergence of analogous formations that we can be sure that reanalysis has taken place.

7.4.4 Contamination or formal assimilation

Semantic association between two words can lead to the change in word form known as contamination. (This is sometimes also called formal assimilation or just assimilation, but should be distinguished carefully from the phonological assimilation discussed in section 7.3.)

most shows the regular development of Old English *māst*, corresponding to Old Frisian *māst*, Middle Dutch *meest*, Old High German *meist*, etc. However, in Old English this form is recorded only in the poorly attested Northumbrian dialect, and the form found in the much better-attested West Saxon dialect is *mǣst*. The vowel in this form cannot easily be explained on phonological grounds, and is probably due to association with the semantically related word *lǣst* 'least'.

French *rempart* 'rampart' is a derivative of *remparer* 'to fortify', but it shows final *-t* as a result of association with *boulevart*, variant of *boulevard*. This was originally the name of a type of defensive fortification, and was probably borrowed from Middle Dutch *bolwerc*, which is related to English *bulwark*; in French the ending was altered as a result of association with words ending in the suffix *-ard*. The final consonant of *rempart* is silent in French, but not in the English borrowing *rampart* which shows final /t/ as a result of a spelling pronunciation.

Viewed historically, *ooze* 'wet mud or slime' and *ooze* 'juice or sap from a plant' are two quite separate words: in Old English the first is *wāse* and the second is *wōs*, and the regular development of each word in modern English would give *oaze* (or *woaze*) and *ooze* (or *wooze*) respectively. The unexpected development of the first word to *ooze* may simply show raising influence of the initial *w-* (which was subsequently assimilated), but it may equally be due to semantic association with *ooze* 'juice or sap from a plant'.[14]

[14] See further Durkin (2006a) 63–5.

Mutual formal influence is probably shown by the words *citizen* and *denizen*. *citizen* is a borrowing from Anglo-French, in which it is ultimately a derivative of *cité* 'city'. The earliest forms in Old French are *citeain*, *citeiain* (from which the modern French form *citoyen* is ultimately developed); in Anglo-French forms of the type *citezein*, *citizein* are found, with *-z-* probably as a result of association with *denzein* 'denizen'. Conversely, the variant *denizein* of *denzein* (a derivative formation from *deinz*, modern French *dans* 'within') is probably the result of association with *citizein*.

Contamination across a large series of words can sometimes provide a plausible explanation for the relationships found among groups of words with expressive meanings, such as the group *piddle*, *paddle*, *pittle*, *tiddle*, *widdle*, etc. encountered in section 4.5.3.

Sometimes we find suggested cases of contamination with no evident semantic motivation. The plant name *mint* is a borrowing ultimately from Latin *menta*. Cognates (or perhaps just parallel instances of borrowing) are shown by Middle Dutch *minte*, Old Saxon *minta*, and, with a sound change known as the High German Consonant Shift, Old High German *minza* (modern German *Minze*). However, there are also forms in Dutch and German with an unexpected stem vowel: Middle Dutch *munte*, *muynte*, *muente* (Dutch *munt*), Old High German *munza* (German regional *Münze*). These forms are very difficult to explain. The explanation usually offered is that they show some sort of formal association with the word for 'coin' borrowed ultimately from classical Latin *monēta* which has the forms Middle Dutch *munte*, *muynte*, *monte*, *moente* (Dutch *munt*), Old High German *muniz* (masculine), *munizza*, *muniza* (feminine; Middle High German *münze*, German *Münze*). This has the virtue of explaining the forms, but has no obvious semantic motivation. (In both cases the modern English cognate has the identical word form *mint*, but this is for the different reason that phonological merger has led to Old English *minte* the plant name and *mynet* 'coin', 'place where money is coined', having identical reflexes in modern English.)

7.4.5 Folk etymology

Where the remodelling of a word involves the replacement of one or more of its syllables by another word with which it is associated semantically this is normally referred to not as contamination but as folk etymology.

sparrowgrass shows a folk-etymological alteration of the word *asparagus*. More accurately, it shows an alteration of *sparagus*, a variant of *asparagus* which shows aphesis or loss of an unstressed initial vowel. In this case, a loanword (ultimately from Greek) which was monomorphemic, unanalysable, and had no obvious link with any other word in English, has been remodelled as a compound of two familiar English words. It even makes a sort of semantic sense: asparagus stalks have at least formal resemblance to grass (in being upright, green, and growing in fields), and it might just about be imagined that sparrows might perch on asparagus stalks or eat them. This sort of very approximate semantic plausibility is often found in folk-etymological alterations which gain a wide currency. However, in the seventeenth century when the form *sparrowgrass* is first recorded we also find a form *sparagrass*, in which the ending has been remodelled after *grass* but where the first two syllables of *sparagus* remain unchanged. (Although it should be noted that while **spara* is not among the recorded forms of the word *sparrow* it is phonologically plausible as a seventeenth-century spelling of that word. Compare e.g. *pilla* for *pillow* in the same period. It is possible that *spara-* in *sparagus* or *sparagrass* was identified with a homophone **spara*, variant of *sparrow* with reduced second syllable, leading to substitution of the form *sparrow*.[15]) Compare also *oke-corn* and *acorn* in section 2.4, where it is the form with only partial remodelling which is current in modern English.

In some cases of folk etymology partial remodelling is the most that is ever found. In section 2.6 we encountered *naseberry*, borrowed from either Spanish *néspera* or Portuguese *nêspera*, but with the ending remodelled as a result of association with words ending in *-berry* such as *blackberry*, *blueberry*, etc. The last two syllables of the word are thus remodelled in a way that makes very good sense semantically (a naseberry or sapodilla is a type of fruit which grows on a tree), but the first part of the word remains an unanalysable unique morph (or cranberry morph). Similarly, *parsnip* shows a borrowing from either Latin *pastinaca* or its reflex French *pasnaie*, but by the time of our earliest examples of the word in Middle English the ending has been remodelled as a result of association with *neep* 'turnip', and so we find the forms *pasneep*, *pasnepe*, etc, and subsequently *pasnip*, *parsnip* with shortening of the vowel in the last syllable (as also in *turnip*). (However, the change in the first syllable from *pasnip* to *parsnip* is unexplained.)

---

[15] For discussion of this etymology along similar lines compare Knappe (2004a) 125–6.

As we saw in the case of *sparrowgrass* and *sparagrass*, some instances of folk-etymological alteration show interesting variation before a canonical form becomes established. *mangrove* 'any of various trees and shrubs which form dense thickets in muddy coastal swamps, tidal estuaries, etc., in tropical and subtropical regions' is probably a borrowing from Spanish *mangue* or *mangle*, which is in turn probably borrowed from a Cariban or Arawakan language. *mangle* is in fact found in English as a borrowing of the Spanish word from the beginning of the seventeenth century. However, much more common is the form *mangrove*, alongside which the forms *mangrowe* and *mangrave* are also found. Of these, *mangrove* apparently shows substitution of English *grove* 'small wood' for the ending of the Spanish word, while *mangrowe* apparently shows the verb *grow*. This association is made punningly in the earliest example of the word in English, in S. Jourdan, *Plaine Description of the Barmudas* (1613) sig. F2v: 'Amongst all the rest there growes a kinde of tree called Mangrowes, they grow very strangely, & would make a man wonder to see the manner of their growing.' The form *mangrave* is less readily explained, unless it simply results from confusion of the form *mangrove*, or shows semantically unmotivated substitution of the word *grave*.

It is important to note that there is nothing intrinsically 'folksy' about the results of folk etymology: *parsnip* is the usual modern English name for this vegetable, *mangrove* is the usual name for this type of tree, and even *sparrowgrass* was the usual term for asparagus during the eighteenth century (although *asparagus* continued in use among botanists). Alternative names have been suggested, such as 'associative etymology' by Ullmann (1962: 101). I would suggest that a drawback of this would be that the same name could equally apply to most of the changes described in sections 7.4.1–4. Arguably etymology is not really involved in the process at all: speakers are, unconsciously, altering word forms in order to create iconic connections with other words, rather than in an effort to explain their origins. However, 'folk etymology' is the usual term, and in spite of the misnomer this seems unlikely to change.[16]

---

[16] Further interesting cases of folk etymology are shown by *crayfish*, *penthouse*, *purblind*, *purlieu*, *sandblind*, *shamefaced*, and perhaps *mushroom*. A fine discussion of the phenomenon is given by Ullmann (1962: 101–5). For a very useful recent overview see Knappe (2004b).

Folk etymology is sometimes described as showing anti-lexicalization, since it runs counter to the tendency towards greater opacity shown by lexicalization, although of course it is not a reversal of lexicalization, since although it increases transparency it does not restore the transparent relationships which existed before a process of lexicalization took place.[17]

The term 'folk etymology' is not normally used to describe changes which involve substitution in a phrase or compound of one word for another which has otherwise become rare or obsolete, although the processes are in fact similar, especially where the word substituted does not provide an exact semantic match. For instance, in Old Icelandic *ragna rǫk*, literally 'destiny of the gods', was remodelled as *ragna røkkr*, literally 'twilight of the gods', with substitution of *røkkr* 'twilight' for the rarer word *rǫk* 'destiny'. If we choose not to call this folk etymology, it is certainly a very closely related process of alteration resulting from reanalysis. (See section 7.7.4 for detailed analysis of a difficult example.) The term is also not normally used to refer to deliberate playful alterations of words, such as *midshipmite* for *midshipmate* or *monkeyrony* for *macaroni* (in the sense 'dandy or fop'), although there is clearly some overlap, and it is not always clear whether a particular alteration has arisen out of playfulness or as a response to the unfamiliarity of a particular word form. Such playful or punning alteration in word form is sometimes referred to as paronomasia. Similar to this, but usually less ambiguous to identify, is the euphemistic remodelling of oaths, exclamations, etc., e.g. *damn it > dash it* (with which compare arbitrary alteration of word forms for similar reasons, e.g. *hell > heck*, etc.). Taboo can lead to remodelling of this sort, as well as to complete replacement of certain lexical items.[18]

7.4.5.1 *Popular explanations of word histories*

The term 'folk etymology' is also sometimes used much more loosely, especially in non-technical usage, to denote any popular explanations of word histories. Such popular theories about word histories abound, for instance the (groundless and completely unsubstantiated) idea that *posh* originates in an acronym **p.o.s.h.* supposedly standing for **port out starboard home*. The story given in support of this is that when people travelled by ship from Britain to India and back again in colonial times a port cabin on the outward journey and a starboard

---

[17] On anti-lexicalization see Brinton and Traugott (2005) 102–3.

[18] On this topic compare e.g. Burridge (2006), Merlan (2006).

cabin on the return journey would give a traveller the best protection from the bright midday sun, and hence tickets providing such accommodation were stamped *p.o.s.h.* Many other popular stories about the origins of words similarly assume that words are acronyms, although in this particular instance there is at least a plausible-sounding scenario. In fact, if conclusive evidence were ever to be found for the use of the expression *port out starboard home* in this context (especially if earlier than the first recorded use of *posh* in *c*1915), and especially if documentary evidence were to be published proving the existence of tickets with *p.o.s.h.* stamped on them, then this story might need to be taken rather more seriously. As it stands, it is simply something of a popular myth, unsubstantiated by any evidence. It is a 'folk etymology' in the sense that it is an explanation of an etymology which is in circulation among 'the folk' but which is taken seriously by very few experts, but it has nothing in common with the associative changes in word form exemplified in section 7.2.5. However, if this story had an impact on the usage of the word *posh*, for instance if people began to spell it *p.o.s.h.*, or began to use the word to designate for example seating shaded from the sun, then this piece of popular etymologizing might indeed have led to folk-etymological influence, albeit of a rather artificial kind.[19]

7.4.6 Changes affecting only the written form of a word

As already noted in the case of French *rempart*, associative changes in word form sometimes affect only the spelling form. *delight* is a borrowing from Old French *delit*, and until the sixteenth century its usual spellings are *delit* or *delite*, but in the sixteenth century a new spelling *delight* is found, by analogy with the spelling of rhyming words such as *light*, *flight*, *bright*, etc. (in which the <gh> spelling historically represents a fricative which had been lost, with compensatory lengthening of the vowel, before this date, hence /lixt/ > /liːt/, eventually > /laɪt/). By the end of the sixteenth century, this spelling had completely ousted the

---

[19] There are groundless stories in circulation about the origins of many other words and phrases, particularly slang and colloquial expressions, such as *codswallop* or *the full monty*. For an entertaining and useful survey of such material see Quinion (2005), although it should be noted that this considers examples of popular explanations of word histories side by side with genuine examples of associative change in word form. On *posh* see also Chowdharay-Best (1971).

spellings without <gh>. We could present this development as a case of proportional analogy (although with *flight*, *bright*, etc. substitutable for *light*):

$$\text{/laɪt/} : light = \text{/dɪlaɪt/} : delight$$

7.4.7 Spelling pronunciation

Such changes in spelling may ultimately also affect the pronunciation of words, as a result of spelling pronunciations, as already seen above in the cases of *merchant* (section 7.2.5) and *rampart* (section 7.4.4). To take a slightly more complex example, *fault* originally had the form *faut* (< French *faute*), but *-l-* was introduced in the spelling as a result of (learned) association with its ultimate etymon Latin *fallere* 'to fail'; subsequently, /l/ was introduced into the pronunciation as well. The same process affects some words with no *-l-* in their etymon: *moult* originally had the form *mout*, and is ultimately from Latin *mūtāre* 'to change'. By analogy with the change in spelling shown by *fault*, *-l-* was introduced in the spelling of this word also, and subsequently /l/ was also introduced into the pronunciation, as a spelling pronunciation.

7.5 Metanalysis

Metanalysis is the redistribution of material across word or morpheme boundaries. It thus affects the form of words, but is neither a sound change nor an instance of associative change in word form. In the history of English examples of metanalysis are frequently found involving the indefinite article *a, an*. Both *adder* and *apron* show the result of the reanalysis of earlier forms *nadder* and *napron* in the combinations *a nadder*, *a napron*, while other words have gained an initial /n/ from the article, such as *newt* (earlier *ewt*; compare *eft* which remains in some modern dialects):

> *a nadder* > *an adder* (hence also *the adder*, etc.)
> *an ewt* > *a newt* (hence also *the newt*, etc.)

The same process is sometimes found with the possessive adjectives *my/mine* and *thy/thine* (as for instance *my nuncle* < *mine uncle*). Widespread literacy and an orthographic standard present a block to this sort of reanalysis across word boundaries, but it is frequent in periods with less widespread literacy and more varied spelling systems. Similar examples are found in medieval French involving the definite article *le, la* before a word beginning with a vowel. A complex history involving metanalysis, associative change in word form, and metathesis is presented by French *omelette* (> English *omelette*):

Middle French *(la) lemelle, (la) lamelle*, literally 'blade, thin plate' (the application to an omelette shows a metaphorical sense development)
>   > (with metanalysis)
(l') alumelle, alumele, alemele
>   > (with suffix substitution)
alumecte, probably also **alemette*
>   > (with metathesis)
amelette
>   > (with initial /o/ probably as a result of semantic association with words derived from Latin *ovum* 'egg')
omelette

7.6 How regular are regular sound changes?

In section 7.1.2 I drew attention to the importance of Verner's Law in explaining apparent exceptions to sound changes, and in the establishment of the 'regularity principle'. This fundamental tenet of neogrammarian work on historical linguistics has been much misunderstood. Essentially, none of the processes that we have encountered so far in this chapter would have been completely alien to the thinking of the Neogrammarians in the late nineteenth century. The Neogrammarians recognized the existence of sporadic sound changes alongside regular sound changes. They also recognized that a sound change which was regular in one dialect might be sporadic in another dialect, or might not occur at all. They saw that dialect-mixing in such a situation would lead to the appearance of irregularity (as we saw in our examination of the Great Vowel Shift and some subsequent developments in section 7.2.3). They observed the importance of analogy and other associative changes in word form in altering the output from sound changes. The 'regularity principle' takes account of all these factors. It assumes that, if none of these factors can be seen to apply, we should not permit reconstructions invoking exceptions to sound changes which otherwise apply in all instances of the qualifying environment.

Since the late nineteenth century, there have been two major developments which to some extent challenge the neogrammarian view of regular sound change.

One arose from some of the earliest work on dialect geography from the late nineteenth and early twentieth centuries. Studies showed that sound changes may sometimes be observed spreading out from one or more focal points, and that this spread may affect some words earlier than it does others. This observation led to the famous slogan *chaque mot a son histoire* 'each word has its own history'.[20] This may at first glance seem something to gladden any etymologist: surely the etymologies in any dictionary are a set of unique word histories, resulting from the interplay of manifold factors. However, if the variability extends to the application of sound changes, then there may be serious implications for our methodology. In particular, there may be a complex interplay between the operation of different sound changes: if change A radiated from place X, and change B from place Y, then they may apply in a different chronological order in different words in different geographical locations, hence giving different output forms.

The second challenge is more recent, and comes from the concept of lexical diffusion developed in the work of Wang and his collaborators from the late 1960s onwards (see especially Wang (1969), Chen (1972)). According to this theory, even within a particular dialect sound changes may come into effect only gradually, affecting some lexical items earlier than others. Most problematically for etymological reconstruction, it is suggested that some sound changes may cease to be operative before they have affected all items in which they may be expected to apply: they may as it were run out of steam. Alternatively they may have failed to affect all eligible items before the commencement of a further sound change which acts upon the outputs of the first change.[21] Modern work on sociolinguistics has greatly reinforced the impression that at least some sound changes operate in this way. The eminent American linguist William Labov has suggested that sound changes can be divided into two basic types, lexically diffusing ones and regular ones (see especially Labov (1981), Labov (1994)), although this idea remains very controversial (see for instance Bybee (2002)). Furthermore, most scholars now accept that sound changes spread through variation in a

[20] The slogan was probably coined by Hugo Schuchardt in the late nineteenth century, although it is often associated most closely with the work of Jules Gilliéron in the early twentieth century: see further Campbell (2004) 212–13.

[21] For useful overview of this topic see McMahon (1994) 46–68.

system. A given sound in a particular word will not change abruptly from a stage where realization A occurs in all instances to a stage where realization B occurs in all instances, but rather we will find an intervening period of variation in which both A and B are found:

$$A > A \sim B > B$$

Some changes will stay at the stage 'A $\sim$ B' for a long time, perhaps indefinitely.

In spite of these considerations, most comparative linguists continue to apply the regularity principle in etymological research. Various arguments have been advanced in support of this position. One eminent Indo-Europeanist comments:

> Another attack on the principle of regularity has come from the field of dialectology. It was observed that sound changes spread, as it were, from word to word, and it seemed that they could stop at any given moment so that a sound might change in some words but remain the same in others. The answer to this problem is that the process of change will ultimately affect all words which the rule marks out for change. Comparative linguistics does not deal with languages still in the *process* of change, but rather, almost exclusively, with languages in which all change that could have taken place is now 'finalized' and 'at rest'.

> (Beekes (1995) 55)

I must confess that I do not find this line of argument entirely satisfactory: there do seem to be well-documented cases of sound changes which have ceased to operate before all words showing the relevant environment have been affected. Uniformitarian principles, i.e. the assumption that languages in the past generally behaved in the same way as languages generally do in the present, make it impossible to rule out the existence of similar situations in earlier periods. In my view a much stronger case for applying the regularity principle in etymological reconstruction is that it offers us much safer results than a model in which we assume the occurrence of irregularities for which we are unable to find specific motivated explanations. The case is well put by Fox:

> Any method, and any model, in linguistic reconstruction as in any other activity, involves a degree of abstraction and idealization if it is to provide solutions to the problems it addresses. We could argue, therefore, that both the uniformity of the proto-language and the regularity principle, in spite of being apparently implausible or even counterfactual, are not, in fact, illegitimate assumptions, *but necessary idealizations*.

> (Fox (1995) 140)

A further point which Fox makes serves as a useful reminder of the most basic function of etymologies in comparative grammars:

In order to determine the nature of linguistic relationships, and to reconstruct earlier forms, it is necessary to proceed *as if* the proto-language were entirely homogeneous, and *as if* sound changes were totally without exceptions, even though we know that this is not necessarily the case.

(Fox (1995) 140)

If one's interest is primarily in establishing the relationships between languages, and not in establishing with certainty the pre-histories of particular linguistic items, then the possibility that application of the regularity principle is leading one to discard some correct etymologies will be of relatively little concern, provided that there remains a sufficiently substantial body of data to make the affiliation of the languages indisputable. However, as soon as we move to the level of individual reconstructions it is as well to bear in mind that in some instances the available data and the application of the available method of reconstruction may well lead to false conclusions. The case is well put by Clackson:

Most Indo-Europeanists would place greater confidence in the reconstructed phonemic system than in many of the reconstructions of individual lexemes or morphological or syntactic phenomena.

(Clackson (2007) 27)

The regularity of sound-change is not an essential factor to ensure the success of the C[omparative]M[ethod], although it has been championed as such since the late nineteenth century. Since the method operates on a majority rule basis, it is possible to reconstruct sounds as long as *most* (if not all) of the sounds in a language change in the same way.

(Clackson (2007) 32)

7.7 Examples of arguments based on word form

Some examples of etymologies where formal difficulties can or cannot be resolved may offer a practical illustration of some of the main points discussed in this chapter. (At the end of chapter 8 we will look at some similar examples involving issues of change in meaning, and draw some contrasts between the two groups of examples.)

7.7.1 Unexplained irregularity: three words with unexpected initial /p/ in English

purse first occurs late in the Old English period, and seems manifestly to be a borrowing from post-classical Latin *bursa*, which has exactly the same meaning, and which is in turn borrowed from ancient Greek *búrsa* 'hide' (a word of unknown origin). The Latin word also gives rise to borrowings in the Romance and other western Germanic languages, but in all of these the expected initial /b/ is found. The initial /p/ in English is perplexing. In Middle English the word shows the following spellings:

> *purs, purse, pursse, purce, pors, porse, porese, porce*, also (rare and late)
> *pours, pourse*

These are very similar to the forms shown by Anglo-French *burse* (from Latin *bursa*), except for the difference of the initial consonant:

> *burse, burs, borce, borse, bource, bours, bourse*

The formal variation shown by the Anglo-French word is entirely what would be expected in the reflex of Latin *bursa* (compare Pope (1934) §632, Short (2007) §6). The Middle English and Anglo-French words also show some very similar semantic developments (e.g. 'scrotum', 'financial exchange', 'allowance', 'money', 'funds'), and it seems clear that the English word at least shows some semantic influence from French; the derivative *purser* similarly seems to show semantic influence from Latin *bursarius* and (Anglo-)French *burser, borser, bourser* (modern French *boursier*). There may also have been some formal influence of Anglo-French *burse* on Middle English *purse*, although the spellings with <o> and <ou> could simply show the result of general French influence on the spelling system of Middle English. For instance *curse*, a word first found in late Old English and of unknown origin, also appears in Middle English with spellings such as *cors*, *curs*, and (very occasionally) *kours*. The initial /p/ in English is, however, very difficult to explain. Troublingly, there are no examples at all with initial <b> in English, except for one instance of *coutte burse* for *cut-purse* in the mid fifteenth century. (In French one form with unvoiced /p/ is recorded from a modern Belgian dialect,[22] but there is no reason to suspect that this shows any connection with the English word.) *burse, bourse* is not found in English until the early fifteenth century, and almost certainly shows a

---

[22] See *Französisches etymologisches Wörterbuch* vol. I 669a at *byrsa*.

later borrowing from (Anglo-)French, chiefly in specialized senses (such as 'scrotum' or, later, 'financial exchange' or 'bursary'). Similarly *bursar* is found only from the early modern English period, much later than *purser*, even though it has since become the usual word in many of the key senses.

One possible explanation for the initial /p/ of English *purse* might be that it is the result of contamination from the etymologically unrelated but semantically close Old English *pusa, posa* 'bag' or its Old Norse cognate *posi*, or alternatively from Old English *pung* 'purse'. However, if so it is surprising that no forms at all are recorded which show the initial /b/ of the Latin word preserved in English, and also that semantic association with (Anglo-)French *burse* did not also lead to at least occasional <b> spellings in Middle English. The situation thus remains unexplained.

In such a situation we must always look for any possible parallels. Dictionaries record extremely rare <b> spellings for words with initial /p/ in the Middle English period, and likewise extremely rare <p> spellings for words with initial /b/, probably showing very rare instances of either voicing or devoicing of the initial consonant, but in no word history are they anything other than very occasional variants. A more promising parallel is perhaps shown by *pudding*. This word is first recorded in English in the thirteenth century, earliest denoting a kind of boiled sausage. (The semantic development to a type of sweet dish is not found until the early modern period, and probably arose from the fact that sweet puddings were originally boiled in a cloth or bag, and hence resembled a sausage in its skin.) The recorded spellings in Middle English are *podding, poddyng, poddynge, poding, podyng, poodyng, pudding, puddyng, puddynge, puding, punding*. The word is perhaps a borrowing of Anglo-French *bodeyn, bodin* (continental French *boudin*) 'sausage'. The ending in *-ing*, which is found in all of the recorded Middle English forms of the word, could show alteration by analogy with other English words with this ending. This could have been facilitated by the variation between /ɪn/ and /ɪŋg/ as realizations of *-ing* that is found in some varieties of Middle English, and becomes much more common later in the history of English. The initial /p/ is, however, very difficult to explain. There could perhaps be contamination from various words denoting things of more or less rounded appearance, such as Old English *puduc* 'wen, swelling' (which has alternatively but rather implausibly been suggested as the etymological basis for the word) or *pod, podge*, or *pudge*, but most of these are first attested much later, and the semantic correspondence is hardly close, basically depending on the idea that a mixture boiled in a cloth or bag may have been associated with almost anything else with a rounded or swollen appearance. We may thus have a parallel for the oddity shown by *purse*, albeit one from several centuries later. However, in the case of *pudding* we should also note that no Middle English forms are recorded with *-in* rather than *-ing*, *-yng*, etc. in the second syllable: this consistency in the spelling forms may perhaps lead us to think that, although there is unlikely to be no link at all between English *pudding* and Anglo-French *bodeyn*, *bodin*, the explanation of the English word as a borrowing from Anglo-French with remodelling of the ending may not be entirely watertight. Additionally, the French word itself has no further etymology, and is also first recorded only in the thirteenth century. Also, unlike *purse*, there is no evidence for subsequent semantic influence of the French word on the English one.

A third English word which shows an initial /p/ but which appears likely to have been borrowed from a word with initial /b/ is the now obsolete word *purrell* 'transverse stripe or bar made by one or a number of coloured weft threads in a web of cloth', which is first attested in the middle of the fifteenth century, and which it is tempting to see as a borrowing of Anglo-French *burel*, *burrelle* 'kind of coarse cloth', (in heraldry) 'barrulet', continental French *burrelle* 'horizontal stripe on a shield'. However, in this instance the semantic correspondence is not exact, and it is perhaps possible that the resemblance is purely coincidental.

We thus have one case, *purse*, where everything except the initial consonant argues very strongly for borrowing from a word with initial /b/. *pudding* provides a less secure second example, and *purrell* may just be a third. Apart from these words, devoicing of initial /b/ seems extremely rare in English (or Latin or French). We certainly do not seem to have sufficient evidence to posit an occasional sound change in a historical grammar of English. Perhaps the etymologies proposed in all three cases are simply wrong, although in the case of *purse* at least such a conclusion seems counterintuitive. Unless and until a better explanation is found, a responsible etymologist can do little more than take note of the difficulty, and ensure that it is flagged prominently in any etymological dictionary entry or other discussion of the etymology of these words.

All three of these words are first recorded in periods of the history of English for which we have reasonably good documentation, and appear to be borrowings from languages for which we also have reasonably good documentation in the relevant periods. Such anomalies are relatively rare in well-documented periods of linguistic history, but this particular puzzle is hardly unique. It is hardly surprising that we also find many unexplained anomalies in periods for which we have very poor documentation, or when we are attempting to reconstruct developments in linguistic prehistory.

7.7.2 Formal difficulties leading to rejection of one etymology and adoption of another

The word *orchard* is found in some of the earliest Old English records, with the forms *ortgeard, orcerd, orcyrd, ordceard, ordcyrd, orceard*, and with the meaning 'a garden (frequently enclosed), especially for herbs and fruit trees'; in modern English the meaning has narrowed considerably. If a word is found in early Old English, then the obvious first place to look for a possible etymology is as an inherited development from proto-Germanic. An initial search seems promising, since we find the following words in other Germanic languages all with similar meanings and at least superficially similar forms:

Middle Low German *wortegarde*, Middle High German *wurzgarte, wurzegarte*, Old Icelandic *jurta-garðr*, Old Swedish *yrtagarþer* (Swedish *örtagård*), Old Danish *urtegard* (early modern Danish *urtegard*), Gothic *aurti-gards*

However, careful inspection of the forms of the word in Old English and in the other Germanic languages shows that the hypothesis of a single origin for all of these is untenable. The Middle Low German, Middle High German, Old Icelandic, Old Swedish, and Old Danish words are readily explained as showing a compound from the Germanic word for 'plant' which is represented by Old English *wyrt* (modern English *wort*, as in plant names such as *St. John's wort*, etc.) and the Germanic word for 'enclosure' which is represented by Old English *geard* (modern English *yard*). This thus gives us a starting point in proto-Germanic as **wurtigard-*.

The forms in Old English and Gothic, however, will not readily support such an analysis: the second element of the word in these two languages certainly seems to be *yard*, but the first element cannot easily be explained as a development from proto-Germanic **wurti-* (modern English *wort*). The Gothic form is *aurti-gards*, with unexplained loss of initial /w/ if **wurti-* is the starting point. In Old English **wurti-* gives *wyrt* (with regular development of /u/ > /y/ by *i*-mutation), but the Old English forms of *orchard* all indicate /o/ as the vowel in the first syllable: *ortgeard, orcerd, orcyrd, ordceard, ordcyrd, orceard*. This is a good example of how misleading it can be to work only from the later forms of words: in Middle English and modern English *wort* does indeed show *o* spellings, but these are only found from the early Middle English period onwards. Such spellings are rather difficult to explain, and it is not altogether certain whether they reflect a change in pronunciation, or simply a spelling convention for /u/; certainly the modern pronunciation /wə:t/ is not developed from /o/ (the pronunciation /wɔ:t/ shows a modern spelling pronunciation); compare similarly *worm* (Old English *wyrm*). What is certain is that these forms are not an Old English phenomenon, and therefore cannot explain Old English *ortgeard* etc.

A compound from *wyrt* and *geard* is indeed attested in Old English, and has the expected form *wyrtgeard*, and the meaning 'a kitchen garden'. This is therefore the formal correspondent to Middle Low German *wortegarde*, Middle High German *wurzgarte*, *wurzegarte*, Old Icelandic *jurta-garðr*, Old Swedish *yrtagarþer*, and Old Danish *urtegard*. As we have seen, Old English *ortgeard*, *orcerd*, *orcyrd*, *ordceard*, *ordcyrd*, *orceard* and Gothic *aurti-gards* cannot easily be traced back to the same origin as the other Germanic words, and therefore another explanation should be sought for the English and Gothic words. Two approaches have been attempted: (i) to see the Old English word as reflecting a variant of the Germanic base of *wort* with a different root vowel (although not all of the problems involved with such an explanation have been satisfactorily resolved); (ii) to see the Old English and Gothic words as showing a separate origin from the other Germanic words, namely a borrowing of Latin *hortus* 'garden' (either independently in each language, or perhaps reflecting an early borrowing in Germanic).

7.7.3 An early distinction in form and meaning pointing to word merger

An adjective *queer* occurs in criminals' slang in the sense 'bad, contemptible, worthless, untrustworthy, disreputable' and later (of coins or banknotes) 'counterfeit, forged'; henceforth I will refer to this as *queer* 'bad'. This appears at first sight to be an obvious semantic development from *queer* 'strange, odd, peculiar, eccentric; of questionable character, suspicious, dubious'; henceforth *queer* 'strange'. This supposition makes good sense chronologically: *queer* 'strange' is first recorded in 1513, and *queer* 'bad' in 1567. However, this easy supposition is dealt a serious blow by the early form history: *queer* 'strange' occurs in the sixteenth and seventeenth centuries only in the expected spellings *queere, quere, quer, queer*, but *queer* 'bad' occurs in the first century of its history only in the spellings *quyer, quyere, quire, quyre, quier*, which suggest a quite different stem vowel (which would give modern English /kwaɪə/), and it does not occur in the forms *queere, queer* until the end of the seventeenth century. We are thus faced with a serious difficulty. A phonological explanation is possible but not overwhelmingly probable: the effects of a following /r/ in either causing vowel lowering or inhibiting vowel raising are well documented for this period (see e.g. Dobson (1968) II 726–60), and we could just be seeing here the selection of a particular variant in the usage of a particular social group (i.e. criminals). However, there are no clear parallels in early modern English for either the raising of the reflex of Middle English /eː/ or the lowering of the reflex of Middle English /iː/ which would be required if we were to explain *queer* 'bad' as a variant of *queer* 'strange' or vice versa. (We encountered what could be interpreted as just such a raising in the case of *friar* in section 1.2.1, but this change occurred several centuries earlier than the period in question here.) When this lack of parallels is placed alongside the consistent distinction in form and meaning which we find up to the late seventeenth century, a conclusion similar to that which we reached in the case of *orchard* begins to appear rather attractive: we possibly have here two different words of separate origin, *queer* 'strange' and not *queer* but *quire* 'bad'. However, we would still have to explain the fact that in modern English both words have the same spelling and pronunciation. Possibly what has occurred here is associative change in word form, leading to merger in a pathway similar to some of those encountered in section 3.5 (see figure 7.2). The difference from the cases considered in section 3.5 is that we have no conclusive evidence from the prior etymology of either form, and this history is hypothesized purely on the basis of analysis of the recorded form and meaning evidence. *queer* 'strange' may be connected etymologically with German *quer* 'transverse, oblique, obstructive, (of things) going wrong (now rare), (of a person) peculiar, etc.', but chronological and semantic difficulties make this far from certain. *quire* 'bad' has no available etymology.

The steps in the argument can be summarized as follows:

- *queer* 'strange' and *queer* 'bad' are close semantically, and have the same form in modern English.

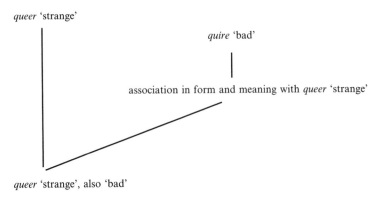

Fig 7.2 Possible merger of two distinct words in the history of *queer*

- But the earliest recorded forms of each show a clear distinction in form: *queer* 'strange' is spelt *queere, quere, quer, queer,* but *queer* 'bad' is spelt *quyer, quyere, quire, quyre, quier.*
- There is no obvious phonological explanation of this difference in form, paralleled by many other words, which would make us happy to see the apparent distinction in form as purely an accident of the historical record.
- It therefore seems possible that there were originally two distinct words, which have merged in modern English as a result of associative change in word form.

7.7.4 A contamination hypothesis

English *maple* and *maple tree* have as their ancestor Old English *mapulder.* The modern form *maple tree* (Old English *mapel trēow*) probably results from substitution of *tree* for the Germanic tree-name suffix *-der.* In fact, this probably occurred as a result of analogy with *apple tree.* In Old English *apulder* 'apple tree' was the only other word which showed the suffix *-der.* It existed alongside *æppel trēow* (modern English *apple tree*), a compound of the words *æppel* 'apple' and *trēow* 'tree'. An *apple tree* is a tree which bears *apples,* but a *maple tree* is not a tree which bears **maples*: the word *apple* is polysemous, denoting both the tree and its fruit, whereas *maple* is not. Nonetheless, the similarity of the word forms, and the fact that only the similar sounding words *mapulder* and *apulder* preserved the suffix *-der,* appears to have led to analogical creation:

apulder : *æppel trēow* (>*apple tree*) = *mapulder* : *mapel trēow* (>*maple tree*)

maple then arose either by a similar process of analogy, or by ellipsis from *maple tree*.

A very similar process very possibly occurred earlier in the history of this word. Old English *mapulder* has an obvious cognate in Old Saxon *mapulder*, but the corresponding word in Old High German is *mazaltra*, *mazzaltra*. Further connections are very unclear, but very slightly favour the assumption that the Old High German form is original. The *z, zz* in the Old High German form should correspond to proto-Germanic **t*, as a result of a sound change known as the High German Consonant Shift, but the Old English and Old Saxon words suggest proto-Germanic **p*. We thus have a situation where some sort of connection seems pretty certain on semantic grounds, but the phonology cannot be reconciled on the basis of regular development of sounds from a common base form. A very plausible resolution of this difficulty was suggested by Bierbaumer, in the course of a detailed study of Old English plant names (1975: 1.100–1): as we have already seen, in Old English (as also in Old Saxon) the *-der* tree-name suffix is otherwise found only in *apulder* 'apple tree', so perhaps the word *mapulder* in these two languages shows a substitution of -*p*- for -*t*- by association with *apulder*, the only other word with the same doubtless rather opaque ending, and which happens to have an otherwise almost identical phonological shape. We might even speculate that there has been confusion about the morpheme boundary, *apul-der* and **matul-der* being perceived as *a-pulder* and **ma-tulder*, hence > *mapulder*.

7.7.5 Unresolved formal difficulties: *polecat*

A multiplicity of form types which have not been satisfactorily reconciled with one another can bedevil attempts at etymological analysis. For example, *polecat*, the name of a small mammal which is probably the ancestor of the domestic ferret, occurs first in the Middle English period (earliest in 1320) with two spelling types, *polcat* and *pulcat*; in the sixteenth century two more types appear, *polecat* and *poulcat*. Middle English *polcat* could be interpreted as a spelling for a form with a long vowel in the first syllable, hence the precursor of later *polecat*, although the existence of a later form *pollcat* suggests that there was also at some point a variant with a short vowel; hence we seem to have evidence for both /pɔlkat/ and /pɔːlkat/. These forms are very difficult to reconcile with either *pulcat* or *poulcat*, which would imply /puːlkat/ and perhaps also /pulkat/. There is no obvious common starting point which would explain all of these forms.

There seems no reason to doubt that in all of these forms the second element of the word is *cat*, the animal presumably being regarded as roughly similar to a cat in its carnivorous habits and size. (As we will see below, French *chat putois* offers at least a parallel in support of this hypothesis.)

One etymological hypothesis might be that the word shows a compound of the same type as *sparrow-hawk*, where the first element denotes a type of food characteristically eaten by the animal denoted by the second element. On this assumption, at least some of the forms might be explained by a borrowing of Old French *poule, polle*, Middle French *poule* 'hen', but this runs into difficulties because a compound of this pattern is unlikely to have been formed in French (especially in view of the premodification of the head of the compound), and borrowing of *poule, polle* into English is not found until the fifteenth century, and is very rare.

Somewhat tantalizingly, *chat putois*, literally 'stinking cat', is found in Old French and Middle French as a name for the polecat, but this can hardly lie immediately behind our English word, although it at least reinforces the assumption that the second element is likely to be *cat*. If we try to explain *polecat* as a compound with a literal meaning 'stinking cat', we might consider as etymon for its first element (Anglo-)French *pulent, pullent* 'stinking, disgusting, dirty', which is at least a little closer formally, but the loss of the second syllable of the French word would be hard to account for.

Crucially, neither of these etymological attempts could explain the full range of forms shown by the word, nor does either of them provide a fully satisfactory explanation for even one of the forms. We can thus summarize a very unsatisfactory state of affairs as follows:

- *polcat, pulcat, polecat,* and *poulcat* all denote the same animal
- These forms are all very similar, differing only in the vowel of the first syllable, but there is no obvious explanation for this variation
- We have no satisfactory etymology for any of these forms

Further than this we cannot really say. It is very tempting to assume that *polcat, pulcat, polecat,* and *poulcat* all show variants of the same word, and that a solution to the etymological puzzle would also lead to a satisfactory explanation of the relationships between the various forms. However, it is unclear whether that explanation would involve phonological developments, or associative changes in word form: perhaps folk etymology has had a part to play here, but without any clear starting point and with no obvious motivation for any of the forms we are essentially left guessing, and the safest course is simply to regard this as an unsolved puzzle.

To take another rather simpler example, *nape* 'back of the neck' (of unknown origin) shows two distinct groups of forms: on the one hand *nape* (and in Middle English also *naape*), and on the other *nalpe, naupe, nawpe* (all in the sixteenth century; the *-au-, -aw-* spellings probably show a diphthong resulting from vocalization of /l/, but this is not certain). The two are normally assumed to show the same word, but the relationship between them has not been explained satisfactorily.

8

Semantic change

In the last chapter we looked in detail at change in word form, and we saw how a systematic approach to this area gives a very solid basis to etymological research. In the present chapter we will turn our attention to change in meaning. As we explored in the early chapters of this book, words have meaning as well as form, and both can and do change over the course of time. However, change in word meaning is generally much less amenable to systematic analysis than change in word form. Semantic changes are notoriously difficult to classify or systematize, and we have no tool comparable to the historical grammar to help us judge what is or is not likely or plausible. Further, although some semantic changes occur in clusters, with a change in one word triggering a change in another, we do not find anything comparable to a regular sound change, affecting all comparable environments within a single historical period. In this respect semantic changes are more similar to sporadic sound changes, but with the major difference that they are much more varied, and show the influence of a much wider set of motivating factors. Additionally, semantic change is much more closely connected with change in the external, non-linguistic world, especially with developments in the spheres of culture and technology. In studying semantic change we must therefore cast our net much wider, although when we come to consider change in the remoter past we will be confronted all too often by problems arising from lack of knowledge about the timeframe and the cultural circumstances within which a particular change occurred.

In this chapter we will look at some of the traditional methods of classifying semantic change, as well as at some more recent approaches, particularly from the standpoint of cognitive linguistics. We will also look at some insights from recent work on grammaticalization, where some of the most impressive advances have been made in identifying major trends. In a recent survey of work on semantic change in comparative linguistics, Sheldon Harrison acknowledges the importance of such work, but comments on the general situation as follows:

> While it may not be entirely fair to say that comparativists have done nothing to clarify the notion 'similar meanings,' we haven't done much . . . We are still very much at the data-collection stage in this endeavour, and are informed in it only by vague senses of what are possible metaphors or metonymies. Sadly, we don't really pay much attention to the meaning side of things. In general, unless a particular meaning comparison grossly offends some very general sense of metaphor, it's 'anything goes' with regard to meaning.

> (Harrison (2003) 219)

In the final section of this chapter we will look at some cases from both historical and reconstructed periods of linguistic history where lack of certainty about the likely course of semantic development poses considerable difficulties for etymological research.

8.1 Meaning change is a common phenomenon

Even the most casual inspection of any historical or etymological dictionary will show that words change in meaning over time. We saw some striking examples in chapter 1 in the histories of *sad*, *deer*, and *treacle*.

Even very basic words can and do show change in meaning. In Old English, as in the earliest stages of other Germanic languages, the word *man* had the senses 'human being' and 'adult male human being', the two only being distinguished by context. Additionally, the words *wer* and *wǣpmann* were available with the meaning 'adult male human being', as distinguished from *wīf* (modern English *wife*) and *wīfmann* (modern English *woman*) in the meaning 'adult female human being'. Neither *wer* nor *wǣpmann* survives beyond the early Middle English period, and we find that during the course of the Middle English period *man* becomes the usual word in the sense 'adult male human being' (and thus the opposite of *woman*), and becomes much less common in the wider sense 'human being'. It becomes obsolete in this sense in the early modern period (last attested in 1597 in Bishop John King 'The Lord had but one paire of men in Paradise'), except in general, abstract, or indefinite uses, as in e.g. 'All men are born equal'. Even this use is now avoided by many people in the light of modern feminist perspectives: it is perceived as excluding women, either implicitly or explicitly, and hence it is avoided and replaced by other constructions which are less ambiguous. This first illustration brings to the foreground three major concerns in the study of meaning change. We need to pay close attention to:

(i)   the relationships between the various meanings shown by a word
(ii) the relationships between different words and their meanings
(iii) the relationships between linguistic meaning and cultural, extralinguistic history

As already noted, a major strand in historical linguistic work over the past several decades has been the study of grammaticalization, the process by which words develop increasingly grammatical meanings and functions over time. *may* has developed from a proto-Germanic verb with the meaning 'to be strong or able, to have power'. From this there developed the (dynamic, or root, modal) sense 'to be able (to do something)', from which in turn developed the (epistemic modal) use describing possibility, e.g. 'it may be the case that', 'this may happen'. We will look at some important generalizations which have been drawn from such processes in section 8.7.2.1; we can state at this point:

(iv) (a) Grammaticalization typically involves increasing internalization or subjectification of meaning
      (b) Such a pathway is characteristic of many other semantic changes

Words denoting material objects in everyday use have also often shown quite dramatic shifts in meaning. *toilet* was borrowed into English from French in the sixteenth century. It earliest denoted various different items made of cloth used for specific purposes, including a cloth cover for a dressing table. From this sense (by metonymy) it also came to denote: all of the items used in dressing; the dressing table itself; the act of dressing or, more recently, of washing and grooming.[1] From the early nineteenth century the word is found denoting a dressing room, or (at first euphemistically) the room in which a lavatory is found, and hence the lavatory itself. Once this sense became established in general use, the senses 'dressing', 'washing', or 'grooming' became very much less frequent, in part because of genuine ambiguity, but in part because of polite avoidance of a word with lavatorial connotations. (Collocations which were frequent in earlier use such as 'a fine toilet table', 'a set of toilet brushes', or 'she is presently at her toilet' would today in most contexts be considered either comical or embarrassing or both. Similarly *eau de toilette* is now normally preferred to the loan translation *toilet water*.) Similar developments can be observed in the development also of the word *lavatory*. We can thus add two further general observations:

(v) The connotations of one meaning of a word can have a dramatic effect on its other uses

(vi) Meaning development can show an intricate connection with technological developments in the material, extralinguistic world

8.2 Polysemy and meaning change

In sections 2.1.4, 3.3, and 3.4 we looked at polysemy, the situation where a single word shows two or more meanings concurrently. The existence of such situations is essential to many of the types of developments in meaning change which we touched on in section 8.1. The interaction between the senses of a word demands the same model for variation in linguistic change which we encountered at various points in our examination of change in word form in chapter 7:

$$A > A \sim B > B$$

That is to say, in the context of change in meaning, a situation where a word has only meaning 'A' is not typically followed by a situation where it has only meaning 'B', but by an intermediate period in which it has both meanings 'A' and 'B'. Investigation of meaning change involves an important corollary

---

[1] For a slightly different interpretation of the early stages of the meaning history of *toilet* see Traugott and Dasher (2005) 58–9.

to this model, which we already saw in outline in chapter 3: although it is possible for both formal and semantic divergence to give rise to two separate words where historically only a single word existed, a much more typical pattern is for semantic change to result in words becoming polysemous, with a set of senses showing often very complex inter-relationships and interconnections which can change and develop over time.

It is likely that most semantic changes are gradual in the same way as those affecting *man* and *may*, that is to say that they proceed little by little chronologically, even when their effects may appear abrupt. We may hypothesize a (metonymic) change by which a word x in period A has the meaning 'nose' (meaning a), but in period B it has the meaning 'chin' (meaning b). In one sense the process must be abrupt in a case like this, since any given use must have either one sense or the other, even if it may be used punningly or with other allusion to the other sense. However, it is likely that, even if each individual use of the word is categorically either the one sense or the other, there will be a period in which polysemy occurs, and some uses are in sense a, others in sense b. Thus while our historical records may only give us evidence for period A (when all examples are in sense a) and for period B (when all examples are in sense b), there is nonetheless likely to have intervened a period X in which both a and b were found.[2]

A powerful model for examining many changes in meaning is provided by prototype semantics, and especially the 'diachronic prototype semantics' presented by Geeraerts (1997).[3] Many traditional models of meaning have looked for invariable components which must be fulfilled by any use of a word in a particular meaning. The difficulties of this traditional approach emerge if we consider a (much-studied) case: the word *fruit* and the semantic category it denotes. We can fairly easily draw up a list of features which most fruits have in common, but we can just as easily find exceptions: a strawberry is unlike many other fruits in that it does not have seeds which are (a) inedible and (b) located centrally, and it also lacks a thick outer skin; similarly, a banana does not have clearly demarcated seeds which are inedible. Prototype semantics resolves these difficulties: having seeds which are inedible and located centrally, and having a thick outer skin, are among the prototypical qualities of a fruit, but this does not mean that every fruit will show all of these qualities. Thus, strawberries and bananas remain very good examples of fruit, because they have many of the other

---

[2] For detailed discussion of such processes see Traugott and Dasher (2005).

[3] See also the essays collected in Geeraerts (2006), and for an overview see also Lewandowska-Tomaszczyk (2007).

qualities typical of the members of this class.[4] The various types of *berry* which we encountered in section 2.6 provide a similar example; see also *petal* in section 5.4. Diachronically, what was peripheral or marginal in one period may become part of the prototypical core of the meaning of a word. If we return to the example of *man*, we could analyse what has happened here diachronically as a case of prototype shift. Formerly, the prototypical meaning was 'human being', with 'adult male human being' as a contextually determined specific meaning. In the Middle English period, the prototype shifted: 'adult male human being' became the prototypical meaning, and generic uses to denote any person irrespective of gender are now understood as showing extended uses of this (and are as such now avoided by many people).

Historical dictionaries normally group together examples on the basis of semantic similarity, but this may mean that a sense has earlier 'outlier' examples, showing uses which were, viewed synchronically, unprototypical, followed by later examples from a period in which this sense has become part of the prototypical use of the word.[5]

A good deal of important recent work on historical meaning change has focused on the relationship between semantics and pragmatics, and on how new word meanings can arise from implicatures which are made when a speaker addresses a hearer, or a writer addresses a reader. Traugott and Dasher (2005) distinguish between: (i) 'utterance-token meanings', i.e. invited inferences which are used innovatively by speakers or writers; (ii) 'utterance-type meanings', i.e. invited inferences or implicatures which have become firmly established in the language (e.g. the causal implicature of *after* in sentences such as *After the trip to Minnesota she felt very tired*); and (iii) 'coded meanings (semantics)', i.e. the conventional meanings of words (Traugott and Dasher (2005) 16–17). In the 'invited inferencing theory of semantic change', new meanings can be seen as developing from 'utterance-token meanings' to 'utterance-type meanings' to 'coded meanings'.[6] It is important to bear in mind the pragmatic contexts of language use whenever considering diachronic semantic change.

[4] For a detailed discussion of this example see Geeraerts (1997) 12–23.

[5] The identification of senses is a controversial subject, and has been approached from a variety of different perspectives. For two views from the standpoint of synchronic lexicography see Hanks (2000) and Kilgarriff (1997). For an overview of the approach of *OED* and many other historical dictionaries see Silva (2000). On the different approaches often taken by semanticists and lexicographers, and the opportunities for fruitful common ground, see Kay (2000), Geeraerts (2007).

[6] On the processes involved see Traugott and Dasher (2005) 35, 38.

8.3 Semantic polygenesis

One consequence of such models of meaning development is that the same meaning may easily arise independently in two different historical periods, a process which Geeraerts calls semantic polygenesis (Geeraerts (1997) 62–8). However, it can be difficult to tell such cases apart from cases where a particular sense was actually in continuous use but there is simply a gap in the historical record. Indeed, even a continuous historical record may conceal a number of separate innovative uses, in the same way that we saw with nonce formation of word forms in sections 2.3 and 3.2.

In assessing such situations we often have to take into account various idiosyncrasies of the historical record of a particular language. For instance, in English there can often be particular problems in deciding whether a sense shows continuity of use when there is a gap in the record between the early modern period and modern regional use, since we know that documentation for most regional varieties of English is almost completely absent between the Middle English period and the nineteenth century. *OED* records *make* in the sense '(of a father) to beget' with a gap between use in *a*1616 in Shakespeare and 1924 in a work of dialect literature. Similarly it records *mannered* in the sense 'having good manners; well-behaved, polite; refined, gracious, sophisticated' with a gap between 1575 and 1829, after which date the sense is found in regional use. In such cases, has the meaning fallen out of use in other varieties but been retained in regional varieties, or has it been created anew in modern regional use?

In other cases polygenesis of the type posited by Geeraerts seems more likely. For instance, *massy* shows the sense 'dense in texture or consistency; compact, substantial' with a gap between 1580 and 1805. Use is found in a variety of different text types in each period, and there is no particular indication either of restricted regional distribution or of revival from the literary record. Therefore in this case the likeliest explanation seems to be that we have independent development of the same meaning in two different periods, although an accidental failure in the historical record cannot be completely ruled out.

8.4 Meaning change in a semantically complex word: *quaint*

In his analysis of the history of the word *quaint*, Samuels (1972: 76) provides a classic account of how the senses of a polysemous word interact with one another diachronically. The following are the main senses which Samuels distinguishes, drawn from the first edition of the *OED*, but collapsing some minor senses together, plus the dates he gives for first and last attestation for each, drawn again from the *OED* (I have added the dates for the corresponding senses from the new edition of the *OED*, so that we can see to what extent Samuels's detailed arguments are still borne out by revised documentation for the word's history):

1 Wise, knowing, skilled, clever: 1250–1728 (now *a*1250–1834)
2 Cunning, crafty, given to scheming: 1225–1680 (now *c*1230–1814)
3 Cunningly or skilfully made (of things), elaborate: 1290–1631 (now *c*1300–1814)
4 Beautiful, pretty, dainty, handsome, fashionable, elegant: 1300–1784 (now *c*1300–1785)
5 (Rarer meanings) proud, haughty: 1225–1430 (now *c*1230–1610) fastidious, prim: 1483–1678 (now 1483–1849)
6 Ingeniously elaborated, refined, smart, full of conceits, affected: 14th cent.–1783 (now *c*1395–1847)
7 Strange, unusual, odd, curious: 14th cent.–1808 (now *c*1325 to present day, but only in regional use after 1808)
8 Unusual but attractive in an old-fashioned way: 1795 to present day (now 1762 to present day)

Samuels's analysis is worth tracing through in detail. He observes that: 'Senses (1), (2), (3) and (5) were all obsolete or obsolescent by the seventeenth century. (2) had been ousted by the developments of (3), which, when transferred from things to persons, resulted in (4), (6) and (7).' If we look at the first dates of each of these senses, Samuels's observations look at first rather odd, since all of the first seven senses are first attested in very roughly the same period. However, *quaint* is a borrowing from French, and comparison with the senses which appear to have been inherited from (Anglo-)French does point rather more to senses 6 and 7 at least being innovations in English, but probably not 4. The corresponding French senses are (as summarized in *OED3*): 'clever, astute, quick-witted, experienced, expert, crafty, cunning, brave, gracious, elegant, pleasant, smart, fashionable, devious, underhand, arrogant, (of a thing) ingenious'. What stands out most from the chronology of the English senses is that, after a long period of stability, sense 8 appears in the mid eighteenth century as the first major new sense in nearly five hundred years, and then between the late eighteenth century and the mid nineteenth century all of the other senses of the word disappear. Samuels's analysis is as follows: '(4) and (7)... combined in (8), and then, *as soon as this had happened*, (4), (6) and (7) vanished'. The revised documentation of the new edition of the *OED* makes Samuels's analysis here even more convincing: the first appearance of sense 8 now antedates rather than postdates the last attestations for senses 4 and 6, thus making it more plausible that the development of sense 8 could have led to the loss of senses 4 and 6.[7] Most important of all is Samuels's analysis of the reason for this development:

Until the late eighteenth century, wide polysemy had been tolerated in this word, but as soon as it was extended to a complex meaning with an individual twist, all the other meanings had to come to an end. The development is pejorative only by comparison with meaning (4), and the reasons for the peculiar twist in sense for this word are probably extralinguistic, e.g. the younger generation might hear the word applied in meaning (4) by their elders to objects, qualities or persons still admired by the older, but not by the younger generation, who would thus come to interpret it in meaning (8).

This explanation surely retains validity, even if the revised dating might make us wonder whether sense 8 might not also have been the immediate cause of the loss of sense 1 as well. So far at least, no explanation has been found as to why this last sense should have arisen in the mid eighteenth century and not before, but once it did it led to a radical adjustment in the range of senses of a word which had shown a high degree of polysemy with relative stability for hundreds of years, with the end result that the word is now practically monosemous, outside certain restricted registers.

8.5 Influence from other words

Our examination of *quaint* has exemplified the relationships among the meanings of a semantically complex word. However, as noted in section 8.1,

---

[7] Senses 2 and 3 both also now have last dates later than the first date for sense 8, although it should be noted that in both cases the later evidence is scarce and clearly archaizing in tone. Samuels does omit one other sense, 'Of an action, scheme, device, etc.: characterized or marked by cleverness, ingenuity, or cunning', for which *OED3* now shows currency from *a*1225 up to the present day. However, *OED3* labels this as 'now rare and arch[aic]', and its post-1800 attestations are all in literary sources, and are also largely in collocations which may to some extent be lexicalized, such as *quaint design* and *quaint device*, suggesting that the assumption remains correct that sense 8 remains the only sense with any genuine currency in everyday language.

the inter-relationships and interaction between the meanings of different words can also be of considerable importance in semantic change. We will consider these in two separate groups: semantic relationships with other words of related meaning, and semantic relationships with other words of similar form.

8.5.1 Relationships with words of related meaning

A good example of how dangerous it can be to try to consider a word's semantic development in isolation from other words in the same semantic field is provided by the word *board*. This is an inherited Germanic word, Old English *bord*, Middle English *bord*. (Old English *bord* originally showed a merger of two distinct words, and the Middle English word probably also showed some semantic influence from (Anglo-)French *bord* and from Old Norse *borð*, but that need not concern us here.)

Middle English *bord* could denote:

a plank or board; an object made of boards (such as a wooden tablet for inscriptions or a wooden tray); a ship; the side of a ship; a shield; a table, including various specific kinds of table for working on or for dining at; hence a meal; (in late Middle English) a board for playing a game on

This summary would be an oversimplification if we wanted to study the meanings of Middle English *bord* in detail, but it suffices to indicate some significant differences from the meanings of modern English *board*. Some specific senses, such as 'a ship' or 'a shield', have become obsolete, and can be regarded as dead offshoots in the word's history: so far as the relationship with other English words is concerned, *board* has simply ceased to be a synonym of *ship* or *shield*. However, the sense 'side of a ship', although itself now obsolete, gave rise to the expressions *on board* and *overboard*, now found in a wide variety of different contexts, including metaphorical uses, e.g. of someone *taking an idea on board* or *throwing something overboard*.

Other changes are rather more complex, and can only be explained adequately when we consider the semantic relationships of *board* with several other English words. (In doing this we adopt an onomasiological approach, as typified by a thesaurus, rather than the semasiological approach typified by a dictionary; although in practice historical dictionaries combine aspects of both approaches.) To take the first of the Middle English meanings listed above, 'a plank or board' would not be a good definition of modern English *board* when it denotes a flat piece of wood used by a builder, precisely because *board* is now usually distinguished in meaning from *plank*, a Middle English borrowing from (Anglo-)French. In modern English a *board* is something which is typically wider and often also thinner than a *plank*, although a *floorboard* may be much closer to the dimensions of a *plank*. In Middle English the two words had much more semantic overlap, although Middle English *planke* is less likely to denote a particularly wide piece of wood than *bord* is. Both words also showed more semantic overlap with *timber* (another word inherited from Old English) than they do in modern English.

Much more complex differentiation has taken place between *board* and another (Anglo-)French loanword, *table*. The complexity of the semantic differentiation which has occurred between these two words can be seen if we also summarize some of the main senses of Middle English *table*:

a plank or board (or various other sorts of pieces of wood, such as posts, splints, etc.); a slab or tablet of stone, wood, or other material, especially one used for writing or painting on; a board for playing a game on; a cleared piece of land for planting crops on; a plate forming part of an instrument; (in building) a floor; a tabular arrangement of words, symbols, etc.; a table (i.e. a piece of furniture consisting of a board supported on four legs); hence a meal, regular daily meals, supply of food in a household

In modern English there is much less overlap between the two words semantically, and some senses which in Middle English could be expressed by either *table* or *board* are now expressed only by *table*, others only by *board* (or by *plank*, or by other words which we have not considered here such as *tablet*). The piece of furniture is in modern English almost always denoted by *table*, but the provision of meals by *board*, especially in collocations such as *board and lodging* or *full board*.

A further important development in the meaning of *board* from the sense 'table' only occurred slightly after the end of the Middle English period, and is still found today, in spite of the loss of the basic sense 'table':

table > (specifically) council table > meeting of a council (at a council table) > the members of a council collectively > the body of people responsible for the governance or administration of a business, institution, etc.

Thus, in the case of *board*, the senses of the word have become rather fragmented. The sense 'table', which forms the link between the senses 'piece of wood', 'regular meals', and 'governing or administrative body' has been lost, except as a deliberate archaism. Similarly, the sense 'side of a ship' is obscured in the now clearly lexicalized expression *on board*, which now has the basic sense 'on the ship' rather than 'onto the ship'. We can thus see a process by which the sort of homonymy which we considered in section 3.3 can arise. (For similar examples compare *office* or the adjective *fair*. See von Wartburg (1969) 112–22 for extended discussion of some further examples, chiefly from French.)

8.5.2 Relationships with words of similar form

We sometimes find that one word's semantic development is affected by association with another word of the same or similar sound which is historically unrelated. This is the mirror image of the process of contamination which we looked at in section 7.4.4, where semantic association affects word form.

The verb *moulder* is a derivative of *mould* 'earth', a word of Germanic descent with cognates of similar meaning in most of the other Germanic languages. Its usual meaning is 'to crumble to dust', but it also shows uses with the meaning 'to rot', as in the following quotation from the *OED*:

1950 T. S. ELIOT *Cocktail Party* II. 129 What have they to go back to? To the stale food mouldering in the larder, the stale thoughts mouldering in their minds.

In such uses it is likely that the word shows semantic association with the etymologically unrelated word *mould* 'woolly or furry growth on food, textiles, etc.'

The meanings of the verb *mean* can be analysed as showing six main branches of development:

to intend, to signify, to mention, to have an opinion, to remember, to go towards

The word is an inherited Germanic verb, and the first four of these sense branches have good parallels among the other Germanic languages. However, 'to remember' and 'to go towards' do not. It is conceivable that they simply show sense developments which happen to have occurred only in English, with no influence from any other word. However, it is also possible that these senses arose through association respectively with the following two words:

- *min* 'to remember' (a borrowing from Norse of a word ultimately related to *mind*)
- *min* 'to intend, to direct one's course, go' (a derivative of Old English *myne* 'mind, intention, remembrance, memory')

These words were not homophones of *mean*, but it is possible that the resemblance in sound led to association or confusion of their meanings. This hypothesis is supported in the case of *min* 'to remember' by the fact that *mean* and *min* with this meaning are often found as variant readings in medieval texts, suggesting that confusion existed between them.

To take another example, Old French *porsuir* (> English *pursue*) is the formal reflex of classical Latin *prōsequī*, which has among its meanings:

to follow, pursue, follow up, continue with, to pursue a claim for, to attend, accompany, to honour or present (someone) with

But the range of meanings shown by Old French *porsuir* is rather wider than would be suggested by the meanings of its Latin etymon:

to follow with intent to overtake and capture, to persecute, to strive for (a circumstance, event, condition, etc.), to besiege, to accompany, escort, to carry on to the end, to accomplish, to pester (someone) in order to obtain something, (of misfortune, etc.) to assail persistently, to follow up (a course of action begun), to seek to obtain (something) through a court of law, (in law) to bring an action against, to proceed along (a path, etc.), to investigate, study

A number of these senses show the likely semantic influence of the formally distinct Old French verb *parsuir* or its etymon classical Latin *persequī*. Among the meanings of *persequī* are:

to seek out, to pursue, to follow with hostility or malignity, to harass, to chase, hunt, to examine, follow up, to go through with or persist in

Among the meanings of Old French *parsuir* are:

to follow with intent to overtake and capture, to search out, to persecute, to complete, to carry out, accomplish, to carry on, continue, to conform to, to comply with

In this instance, the two Latin verbs ultimately show different prefixed forms, in *prō-* and *per-* respectively, of the same verb, *sequī* 'to follow'. In Old French the formal reflex of the one, *porsuir*, appears to have borrowed senses from the other, *parsuir* (which ultimately became obsolete). The situation is thus very similar to a merger in word form (compare section 3.5), but what appears to have happened here is that instead of the two words becoming indistinguishable in form, the one word acquired additional meanings from the other, which subsequently became obsolete. (The formal association of the two words may have been aided by the fact that in the heavily abbreviated writing typical of many medieval manuscripts the abbreviations for *per-* and *pro-* were very similar. Compare section 7.2.5 on the identical abbreviations used for *per-* and *par-*.)

8.6 Some basic types of change

As noted at the beginning of this chapter, one of the main concerns in historical semantics has traditionally been the classification of different types of semantic change. This is obviously of great importance for etymological research: if we want to know whether a particular semantic change is likely to have occurred in one word history, it will be crucially important to know whether similar changes have occurred in other word histories. However, identifying similarity is a far from simple matter. If we compare the situation with sporadic sound changes, it is usually relatively simple to identify cases of metathesis, for example. However, in the case of semantic change it can be much more difficult to identify the exact circumstances of change in any given instance, or to pinpoint when a change has occurred. As we have seen from the examples already considered, a great many different factors can be at play in the semantic development of a word.

In this section we will look at some of the typical processes of semantic change which are most commonly identified in the scholarly literature: broadening, narrowing, pejoration, amelioration, metaphor, and metonymy.[8] It is important to note that these are not hard and fast categories. Some scholars identify additional distinct categories, while others would collapse some of those presented here.[9] Additionally, there is often ambiguity as to which category a particular example belongs to.

As a final but important proviso, we should note that these are strictly only the outcomes of semantic change, rather than the mechanisms themselves, which we have already touched on in section 8.2.[10]

---

[8] For an overview of the history of scholarship in this area see Traugott and Dasher (2005) 51–104.

[9] For a very useful analysis of some of the key issues see Traugott (2006).

[10] For a slightly different perspective on this question compare also Fortson (2003) 650.

8.6.1 Broadening

Broadening is the process by which a word comes to have wider semantic application. We could put this another way, and say that a restriction on the meaning of a word is lost, or that meaning becomes less specific. Sometimes the term generalization is used instead.

French *arriver* (> English *arrive*) has the same basic meaning in modern French as in English. However, when it is first attested in Old French in the eleventh century it has the sense 'to disembark, to reach the river bank, to land'. It is either the reflex of or is formed on the model of post-classical Latin *arripare*, which is found in the same sense from the ninth century, and is formed from classical Latin *ad* 'to, at' and *rīpa* 'river bank'. Subsequently the meaning was broadened to reaching any sort of destination, or to put it another way, the restriction to 'river bank' or to 'travel by water' was lost. (This broader sense is attested in French from the second half of the twelfth century, but the evidence of some of the other Romance languages suggests that it actually developed earlier in Latin.)

German *Limonade* is a seventeenth-century borrowing from French *limonade* 'lemonade'. However, in the nineteenth century the sense became broadened to any kind of soft drink. Thus in modern German one finds compounds such as *Orangenlimonade* 'orange soft drink', and lemonade itself is now often distinguished as *Zitronenlimonade*, a new compound with *Zitrone* 'lemon' as its first element. In this instance the broadening of the meaning of *Limonade* was probably facilitated by the semantic shift of German *Limone*, which is a fourteenth-century borrowing from French *limon* 'lemon', but which now has the sense 'lime' in standard German.

Similarly, in some varieties of modern Scottish English, *ginger*, originally by ellipsis from *ginger beer*, is found in broadened use denoting any fizzy soft drink. (See *Scottish National Dictionary* Supplement, and compare Smith (1996) 117.) In other varieties of Scottish English, *juice* has the broadened sense 'soft drink', with the result that for instance a drink made from the juice of oranges, rather than simply having an orange taste, is typically distinguished as *fresh orange* rather than *orange juice*. (For examples see the SCOTS corpus at http://www.scottishcorpus.ac.uk/.)

Related to broadening is bleaching, where the semantic content of a word becomes reduced as the grammatical content increases, for instance in the development of intensifiers such as *awfully, terribly, horribly* (e.g. *awfully late, awfully big, awfully small*) or *pretty* (*pretty good, pretty bad, pretty small*, etc.), or earlier in the history of English *very*: this originally meant 'truly', and was a conversion during the Middle English period from *verrai* 'true', which was borrowed from (Anglo-)French *verrai* (modern French *vrai*). (Compare also section 8.7.2.1 on *very*.)

8.6.2 Narrowing

Conversely, narrowing is the process by which a word comes to have more restricted application. Or we could put this another way, and say that a restriction has been added to the meaning, or that meaning becomes more specific. Sometimes the term specialization is used instead.

We encountered in section 1.3.3 the narrowing of *deer* from 'animal' to 'deer', a particular type of animal. Similarly, *meat* shows a slow process of change in its history within English from 'food in general' to 'flesh of an animal (as food)', replacing *flesh* in general use in this sense. In section 3.1 we saw narrowing in the case of *poke* from 'bag, small sack' to 'small bag or pouch worn on the person' to 'purse, wallet'.

herb is an early Middle English borrowing from French. In early use it has two main senses:

- any plant whose stem is not woody or persistent (i.e. anything not a tree or a shrub)
- any plant whose leaves, or stem and leaves, are used for food or medicine, or in some way for their scent or flavour

The first of these has been lost, except for very restricted technical use in botanical registers, and the core meaning today is the narrower second one, which has narrowed further to exclude e.g. green vegetables. In this instance a full investigation of the meaning development would need to look also at the meanings of other terms in the same semantic field, such as *plant*, *wort*, *weed*, or indeed *tree*, *shrub*, as we did in the case of *board* in section 8.5.1.

8.6.3 Pejoration and amelioration

Pejoration and amelioration (or sometimes melioration) describe the acquisition respectively of less positive or more positive meanings. The main importance of these processes is the effect that they tend to have on the other senses of a word. This is particularly the case with pejoration.

We saw in section 8.4 how the development of the meaning 'unusual but attractive in an old-fashioned way' had a dramatic effect on the use of *quaint* in such senses as 'beautiful, pretty, dainty, handsome, fashionable, elegant'. A similar pressure is likely to have occurred in the history of the word *silly* in English, which has developed in meaning as follows:

happy, blessed, pious
> innocent, harmless, helpless, weak, deserving of pity
> feeble-minded, foolish, stupid

We do not know the circumstances of the extensions of meaning which occurred or their motivation, but it is likely that at each stage in this development the establishment of the new senses led to the loss of the older ones. (For the classic account of this word history, and an often reproduced diagram illustrating it, see Samuels (1972) 65–7.)

Pejoration and amelioration are both frequent in words denoting social ranks, positions, etc. The sense development of English *knave* can be summarized as follows:

boy
> (with narrowing)
young male servant
> (with broadening)
any (low status) male servant
> (with pejoration)
base and crafty rogue

Similarly *churl* shows a development from 'male human being' to 'freeman of the third and lowest rank' to 'serf, bondman' to 'peasant, countryman' to 'impolite and mean-spirited person'. A semantic history such as this one shows the close connection between meaning change and social and cultural history. The development from 'peasant, countryman' to 'impolite and mean-spirited person' reflects the low esteem in which the working people of the countryside have often been held. Similarly the meaning of *villain* has developed from the general meaning 'serf' to denoting someone whose behaviour is criminal or reprehensible.[11]

Amelioration is sometimes found in the names of military ranks. For instance *marshal* originally denoted 'a person in charge of the upkeep of horses' (the first element is cognate with *mare*), gradually coming to be the

---

[11] Another interesting group of words to investigate are forms of address such as *Mr*, *Mrs*, French *monsieur*, *madame*, German *Herr*, *Frau*.

title of high offices in the royal household and in the army because of the importance of the horse in the medieval state, and particularly of cavalry in medieval warfare. As we saw in section 4.4.3, *major* was originally a clipped form of *sergeant-major*, but *major* now denotes a rather higher ranking officer than it did in early use, while *sergeant-major* denotes a considerably lower ranking one.

A very interesting example is provided by comparison of English *knight* with German *Knecht*. The two words are cognate, and both earliest have the meaning 'boy'. However, the semantic development shown in each language in the course of the medieval period is radically different:

German *Knecht*

> boy, lad
> > boy or lad employed as a servant or attendant
> > servant, farm labourer, menial

English *knight*

> boy, lad
> > boy or lad employed as a servant or attendant
> > high-ranking (originally military) attendant or follower of the monarch or of another person of very high status

Examples like this one show the severe limits on predictability in semantic change. In each case the semantic development is easily understood in terms of the social and cultural history of the Middle Ages, but in the two languages the outcomes are radically different, even though the two societies concerned were identical in all of the respects which are relevant here, and English *knight* could have developed the meaning 'servant, farm labourer, menial' just as German *Knecht* could have developed the meaning 'high-ranking attendant or follower'. See further section 8.7.1 on this topic. (In fact in modern German the word for a knight is *Ritter*, showing semantic specialization, at first in Low German or Dutch, of a word which originally had the broader meaning 'rider'.)

A word often develops a pejorated sense through generalization of the connotative meaning of a collocation in which it frequently occurs. In section 7.2.5 we encountered *arrant* 'notorious, downright', which originated as a variant of *errant* 'wandering'. This pejorated narrowed sense developed from the connotative meaning of the frequent collocation *errant rogue* or *arrant rogue*, originally 'an outlawed roving robber', hence 'a common or out-and-out thief'. As a result of reanalysis the word came to be used analogously in other collocations with a depreciative sense, e.g. *arrant traitor*, *arrant knave*, *arrant ass*.

8.6.4 Metaphor and metonymy

The terms 'metaphor' and 'metonymy' both date back to antiquity as terms of rhetorical analysis, the names of traditional 'figures of speech'. In this tradition, a metaphor is an implicit comparison, as contrasted with a simile or explicit comparison. In a metaphor one thing, sometimes called the 'tenor', is referred to by the name of another, sometimes called the 'vehicle'. A metonymy shows the extended use of a term to denote something which is conceptually contiguous with the thing which it normally denotes.

In linguistics, the same terms are used to denote two typical processes of semantic change. (For examples see the following two sections.) The same definitions as given in the last paragraph remain valid, but the conception of the processes is rather different. Crucially, they are not perceived, as in the rhetorical tradition, as conscious stylistic devices belonging to heightened language, but as largely unconscious processes in meaning development, just like narrowing, broadening, pejoration, or amelioration.

In the cognitive linguistics tradition which emerged in the last decades of the twentieth century, metaphor and metonymy have a very important role. In this tradition, the metaphors and metonymies seen in actual linguistic usage are regarded as reflections of more fundamental mappings in the mind, i.e. as reflections of the ways in which people conceptualize the world and process abstract thought. In the very influential conceptual metaphor theory associated with George Lakoff and advanced especially in Lakoff and Johnson (1980; 2nd edn. 2003), the particular metaphorical expressions which we can trace in language are grouped and analysed as reflections of deeper conceptual metaphors. For instance, the conceptual metaphor 'THE MIND IS A CONTAINER' gives rise to expressions such as 'why can't you get that into your head?' In a good deal of more recent work in cognitive linguistics, the focus has shifted to metonymy as an even more basic linguistic process, and some have sought to analyse metaphor in terms of underlying metonymical processes.[12] However, whichever theoretical position is adopted, the crucial point is that it is assumed that the metaphorical and metonymical meaning developments found in the histories of particular

---

[12] For discussion and references see Traugott and Dasher (2005) 27–9.

words are not accidental, one-off affairs, but instead reflect characteristic patterns of thought. This is potentially of very great importance for work in etymology, because identification of such typical patterns would in theory provide a means of assessing the plausibility of the meaning development assumed in a particular word history. However, it should be stressed that such work is still in its infancy.

8.6.4.1 *Metaphor*   Some examples will show how the three approaches sketched in the preceding section can in practice overlap.

In classical Latin *quadrivium* meant a crossroads, a place where four roads meet, and *trivium* meant a place where three roads meet. In the early Middle Ages, we find metaphorical use of these two words to denote the two great divisions of the Seven Liberal Arts in the field of education: the advanced *quadrivium*, consisting of four subjects, and the more elementary *trivium*, consisting of three subjects. We can see how this metaphor can easily be analysed in terms of the traditional rhetorical figure of metaphor: a term is taken from one sphere, usually a more concrete one, and applied in a new one, usually a more abstract one; hearers recognize that this is a novel usage but also understand its meaning relatively easily. *quadrivium* in this use is first found in the works of the philosopher Boethius in the early sixth century, and may even have been coined by him. However, if we look at this metaphor from the perspective of cognitive linguistics, it is tempting to see motivation for it in the widespread conceptual metaphor 'KNOWLEDGE IS A JOURNEY'. From such a perspective, these metaphorical uses of *quadrivium* and *trivium* readily arise and are readily understood precisely because they are motivated by an underlying conceptual metaphor.

Many other metaphors express much more fundamental meaning relations. For instance, the expression *I see what you mean* depends upon the association between the physical sense of sight and mental cognition which is reflected also in the traditional saying *seeing is believing*. Investigation of the etymologies of verbs meaning 'to know' or 'to understand' shows this same association repeated over and over again, in different languages and in different cultures. (See further section 8.7.2.2 below.)

What were originally metaphorical uses often come to be apprehended as primary meanings of words, so that their metaphorical origin can only be recovered through etymological research. We looked at cases such as *crane* 'type of bird' and *crane* 'type of machine' in section 3.4, and also cases where there is a formal split, as between *flower* and *flour* in section 3.6. The names of many abstract concepts are metaphorical in origin, and concrete to abstract is a very common pathway for metaphorical change: for instance, *line* 'long straight mark or band' is originally a metaphorical development of *line* 'piece of cord or string'.

8.6.4.2 *Metonymy*   Meaning change through contiguity, whether physical or conceptual, is extremely common. Classical Latin *trivium* 'place where three roads meet' also has the meaning 'public square or meeting place': a public square is typically located at the meeting place of several roads, and hence is physically contiguous; unlike the metaphorical meaning development examined in the preceding section, both concepts belong to the same semantic field. If we now take a less obvious example, the adjective formed from classical Latin *trivium* is *triviālis* 'of the cross-roads, of the public square or meeting place' hence 'everyday, commonplace, vulgar, trivial' (> English *trivial*). We could see this meaning development also as metonymic, since there is contiguity in the conception of the public square as a place where one encounters the commonplace, and also the vulgar (from certain social standpoints). Alternatively, we could interpret the change shown by this word as broadening: 'met with in the public square and hence commonplace' broadening to 'commonplace (in any context)'.

In some cases of metonymic change a part or an attribute can refer to the whole, for instance *bigwig* 'important person', or the idiom *he hadn't a stitch on* 'he was naked'. Such changes are sometimes classified as showing a distinct category, synecdoche. French *bureau* shows two such changes in its historical sense development:

type of baize cloth > desk > office

Another classic example of this type of change is provided by Japanese *mikado* 'emperor', a metonymic use of a word literally meaning 'exalted gate', hence specifically the gate of the imperial palace. This has a striking parallel in Ottoman Turkish *bāb-i 'ālī*, literally 'high or exalted gate', applied specifically to the residence of the Grand Vizier and hence metonymically to the Grand Vizier's government. (A loan translation in French gave rise to similar use of *porte* 'gate' or more fully *la Sublime Porte* to refer to the court of the Ottoman sultanate, and hence *the Sublime Porte* also in English.) A slightly less close parallel is provided by ancient Egyptian *pr-'o* 'pharaoh', literally 'great house'.

In another frequent type an activity or product is named metonymically from a tool or instrument. For instance, *tongue* 'language' has many parallels cross-linguistically.[13] Another typical pattern is use of the name of a container for its typical contents, as in the development from 'purse, wallet' to 'roll of banknotes, money' in the case of *poke* (see section 3.1).

Metonymic changes, like other meaning changes, are often most usefully examined in relation to other changes affecting a group of words. A classic example is provided by names for the hip, thigh, and lower leg in Latin and the western Romance languages. Latin *crus* 'lower leg' was replaced in the various Romance languages by forms developed from two different words which both originally denoted parts of the legs of animals: compare on the one hand French *jambe* and Italian *gamba* (both from post-classical Latin *gamba* or *camba* 'pastern of a horse') and on the other Spanish *pierna* and Portuguese *perna* (both from Latin *perna* 'leg of mutton, ham'); we could perhaps analyse this as either metonymic change or broadening. Latin *femur* 'thigh' was replaced by the reflexes of Latin *coxa* 'hip' giving French *cuisse*, Italian *coscia*, Portuguese *coxa*, all 'thigh'; this is thus a clear example of metonymic change (unless we assume an unattested intermediate stage where the word meant both 'hip' and 'thigh', in which case we would have broadening followed by narrowing). This change may perhaps have been motivated by embarrassing homonymy between the reflexes of *femur* and the reflexes of *fimus* 'dung' (compare section 3.8). (Latin *coxa* 'hip' was in turn replaced in this meaning by a borrowing from a West Germanic form **hanka* giving French *hanche*, Italian *anca*, Spanish *anca*, Portuguese *anca*.)[14]

8.7 Is semantic change predictable?

8.7.1 Semantic divergence in different languages

Two words with the same origin often develop semantically in different ways in different languages. In section 8.6.3 we contrasted the amelioration of English *knight* with the pejoration of its German cognate *Knecht*.

The English adjective *rank* is cognate with Middle Dutch *ranc* and Middle Low German *rank*, and is probably ultimately from a variant of the same Indo-European base as *right*, with a basic sense 'upright' in

---

[13] Compare Ullmann (1962) 226 and further references there.

[14] For further discussion of this group of examples see von Wartburg (1969) 118.

proto-Germanic. Dutch and Low German both show the basic sense 'slim, slender', with the additional connotative meaning 'lank, weedy' in Dutch and the technical meaning '(of a ship) heeling, listing' in Low German. In English the word has shown radically different semantic development, showing a group of senses (now mostly obsolete) developed from the meaning 'strong, vigorous', such as 'proud', 'showy', 'impetuous', 'brave', and other senses which refer to full or large size, such as 'vigorous or luxuriant in growth', 'copious', 'excessively large', 'gross', 'luxuriant', 'of coarse quality'.

We also find many cases where a borrowed word and its donor develop in very different ways. English *qualify* is borrowed from French *qualifier* and its etymon post-classical Latin *qualificare* (compare section 6.5). In English the word has two main branches of semantic development:

- to invest with a quality or qualities (hence to become eligible for something etc.)
- to modify or moderate in some respect (hence to mitigate etc.)

French lacks anything similar to the second branch, and in Latin the sense 'to modify' appears to be restricted to British sources. From the available evidence, it appears that one of the major components of the word's meaning in English, 'to modify or moderate', can be traced back to Latin as used in Britain, but has no parallel outside Britain.

magazine is a borrowing ultimately from Arabic *maḵzan*, *maḵzin* 'storehouse'; the word entered English directly from French *magasin*, and it probably came to French from Italian *magazzino*, thus:

Arabic *maḵzan*, *maḵzin* > Italian *magazzino* > French *magasin* > English *magazine*

The word shows numerous sense developments in both English and French. In each language there is one major strand of semantic development which is not shared by the other language. In French the word shows the semantic development:

storehouse > place where merchandise is sold > shop

In English it shows the development:

storehouse
> book providing information on a specified subject or for a specified group of people

> periodical publication containing articles by various writers; especially one with stories, articles on general subjects, etc., and illustrated with pictures, or a similar publication prepared for a special-interest readership

This latter sense was borrowed back into French, usually distinguished in form as *magazine*, while the French sense 'shop' is not found in English.

Semantic divergence of this sort can thus be observed even in etymologically related groups of words, in very similar societies, even when there is frequent and intimate contact between the societies concerned. (Compare section 6.6 on the frequent continuing semantic influence of French words on the development of English words long after an initial borrowing.) This is of course in many ways similar to the situation with sound change and other changes in word form, which can lead to radical divergence in form between related words in different languages, or indeed in different varieties of a single language. However, the greater unpredictability of semantic change can result in much greater challenges for etymological research. The case is well put by Trask in a discussion of the very different semantic histories of the cognate words English *clean* and German *klein*:

English and German are fairly closely related, and, by the usual correspondences, these words ought to be cognate – and yet the German word means 'small'. Is it really possible that two such dissimilar meanings could arise from a single source? Could we just be looking at two unrelated words whose resemblance is the result of chance? As it happens, we have abundant textual evidence for earlier German, and the earliest attested sense of the German word is 'bright, shining'. With some assistance from the texts, therefore, scholars have concluded that the German word has undergone an extraordinary sequence of semantic shifts, roughly 'shining' > 'clean' > 'fine' > 'delicate' > 'small'. Everyone is therefore satisfied that the words really are cognate – but, if there had been no textual evidence to consult, possibly very few linguists would have been happy to accept such a seemingly bizarre shift in meaning, and we would remain uncertain whether the two words were actually cognate at all.

(Trask (1996) 229; reprinted Millar (2007) 281)

8.7.2 Some regular patterns

The situation presented so far in this chapter poses some serious challenges for etymological research. As we have seen, two words which are of identical etymology can develop in different ways in different languages, even when cultural and historical circumstances are very similar. Extralinguistic historical and cultural factors can have an enormous impact on the semantic development of words. Within the linguistic system, semantic development is affected by the relationships between the senses of an individual word, and also by the relationships between the meanings of different words. Semantic development may even be affected by association with other words of similar form.

In our classification of different types of semantic change, we have looked at six different categories, but we have noted that it is sometimes difficult to assign a particular change to one category or another. Also, four of the typical types of change, narrowing and broadening, and pejoration and amelioration, are essentially opposites, preventing any simple generalizations about the typical direction of change.

More fundamentally, when we attempt to evaluate whether a particular etymology is semantically plausible, we need to establish the likely pathway of semantic change. For this purpose, these categories are too broad to serve as useful tools.

More promising are some of the ideas from conceptual metaphor theory which we touched on in section 8.6.4. If some examples of metaphorical change, from different periods and in different languages, can plausibly be grouped together as showing manifestations of a more widespread underlying conceptual metaphor, then this may help us to make hypotheses about other semantic changes which may have occurred in less well-documented cases. We will look at an extended example in section 8.7.2.2. First, though, we will look at some perspectives which have developed in recent decades from another major field of linguistic research: grammaticalization studies.

8.7.2.1 *Increasing subjectification of meaning*   In important work originally grounded in the study of meaning development in grammaticalization, Elizabeth Traugott has drawn attention to some important tendencies in semantic change which are of much wider application. The following is the formulation set out in Traugott (1989):

Tendency I: Meanings based in the external described situation > meanings based in the internal (evaluative/perceptual/cognitive) described situation.

This subsumes most of the familiar meaning changes known as pejoration and amelioration...

Tendency II: Meanings based in the external or internal described situation > meanings based in the textual and metalinguistic situation.

By 'textual situation' I mean the situation of text-construction. Examples include the development of lexical and morphological forms into connectives coding cohesion,

as in the shift from *þa hwile þe* 'the time that' (coding an external described situation) > 'during' (coding the textual situation). By 'metalinguistic situation' I mean the situation of performing a linguistic act. Examples include the shift from a mental-state to a speech-act verb meaning; for instance, in the early 1500's *observe* had the mental-verb meaning 'perceive (that)' (coding an internal described situation), and by 1605 it had come to be used as a speech-act verb in the sense 'state that' (coding the metalinguistic situation).
Tendency III: Meanings tend to become increasingly based in the speaker's subjective belief state/attitude toward the proposition.

This tendency subsumes the shift of temporal to concessive *while* and a large number of other changes. Among them is the development of scalar particles such as *very*: borrowed in Middle English from Old French *verai* 'true' (a cognitive evaluation), in Early Modern English it became a scalar particle as in *the very height of her career* (a subjective evaluation)

(Traugott (1989) 34–5)

Traugott identifies what these three tendencies have in common as the increasing 'subjectification' of meaning, a process in which speakers or writers 'come over time to develop meanings for L[exemes] that encode or externalize their perspectives and attitudes as constrained by the communicative world of the speech event, rather than by the so-called "real-world" characteristics of the event or situation referred to' (Traugott and Dasher (2005) 30). We saw an example in section 8.1 in the meaning development shown by the modal verb *may*:

'to be strong or able, to have power'
> the (dynamic, or root, modal) meaning 'to be able (to do something)'
> the (epistemic modal) meaning 'it may be the case that', 'this may happen'

Compare also the development of *must* from (deontic modal) 'you must do this' to (epistemic modal) 'this must surely happen soon'.

An example of the usefulness of this sort of framework in etymological research is provided by the etymology of English *merry*. This is an inherited Germanic word. The same proto-Germanic base gives rise to Middle Dutch *mergelijc* 'pleasant, agreeable', and also the English derivative noun *mirth* which similarly has a parallel in Middle Dutch *merchte, merechte* 'joy, pleasure'. A good formal match is provided by Old High German *murg* 'short', and Gothic *gamaurgjan* 'to shorten', which have Indo-European cognates with similar meanings, including Sanskrit *muhur* 'suddenly', Avestan *mərəzu-* 'short', Sogdian *mwrzk* 'short', and ancient Greek *brachús* 'short'. The problem is how to connect the English and Dutch words with the others semantically. A hypothetical semantic development from 'short' to 'that shortens or whiles away time' to 'entertaining, pleasant' is made much more convincing by an extensive set of parallels in English and in other Germanic languages: English *pastime*; use of English *short* 'to shorten' in the sense 'to make to appear short, to beguile (the time, the way) with sport or stories' (and similar uses of the related *shorten* and obsolete *shurt*); Middle High German *kurzwīle* (from *kurz* short and *wīle* period) 'short while, whiling away of time, pastime, pleasure'; Old Icelandic *skemta* 'to amuse, entertain' (from *skammur* 'short'). We can also see that this works well in terms of the subjectification of meaning: all of these meaning changes show a shift from 'objectively short in duration' to 'apparently short, in a way which is pleasant for the speaker'.

However, this sort of framework rather conspicuously excludes a good many of those semantic changes which depend upon extralinguistic factors, as Traugott and Dasher acknowledge:

> Irregular meaning changes seem to occur primarily in the nominal domain, which is particularly susceptible to extralinguistic factors such as change in the nature or the social construction of the referent. For example, the referents of towns, armor, rockets, vehicles, pens, communication devices, etc., have changed considerably over time, as have concepts of disease, hence the meanings attached to the words referring to them have changed in ways not subject to linguistic generalization.
>
> (Traugott and Dasher (2005) 3–4)

Scientific and technological advances of the kind exemplified here have an enormous impact on the semantic development of many words, especially nouns (numerically by far the largest class in the lexicon of any language). As we have already seen, this is by no means the only area where cultural and historical factors are crucial to explaining semantic change.

Additionally, problems arise for etymological research from just how broadly applicable the process of subjectification is. If it is indeed common to many instances of semantic change this is a major insight in linguistic research. However, this is less of a virtue for the particular requirements of etymological research. Where we find respectively less and more subjective meanings, Traugott's research helps us to see the likelihood that the more subjective meaning has developed from the less subjective one. However, many of the most perplexing problems can arise in trying to identify the specific pathway by which such change has occurred.

An example of this is provided by the word *pagan*. It has not been seriously doubted that post-classical Latin *paganus* 'pagan' (> English *pagan*) ultimately shows a semantic development of classical Latin *pāgānus* 'of or belonging to a country community, civilian', also (as noun) 'inhabitant of a country community, civilian (opposed to *mīles* soldier)'. This probably occurred in the fourth century AD. The meaning development was almost certainly from less to more evaluative: 'of or belonging to a country community' is a relatively neutral term in comparison with 'pagan', the defining characteristic of the non-Christian other from the perspective of the early Christian Church. However, the precise path of the semantic change is much less certain. *OED* summarizes three main possibilities (I omit supporting examples for the first and third theories from the ancient historian Orosius in the early fifth century):

(i) The older sense of classical Latin *pāgānus* is 'of the country, rustic' (also as noun). It has been argued that the transferred use reflects the fact that the ancient idolatry lingered on in the rural villages and hamlets after Christianity had been generally accepted in the towns and cities of the Roman Empire.

(ii) The more common meaning of classical Latin *pāgānus* is 'civilian, non-militant' (adjective and noun). Christians called themselves *mīlitēs* 'enrolled soldiers' of Christ, members of his militant church, and applied to non-Christians the term applied by soldiers to all who were 'not enrolled in the army'.

(iii) The sense 'heathen' arose from an interpretation of *pāgānus* as denoting a person who was outside a particular group or community, hence 'not of the city' or 'rural'.

(OED3 at *pagan* n. and adj., etymology section)*

Here the main problem is a gap in our evidence: we simply do not have the crucial early examples of the use of the word in its new sense that would enable us to see the exact circumstances of its development. We have a good knowledge of what the word meant in classical Latin, and we have some knowledge of the cultural circumstances of the period, but this is not sufficient to categorically confirm or deny any of these three possibilities. Further close study of the documentary evidence concerning Christian culture in this period could perhaps help to resolve the issue, but as the question was already debated by the time of Orosius in the early fifth century it is perhaps unlikely that we will ever reach any definitive answer.

8.7.2.2 *Metaphor in cognitive linguistics*   In a now classic study in a chapter of her 1990 book *From Etymology to Pragmatics*, Eve Sweetser examines 'English perception-verbs in an Indo-European context' (Sweetser (1990) 23–48). This study is grounded in the assumption from cognitive linguistics (common to much other linguistic work as well) that the way the human mind structures perceptions of the external world is reflected to some extent in linguistic structures:

> Linguistic categorization depends not just on our naming of distinctions that exist in the world, but also on our metaphorical and metonymic structuring of our perceptions of the world.

(Sweetser (1990) 9)

Very interestingly for our purposes, Sweetser looks at both bidirectional and unidirectional relationships. For instance, two common semantic sources for vision verbs are identified as:

(a) metaphors of physical touching or manipulation, such as English *to catch sight of* or Latin *percipere* (> English *to perceive*), which is formed < *per-* 'thoroughly' and *capere* 'to take, seize, lay hold of'

(b) metaphors of control; e.g. English *wake*, *watch*, and (via French and Latin) *surveillance* and *vigil* are all derived from an Indo-European root with the probable sense 'to be strong, to be lively', as shown for example by Latin *vegēre* 'to rouse, excite, to be lively or active', *vigēre* 'to be vigorous' (see Sweetser (1990) 32–3)

Of these, source (a) appears to be unidirectional, words for physical touching or manipulation giving rise to vision verbs but not vice versa, whereas the relationship in (b) appears to be bidirectional, as shown e.g. by English *to keep an eye on someone* which shows development from 'sight' to 'oversight, control'.

Similarly, words for physical sight give rise to words for knowledge or intellection, arising from the role of vision as a primary source of data, hence *I see what you mean* or again *perceive*. However, the reverse does not appear to be the case, and so this relationship may be seen to be (as a general rule) unidirectional. A rare exception is perhaps shown by English *recognize*, which shows the development:

'to acknowledge'
> 'to identify (something which has been known before)'

> 'to identify (a person from their physical appearance)'

In the case of meaning developments from 'to hear' to 'to listen to, to heed' (and thence to 'to obey'), there is a rather stronger counterexample in French *entendre* 'to hear', a development from the earlier sense 'to take heed of, to understand', ultimately from Latin *intendere* 'to stretch out, to direct one's attention to' (see Sweetser (1990) 34–5).

Traditionally minded etymologists may find much that is reassuringly familiar in Sweetser's approach. Clearly a fundamental factor is the collecting and classifying of examples, in order to establish which changes in meaning are common and thus likely to be found also in other, less well-evidenced, cases. Many of her observations are based on the analysis of changes occurring during the documented histories of words (as with French *entendre*) or which can be inferred reasonably confidently from the composition of complex words (as with Latin *percipere*, formed from *per-* and *capere*). In such cases the analysis is generally uncontroversial, and the desiderata for further research seem clear:

(i) analysis of meaning developments which cross other semantic fields (or domains, as the underlying relationships between meanings are normally called in the cognitive linguistics tradition)

(ii) analysis of further cross-linguistic data, in the areas studied by Sweetser (since the set of data on which her observations are based is relatively small)

In the almost two decades since the publication of Sweetser's 1990 study, there has been relatively little work in this direction, either inside or outside the cognitive linguistics tradition.[15] This is regrettable, since the identification of pathways of semantic change which occur frequently cross-linguistically would provide a powerful aid to further etymological research.

Much of Sweetser's work focuses on meaning change in the reconstructed past, often at the level of reconstructed Indo-European roots. This is rather more controversial, and we will consider this in the following section.

8.7.2.3 *Reconstructing meanings and changes in meaning*   In etymological reconstruction at the level of proto-languages, it is customary to reconstruct roots, which are assigned glosses, reflecting what is taken to be the common meaning shown by the words derived from this root. Thus in

---

[15] For a recent contribution see Allan (2008).

Pokorny (1959–69), which remains the standard comparative dictionary of Indo-European etymology, a reconstructed root with a gloss stands at the head of each entry.[16] The same is found in smaller comparative dictionaries such as Watkins (2000). It is worth looking in a little detail at what sorts of entities these roots are and what the glosses assigned to them are intended to convey. Hence for a moment we will turn aside from semantics and take up some topics in morphology which we touched on in chapter 4.

In some cases, a complete word has parallels in several branches of Indo-European, and can be reconstructed with some confidence for the parent language. This is the case with the kinship terms *mother*, *father*, *brother* which we looked at in section 1.2.4. Each word has cognates in a number of other branches of Indo-European, and we can reconstruct the proto-Indo-European words *mātēr*, *pǝtēr*, *bhrātēr*. We can recognize *-tēr-* as a termination common to all of these words, although we cannot establish any further etymology for the roots to which it is attached with any confidence.

In the majority of cases, the situation is rather different, and what we find reflected among the 'cognates' are in fact the scattered remains of a morphological family, showing various different suffixes and various different modifications of the root; that is, the words that survive are cognates only at one or more removes. The typical morphology of a word in proto-Indo-European can be represented as follows:

a root, with a certain ablaut grade;
perhaps + an extension (which did not usually alter meaning);
usually + a suffix (which conveyed information about word class and
   often also about meaning, and which could also show ablaut
   variation);
+ inflectional endings

The root is common to all words in the same morphological family, but various differences of meaning and/or grammatical function are conveyed by differences of ablaut grade and suffixation. The words belonging to any such family which survive in the various documented Indo-European languages will typically reflect only a small fragment of the original family. Often we will find that one derivative formation survives in one language, a second in another language, a third in another language, and so on. In each case there will probably also have been subsequent morphological and semantic

---

[16] Compare note 18 below on the urgent need for revision of this dictionary.

change, between the proto-Indo-European stage and the stage reflected by our documented words. By comparative analysis of the morphological and phonological histories of many other words, we may be able to establish that this set of words can plausibly be referred to the same Indo-European root, showing suffixes whose function we may or may not be able to reconstruct with some confidence. However, this is not necessarily the same thing as being certain of exactly what the historical sequence of derivational relationships was in a group of related words, nor exactly how their meaning development unfolded.[17] As we saw in chapter 4, study of the recorded history of languages shows that there are many possible permutations for the relationships among a group of morphologically related words. The 'meaning' that can be reconstructed for a proto-Indo-European root is typically no more than the semantic common denominator for a set of words which we can plausibly refer to a single root. The case is well put by Watkins:

A word of caution should be entered about the semantics of the roots. It is perhaps more hazardous to attempt to reconstruct meaning than to reconstruct linguistic form, and the meaning of a root can only be extrapolated from the meanings of its descendants. Often these diverge sharply from one another, and the scholar is reduced in practice to inferring only what seems a reasonable, or even merely possible, semantic common denominator. The result is that reconstructed words, and particularly roots, are often assigned hazy, vague, or unspecific meanings. This is doubtless quite illusory; a portmanteau meaning for a root should not be confused with the specific meaning of a derivative of that root at a particular time and place. The apparent haziness in meaning of a given Indo-European root often simply reflects the fact that with the passage of several thousand years the different words derived from this root in divergent languages have undergone semantic changes that are no longer recoverable in detail.

(Watkins (2000) xxi)

It is in this context that work such as Sweetser's (see section 8.7.2.2) can encounter some difficulties, if cognitive motivations are sought for meaning changes reconstructed for the remote linguistic past. At the very least, we must exercise caution if much of the support for thinking that a particular meaning change is natural or is frequent cross-linguistically depends upon reconstructed stages of linguistic history.[18]

---

[17] For a useful discussion of this topic see Clackson (2007) 190–1.

[18] Sweetser (1990) is very critical of the semantic side of much work in Indo-European etymology, and exemplifies this by commenting on material taken from Pokorny (1959–69). However, it should be noted that those entries from Pokorny on which she comments

8.8 Some practical examples

Just as we looked in section 7.7 at practical examples of etymological arguments based on word form, we will look in this section at some practical examples of arguments based on word meaning.

8.8.1 Parallel semantic developments lending support to an etymology

We have already noted that an important step in establishing support for a particular etymology can be finding another word history which appears to show a similar semantic development.

Italian *marrone* 'a chestnut' (from which French *marron* was borrowed, and thence ultimately the English colour term *maroon*) is of uncertain etymology. One suggestion is that it comes from a common Romance base with the meaning 'stone, rock', and this can perhaps be supported by a semantic comparison with the Spanish dialect word *berrueca* 'a large kind of chestnut' which is related to Spanish *berrueco* 'rocky reef'.

Modern English has numerous words meaning 'drunk, intoxicated with alcohol' which result from metaphorical uses of past participles of verbs referring to various types of physical harm, such as *smashed, stoned* (now more commonly used with reference to drugs), *wrecked*, etc. These parallels lend weight to the hypothesis that recent British slang *mullered* 'intoxicated' (recorded from 1995) is derived from *muller* 'to ruin, wreck, or destroy' (recorded from 1990, and very probably of Romani origin, from a verb ultimately related to Sanskrit *mr̥-* 'to die').

The Caribbean English word *mesple*, denoting the sapodilla, a type of evergreen tropical American tree with edible fruit, probably ultimately shows a borrowing of Dutch *mispel* denoting the medlar, a small bushy tree related to the rose which bears apple-like fruits. This supposition is supported by the fact that Caribbean English also has the name *naseberry* for the sapodilla (as already touched on in sections 2.6 and 7.4.5), showing a borrowing of Spanish *néspera* and Portuguese *nêspera* 'medlar' with

critically (Sweetser (1990) 24–5), '1. *ken-*' and '*kwelp-*', involve etymologies which are accepted by very few other researchers, partly on the basis of semantic implausibility. On this difficult area of research compare also the useful discussion in Fox (1995) 201–6. On Pokorny's dictionary compare Ringe (2006) 65: 'Pokorny 1959 is badly out of date; moreover, it errs extravagantly on the side of inclusion, listing every word known to the author that might conceivably reflect a PIE [proto-Indo-European] lexeme if one's etymological standards are not too strict.'

remodelling of the ending of the word as a result of association with words ending in *-berry*. In this instance, *mesple* and *naseberry* both arose in the same geographical area, but in different historical periods, *naseberry* being first found in 1679, while *mesple* is not found until 1979, and probably entered English through Dutch Creole. It is therefore likely that the two cases are genuine parallels, rather than that the one has provided a model for the other.

8.8.2 Formal similarity, but no plausible semantic connection

English *nick* 'to make a notch or cut in (something)' corresponds exactly in form to Middle Dutch *nicken* 'to bow, to bend', Middle Low German *nicken* 'to bend over, sink down', Middle High German *nicken* 'to bend, press down', but no convincing semantic connection can be made.

prank 'a malicious trick; a wicked deed; a deception or scheme intended to harm, a hoax; a magical trick or feat, a conjuring trick, a practical joke, a lark, a capriciously foolish act' is of unknown origin. The obvious etymology on a formal basis would be to attempt to connect the word with the verb *prank* 'to dress or deck in a smart, bright, or ostentatious manner, to decorate, to dress up, to give a particular (misleading) appearance to, to embellish, to make an ostentatious display (with), to show off, to behave ostentatiously', but it is hard to establish any semantic connection, unless it is perhaps via the meanings 'deception' and 'to dress up, to give a particular (misleading) appearance to'.

It is useful to contrast the situation in both of these cases with the sorts of arguments on the basis of word form that we encountered in chapter 7. If there were a formal difficulty, there would at least be a clear procedure for identifying the difficulty, and for trying to resolve it. We would look for possible explanations from what is known about the phonological history of other words in the same period, or from formal developments which are typologically common. Even if this did not lead to a solution, it would allow us to clarify the difficulty, e.g. 'perhaps related, but the difference in the stem vowel is difficult to explain'. Our present state of knowledge about what is and is not likely in semantic change seldom allows us even to formulate the difficulties as precisely as this.

In section 2.4 we looked at words which originated as lexicalized compounds, although this fact may be entirely opaque from the modern form and meaning of the word. In some instances we may suspect such a history, but be unable to provide any semantic explanation for the compound. *prial* 'three of a kind (especially in cards)' occurs earliest in the sixteenth and seventeenth centuries in the following forms:

parriall, paire royall, paroyal, paroyall, parreiall, par-royall, perryal, perryall, pair royal

Comparison with the recorded form history of *pair* and *royal* points strongly to the word being a lexicalized compound of these two words, but if so the semantic motivation is unclear. There seems no reason why a 'royal pair' should number three; perhaps we might speculate that it is because 'royal' is good, and three cards are better than a pair, but this seems tenuous, and is unsupported by other similar uses of *royal*. Perhaps it could be connected with the fact that there are three court cards, i.e. king, queen, and jack, in each suit (compare much later terms such as *royal flush*), but this does not really explain why three of a kind should be called a royal pair. (The term *royal pontoon* occurs in the card game pontoon, denoting a hand of three sevens which beats all pairs totalling twenty-one which would otherwise win the game, but is first recorded very much later.) The postposition of the adjective, i.e. the fact that the compound appears to be *pair royal*, not **royal pair*, would perhaps suggest that it is modelled on a compound or phrase in a language in which adjectives normally follow the nouns they modify (perhaps French, given the date and cultural context), but no such model has been identified. Of course, it is always possible that there may be no historical connection with *pair* and *royal* at all, and this form may simply show a folk-etymological alteration.

We can also encounter similar difficulties with apparent derivative formations. *potty* appears to be a derivative of the noun *pot* 'vessel (of earthenware, etc.)' in the adjective-forming suffix *-y*, and this readily explains the word in its (rare) sense 'of tea: that tastes of the pot; strong, stewed' (recorded in 1901 in an isolated example). However, the semantic connection is harder to trace in the case of two groups of depreciative senses shown by *potty*:

(a) feeble, indifferent; petty, insignificant, unimpressive; easy to manage, accomplish, or deal with; easy, simple. (Recorded from the mid nineteenth century; now rare.)
(b) crazy, mad; out of one's mind; eccentric; madly in love; madly enthusiastic (about), madly keen (on). (Recorded from the early twentieth century.)

Group (a) senses, which are recorded from the mid nineteenth century onwards, were perhaps suggested by *tin-pot* in its metaphorical sense 'of little worth' (recorded from the early nineteenth century), although there is perhaps also some semantic association with *petty* on the basis of similarity of word form (compare section 8.5.2): crucially, though, there is little to help us decide the likelihood of this, other than the researcher's own intuitions about what is or is not plausible, and that is not a very satisfactory basis for etymological decision making. *potty* in these meanings could conceivably be a different word of different origin, perhaps a variant of *petty*, maybe as a result of some association with *pot* or (as seems more likely on semantic grounds) *tin-pot*.

Group (b) senses, recorded from the early twentieth century onwards, were perhaps suggested by earlier metaphorical formations such as *cracked-pot* or *crack-pot*, and by proverbial expressions which similarly conceptualize the head of a foolish person as a cracked pot. Here we may perhaps feel on rather more promising ground in assuming that these senses of *potty* do show a derivative of the word *pot*, since not only do we have a group of potential models, but we can also make a link with the broader conceptual metaphor 'THE MIND IS A CONTAINER' which has been suggested in research on conceptual metaphor theory.

8.8.3 One word or two?

In some cases a historical or etymological dictionary may group material together as probably showing a single word history, but at the same time flag uncertainty about whether this is in fact the case. The verb *pink* shows various senses which the *OED* groups under the heading 'senses related to cutting or piercing', plus a further sense 'to adorn, beautify; to deck, trick (out)' (earliest recorded in 1558) which it is difficult to relate to the other uses. It is possible that it may show a development from the earliest recorded sense of the word, 'to ornament (cloth or leather) by cutting or punching eyelet holes, slits, etc., especially to display a contrasting lining or undergarment; to perforate' (earliest recorded in 1486; compare the use of modern *pinking shears* partly for decoration and partly to prevent material from fraying). Alternatively it is quite possible that it may show an independent and unrelated word.

Similarly, *pickle* meaning (in baseball) 'to hit (the ball) very hard' seems to be a specific sense of *pickle* 'to preserve in pickle', but if so the semantic motivation is rather unclear. Cases like these really differ from *prank* or *nick* in section 8.8.2 only in the respect that lexicographers have felt the balance of probabilities more in favour of a common origin, but a completely satisfactory explanation remains elusive.

English *as thin as a rake* (earliest recorded in late Middle English in Chaucer) is usually assumed to show a metaphorical application of the tool name *rake*, the spokes or teeth at the end of the long handle presumably suggesting a skeletal appearance. However, this interpretation has been challenged by (among others) Lockwood, who suggests that the metaphor is unlikely:

> Perhaps it was on a summer's day as we were raking together the cuttings on the lawn, or perhaps we were just watching some one else perform this laudable service, when quite suddenly the familiar phrase 'thin as a rake' crossed our minds. How often has one heard that expression! How naturally it comes! But, on this particular occasion, why we cannot say, we paused to wonder what on earth was thin about a rake. True, it has a long slender handle, but one doesn't associate even the most slender handle with thinness. Furthermore other implements, such as a hoe, have similar handles, but nobody says 'thin as a hoe'. The really distinctive things about a rake are its teeth. It is on these that attention is concentrated. They may be strong, sharp, they may be worn, bent or broken, but are they ever thin? However one looks at it, thinness is definitely not a property of a rake.

> (Lockwood (1995) 169)

Lockwood (1973, also 1995) instead suggests that *as thin as a rake* reflects a borrowing from a Scandinavian language of a word related to Norwegian (Nynorsk) *rak* 'skeleton, dead body, emaciated animal' and probably also to Old Icelandic *hrak-*, recorded in the derivatives *hrakligr* 'wretched' and *hrakmagr* 'wretchedly thin' (see summary in Lockwood (1995) 169–71); this is probably ultimately related to Old Icelandic *hrekja* 'to worry, vex'. A similar borrowing could perhaps be reflected by English regional *rackling*, *reckling*, or *rickling* 'small or weak animal, runt', with *i*-mutation caused by the suffix. If this etymology is adopted, a formal problem remains, since such a borrowing would show a short vowel, but *rake* in *as thin as a rake* shows a long one. Lockwood explains the long vowel as resulting from folk-etymological association with *rake* (the tool); this is plausible, since as we have seen in section 7.4.5 folk-etymological associations often show little or no semantic component, and substitution of *rake* for **rak* may have been motivated simply by the fact that **rak* did not survive outside this expression in English and hence the expression was opaque. However, the fundamental difficulty is in deciding whether the metaphor *as thin as a rake* (i.e. as the tool) is in fact inherently implausible: some researchers have found it plausible, others not. There are no very exact semantic parallels:

perhaps compare *as thin as a rail/toothpick/lath*, although these objects are obviously all thin for their whole length. Study of medieval images of rakes shows that they typically were more similar to a modern soil rake than to a modern lawn rake, i.e. they generally had a straight cross-beam at the end with stout teeth attached, rather than the fan-shaped pattern of slender spokes shown by a modern lawn rake. They were typically used by peasants who could not afford the larger and heavier harrow which was pulled by a beast of burden. Lightness and slenderness of construction would have been essential, so that the tool could be conveniently drawn across the earth. (We will look further at this sort of approach based on study of the material culture of the past in section 8.10.) The *Middle English Dictionary* also includes 'hoe' among the meanings it records for Middle English *rake*. We might note that a hoe is characteristically thin for its whole length, having only a small blade at one end. However, we have already seen that Lockwood comments (correctly) 'nobody says "thin as a hoe"'. Unless convincing parallels can be found, it is hard to see what evidence can convince the doubters that the metaphor is plausible after all. It is even harder to see what could convince those who find the metaphor plausible that Lockwood is correct and an alternative etymology should be sought.

8.9 Arguments based on form and meaning contrasted

As we have seen from the practical examples in section 8.8, semantic change often presents problems for etymological research of a quite different nature from those presented by change in word form. Work in semantics lacks any tool comparable to the historical grammar, enabling us to assess any hypothesized change against the background of the known phonological and morphological history of a particular language. This is largely because semantic change does not affect groups of words simultaneously or within a defined historical period. Instead it affects words individually. In this respect it is more like sporadic sound changes, such as metathesis in English. However, it is unlike these in its complexity, and in the extent to which semantic change in one word may be shaped by the meaning relationships with a large group of other words. In this respect probably every instance of semantic change is unique, even though we may be able to identify general tendencies, and also find specific parallels in other periods or in other languages which at least show a reasonable degree of similarity. A diagram can be useful in

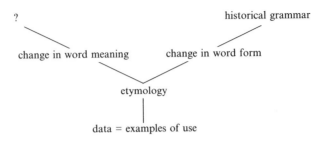

Fig 8.1 A framework for etymological research

summarizing the basic differences between change in word form and change in word meaning as they affect etymological research – see figure 8.1.

We employ etymological reasoning as a tool in interpreting data of actual linguistic usage, in order to establish a coherent word history. This will necessarily involve analysis of both change in word form and change in word meaning. So far as change in word form is concerned, this analysis will involve interaction with historical grammar. The term historical grammar has two related meanings: it is the name of a methodology, and it is also the name of an artefact of linguistic historiography, whether that exists in the form of a single book, or more realistically in the form of many separate books, plus contributions to the literature in articles etc. Etymological hypotheses can be assessed against the existing body of data in the historical grammar (in this second sense), employing the methodology of historical grammar (in the first sense); new discoveries or reassessments can then be incorporated in the body of knowledge in the historical grammar (in the second sense). If we turn now to meaning change, the methodology of historical semantics exists, and has been the main topic of this chapter, but there is no corresponding artefact of linguistic historiography to which we can refer. There is no 'historical semantics' of English or any other language analogous to the historical grammar. We can look for cases of parallel developments in the scholarly literature or in historical dictionaries. Here tools such as the *Historical Thesaurus of English* now available for the English language are an invaluable aid, in allowing us to explore how similar meanings have developed in other word histories at different times. However, there is no systematic classification of changes to which we can refer, for the simple reason that no theoretical approach has been found which makes this possible, and the number of variables at play in any semantic change makes it very unlikely that such an approach could ever succeed.

8.10 Etymology and extralinguistic factors

As we noted in section 8.7.2.1 and at various other points in the course of this book, one of the most significant factors influencing many instances of meaning change, and reducing the extent to which we can identify regular patterns of change, is interaction with external, non-linguistic cultural and material history.

An important trend in etymological research in the early twentieth century was what is known by the German name *Wörter und Sachen*, 'words and things'. This was the name of a journal founded in 1909. The scholarly tradition associated with this journal stressed the importance of looking at connections between word histories and the history of material culture, and also of looking at what linguistic history can reveal about the material (and intellectual) culture of the past.[19] We saw in section 8.1 how the semantic development of the word *toilet* is closely correlated with the development of dressing and bathing habits in Western culture, and subsequently with the development of sanitary arrangements. If we were trying to trace the history of the word *toilet* from scratch, we would have to piece together all of this information about cultural history in order to be able to trace the semantic history of the word in its proper cultural context. In investigating *as thin as a rake* in section 8.8.3 we touched on how an examination of medieval tool shapes and functions can be helpful in examining a difficult etymology. However, when we are studying earlier or less well-documented stages in linguistic history, we often find that difficulties in specifying precisely when and where a particular linguistic development occurred make it very difficult to correlate linguistic and material culture in the way that we would ideally like to do.

English *plough* provides a good illustration. It is helpful to look in a little detail at some of the documentation offered in *OED3* for this etymology. Late Old English *plōh*, *plōg* is related to words in other Germanic languages, summarized in *OED* as follows:

Old Frisian *plōch*, *plōg* (West Frisian *ploege*, *ploech*, North Frisian *pluwge*), Middle Dutch *ploech* (Dutch *ploeg*), Middle Low German *plōch*, *plūch*, Old High German *phluog* (8th cent.; Middle High German *phluoc*, German *Pflug*), Old Icelandic *plógr* (in the poem *Rígsþula*, which was perhaps composed in the 10th cent., but shows probable reworking, perhaps in England, in the 11th cent.; also in Skaldic poetry of

---

[19] On the history of this movement from the perspective of etymological research see especially Malkiel (1993).

the mid 11th cent.), Norn (Shetland) *plug*, Old Swedish *plogher* (Swedish *plog*), Old Danish *plogh* (Danish *plov*), all in sense 'plough'.

OED goes on to comment on possible further relationships:

The Germanic words are apparently related also to post-classical Latin *plovum* (mid 7th cent.), Italian regional (northern) *piò*, and perhaps also to classical Latin *plaumorati* (in an isolated attestation in Pliny, where it is apparently a loanword, and refers to a new type of plough with two wheels in use in Gaul; the word is sometimes regarded as plural (or genitive singular) and a (nominative) singular *plaumoratum* constructed, but the context is unclear).

In the surviving Old English records the word is not found at all denoting the implement, although currency in this sense may be implied by the (rare and only late Old English) compounds *plōgesland*, *plōgaland* 'ploughland' and *plōgagang* 'plough-gang'. The word is found (again rarely and only in late Old English) in the senses 'name given to a unit of land capable of being tilled by a team of oxen in a year' and 'team of horses or oxen used for ploughing'. The usual Old English word for a plough is *sulh*, which survived in western and south-western English dialects as *sullow*. These were the geographical areas generally least influenced by Norse settlers, and this, combined with the late date of attestation, and the fact that apparently secondary senses occur earlier than the apparently basic sense denoting the implement, has led to a frequent supposition that the English word is a borrowing from Norse. However, early evidence for the word in the Scandinavian languages is also scarce, hence the philological details about the early occurrences of the word given in the *OED* listing of forms quoted above, although the situation is complicated by the general scarcity of very early documentation for these languages. The *OED* comments as follows:

The word also does not appear to be early in the Scandinavian languages, where the earlier name appears to have been *arðr* ... which survives in Norwegian as *ar* a small plough (... hence perhaps originally denoting an earlier and simpler implement than the *plógr*), and it has been suggested by some scholars that the early Scandinavian word was in fact a borrowing from Old English. The word is also not found in Gothic, which has *hoha*. It is perhaps most likely that the word occurred earliest in continental West Germanic (but not English, and not originally in either East Germanic or North Germanic), and was borrowed thence, either directly or indirectly, into both Old English and early Scandinavian. However, even this much is far from certain.

The connections between the Germanic words, post-classical Latin *plovum*, and classical Latin *plaumorati* are also much disputed, as are the possible connections between these and various words in Slavonic languages and Albanian which *OED* summarizes as follows:

Compare Old Russian *plug"* (Russian *plug*), Polish *plug*, Czech *pluh*, Lithuanian *pliūgas, plūgas* (probably all < German or other Germanic languages, although some have argued that these show an inherited Slavonic word ultimately of Indo-European origin); compare also Albanian *plug* plough. Perhaps compare also Albanian *plor*, Albanian regional (Tosk) *plúar*, (Gheg) *plúer* ploughshare, tip of a wooden plough, of uncertain origin.

On the possibilities of establishing a secure further etymology *OED* comments:

As regards the further etymology, attempts have been made (in spite of the difficulties posed by the initial *p* and by the restricted distribution among Germanic languages) to regard the word as an inherited item in Germanic, and hence to link it with either of two different Indo-European bases, or alternatively with the Germanic base of German *pflegen* . . . ; alternatively, it has been explained as a loan either from another Indo-European language (perhaps Gaulish in view of Pliny's *plaumorati*) or from a non-Indo-European language. It seems unlikely that a consensus view will be reached.

(On the problems posed by Germanic words with initial *p*- compare section 6.8.)

If we now consider the possibilities for a *Wörter und Sachen* approach, we can see that assumptions about changes in ploughing technology, or about naming of different types of ploughs, occur at various points in this etymology. Pliny identifies *plaumorati* as the name of a particular type of plough which is new and is used in Gaul. Old English and Old Norse both appear to have had earlier names for the plough, and it is tempting to imagine that the borrowing of a new word reflects a technological distinction, although as we have seen from examples in chapters 5 and 6 this is not necessarily the case. The absence of the word in Gothic as well suggests that the word may well have been a borrowing into continental West Germanic, probably after the date when English was already established in England, and this in turn could reflect a technological distinction of some sort. It is possible that collaboration with archaeologists or ancient or medieval historians might provide further leads in this case, but this is perhaps unlikely, since at each of the important junctures in the history of this word we are looking at really rather broad historical periods, and there are also basic uncertainties about the chain of events and their causation. At each of these junctures, borrowing may or may not have occurred; if it did, it may or may not have been because of a difference in technology, or because the word was useful in marking an existing technological distinction, and it could have happened at any point in a period of several centuries or more.

Such uncertainties plague attempts to apply a *Wörter und Sachen* approach at a considerable time depth, especially when one is dealing with early history or pre-history, although they do not mean that the endeavour is not worthwhile. Celebrated achievements have been made in the study of Indo-European kinship terms, for instance, and in the exploration of the wider vocabulary of social relations within the household. It is no coincidence that (as noted in section 8.7.2.3) this is a semantic field where we are able to reconstruct a number of Indo-European word forms (rather than simply root forms) and their associated meanings with reasonable confidence. For recent summaries and further references to work on reconstructing Indo-European culture and society through linguistic reconstruction see Mallory and Adams (2006), or Fortson (2004) 16–47. Particular problems arise when one tries to assess the significance of the absence of a reconstructable word with a particular meaning, as noted by Ringe:

The most difficult problem is assessing the gaps that we inevitably find. For instance, it comes as no surprise that there was no PIE [proto-Indo-European] word for 'iron', since there are numerous indications that PIE was spoken before the Iron Age. But what about the fact that there is also no reconstructable word for 'finger'? Obviously speakers of the language had fingers, and they must have had a word for them; the fact that we cannot reconstruct it can only be the result of its loss in all the major subgroups (or all but one). The hard fact is that linguistic evidence relentlessly degrades and self-destructs over time, and that imposes an inexorable limit on what can be reconstructed.

(Ringe (2006) 65–6)

An area of etymological research where the consideration of external, non-linguistic factors is unavoidable is the study of the etymology of names. These in turn are often inter-related with the etymologies of other words. A good example of this interaction is found in the etymology of the English word *penguin*, which is first attested in 1577 denoting a penguin, and in 1578 denoting the great auk, a now-extinct bird of the northern hemisphere which in its appearance and habits closely resembled penguins (which are found only in the southern hemisphere). The word is found in several other European languages within a few decades of its first appearance in English, but in all of these it probably shows a borrowing from English, either directly or indirectly. Welsh *pengwin* 'great auk' is probably also from English, although in fact the likeliest etymon of the English word is Welsh *pen gwyn* 'white head'. In spite of the chronology of the earliest attestations, it is likely that the English word earliest denoted the great auk, and was subsequently transferred to the penguin. However, this explanation encounters a difficulty, since the great auk did not have a white head. A possible solution to this problem lies in a place name, *Penguin Island* in Newfoundland. This is first recorded in 1589 (as *Island of Penguin*), although in a reported narrative of events which took place fifty years earlier. The immediate assumption seems simply to be that the place was so called because many great auks were encountered there. Thus if the place name did date from the early sixteenth century that might help us to antedate the word *penguin* and demonstrate that its earliest meaning was indeed 'great auk' and not 'penguin', but it would not help solve the etymological difficulty. However, another meaning of Welsh *pen* is 'headland', and it is thus possible that *Penguin Island* may reflect a Welsh name meaning 'white headland', a supposition which is supported by a 1584 reference (in an account of a mythical medieval voyage) to 'the white rocke of Pengwyn'. Welsh speakers were certainly present in the European voyages of exploration to this area, as also were Breton speakers in large numbers. In Breton a place name 'white headland' would have differed from the Welsh only in spelling; hence the place may plausibly have been given either a Welsh or a Breton name, which was subsequently adopted in English as well.[20] *penguin* 'great auk' would therefore derive from the place name, rather than vice versa. This etymology illustrates some fundamental points about name etymologies: *Penguin Island* refers to an entity, in this instance a particular place in North America; when the name was originally given, it was probably a descriptive name of some sort, but we cannot infer from the name's subsequent use what the original basis for the name may have been, nor even which language the name was originally given in.

In the next chapter we will look in more detail at the etymologies of names, and in particular at the connections they often entail between intralinguistic and extralinguistic factors.

---

[20] For all of the documentation drawn upon here see *OED3* at *penguin* n., and for further discussion of the underlying research see Thier (2007). For other recent studies very much in the *Wörter und Sachen* tradition by the same author see (on *paddle*) Thier (2005) and (on *sail* and related issues) Thier (2003a, 2003b).

9

Etymology and names

In chapter 8 we examined various aspects of the interaction between etymology, semantic change, and extralinguistic cultural and historical factors. In this final chapter we will look in a little detail at the etymologies of names, and at how these interact in interesting ways both with the etymologies of other words in a language, and with external, extralinguistic historical data. As we will see, the study of name etymologies depends to an unusual degree on close consideration of extralinguistic factors, but conversely also has an unusually large and direct contribution to make to the study of non-linguistic history.

9.1 How and why are names different?

Names differ from other items in the vocabulary of a language in various significant ways:[1]

---

[1] The grammatical analysis of names is a difficult and contentious area, which has an impact on many aspects of terminology, such as whether to distinguish (as I have here)

(i) A name denotes a place or an individual (or another entity, such as a people, an organization, etc.).

There is a clear one-to-one relationship between a place name and the place which it denotes, although of course a place may have more than one name, and the same name form may occur as the name of more than one place. Almost all studies of place names treat the names of different places as distinct and different names, even if they are identical in form. From a diachronic perspective, there are very strong reasons for doing this, since homonymous place names often have quite different origins (see section 9.2 for an example). Even when the etymology of two place names is identical, they will normally have been named at different times by different people, in response to a different set of social, historical, and geographical circumstances.

The same considerations apply in theory to personal names, although there are complicating factors. Most important is the sheer weight of numbers: there are ordinarily far more people in a community than there are named places, even in a single historical period, and this becomes exponentially more so when we look across a number of generations. Additionally, in many societies there is an inherited aspect to names, as is most clearly shown by modern surnames. Many studies of personal names, including the majority of dictionaries, focus on distinct name forms rather than on the names of individual people, although in doing so they lose a very important level of detail. Studies of personal names thus generally focus on the types rather than the tokens.

(ii) Names are often referred to as having 'meanings', but it is important to be clear about what this means.

The basic function of a name is to refer to the particular place, person, etc. which it names. Many (but not all) scholars call this property of a name its reference, as distinct from the denotation of a word such as *man*: put very briefly, *man* denotes any of a whole class of individuals showing certain defining characteristics (compare section 8.2 on the complexities of this in practice), whereas *London* or *Eric* refer only to particular places or individuals who bear this name. This question involves a number of difficult issues, but fortunately need not concern us further here.[2]

between 'names' and 'other words', or between 'proper nouns' and 'common nouns'. For two important recent studies see Anderson (2007) and Coates (2006b).

[2] For starting points on this topic see again Anderson (2007) or Coates (2006b).

When the 'meaning' of a name is referred to in philological or etymological work, normally something rather different is meant. We can observe, entirely uncontroversially, that the vast majority of names are not arbitrary in origin. A place name usually refers to some attribute of the place denoted, or of its inhabitants/founders/rulers etc., even if the connection may be as remote as that it takes its name from that of another place in the colonizers' home country, e.g. *New South Wales* or *New Jersey*. Some personal names originally refer to some attribute of a person so named, although they may then be transferred to many other people who do not have this attribute. Alternatively they may be chosen because they refer to qualities which are particularly esteemed, or simply because they are deemed to have an impressive or pleasant 'ring' to them. The identification of the component parts of a name, and of their meaning or function as common words, is often referred to as giving the 'meaning' of a name. Such 'meanings' of names are strictly 'etymological meanings'. Access to such meanings often depends upon knowledge about the circumstances under which a name was first given. In the case of a nickname, for instance, these circumstances may become opaque very rapidly, and easily within an individual's lifetime.[3] Additionally, while the reasons lying behind a particular name may be transparent to some speakers, they may be completely opaque to others: thus, in a single historical period, a name may be 'meaningful' to some speakers, but not to others. Crucially, it does not hinder the efficient functioning of a name in referring to a particular place, person, etc. if its original 'meaning' has become confused, forgotten, or otherwise misinterpreted. However, names may also be 'meaningful' in the connotations that they convey: for instance, in England in the centuries after the Norman Conquest given names of continental origin (including a number of names ultimately of Germanic or classical origin alongside many biblical names) become much more frequent than names inherited from the Old English naming tradition, reflecting complex patterns of social prestige, but not implying any knowledge or awareness of the etymological 'meanings' of these names.[4]

(iii) Related to point (ii), because names are so easily dissociated from their original 'meaning', and hence from any connection with other

---

[3] For an entertaining and informative account of some modern nicknames from a philologist's perspective see Clark (1981).

[4] Compare Clark (1992b) and, for examples of more detailed examination of the records from particular localities, Clark (1976, 1982).

etymologically related words, they are particularly prone to sound change and to folk etymology and other types of associative change in word form.

This is well put by the medievalist and philologist Cecily Clark:

Names..., although ultimately derived from ordinary meaningful elements of language, have by definition ceased to carry any 'sense' as normally understood. This obviates maintenance of formal links or analogies with the related lexical items and so... allows free rein to tendencies, elsewhere curbed, towards assimilation or dissimilation, elision and syncope, procliticization, folk-etymology... and so on.

(Clark 1991, reprinted 1995: 150)

This factor makes it particularly important that work on names should always take very careful note of the earliest forms of a name that we can find recorded, and that the names researcher has a good grasp of the philology (i.e. the historical and linguistic peculiarities) of the documents in which the name is recorded. A good deal of extralinguistic historical knowledge and expertise is also very often required. Conversely, when names from the past are preserved in oral or literary traditions, they may sometimes preserve earlier linguistic forms (e.g. they may fail to show the effects of subsequent otherwise entirely regular sound changes), but this is an area where one must always proceed with caution.

9.2 Two villages called *Harvington*

English place names with the ending *-ington* are very common. The *-ton* element represents the Old English word *tūn*, modern English *town*, although in Old English the word normally denotes a much smaller settlement than a town. It is an inherited word, found in West and North Germanic languages, and probably originally had the sense 'fence', as does its modern German reflex *Zaun*. In Old English the meaning 'enclosure' is also recorded, but the sense 'fence' is not. The sense development was probably from 'fence' to 'enclosure' to '(small) settlement'.

The *-ing-* element in English place names ultimately reflects a Germanic suffix which normally has the senses 'belonging to', 'of the kind of', 'possessed of the quality of', 'descended from, son of'. We might therefore guess from the modern form of the name that a place called *Harvington* would originally have had the meaning 'settlement connected with or named after' or 'settlement connected with the followers of' someone whose name might ultimately have given rise to the first syllable of the place name.[5] Compare *Paddington* 'settlement connected with or named after Padda'.

There are in fact two villages which today have the name *Harvington* in Worcestershire. One is in the north of the county between the towns of Kidderminster and Bromsgrove, and the other is in the south-eastern corner of the county, between the towns of Evesham and Stratford-upon-Avon. Neither of them is in fact a name of the type which I have just described. The crucial information is given in the Worcestershire volume (Mawer, Stenton, and Houghton 1927) of the English Place-Name Society's monumental (and as yet unfinished) survey of English place names. The *Harvington* near to Kidderminster is recorded in the following forms in the *EPNS* volume:

> *Herwynton* (1275, 1311, 1327), *Herewinton* (1275, 1326, 1342), *Horinton* (1323), *Herwyngton* (1325), *Harwynton* (1545)

The balance of these early forms points to the -*g*- not being original; it probably arose as a inverse spelling as a result of the frequent occurrence of -*in* as a variant of -*ing* (compare section 7.7.1). We can therefore probably discard the hypothesis that this is an -*ington* type name. Instead, the early forms suggest that this is from a woman's name, *Herewynn*, so 'settlement of Herewynn' (or farm, manor, village, or whatever else may be denoted by -*ton* in this particular instance). However, no likely historical person of this name who might have given her name to the village has been identified. This is a very typical situation in name studies. The personal name *Herewynn* is itself of a very ancient type, common in the Germanic languages, which is made up of two components, and hence is called dithematic (see further section 9.3); in this instance the two elements are probably Old English *here* 'army' and *wynn* 'joy'. The modern form of the place name shows the effects of two sound changes, in addition to association with names of the -*ington* type: (i) the late Middle English lowering of /e/ to /a/ before /r/ which we encountered in section 7.2.5; and (ii) a change of /w/ to /v/ which is less easy to explain, but which is paralleled by some other place names.

The name of the village called *Harvington* near to Evesham has an even more surprising history. In this case the early forms, as given in the *EPNS* volume, are:

> *Herverton* (709, in a late copy; 1275), *Hereford* (799, 804 in late copies), *Herefordtun juxta Avene* (964 in a late copy), *Herferthun* (1086), *Hervertona*

---

[5] On the distinction between the two types 'settlement connected with or named after' and 'settlement connected with the followers of' see Cameron (1996) 148.

(*c*1086), *Herwerton* (1227), *Hervorditun* (1240), *Herfertun* (1240), *Herfortun* (1249), *Hervington* (1508), *Harvington* (sixteenth century)

The early forms show us immediately that this is not an original -*ington* name; in this case, the common place-name element -*ing*- has been substituted for -*er*- or -*or*- in a position of low stress. The earliest forms point to an etymology from Old English *here* 'army' and *ford* 'ford', and in this case the etymology is supported very strongly by archaeological evidence: if one descends the hill on which the oldest part of the village stands and follows a minor road for some half a mile there is indeed a very substantial ford crossing the river Avon. The name of this village is thus etymologically identical with that of the county town of *Hereford* in the neighbouring county of Herefordshire. This is probably the reason for the distinguishing use of the name of the river in the longer form of the name *Herefordtun juxta Avene*, in which the Latin preposition *juxta* 'beside' is used in the same way as English *upon* is used in the name of nearby *Stratford-upon-Avon* (which is thus distinguished from the numerous other English places with the name *Stratford*, all from Old English *strǣt* 'street, Roman road' plus *ford* 'ford': see further section 9.6).

We can thus see that in neither case are the initial assumptions that we might make from the modern form *Harvington* borne out by the historical data. The two names have different origins, and different forms in their earlier histories, although none of this information would be recoverable if we had only the modern name forms to work from.

9.3 Change in word form shown by names

Names, as linguistic units, naturally show many of the same processes of phonological change as any other linguistic unit; in fact they very often give crucial information about dialect developments that is inaccessible by other means. However, as with all other aspects of name studies, caution must often be exercised.

In section 7.3 we encountered the surname *Neldare* < *Needler* as an example of metathesis. If a similar metathetic change occurred in the agent noun *needler* it is likely that the form *needler* would be restored by analogy with the base word *needle*. However, in a surname, which is hereditary and is probably no longer borne by someone with the occupation to which its etymological 'meaning' refers, there is no such block on the operation of sound change.

Many English place names originated as a topographic phrase with the basic structure '[somewhere] at the something', thus containing the preposition *at* (Old English *æt*) followed by the dative case of either the masculine/neuter or the feminine of the definite article *the*, hence Old English *æt þǣm* or *æt þǣre*.[6] As a result of low stress on the definite article, Old English *æt þǣm* or *æt þǣre* become reduced in Middle English to *atten* and *atter* respectively, which both later become *atte* (compare *Stratford atte Bowe* in section 9.6 and the personal name *Peter atte Peat* in section 9.5). In a number of place names metanalysis (see section 7.5) occurred at the stage *atten* or *atter*. Hence *Nash* (as the name of three different places in Buckinghamshire, Herefordshire, and Shropshire) arises from *atten ashe* 'at the ash tree'. *Ricknield Street*, a Roman road, takes its name from that of the ancient trackway *Icknield Way*, but with transfer of *-r* from the inflected definite article: *atter Icknield* > *atte Ricknield*.[7]

Name studies may also give evidence for sound changes and other developments which have little or no parallel elsewhere in a language. A number of English place names show endings which have developed from Old English *-ceaster*, ultimately reflecting Latin *castrum* 'fort'. Some of these, e.g. *Chester, Winchester, Manchester, Rochester*, show the pronunciation/-tʃɛstə/ which would be expected for the modern reflex of an Old English word of this form. Others show the pronunciation /-stə/, e.g. *Gloucester* /ˈɡlɒstə/, *Bicester, Leicester, Worcester, Alcester, Frocester*, and *Towcester*. (*Cirencester* shows /ˈsaɪərənsɛstə/, but this is usually taken to show the result of a modern spelling pronunciation; the same explanation probably applies to /ˈɔːlsɛstə/ sometimes heard for *Alcester*.) Explaining the difference between names in /-tʃɛstə/ and in /-stə/ has long been a problem. One theory previously favoured was that /-sɛstə/ in *Gloucester* etc. reflected sporadic substitution of /s/ for /tʃ/ by native speakers of French but not of English, who lacked this sound in their own speech. In an important paper, Cecily Clark demonstrated not only that /tʃ/ was certainly current in Anglo-Norman (and in continental French) in the period in question, but also that the distribution of the names with /-tʃɛstə/ and /-stə/ makes

---

[6] For discussion of the difficulties of analysis posed by such names, i.e. whether in a given instance they should be interpreted as names or as descriptive phrases, see Coates (2006b) 367, 370.

[7] For these, and further, examples see Cameron (1996) 95–6, 156.

little sense in terms of the socio-cultural history of the towns and cities concerned: 'socially, it is hardly obvious why Bicester or Towcester should seem to have been more of a hotbed of "Anglo-Norman influence" than, of all places, Winchester' (Clark 1991, reprinted 1995: 152). What makes much more sense is an explanation of these name forms as showing a sound change which sometimes occurred in a position of low stress, an observation supported also by the fact that a number of these names vary between forms with *-chester* and forms with *-cester* until late in the Middle English period.

It thus appears that *Cirencester*, *Gloucester*, etc. show a sporadic sound change which happens to be exemplified in the surviving documentation only by proper names. However, there are also instances of developments which appear to have been confined to proper names, and did not occur elsewhere in the linguistic system. The personal names scholar Peter McClure, in a paper on hypocoristic or pet-forms of personal names in the Middle English period, discusses the processes of abbreviation, extension, and substitution often shown by such forms. Some of the processes grouped by McClure under the cover term of 'abbreviation' will be surprising to those who are not personal names specialists:

> The most characteristic aspect of abbreviation is that deletion can affect segments of any length, from the loss of a single phoneme to the elision of any sequence of weakly stressed phonemes, syllables or morphemes, and that it can occur in any position, whether initial (*aphesis*, as in *Col* for *Nicol* and *Naud* for *Reynaud*), medial (*syncope*, as in *Maret* for *Margaret* and *Phip* for *Philip*), final (*apocope*, very common as in *Bet* for *Be(a)trice*, *Gef* for *Geoffrey*, *Teb* for *Tebald* and *Mal* for *Mald*), or multi-positional (as in *Til* for *Matilde*, *Ib* for *Isabel* and *Heb* for *Herbert*).
>
> (McClure (1998) 108–9)

Some of these developments are not very uncommon typologically but are rare outside names in Middle English (compare section 4.4.3 on clippings). Others, for instance *Ib* < *Isabel*, would be very surprising developments in any language in any period; for parallels we might have to look perhaps to child language, or to cases of conscious remodelling of words, as for instance in the coining of the names of drugs or other products in contemporary English. Clearly, an etymologist will often need to approach these sorts of hypocoristic personal names with a different set of assumptions from those made when etymologizing general vocabulary items. The same is true of some of the vowel and consonant alternations which McClure exemplifies under the heading of 'substitution', such as *Mog* for *Mag* or

Gep for *Gef*, or rhyming forms such as *Dick* for *Rick* or *Pog* for *Mog* (McClure (1998) 109).[8]

Under 'extension', McClure exemplifies how personal names can also have extended forms with endings which constitute a system distinct from the regular derivational morphology of Middle English:

> Extension is typically morphemic, by the addition of vocalic suffixes such as -*y*, -*in*, -*on*, -*un*, -*el*, -*et* and -*ot*, double vocalic suffixes such as -*elet*, -*elot*, -*elin*, -*onel*, -*inet* and -*inot*, and *k* suffixes such as -*k*, -*kin*, -*cok*, -*cot* and -*cus*. These diminutivising suffixes are sometimes added to a full name (e.g. *Philipot*) but more often to a short form, including abbreviated forms of existing pet-names (e.g. *Potkin*). Most suffixes are found added to names of either gender.
>
> (McClure (1998) 109)

While some (although not all) of these endings can be etymologized as arising from productive suffixes forming diminutive nouns in Middle English, they nonetheless constitute a system of their own, often owing as much or more to foreign naming patterns as to the noun morphology of English. If we turn to an earlier historical period, another system distinct from that of the general vocabulary is shown by the system of name 'themes' found in early Germanic personal names. These are generally derived from general vocabulary items, but in their typical combination in 'dithematic' names (like *Herewynn* in section 9.2) they are often used with little regard for the semantics of the 'compound' thus formed, with the choice of 'themes' being determined instead by onomastic factors such as kinship, etc. In a particularly clear example, St. *Wulfstān*, literally 'wolf stone', was the son of a man called *Æðelstān*, literally 'noble stone', and a woman called *Wulfgifu*, literally 'wolf gift'. (See Clark (1992a) 456–62.)

However, names do not exist entirely in isolation from the rest of the linguistic system, and we sometimes encounter instances of the influence of name morphology on non-name morphology. For instance, the etymology of German *Quarz* is probably best explained by a hypocoristic suffix which is mostly found in pet-forms of personal names. It is presented in *OED* as follows:

> German *Quarz* (earlier also *Querz*; first half of the 14th cent. in Middle High German (Bohemia) as *quarz*), of uncertain origin: perhaps a pet-form (with -*z*, hypocoristic suffix) of Middle High German *querch*, variant of *twerc* dwarf (see DWARF n. and adj.); compare *Fritz*, pet-form of *Friedrich*, *Heinz*, pet-form of *Heinrich*, etc. For the

---

[8] For a wealth of similar medieval surname data, approached primarily from the perspective of a genealogist, see Redmonds (2002) 121–68 and 205–14.

association of dwarfs with German mineral names see discussions at KUPFERNICKEL n. and COBALT n.; compare also Norwegian *dvergstein* quartz, lit. 'dwarf-stone'.

The etymologies of hypocoristic forms can be very difficult to establish. It can also be difficult to establish which full name forms hypocoristics corresponded to in synchronic use. An essential tool in the latter task is prosopography, identifying individuals in the historical record and, if possible, finding individuals who have been identified at different times by both a full form and a hypocoristic. However, even this is not necessarily conclusive for the etymology of the hypocoristic, since it is possible that a form which was originally a formation from one name may have come to function as a hypocoristic corresponding to another. A notoriously difficult case is *Jack*, in recent times the most popular male forename in Britain. From the Middle English period onwards this occurs in frequent use as a hypocoristic form for people named *John*, but scholars have differed over whether it originated as a development from the name *John* or from *James*. McClure (2003) argues, on the basis of prosopographical and linguistic evidence, that *Jack* did originate ultimately from *John*, although probably not within English: it probably shows borrowing from northern Old French *Jakke*, which is probably from an unattested form *Janke* (compare attested *Hanke*) < *Jan* < *Jehan* < Latin *Johannes*.

9.4 Which language does a name belong to?

It is something of an open question whether names can truly be said to belong to any language. We can adduce certain pieces of evidence which appear to suggest quite strongly that they do. For instance, the same place or the same person may be referred to by different names in different languages: the German city of *München* is called *Munich* in English, the English capital *London* is *Londres* in French, while numerous medieval monarchs and other figures known as *Louis* in French are known as *Ludwig* in German. However, in most cases a more-or-less settled modern practice is only the outcome of a process of standardization; for instance, English *minikin*, the name of a type of lute string which Munich was famous for producing in the sixteenth century, is from *Miniken*, an older form of the name of the city in English, which itself reflects German *Münichen*, an older trisyllabic form of the place name. Naturalized name forms of the *Munich* type also often undergo a process of 'de-naturalization' by association with the form in the majority language of the place named: *Rome*, the English name of the Italian capital city, formerly showed the effects of the Great Vowel Shift, with a pronunciation /ruːm/, but now invariably has /əʊ/ restored by analogy with the pronunciation of Italian *Roma* and with the pronunciation of other English words of similar spelling, such as *home* or *dome*. The English name of *Milan* (Italian *Milano*) now very rarely has stress on the first syllable, although this was formerly very common (and is reflected by the derivative *milliner*: see section 9.7). English *Leghorn* for Italian *Livorno* (formerly *Legorno*) is now almost completely obsolete, being replaced by the Italian name. English *Florence*, however, shows no signs of replacement by Italian *Firenze*, nor does English *Venice* by Italian *Venezia*.

Much more commonly, names will differ only in small ways in pronunciation, showing assimilation to the sound system of another language, and crucially this degree of naturalization may differ from speaker to speaker, and from period to period. If we look at realizations of the same name in different dialects or varieties within a language, the differences will in many instances be as great or greater, as for instance in pronunciations of place names such as *Doncaster* with or without pre-fricative lengthening (hence with either /a/ or /ɑː/ in the second syllable) or with or without final /r/.

In languages which show a greater degree of nominal inflection, each name will generally be assigned to a particular morphological class, and hence is more clearly identified as belonging to the grammatical system of the language. However, grammars of highly inflected languages such as Latin indicate that names are frequently assigned to minor morphological classes either reflecting the morphology of foreign languages or showing a restricted set of inflections. (Compare e.g. Leumann (1963) on names in the grammatical system of Latin.)

Such issues can sometimes pose practical problems if we attempt to use names as evidence for the currency of words. For instance, in medieval England we find numerous surnames such as *Mariner* or *Messenger* which could reflect either Middle English or Anglo-French occupational terms. Such names may be encountered in documents which are in Middle English, Anglo-French, or (more typically) Latin, but this does nothing to identify which language the name originated in. Additionally, an instance of such a name could show a by-name, describing the occupation of the person bearing it, or it could be an inherited surname. In some cases it could be an inherited surname but also be the same as its bearer's occupation, since the same occupation was often followed by successive generations of a family. Normally all we can be certain about with such names is that they imply the currency of the corresponding occupational term in one of the vernacular languages of medieval England, but we cannot be certain which. (For further discussion of these and other examples see Simpson, Weiner, and Durkin (2004); on the difficulties of Middle English surname and by-name evidence in general see Clark (1992b).)

9.5 Names as evidence for lexis

Often a name or a group of names will provide the earliest evidence for the existence of a word, or of a sense of a word. The etymologizing of names can thus provide crucial primary evidence, on which new etymologies can be constructed or against which existing etymologies can be tested.

peat, a word of very uncertain etymology, is first attested contextually in 1333, but earlier currency is implied by place names such as *Petepottes* (*c*1200 in Cumberland, probably showing *peat pot* 'a hole from which peat has been dug') and surnames such as *Peter atte Peat* (1326; a prepositional surname 'at the peat'). Here both *Petepottes* and *atte Peat* give some important linguistic context, which helps make the identification of these names as showing the word *peat* much more secure: *Petepottes* appears to show a compound word, apparently with the plural of *pot* as its second element, thus narrowing down considerably the possibilities for the identity of the first element; *atte Peat* is a prepositional surname, and so *Peat* in this name must refer to some place descriptively.

The verb *pave* is recorded in contextual use from *c*1325 (and is a borrowing from (Anglo-)French), but its derivative *paved* has been identified in 1313 in a Cheshire field name *Le pauedelake* (showing the probable meaning 'stream with a gravelly bed': see further Hough (2001)). Again, the linguistic context provided by the name *Le pauedelake* is essential: *paved* is almost certainly an adjective, formed with the suffix *-ed*, and modifies *lake* in one of its Middle English meanings, hence the possibilities for the identity of *pave* are narrowed considerably.

pad 'toad', which is now found only in regional use, has cognates in various other Germanic languages (such as Middle Dutch *padde* or Old Icelandic *padda*), but is first recorded in contextual use only in the twelfth century (in the Peterborough continuations of the *Anglo-Saxon Chronicle*). The supposition that it existed in Old English, rather than being borrowed from one of the other Germanic languages, is supported by the existence of an Anglo-Saxon personal name *Padda*, which probably originated from this word. As such, it would fit into a naming pattern which was productive in this period.[9]

In some cases such examples may also show formal variation which is not documented for the word in contextual use. For instance *queach* 'a dense growth of bushes, a thicket' is first recorded in contextual use in 1486, but is probably attested earlier in place names such as *Thirsqueche* (Northamptonshire, 1292), *La queche* (Worcestershire, 1307), *Quechefen* (Northamptonshire, 1330), and earliest of all, in a form apparently showing rounding of the vowel and assimilatory loss of /w/, *Cocheworth* (Sussex, 1265).

In other cases matters may be much less clear. For instance, *big* is first recorded c1300. It probably earliest had the meaning 'strong, sturdy, mighty', from which the meaning 'large' subsequently developed, although this is not certain since the earliest senses of the word are close in date and various different directions of semantic change would be plausible. The earliest examples of the word are all from northern texts. The date and early localization of the word suggest borrowing from Old Norse as a possible origin. There is no obvious etymon recorded in the early stages of any of the Scandinavian languages, but in modern Norwegian regional use we do find *bugge* (noun) 'mighty man' and *bugga* (adjective) 'rich, wealthy, powerful'. It is possible that the Middle English word could show a borrowing from an Old Norse precursor of this word, or more likely from a morphological variant of this word showing a suffix causing *i*-mutation, which would explain the forms shown by the English word very well (although we should note that there is no secure etymology for Norwegian *bugge* and *bugga*). However, there is some evidence from personal names which rather complicates the picture. From the first half of the eleventh century onwards we find a by-name or surname of the form *Bigga*, *Bigge*, earliest in southern counties, especially Kent. It is tempting to see this as reflecting a name on the same pattern as *Padda* above, and if so a formation from *big* would be very plausible semantically; that is, we can conceive of a person being called 'strong, sturdy, mighty', or for that matter 'big'. The localization of the

---

[9] It would be possible to list many hundreds of other examples where names provide crucial early evidence for a word. For other interesting examples, just from among words with initial *p-*, see the *OED* entries for *pike* n.[1], *pike* n.[3], *pick* v.[1], *pierce* v., *poll* n.[1], *polled* adj., *pommely* adj., *pont* n.[1], or *pritchel* n.

names and the stem vowel which they show do, however, raise difficulties for the assumption of any connection with an Old Norse cognate of Norwegian *bugge* and *bugga*: we would expect an Old English borrowing to show the stem vowel *y* (later developed to *i* in some dialects of Middle English), and we would expect a localization in the areas of heaviest Norse settlement in the northern and eastern counties, rather than in the south. We thus arrive at a difficulty which is not uncommon when we attempt to use names as lexical evidence: we cannot be certain that *Bigga*, *Bigge* as a name has any connection with *big*; from the point of view of the English evidence, it is plausible both formally and semantically, but there is no positive support for this assumption. The suggested etymological connection between *big* and Norwegian *bugge* and *bugga* is similarly plausible but not of an overwhelming probability. We are thus left with a rather unsatisfactory conclusion: we may have a (slightly tenuous) etymology for *big*, or we may have some personal name evidence which pushes the word *big* back to slightly before the Norman Conquest, but we cannot very easily reconcile the two (and of course, both may in fact be wrong).

9.6 Names as evidence for word meaning

Middle English *bowe* 'bow' shows a number of specialized senses denoting various things with a curved shape. One of these is 'arch of a bridge'. In place names we may also find evidence for a further metonymic extended sense 'arched bridge', as in the name of *Bow* in East London, which was earlier called *Stratford atte Bowe*. In this particular instance the bridge referred to by the name was probably built during the reign of Henry I (1100–35). As in the name of *Stratford-upon-Avon* (see section 9.2), we have here an extended form of a place name which was originally simply *Stratford*, with the addition of *atte Bowe* 'at the arched bridge' in order to distinguish this name from the many other *Stratford*s in England (especially in this instance another place of the same name on the opposite bank of the River Lea in Essex, formerly distinguished as *Stratford Langthorn* and now simply *Stratford*).

More controversially, analysis of the places denoted by descriptive topographical place names may perhaps yield information about the precise meanings of topographical vocabulary at the time when the name was given. Pioneering work on the semantics of English topographical place names has been done by Margaret Gelling, latterly in collaboration with Ann Cole, as exemplified in Gelling and Cole (2000). For instance, in a section on 'hills, slopes and ridges' analysis of place names in Old English *beorg* (modern English *barrow*) gives rise to the following observation:

> It cannot be claimed that every beorg name in the country has been matched to its visual setting, but this has been done in a sufficiently large number of instances for it to be asserted confidently that the defining characteristic of a *beorg* is a continuously rounded profile. This probably explains the use of the word for tumuli in the southern half of England, which led to the adoption of *barrow* as a technical term by archaeologists. Many tumuli would be *beorg*-shaped.
>
> (Gelling and Cole (2000) 145)

Gelling acknowledges, however, that this contradicts the likely reconstructable meaning for the Germanic word from which this is derived, which is 'mountain'. Therefore, if the observation about the use in place names is correct, it is nonetheless uncertain how far this should apply to the general use of the Old English word. On the basis of the literary records the *Dictionary of Old English* records the much wider range of senses 'mountain, hill; mountain range; mountain (with name specified); cliff, headland, promontory; barrow, tumulus, burial mound (both Saxon and pre-Saxon, frequent in charters); heap, pile, mound'. However, for the Middle English period the *Middle English Dictionary* records a narrowed range of senses ('hill, mound, barrow') much closer to that suggested by Gelling's analysis of place names (although in the Middle English period the semantic influence of the cognate Old Norse *berg* must also be taken into account).

9.7 Names as etymons

Some etymologies from names are very well known. For instance, the company name *Hoover* has come to be used not just as a generic word for a vacuum cleaner, but has also given rise (by conversion) to a verb for the associated activity. The second element of *tarmacadam* is the surname of John Loudon *McAdam*, the Scottish surveyor who invented this type of road surface. The *margherita* pizza takes its name from *Margherita* Teresa Giovanna of Savoy, Queen of Italy, having been created and named in her honour in June 1889 by Raffaele Esposito, a Neapolitan pizza maker. *paparazzo* 'freelance photographer who pursues celebrities to take photographs of them' is from the name of a character who is a society photographer in Federico Fellini's 1960 film *La Dolce Vita*.

Words are often formed from names in combination with derivative suffixes, or as an element in a compound. Thus very many names of plants, minerals, etc. are named after their discoverers, or in honour of important figures in a particular field of study, or for reasons of political prestige, as *poinsettia* (from the name of *Poinsett*, a US minister to Mexico) or *fuchsia* (from the name of the German botanist *Fuchs*), or from the names of the places where they were discovered, as *maldonite* (from the name of *Maldon* in Australia, where this alloy was discovered) or *pandaite* (similarly from the name of *Panda* Hill in Mbeya, Tanzania). *nessberry*, denoting a North American soft fruit similar to a loganberry, shows a late nineteenth-century addition to the *-berry* words which we encountered in section 2.6. The first element is from the name of Helge *Ness*, the horticulturist who first raised this type of fruit. Similarly we find *loganberry*, *veitchberry*, *youngberry*, *boysenberry* (all from surnames), and (from place names) *tayberry*, *tummelberry*, *marionberry*, *worcesterberry*. We encountered *sadism* and related words in section 4.3.1; *masochism* is similarly from a personal name, that of the Austrian writer Leopold von Sacher-*Masoch*. *malapropism* is from the name of the character Mrs *Malaprop* in Sheridan's 1775 play *The Rivals*, who is characterized by her confusion in the use of long words; in this instance the name was itself created by Sheridan from the word *malapropos* 'inopportune, inappropriate'.

milliner shows semantic specialization of a derivative of a place name. Middle English *milener* means simply 'person from Milan' (with the stress on the first syllable, noted in section 9.4). In early modern English it shows a sense development summarized as follows by *OED*: 'Originally: a seller of fancy wares, accessories, and articles of (female) apparel, esp. such as were originally made in Milan. Subsequently: spec. a person who designs, makes, or sells women's hats.' The sense 'person from Milan' (which usually shows the form *milaner* in later use) becomes obsolete at the end of the nineteenth century, being replaced by *Milanese*.

9.8 Names and non-linguistic history

We can see some of the potential for interaction between the study of name etymologies and the study of external, non-linguistic history if we take a

brief look at some material from the introduction to the English Place-
Name Society survey volume for the former English county of Rutland.
Here Barrie Cox, one of the scholars who have done most to establish the
relative chronology of various types of names in the early period of the
Anglo-Saxon settlement of England, puts this research to daring use. He
sets out first the relevant methodology:

> An analysis of place-names appearing in Old English records to 730 AD indicates
> that of those surviving in Rutland, the following may be considered to be very early:
> habitation names in *hām* 'a village, an estate' and nature names in *dūn* 'a large hill'.
> Place-names in which -*inga*-, the genitive plural of the folk-name-forming suffix -*ingas*,
> is compounded (especially in -*ingahām*) may be only slightly later than these.
>
> (Cox (1994) xxiv)

With the methodology thus clearly established, it can be deployed in combination with other, non-linguistic evidence to give a composite picture, as
in the following paragraph where names showing these elements are related
to the pattern of Roman roads and to the Romano-British and early Anglo-
Saxon archaeology of the county:

> In the east on Ermine Street and Sewstern Lane are Clipsham and Greetham, while
> Luffenham ... lies on the postulated Roman road running south to Turtle Bridge. Two
> names with -*inga*-, Empingham (from -*ingahām*) and Tinwell (from -*ingawella*) also lie
> on these roads. Uppingham (again from -*ingahām*) seems isolated, but an original large
> estate with a name in -*hām*, i.e. *Thornham*, appears to have lain to its north and east.
> The Glaston pagan Anglo-Saxon cemetery may have related to this lost estate. Clip-
> sham, Empingham and Tinwell are also villa locations, while Greetham has a Roman
> kiln which probably represents an as yet undiscovered Romano-British habitation site.
> The three Rutland names in *dūn*, Hambleton, Lyndon and Barrowden, march with
> parishes with names in *hām*. Hambleton ... may well have been the location of the
> Anglian *caput* of the entire territory. Ketton is also early. With its name probably
> based on a pre-Anglian root, this parish lies astride the Great Casterton to Tixover
> Roman road and is surrounded by names in *hām*, *dūn* and -*inga*-.
>
> (Cox (1994) xxiv–xxv)

This sort of synthesis of etymological data with historical and archaeological data is exciting. Equally exciting are the conclusions that Cox is
able to draw from the early Scandinavian settlement names in the county.
Work on Scandinavian place names in England, particularly by Kenneth
Cameron, has shown that among the very earliest are so-called *Grimston-*
hybrid names. These show a Scandinavian personal name as the first element, and Old English *tūn* as the second element. From careful examination
of the sites of these villages, it has been established that they were existing

Anglo-Saxon villages which came under the overlordship of the bearers of the Viking personal names which are reflected in their modern names.[10] A slightly later layer of Scandinavian place names is shown by names in Old Norse *bӯ* 'farm, village'. These are frequently found in less favourable sites alongside villages with English names in slightly better locations, hence probably reflecting subsequent settlement by Scandinavian incomers, as opposed to the initial phase of appropriation of existing settlements shown by the *Grimston*-hybrid names. Cox draws some important historical conclusions from the scarcity of both types in Rutland in comparison with other parts of the Danelaw (the area of Scandinavian control):

The place-name evidence as a whole indicates that Scandinavians were excluded polit-ically from Rutland at the time of the disbanding of the Danish army in the East Midlands in 877, the indicator of whose settlement is the Grimston-hybrid name-type, and excluded also during the subsequent colonization phase which is recorded by place-names in *bӯ*. There are no Grimston-hybrids in the real sense in Rutland and no names in *bӯ* compounded with Scandinavian personal names, a remarkable contrast with the surrounding territories.

(Cox (1994) xli)

[10] In Cameron's more recent work these are in fact referred to instead as *Toton*-hybrids, because it was realized that some of the places called *Grimston* did not show the same origin: see Cameron (1996) 74–5. For important work on the evidence for the nature and extent of linguistic contact between English and Norse speakers which is yielded by place names see Townend (2002).

10

Conclusion

We have defined etymology as the tracing of word histories. It focuses especially (but not exclusively) on those areas where there is a doubt about a stage in a word's history, or where the documentary record fails us, e.g.:

- we have reached the extreme limit of the documentary record of a word's history, and are attempting to reconstruct its pre-history
- there is a gap in the documentary record of a word's history, and we are attempting to reconstruct what occurred in that gap
- there is no gap at all in the documentary record, but the nature of the historical development is not clear, and we must find an explanation for how a set of forms or meanings are related to one another

We solve difficult cases largely by comparison with what has happened in simpler and better-documented cases. Therefore little in the field of word histories will be outside the interests of an etymologist.

Words are the units studied by etymologists, and this raises some difficult issues. The problems in deciding whether some particular items are words or phrases are of little practical importance for etymologists, since many phrases also have unpredictable meanings which we will need to account for. A more difficult problem is posed by the fact that the lexis of any language is almost limitless, with new words formed according to productive word-forming processes constantly occurring in actual language use. Etymologists need to be aware of the word-forming processes which are productive in a given language in a given period, but (except when the surviving corpus is very small) they will not be able to pay attention to every word which is produced by those productive processes. We arrived at a priority list of words for etymological attention:

- any monomorphemic words
- any word containing a cranberry morph
- any word with a form not explicable by currently productive word-formation processes
- any word in which the semantic relations between its elements is opaque

It is often desirable also to add to this list other words or phrases which have a non-predictable, institutionalized meaning.

Some words can show enormous variation in form and/or meaning. Etymological research will not be successful if we do not pay careful attention to the full range of formal and semantic variation shown by each word. Not all words show a simple linear history. Some words split and others merge. Polygenesis, of both words and meanings, is probably very widespread. Some words show large discontinuities in the historical record. In some cases this is almost certainly accidental, in others it probably points to two separate word histories. Distinguishing between such cases is often very difficult.

It is very important to understand the range of word-forming processes found in a language in a given period. In many cases more than one analysis is possible of how a word was formed, and keeping an open mind on such questions can often lead to new and more satisfactory etymological explanations of the histories of particular words or groups of words. Some words are onomatopoeic, and show a non-arbitrary connection between word form and sounds in the external, non-linguistic world. The identification of such items presents considerable challenges for etymological research, since the connection between word form and non-linguistic sounds is often rather tenuous, and is sometimes made more opaque by subsequent phonological change. Tracing the histories of onomatopoeic words is further complicated by the fact that they sometimes fail to show sound changes which are otherwise regular, because of the strength of the association with non-linguistic sounds. Some words are commonly perceived as expressive or onomatopoeic, but in fact show no obvious connection with sounds in the non-linguistic world. Many such words derive their perceived expressive quality from sound combinations which they share with other words of similar meaning, although they are not related to them in any way which can be explained by regular word-formation processes. Many scholars invoke the controversial concept of the phonaestheme to explain some such cases.

Borrowing is a frequent origin of new words in most languages. It is easy to understate its potential complications. We will usually need to distinguish between loanwords, loan translations, semantic loans, and loan blends, although it is often difficult to determine which process has occurred, or indeed whether borrowing has occurred at all. We will also often need to distinguish the immediate donor language from the language in which a word ultimately originates. Borrowings occur in a particular historical and cultural context, and the better we can understand this, the fuller our understanding of a linguistic borrowing will be. Some borrowed words show subsequent semantic or formal influence from the donor, while other words are borrowed twice in two different historical periods. Borrowing is often a very complex process, in which an initial interlinguistic borrowing between languages is normally followed by intralinguistic borrowing as a word spreads within a language. The motivation and other circumstances may vary considerably in each stage of this process. It can also at times be difficult to distinguish borrowing from lexical transfer (when a group of speakers abandon one language for another), and also from code-switching.

The histories of particular words are often closely interlinked. This may be semantic, as with *board* and *table*, or it may be formal, as happens in associative change in word form.

However complex and controversial its mechanisms may be, sound change provides the most important tool available to any etymologist. Whether we adhere to the regularity principle, or adopt a lexical diffusionist model, or any of various other theoretical positions, it remains the case that we can often group together sets of words which all show the same change in broadly the same chronological period. These can be analysed and conclusions can be drawn from them in a historical grammar. Individual word histories may indicate the chronological sequence in which particular sound changes occurred, and hence provide the historical grammar with the evidence for a relative chronology, albeit in many cases only a very tentative one. The incidence of some sound changes is sporadic or isolated, but such cases generally belong to types for which we can find parallels in other periods or in other languages. Sometimes we find unaccountable developments, such as the initial /p/ of *purse*, but these are relatively few. Associative changes in word form can be more idiosyncratic and more difficult to trace, but normally they arise through some association in meaning between two or more words, and this usually provides the key to identification.

Words have meaning as well as form, and etymological research cannot be pursued without close attention to both.

If we took the view that homonymy was a very unlikely state in earlier stages of language history, then we might reasonably conclude that if tracing two separate word histories leads to an identical word form, our task is then simply to find the semantic common denominator and explain how the two words are likely to have diverged from a common point of origin. However, since we have concluded that homonymy appears to have been common in the past just as in the present, then we must also ask ourselves whether two identical word forms are connected at all, rather than just how they are connected.

Change in meaning presents many problems not presented by change in word form. It affects words individually, but in ways which often result from complex inter-relationships with the meanings of other words, often including aspects of both referential and non-referential meaning (such as register or stylistic level), and also often showing a close connection with developments in non-linguistic social and cultural history. There is no tool comparable to the historical grammar enabling us to group and categorize semantic changes, and it is hard to imagine how one could be conceived. Nonetheless, our best measure of whether a particular hypothesized meaning change is plausible is whether we can find cases of similar changes in well-documented word histories.

Etymology can be a very demanding area of research, drawing on many different aspects of linguistics. It also draws at times on a good deal of non-linguistic information, about the transmission of texts or other sources of data, or about developments in social or cultural history. For this very reason it can also be extremely rewarding. Few areas of study offer points of contact with so many other fields. A discovery in etymology often depends upon insights drawn from many different areas of research, and often has the potential to illuminate questions in many linguistic sub-disciplines or beyond. Etymology is a crucial tool for investigating the language and thought of the past. It opens up a field of research where a very great deal remains to be discovered. And like all the best intellectual pursuits, once the bug is caught, it is likely to remain with one for life.

Glossary

The following is a very selective list, chiefly of terms which occur frequently in the text, especially those whose meaning could be confused. See also in the index for other terms which are discussed and defined in the main text of the book. The words which are included here are defined narrowly from the point of view of their usage in etymological research. For general dictionaries of linguistics, which offer definitions which reflect the full range of use in linguistic writing, see Matthews (2007) or Crystal (2008), or (expressly from the perspective of historical and comparative linguistics) Trask (2000).

< Developed from, comes from. Used in this book to link forms which are related by direct phonetic descent, by borrowing, or by word formation processes, as well as to represent the stages in the semantic development of a word. By some scholars used only to link forms related by direct phonetic descent: see 1.2.1.

> Develops to, gives. See further under '<' above.

ablaut Realization of grammatical or derivational relationships through vowel alternation in the root (i.e. a type of root allomorphy); used especially as the name of a process of this type which was highly productive in proto-Indo-European: see 4.4.1.

affix see **affixation**

affixation Addition of **bound forms** or **affixes** to words (or other morphological bases) in order to form derivative words (i.e. as a word formation process) or in order to realize grammatical distinctions (i.e. **inflection**). An affix added to the beginning of a word or stem is called a prefix, and one added to the end of a word or stem is called a suffix. Infixes, which interrupt a morphological base, are also sometimes found, as are circumfixes, which involve addition simultaneously of material at the beginning and the end of a base. See 2.2.3, 4.1.

after In etymologies = 'on the model of'.

amelioration Acquisition of more positive meaning. See 8.6.3.

analogy Alteration of existing forms or meanings (analogical change) or creation of new forms or meanings (analogical creation) on the basis of parallels elsewhere in the linguistic system. **Proportional analogy** shows the pattern A : B = X : Y, where Y is the altered or newly created form. See 7.4, 7.4.1.

analysable (Of a word) capable of being analysed (by speakers) into its constituent morphemes. See 2.1.1.2, 2.2.1, 2.2.4, 2.3, 2.4, 2.6, 2.7. Compare **monomorphemic**, **transparent**.

assimilation (In sound change) a change by which two consonants become more similar or identical in articulation: see 7.3. Compare **dissimilation**. Sometimes also used in etymology to denote the type of associative change in word form also known as **contamination** (see 7.4.4).

associative change in word form Change in word form resulting from **analogy**, **levelling**, **contamination**, or **folk etymology**. See 7.4.

back formation A word-formation process in which reanalysis of an existing word as showing a particular affix leads to the creation of a new word which is taken to be its morphological base; e.g. *peddle* < *pedlar*. See 4.4.5.

base (In morphology) the word form or stem form on which **affixation** operates. See 4.1.

bleaching A type of meaning change in which the semantic content of a word becomes reduced as the grammatical content increases: see 8.6.1.

blend A type of word formation in which two truncated word stems combine to form a new word, e.g. *smog* < *smoke* and *fog*. See 4.4.4.

blocking (In word formation) prevention of the general adoption of a new word by the prior existence of a synonym. See 4.2.

borrowing Process by which a language takes a word, meaning, phrase, construction, etc. from another language. Types of borrowing include **loanword**, **loan translation**, **semantic loan**, **loan blend**. See 5.1. Compare **transfer**.

bound form A morpheme which can only occur as a component of other words, rather than on its own as an independent word form. See 4.3.1.

broadening Process by which a word comes to have wider semantic application. See 8.6.1. Compare **narrowing**.

calque = **loan translation**

circumfix See **affixation**

clipping A process of shortening of a word form without change of meaning or word class, usually leaving a form which is morphologically incomplete or **unanalysable**. See 4.4.3. Compare **ellipsis**.

code-switching Phenomenon where bilingual speakers switch between use of one language and use of another, in the knowledge that they are addressing others who also have some knowledge of each language. See 6.9.

cognate Developed from a common ancestor. Among the cognates of Old English *sǣd* are Old Dutch *sat*, Old Saxon *sad*, Old High German *sat*, Old Icelandic *saðr*, Gothic *saþs*; these words are all cognate. See 1.2.3.

combining form A type of **bound form** which occurs only in compounds, typically combined either with an independent word or with another combining form; used especially of such elements ultimately derived from Latin and Greek occurring in modern European languages, which are sometimes called **neo-classical combining forms**. See 4.3.1.

complex (Of a word) consisting of more than one **morpheme**. See 2.2.1. Compare **monomorphemic**.

compounding The combination of two words to form a new word, especially when this preserves all of the phonetic substance of each word or its morphological stem. See 2.2.3, 4.3.

conditioned (Of a sound change) only occurring in a particular phonetic context in a word. See 7.2.2. Compare **isolative**.

contamination A type of associative change in word form resulting from semantic association between two words, e.g. Old English *mǣst* 'most' occurring in place of the expected form *māst* as a result of semantic association with *lǣst* 'least'. See 7.4.4. Compare **analogy**, **folk etymology**.

conventional (Of meaning) established, not inferred afresh from context each time a word is encountered; = **institutionalized**.

conversion The process by which a word in one class gives rise to an identical word form in another word class. See 4.4.2.

cranberry morph An **unanalysable** element occurring in a word which otherwise has the appearance of being an analysable compound or derivative. See 2.6.

denotatum The thing, concept, etc. which a word denotes or refers to.

derivation Word formation by **affixation**. (Sometimes used much more broadly as a synonym of **etymology**.)

derivative A word formed by **affixation** (i.e. **derivation**). (Sometimes used much more broadly to denote any word form developed historically from another word form.)

diagrammatic iconicity A type of **iconicity** which involves associations and connections entirely within the world of linguistic signs. See 4.5. Compare **imagic iconicity**.

diphthong A vowel which changes in quality perceptibly within a single syllable, as opposed to a **monophthong** (or pure vowel). Thus *pine* /paɪn/ shows a diphthong, while *pin* /pɪn/ and *preen* /priːn/ both show monophthongs.

dissimilation (In sound change) a change by which two consonants become less similar in articulation: see 7.3.

donor In a borrowing situation, the language from which another language borrows. See 5.1.

doublet Each word in a group of two or more words which all show the same ultimate etymology. See 6.7.

ellipsis The shortening of an existing compound or phrase so that one element comes to take on the previous meaning of the whole compound or phrase. See 4.4.3. Compare **clipping**.

etymology The tracing of the form and meaning history of a word, where there is a doubt about a stage in a word's history, or where the documentary record fails; (an account of or hypothesized explanation for) the form and meaning history of a word. See 1.1, and chapter 10.

etymon The antecedent form of a word. Frequently a distinction is made between an immediate etymon, i.e. the direct parent of a particular word, and one or more remote etymons. Thus Old French *frere* is the immediate etymon of Middle English *frere* (modern English *friar*); Latin *frāter*, *frātr-* is a remote etymon of Middle English *frere*, but the immediate etymon of Old French *frere*.

folk etymology A type of associative change in word form in which one or more syllables of a word are replaced by another word, especially where some semantic association is perceived or felt to exist. See 7.4.5. Compare **contamination**, **analogy**.

grammaticalization The process by which words develop meanings and functions which are more grammatical. See 3.4, 8.1, 8.7.2.1.

harmful homonymy = homonymic clash

homograph A word which is identical in written form to another unrelated word, but is not necessarily identical in pronunciation.

homonym A word which is identical in form to another unrelated word. (Sometimes used of words which are identical only in spoken form = **homophone**.) See 2.1.4, 3.8.

homonymic clash A situation where **homonyms** exist, especially where this results in ambiguity. Hence a (contested) mechanism which tends to reduce the incidence of such clashes. See 3.8.

homonymiphobia = **homonymic clash**

homonymy The state of being a **homonym** of another word. A situation where two or more homonyms exist.

homophone A word which is identical in pronunciation to another unrelated word, but is not necessarily identical in written form.

iconic That shows **iconicity**.

iconicity The property of a linguistic form (or construction etc.) whose form reflects a semantic connection either with the external, non-linguistic world (**imagic iconicity**) or within the linguistic system (**diagrammatic iconicity**). See 4.5; also 1.3.2.

imagic iconicity A type of **iconicity** which involves a connection between linguistic form and the external, non-linguistic world. Onomatopoeic words show this type of iconicity. See 4.5. Compare **diagrammatic iconicity**.

imposition = **transfer**

i-**mutation** (In Old English and most of the other early Germanic languages) raising and/or fronting of a vowel which occurred when an /i/ or /j/ followed in the next syllable See 7.2.4; also 4.4.1.

infix See **affixation**

inflection A change in word form (especially an ending) which realizes a grammatical distinction. See 2.1.4.

institutionalized (Of a word) being the usual or conventional word occurring in a given meaning in a given context; (of a meaning) being the usual or conventional meaning of a given word in a given context. Compare 2.1.4, 2.3.

internal borrowing Borrowing which occurs within a language; spread of a word, meaning, construction, etc. See 6.4.

i-**umlaut** = *i*-**mutation**

isolative (Of a sound change) not determined by any particular phonetic context in the word. See 7.2.1. Compare **conditioned**.

levelling Generalization of a single (stem or inflectional) form to different parts of a **paradigm**, by **analogy**. See 3.1, 7.4.2.

lexeme A unit comprising one or more word forms which realize different grammatical forms of a single word; often represented in small capitals. E.g. *giraffe* and *giraffes* are word forms of the lexeme GIRAFFE; *man* and *men* are word forms of the lexeme MAN; *be, was, is,* and *are* are word forms of the lexeme BE. See 2.1.4.

lexical diffusion The spread of a sound change gradually from one lexical item to another, rather than affecting all items showing the same phonetic environment simultaneously. See 7.6.

lexical gap A situation where a particular slot in the set of possible (or expected) meaning relations in a language is not filled by any word form, thus (hypothetically) creating a gap which (from a functionalist perspective) requires to be filled. See 1.2.1, 5.3.

lexical item = **lexeme**. Sometimes also used to denote a broader class including idioms and other multi-word expressions: see 2.1.5.

lexicalization Process by which words become **opaque** in form or meaning, or both. See 2.3.

lexicalized That has undergone **lexicalization**.

lexis Vocabulary, words collectively. The lexis of a language is those words in use in that language, usually in a specified time period and in a specified place.

loan blend A borrowing of a complex word with substitution of one or more native morphs for morphs in the borrowed word. See 5.1.4.

loan translation A borrowing which shows replication of the structure of a foreign-language word or expression by use of synonymous word forms in the borrowing language. See 5.1.2.

loanword A borrowing of a word form and its associated word meaning, or a component of its meaning. See 5.1.1.

merger (As a type of sound change) loss of a distinctive contrast between two phonemes. See 7.2.3. Also (in lexicology) collapse of two distinct **lexemes** as a single **lexeme**. See 3.5.

metanalysis The redistribution of material across word or morpheme boundaries, e.g. *a nadder* > *an adder*. See 7.5.

metathesis A type of sound change in which a particular sound changes its position in the sequence of sounds in a word. See 7.3.

monomorphemic Consisting of only one **morpheme** or meaningful unit, e.g. *friar*, *sad*, *deer*. See 2.2.1. Compare **analysable**.

monophthong see **diphthong**

morpheme A minimal meaningful unit within a complex word. Compare **monomorphemic**, **complex**, **analysable**.

narrowing Process by which a word comes to have more restricted semantic application. See 8.6.2. Compare **broadening**.

naturalized (Of a word, in a borrowing situation) showing adaptation to the borrowing language (usually phonological adaptation). See 5.1.

neo-classical combining form see **combining form**

nonce (Of a word form, etc.) 'one-off', used on one occasion only. See 2.1.3, 2.3.

obstruent Any consonant which is formed with an obstruction of the airflow, i.e. a stop (in English /p, b, t, d, k, g,/), an affricate (in English /tʃ, dʒ/), or a fricative (in English /f, v, s, ʃ, z, ʒ/).

onomatopoeia A form of **imagic iconicity** in which the form of a linguistic sign echoes a sound in the external, non-linguistic world with which it is associated in meaning. See 4.5.

opaque (Of the meaning relation between the component parts of a word) not readily understood, not transparent. See 1.3.2, 2.3. Compare **transparent**.

paradigm The set of grammatical forms shown by a word. See 2.1.4.

pejoration Acquisition of less positive meaning. See 8.6.3.

phonaestheme (In the analysis adopted in this book) a sequence of sounds (not constituting a morpheme) found in a group of semantically similar words and which speakers identify as reflecting the perceived semantic similarity between these words, even though the words in the group often have no historical relationship with one another. See 4.5.3.

polygenesis Independent development of the same form or meaning in two different times and/or places. See 3.2, 8.3.

polysemous Showing more than one (conventional, established) meaning. See 2.1.4, 8.2.

pragmatics (The study of) the specific meanings shown by words, constructions, etc. in the context of a particular instance of language use, including implicatures as well as literal meanings. See 8.2.

prefix see **affixation**

productive (Of an affix, or a word formation process, etc.) that enters freely into the production of new words. (The term is not used in the same way by all scholars.) See 2.1.3, 2.2.4.

proportional analogy see **analogy**

reanalysis An analysis of the meaning or composition of a word or other linguistic unit which runs counter to its actual historical development. Reanalysis is often followed by new analogical formations, and can be identified most easily through these: e.g. Middle English *handiwork* < Old English *handgeweorc* < *hand* + *geweorc* was reanalysed as showing *hand*, *-y*, and *work*, hence giving rise (by **analogy**) to *handy* 'done by hand'. See 1.3.2, 4.1.1, 4.4.5, 7.4.3.

reflex The linear historical development of an earlier form, e.g. modern English *sad* is the reflex of Old English *sæd*. See 1.2.2.

register A set of distinctive linguistic usages employed by a particular social group, the members of a particular trade or profession, etc., or within a particular field of study etc.

regular (Of a sound change) occurring systematically in all or nearly all words which show the qualifying environment. See 7.1, 7.6.

root A basic, **unanalysable** form from which other word forms have been derived. In proto-Indo-European, roots typically have the structure CVC, and words derived from them typically show a variety of different root extensions and derivative suffixes. See 1.2.4, 4.4.1, 8.7.3.

semantic field A set of related meanings in a particular subject field, area of human experience, etc. See 8.5.1.

semantic loan An instance of extension of the meaning of a word as a result of association with the meaning of a partly synonymous word in another language. See 5.1.3.

specialization (as a type of meaning change) = **narrowing**

spelling pronunciation A pronunciation which arises from the written form of a word, rather than by regular historical phonetic development. See 7.4.7.

sporadic (Of a sound change) not occurring with regularity or in a pattern typical of lexical diffusion; affecting particular words individually or sporadically at widely separated times. See 7.3.

stem The form in a **paradigm** to which **affixes** are added.

stylistic level A set of distinctive linguistic usages employed in a particular social situation, e.g. formal language, informal language, slang, literary language, etc.

suffix see **affixation**

synonym A word which shares a meaning with another word, i.e. the two words show **synonymy**. See 4.2.

synonymy The situation where two words share a meaning. See 4.2.

token Each of the units in a sample of data. Opposed to **type**, each of the distinct varieties of unit in a sample of data. In *the cat sat on the mat* there are six tokens, but only five types (because *the* occurs twice).

transfer Process by which words enter a language during a process of language shift, when a group of speakers are abandoning one language for another. See 6.3. Compare **borrowing**.

transparent (Of the meaning relation between the component parts of a word) readily understood; (of a complex word) showing a clear form and meaning relationship between its component parts. See 1.3.2, 2.3. Contrasted with **opaque**. Compare **analysable**.

unanalysable That is not **analysable**.

unique morph = **cranberry morph**

word (As used in this book) normally = **lexeme**; see 2.1.4, and also 2.1.1, 2.1.2, 2.1.3.

Suggestions for further reading

This book has largely looked at etymological research in the context of those areas of the much broader field of historical linguistics which bear most directly on etymology. The best approach to further reading is hence to pursue the references given to fuller discussions of each topic, although the reader who is specifically interested in etymology will often need to ask questions for herself about what the impact of particular issues is on etymological research, since this is seldom a major focus in the general historical linguistic literature.

Some useful introductory accounts of issues in historical linguistics are listed in the introduction. Solid introductions to many topics can also be found in the fourteen volumes of Brown (2006). At a slightly more advanced level, some very illuminating discussion of many of the topics featured in this book can be found in Anttila (1989), Hock (1991), McMahon (1994), Lass (1997), or the essays in Joseph and Janda (2003).

On issues to do with morphology and word formation, Bauer (2003) is extremely informative. With a focus on English, Bauer (1983), Adams (2001), Plag (2003), and Booij (2007) are all valuable, especially for the contrasting perspectives that they bring to bear on some topics. Marchand (1969) remains an invaluable treasure trove of examples of English word formation, with many very insightful analyses.

There are few studies dedicated to issues to do with lexical borrowing which are not tied to consideration of a particular language or language group, although Thomason (2001) is a very useful general introduction to the wider field of contact linguistics. The somewhat dated surveys in Serjeantson (1961) and Sheard (1954) give useful overviews of the history of borrowing in English, but should be supplemented by the various volumes of the *Cambridge History of the English Language* (Hogg 1992a, Blake 1992, Lass 1999b, Romaine 1998), and by more specialist discussions referenced in chapters 5 and 6. (For very valuable theoretical perspectives, albeit focusing on a relatively narrow set of data, see Dance 2003).

On issues of change in word form see the general books on issues in historical linguistics listed above. Hoenigswald (1960), Anttila (1989), and

Hock (1991) are very useful for detailed (if at times demanding) accounts of some of the core methodology, and McMahon (1994), Lass (1997), and Joseph and Janda (2003) for some illuminating perspectives. As in all areas, reading of material written from a variety of different theoretical perspectives is to be warmly recommended for the broader understanding that it brings. Specifically on English, the various volumes of the *Cambridge History of the English Language* again provide an ideal starting point for the more advanced student. Fortson (2004) and Mallory and Adams (2006) offer excellent starting points for comparative Indo-European studies.

On semantic change, Traugott and Dasher (2005) has already proven hugely influential, and also provides an invaluable overview of important earlier work in the field. However, it is a demanding book for beginners, who will want to begin with some of the accounts in more general books on historical linguistics and language change such as Campbell (2004) or McMahon (1994). Although older, Ullmann (1962) is highly recommendable, especially for its wealth of examples (largely from Romance languages and English).

On names, useful pointers for reading and research are found in the following articles from Brown (2006): Hough (2006), Hanks (2006a), Hanks (2006b); see also Anderson (2007).

There are relatively few books specifically about etymology, and few recent books which examine etymological questions extensively. Malkiel (1975) and Malkiel (1993) are very good on different approaches, and on the nineteenth- and twentieth-century history of the field. A general book about historical linguistics written by a very eminent etymologist is von Wartburg (1962; English translation 1969). Another study by a linguist who has spent much of a distinguished career examining questions of word form and word meaning is Samuels (1972), which I have cited at numerous points in the course of this book. Both books offer a host of highly stimulating examples (von Wartburg largely from the Romance languages, and Samuels largely from English), and can be very warmly recommended. Both are also written from a standpoint which is rather more accepting of what can be broadly classed as functionalist approaches to linguistic questions than the standpoint that I have adopted at some points in this book (compare e.g. section 3.8 and the references to von Wartburg's and Samuels's contributions given there). Readers may find the difference of perspective informative. On etymology more generally see also further discussion and references in Durkin (2006d).

Introductory accounts of issues in the history of English geared particularly towards work on English etymology are offered by Bammesberger (1984) and Lockwood (1995), which both end with useful selections of etymologies presented in a little detail.

Finally, one of the best places to learn more about etymology, and even to make discoveries and establish new connections, is in the pages (physical or electronic) of historical and etymological dictionaries. To even begin giving a listing of recommended dictionaries for each language would stretch the size of this book beyond all reasonable bounds, but any reader who has completed this book will easily be able to navigate among the many dictionaries in any good library and find some fruitful places for further investigation. (For some help with interpreting the conventions employed in etymologies in the new edition of the *OED* see Durkin (1999, 2004).)

References

Aarts, Bas and McMahon, April M. S. (eds.) 2006. *The Handbook of English Linguistics*. Oxford: Blackwell.

Adams, J. N. 2008. *The Regional Diversification of Latin 200 BC–AD 600*. Cambridge: C.U.P.

Adams, Valerie 2001. *Complex Words in English*. London: Longman.

Adamson, Sylvia 1999. 'Literary language', in Lass (1999) 539–653.

Aitchison, Jean 2003. *Words in the Mind: An Introduction to the Mental Lexicon*, 3rd edn. Oxford: Blackwell.

Algeo, John 1998. 'Vocabulary', in Romaine (1998) 57–91.

Alinei, Mario 1995. 'Thirty-five definitions of etymology: or, etymology revisited', in Werner Winter (ed.) *On Languages and Language: The Presidential Addresses of the 1991 Meeting of the Societas Linguistica Europaea*. Berlin: Mouton de Gruyter, 1–26.

Allan, Kathryn 2008. *Metaphor and Metonymy: A Diachronic Approach*. Oxford: Blackwell.

Anderson, John M. 2007. *The Grammar of Names*. Oxford: O.U.P.

The Anglo-Norman Dictionary, 1977–1992; 2nd ed. 2005–. Ed. Louise W. Stone, T. B. W. Reid and William Rothwell; 2nd ed. William Rothwell, Stewart Gregory, and Dawid Trotter. London: The Modern Humanities Research Association.

Anttila, Raimo 1989. *Historical and Comparative Linguistics*, 2nd edn. Amsterdam: John Benjamins.

—— 2003. 'Analogy: the warp and woof of cognition', in Joseph and Janda (2003) 425–40.

Baayen, Harald R. and Renouf, Antoinette 1996. 'Chronicling The Times: productive lexical innovation in an English newspaper', in *Language* 72: 69–96.

Backhouse, Anthony E. 1993. *The Japanese Language: An Introduction*. Oxford: O.U.P.

Bammesberger, Alfred 1984. *English Etymology*. Heidelberg: Winter.

Barber, Charles 1996. *Early Modern English*, 2nd edn. Edinburgh: E.U.P.

Barnhart, Robert K. 1989. 'Dating in etymology', in *Dictionaries* 11: 53–63.

Bauer, Laurie 1983. *English Word-Formation*. Cambridge: C.U.P.

—— 1998a. 'When is a sequence of two nouns a compound in English?', in *English Language and Linguistics* 2: 65–86.

—— 1998b. 'Is there a class of neoclassical compounds, and if so is it productive?', in *Linguistics* 36: 403–22.

—— 2001. *Morphological Productivity*. Cambridge: C.U.P.

—— 2003. *Introducing Linguistic Morphology*, 2nd edn. Edinburgh: E.U.P.

—— 2006a. 'Compounds and minor word-formation types', in Aarts and McMahon (2006) 483–506.

—— 2006b. 'Competition in English Word Formation', in Ans Van Kemenade and Bettelou Los (eds.) *The Handbook of the History of English*. Oxford: Blackwell, 177–98.

Baugh, Albert C. and Cable, Thomas 2002. *A History of the English Language*, 5th edn. London: Routledge.

Beekes, R. S. P. 1995. *Comparative Indo-European Linguistics: An Introduction*. Amsterdam: Benjamins.

Bennett, J. A. W. and Smithers, G. V. 1968. *Early Middle English Verse and Prose*, 2nd edn. Oxford: O.U.P.

Bierbaumer, Peter 1975–79. *Der botanische Wortschatz des Altenglischen*, vols. 1–3. Frankfurt am Main: Lang.

Björkman, Erik 1900. *Scandinavian Loan-Words in Middle English*. Halle: Niemeyer.

Blake, Norman (ed.) 1992. *The Cambridge History of the English Language*, vol. II: *1066–1476*. Cambridge: C.U.P.

Bloomfield, Leonard 1933. *Language*. New York: Henry Holt.

Bolinger, Dwight 1950. 'Rime, assonance, and morpheme analysis', in *Word* 6: 117–36.

Booij, Geert 2007. *The Grammar of Words: An Introduction to Linguistic Morphology*, 2nd edn. Oxford: O.U.P.

Brinton, Laurel J. and Traugott, Elizabeth Closs 2005. *Lexicalization and Language Change*. Cambridge: C.U.P.

Britton, Derek 2007. 'A history of hyper-rhoticity in English', in *English Language and Linguistics* 11: 525–36.

Brown, Cecil H. 1999. *Lexical Acculturation in Native American Languages*. Oxford: O.U.P.

Brown, Keith (ed.) 2006. *Encyclopedia of Language and Linguistics*, 2nd edn. 14 vols. Oxford: Elsevier.

Burnley, David 1992. 'Lexis and semantics', in Blake (1992) 409–99.

Burridge, Kate 2006. 'Taboo, Euphemism, and Political Correctness', in Brown (2006) XII: 455–62.

Bybee, Joan 2002 'Word frequency and context of use in the lexical diffusion of phonetically conditioned sound change', in *Language Variation and Change* 14: 261–90.

Bynon, Theodora 1977. *Historical Linguistics*. Cambridge: C.U.P.

Cameron, Kenneth 1996. *English Place Names*, new edn. London: Batsford.

Campbell, Alistair 1959. *Old English Grammar*. Oxford: O.U.P.

Campbell, Lyle 2003. 'How to show languages are related: methods for distant genetic relationship', in Joseph and Janda (2003) 262–82.

—— 2004. *Historical Linguistics: An Introduction*, 2nd edn. Edinburgh: E.U.P.

Cannon, Garland and Warren, Nicholas 1996. *The Japanese Contributions to the English Language: An Historical Dictionary*. Wiesbaden: Harrassowitz.

Cassidy, Frederic G. 1966. 'Multiple etymologies in Jamaican Creole', in *American Speech* 41: 211–15.

Chambers, J. K. and Trudgill, Peter 1998. *Dialectology*, 2nd edn. Cambridge: C.U.P.

Chambers, W. Walker and Wilkie, John R. 1970. *A Short History of the German Language*. London: Methuen.

Chen, Matthew 1972. 'The time dimension: contribution toward a theory of sound change', in *Foundations of Linguistics* 8: 457–98.

Chowdharay-Best, George 1971. 'Posh', in *Mariner's Mirror* 57: 91–2.

Clackson, James 2007. *Indo-European Linguistics: An Introduction*. Cambridge: C.U.P.

Clark, Cecily 1976. 'People and languages in post-Conquest Canterbury', in *Journal of Medieval History* 2: 1–33; reprinted in Clark (1995) 179–206.

—— 1981. 'Nickname-creation: some sources of evidence, "naïve" memoirs especially', in *Nomina* 5: 53–72; reprinted in Clark (1995) 351–61.

—— 1982. 'The early personal names of King's Lynn: An essay in socio-cultural history. Part 1 – baptismal names', in *Nomina* 6: 51–71; reprinted in Clark (1995) 241–57.

—— 1991. 'Towards a reassessment of "Anglo-Norman influence on English place-names"', in P. Sture Ureland and George Broderick (eds.) *Language Contact in the British Isles: Proceedings of the Eighth International Symposium on Language Contact in Europe*. Tübingen: Niemeyer, 275–95; reprinted in Clark (1995) 144–55.

—— 1992a. 'Onomastics', in Hogg (1992a) 452–89.

—— 1992b. 'Onomastics', in Blake (1992) 542–606.

—— 1995. *Words, Names and History: Selected Papers*, ed. Peter Jackson. Cambridge: D. S. Brewer.

Coates, Richard 2006a. 'Behind the dictionary-forms of Scandinavian elements in England', in *Journal of the English Place-Name Society* 38: 43–61.

—— 2006b. 'Properhood', in *Language* 82: 356–82.

Collinge, N. E. 1985. *The Laws of Indo-European*. Amsterdam: Benjamins.

Cooper, Brian 2008. 'Contribution to the study of a euphemism in the intimate lexis of Slavonic and Germanic languages', in *Transactions of the Philological Society* 106: 71–91.

Corominas, Juan and Pascual, José A. 1980. *Diccionario crítico etimológico castellano e hispánico*, vols. I–III. Madrid: Gredos.

—— 1981. *Diccionario crítico etimológico castellano e hispánico*, vol. IV. Madrid: Gredos.

—— 1983. *Diccionario crítico etimológico castellano e hispánico*, vol. V. Madrid: Gredos.

—— 1991. *Diccionario crítico etimológico castellano e hispánico*, vol. VI. Madrid: Gredos.

Cox, Barrie 1994. *The Place-Names of Rutland*. Nottingham: English Place-Name Society.

Croft, William and Cruse, D. Alan 2004. *Cognitive Linguistics*. Cambridge: C.U.P.

Crystal, David 2008. *A Dictionary of Linguistics and Phonetics*, 6th edn. Oxford: Blackwell.

Dalton-Puffer, Christiane 1996. *The French Influence on Middle English Morphology: A Corpus-based Study of Derivation*. Berlin: Mouton de Gruyter.

Dance, Richard 2003. *Words Derived from Old Norse in Early Middle English: Studies in the Vocabulary of the South-West Midland Texts*. Tempe, Ariz.: Arizona Center for Medieval and Renaissance Studies.

Datations et documents lexicographiques: Matériaux pour l'histoire du vocabulaire français 1959–65, 2nd series 1970–. Eds. Bernard Quemada and P. Rézeau. Paris: Klincksieck. Searchable online at: http://atilf.atilf.fr/jykervei/ddl.htm

Daulton, Frank E. 2008. *Japan's Built-in Lexicon of English-based Loanwords*. Clevedon, UK: Multilingual Matters.

Dekeyser, Xavier 1986. 'Romance Loans in Middle English: a re-assessment', in Dieter Kastovsky and Aleksander Szwedek (eds.) *Linguistics across Historical and Geographical Boundaries*. Berlin: Mouton de Gruyter, 253–66.

The Dictionary of Old English, 1994–. Ed. Antonette diPaolo Healey. Toronto: Pontifical Institute of Mediaeval Studies.

Dietz, Klaus 2003. 'Romanisch-Germanische Sprachbeziehungen', in Heinrich Beck, Dieter Geuenich, and Heiko Steuer (eds.) *Reallexikon der Germanischen Altertumskunde*, vol. 25. Berlin: de Gruyter, 242–46.

Dobson, Eric J. 1968. *English Pronunciation 1500–1700*, 2nd edn. 2 vols. Oxford: O.U.P.

Durkin, Philip 1999. 'Root and branch: revising the etymological component of the *OED*', in *Transactions of the Philological Society* 97: 1–49.

—— 2002a. ' "Mixed" etymologies of Middle English items in OED3: some questions of methodology and policy', in *Dictionaries: the Journal of the Dictionary Society of North America* 23: 142–55.

—— 2002b. 'Changing documentation in the third edition of the *Oxford English Dictionary*: sixteenth-century vocabulary as a test case', in Teresa Fanego, B. Méndez-Naya, and E. Seoane (eds.) *Sounds, Words, Texts and Change: Selected Papers from 11 ICEHL, Santiago de Compostela, 7–11 September 2000*. Amsterdam: Benjamins, 65–81.

—— 2004. 'Loanword etymologies in the third edition of the *OED*: some questions of classification' in Christian Kay, Carole Hough, and Irené Wotherspoon (eds.) *New Perspectives on English Historical Linguistics*, vol. II: *Lexis and Transmission*. Amsterdam: Benjamins, 79–90.

—— 2006a. 'Loanword etymologies in the third edition of the *OED*: the benefits of a consistent methodology for the scholarly user', in Ritt et al. (2006) 61–75.

—— 2006b. 'Lexical borrowing in present-day English', in *Oxford University Working Papers in Linguistics, Philology and Phonetics* 11: 26–42.

Durkin, Philip 2006c. 'Lexical splits and mergers: some difficult cases for the *OED*', in Graham D. Caie, Carole Hough, and Irené Wotherspoon (eds.) *The Power of Words: Essays in Lexicography, Lexicology and Semantics in Honour of Christian J. Kay*. Amsterdam: Rodopi, 57–66.

—— 2006d. 'Etymology', in Brown (2006) IV: 260–7.

Durkin, Philip 2008. 'Latin loanwords of the early modern period: how often did French act as an intermediary?', in Richard Dury, Maurizio Gotti, and Marina Dossena (eds.) *Selected Papers from the Fourteenth International Conference on English Historical Linguistics (ICEHL 14), Bergamo, 21–25 August 2006*, vol. II: *Lexical and Semantic Change*. Amsterdam: Benjamins, 185–202.

Early English Books Online: see http://eebo.chadwyck.com/home

Fischer, Andreas 1999. 'What, if anything, is phonological iconicity?', in Nänny and Fischer (1999) 123–34.

—— 2003. 'Lexical borrowing and the history of English: A typology of typologies', in Dieter Kastovsky and Arthur Mettinger (eds.) *Language Contact in the History of English*, 2nd. rev. edn. Frankfurt am Main: Lang, 97–115.

Fischer, Olga and Nänny, Max 1999. 'Introduction: iconicity as a creative force in language use', in Nänny and Fischer (1999) xv–xxxvi.

Fortson, Benjamin W. 2003. 'An approach to semantic change', in Joseph and Janda (2003) 648–66.

—— 2004. *Indo-European Language and Culture: An Introduction*. Oxford: Blackwell.

Fox, Anthony 1995. *Linguistic Reconstruction: An Introduction to Theory and Method*. Oxford: O.U.P.

Französisches etymologisches Wörterbuch: Eine Darstellung des galloromanischen Sprachschatzes, 25 vols., 1922–1978; 2nd. edn. in course of publication. Founding editor Walther von Wartburg. Basel: Zbinden.

Geeraerts, Dirk 1997. *Diachronic Prototype Semantics: A Contribution to Historical Lexicology*. Oxford: O.U.P.

—— 2006. *Words and Other Wonders: Papers on Lexical and Semantic Topics*. Berlin: Mouton de Gruyter.

—— 2007. 'Lexicography', in Geeraerts and Cuyckens (2007) 1160–74.

—— and Cuyckens, Hubert (eds.) 2007. *The Oxford Handbook of Cognitive Linguistics*. Oxford: O.U.P.

Gelling, Margaret and Cole, Ann 2000. *The Landscape of Place-Names*. Stamford: Shaun Tyas.

Giegerich, Heinz 2004. 'Compound or phrase? English noun-plus-noun constructions and the stress criterion', in *English Language and Linguistics* 8: 1–24.

Gilliéron, J. and Roques, Mario 1912. *Études de géographie linguistique d'après l'Atlas linguistique de la France*. Paris: Champion.

Godefroy, Frédéric 1881–1902. *Dictionnaire de l'ancienne langue française et de tous les dialectes, du IXe au XVème siècle* 10 vols. Paris: F. Vieweg, Emile Bouillon.

Görlach, Manfred 1999. 'Regional and social variation', in Lass (1999) 459–538.

—— (ed.) 2001. *A Dictionary of European Anglicisms: A Usage Dictionary of Anglicisms in Sixteen European Languages*. Oxford: O.U.P.

—— (ed.) 2002a. *English in Europe*. Oxford: O.U.P.

—— 2002b. *Explorations in English Historical Linguistics*. Heidelberg: Winter.

Hanks, Patrick 2000. 'Do word meanings exist?', in *Computers and the Humanities* 34: 205–11.

—— 2006a. 'Personal names', in Brown (2006) IX: 299–311.

—— 2006b. 'Proper names: linguistic status', in Brown (2006) X: 134–7.

Harrison, Sheldon P. 2003. 'On the Limits of the Comparative Method', in Joseph and Janda (2003) 213–43.

Haugen, Einar 1950. 'The analysis of linguistic borrowing', in *Language* 26: 210–31.

Heidermanns, Frank 1993. *Etymologisches Wörterbuch der germanischen Primäradjektive*. Berlin: Mouton de Gruyter.

Hickey, Raymond 2006. 'Productive lexical processes in present-day English', in Christian Mair and Reinhard Heuberger (eds.) *Corpora and the History of English: Papers Dedicated to Manfred Markus on the Occasion of his Sixty-Fifth Birthday*. Heidelberg: Winter, 153–68.

A Historical Thesaurus of English: online version searchable at http://libra.englang. arts.gla.ac.uk/historicalthesaurus/; paper publication forthcoming, Oxford: O.U.P.

Hoad, Terry F. 1993. 'On the role of some questions of semantics in etymological explanations', in Rolf H. Bremmer and Jan Van Den Berg (eds.) *Current Trends in West Germanic Etymological Lexicography*. Leiden: Brill, 117–32.

Hock, Hans H. 1991. *Principles of Historical Linguistics*, 2nd edn. Berlin: Mouton de Gruyter.

—— 2003. 'Analogical change', in Joseph and Janda (2003) 441–60.

Hoenigswald, Henry M. 1960. *Language Change and Linguistic Reconstruction*. Chicago: University of Chicago Press.

—— 1978. 'The *Annus Mirabilis* 1876 and Posterity', in *Transactions of the Philological Society* 76: 17–35.

Hogg, Richard M. 1982. 'Two geminate consonants in Old English?', in John Anderson (ed.) *Language Form and Linguistic Variation: Papers Dedicated to Angus McIntosh*. Amsterdam: Benjamins, 187–202.

—— (ed.) 1992a. *The Cambridge History of the English Language*, vol. I: *The Beginnings to 1066*. Cambridge: C.U.P.

—— 1992b. *A Grammar of Old English*, vol. I: *Phonology*. Oxford: Blackwell.

—— 2006. 'English in Britain', in Richard M. Hogg and David Denison (eds.) *A History of the English Language*. Cambridge: C.U.P., 352–83.

Hopper, Paul J. and Traugott, Elizabeth Closs 2003. *Grammaticalization*, 2nd edn. Cambridge: C.U.P.

Hough, Carole 2001. 'ME *paved* in a Cheshire field-name', in *Notes and Queries* 246: 371.

—— 2006. 'Place Names', in Brown (2006) IX: 613–20.

Hunt, Tony 2000. 'Code-switching in medical texts', in David A. Trotter (ed.) *Multilingualism in Later Medieval Britain*. Cambridge: D. S. Brewer, 131–47.

Joseph, Brian D. and Janda, Richard D. (eds.) 2003. *The Handbook of Historical Linguistics*. Oxford: Blackwell.

Kastovsky, Dieter 1992. 'Semantics and vocabulary', in Hogg (1992) 290–408.

Katamba, Francis 2005. *English Words*, 2nd edn. London: Routledge.

Kaunisto, Mark 2007. *Variation and Change in the Lexicon: A Corpus-based Analysis of Adjectives in English Ending in -ic and -ical*. Amsterdam: Rodopi.

Kay, Christian J. 2000. 'Historical Semantics and Historical Lexicography: will the twain ever meet?', in Julie Coleman and Christian Kay (eds.) *Lexicology, Semantics and Lexicography: Selected Papers from the Fourth G. L. Brook Symposium*. Amsterdam: Benjamins, 53–68.

Kilgarriff, Adam 1997. 'I don't believe in word senses', in *Computers and the Humanities* 31: 91–113.

Kiparsky, Paul 2005. 'Analogy', in William J. Rawley (ed.) *International Encyclopedia of Linguistics*. Oxford: O.U.P., vol. I: 77–83.

Knappe, Gabriele 2004a. 'Hören – Zuhören – Hineinhören – Verhören? – Anmerkungen zur Rolle der Perzeption in der sogenannten Volksetymologie', in Margarete Imhof and Daniela Ulber (eds.) *Aktuelle Perspektiven schulpsychologischer Praxis und Theorie*. Osnabrück:Der Andere Verlag, 115–30.

—— 2004b. 'Greyhounds are not grey: On folk-etymological change and its role in the history of English', in Christoph Bode, Sebastian Domsch, and Hans Sauer (eds.) *Anglistentag 2003 München: Proceedings of the Conference of the German Association of University Teachers of English*, volume XXV. Trier: Wissenschaftlicher Verlag, 491–505.

Koerner, E. F. K. 1999. *Linguistic Historiography: Projects and Prospects*. Amsterdam: Benjamins.

Krahe, Hans 1969. *Germanische Sprachwissenschaft*, vol. III: *Wortbildungslehre*, 7th edn. revised by Wolfgang Meid. Berlin: Mouton de Gruyter.

Labov, William 1981. 'Resolving the Neogrammarian controversy', in *Language* 57: 267–308.

—— 1994. *Principles of Linguistic Change: Internal Factors*. Oxford: Blackwell.

Lahiri, Aditi and Dresher, B. Elan 1999. 'Open syllable lengthening in West Germanic', in *Language* 75: 678–719.

Laing, Margaret and Lass, Roger 2008. *A Linguistic Atlas of Early Middle English, 1150–1325*, version 1.1 [http://www.lel.ed.ac.uk/ihd/laeme1/laeme1.html]. Edinburgh: The University of Edinburgh.

—— and Williamson, Keith (eds.) 1994. *Speaking in our Tongues: Medieval Dialectology and Related Disciplines*. Cambridge: D. S. Brewer.

Lakoff, George and Johnson, Mark 1980. *Metaphors We Live By* (2nd edn. 2003). Chicago: University of Chicago Press.

Lass, Roger 1980. *On Explaining Language Change*. Cambridge: C.U.P.

—— 1984. *Phonology: An Introduction to Basic Concepts*. Cambridge: C.U.P.

—— 1992. 'Phonology and morphology' in Blake (1992) 23–155.

—— 1994. *Old English: A Historical Linguistic Companion*. Cambridge: C.U.P.

—— 1997. *Historical Linguistics and Language Change*. Cambridge: C.U.P.

—— 1999a. 'Phonology and morphology', in Lass (1999b) 56–186.

——(ed.) 1999b. *The Cambridge History of the English Language*, vol. III: *1476–1776*. Cambridge: C.U.P.

——2007. 'The Corpora of Etymologies and Changes', in Lass and Laing (2007).

Lass, Roger and Laing, Margaret 2007. *A Linguistic Atlas of Early Middle English, 1150–1325: Introduction* [http://www.lel.ed.ac.uk/ihd/laeme1/laeme1.html]. Edinburgh: The University of Edinburgh.

Lepschy, Giulio 1994a. *History of Linguistics*, vol. I: *The Eastern Traditions of Linguistics* (first published in Italian 1990). London: Longman.

—— 1994b. *History of Linguistics*, vol. II: *Classical and Medieval Linguistics* (first published in Italian 1990). London: Longman.

—— 1998. *History of Linguistics*, vol. III: *Renaissance and Early Modern Linguistics* (first published in Italian 1992). London: Longman.

Leumann, Manu 1963. *Lateinische Laut- und Formen-Lehre*. Munich: Beck.

Lewandowska-Tomaszczyk, Barbara 2007. 'Polysemy, Prototypes, and Radial Categories', in Geeraerts and Cuyckens (2007) 139–69.

Lockwood, William B. 1973 'More English etymologies', in *Zeitschrift für Anglistik und Amerikanistik* 21: 414–23.

—— 1995. *An Informal Introduction to English Etymology*. London: Minerva Press.

Macafee, Caroline 2002. 'A History of Scots to 1700', in *A Dictionary of the Older Scottish Tongue*, vol. XII: xix–clvii (see also http://www.dsl.ac.uk/dsl/).

Machan, Tim W. 2003. *English in the Middle Ages*. Oxford: O.U.P.

Mahootian, Shahrzad 2006. 'Code switching and mixing', in Brown (2006) II: 511–27.

Mair, Christian 2006. *Twentieth-century English: History, Variation, and Standardization*. Cambridge: C.U.P.

Malkiel, Yakov 1975. *Etymological Dictionaries: A Tentative Typology*. Chicago: University of Chicago Press.

—— 1979. 'Problems in the diachronic differentiation of near-homophones', in *Language* 55: 1–36.

—— 1993. *Etymology*. Cambridge: C.U.P.

Mallory, James P. and Adams, Douglas Q. 2006. *The Oxford Introduction to Proto-Indo-European and the Proto-Indo-European World*. Oxford: O.U.P.

Marchand, Hans 1969. *The Categories and Types of Present-Day English Word-Formation: A Synchronic-Diachronic Approach*, 2nd edn. Munich: Beck.

Martinet, André 1937. *La gémination consonantique d'origine expressive dans les langues germaniques*. Copenhagen: Levin & Munksgaard.

Matthews, Peter H. 2007. *The Concise Oxford Dictionary of Linguistics*, 2nd edn. Oxford: O.U.P.

Mawer, A., Stenton, F. M., and Houghton, F. T. S. 1927. *The Place-Names of Worcestershire*. Nottingham: English Place-Name Society.

McClure, Peter 1998. 'The interpretation of hypocoristic forms of Middle English baptismal names', in *Nomina* 21: 101–32.

—— 2003. 'The kinship of Jack: I, Pet-forms of Middle English personal names with the suffixes -kin, -ke, -man and -cot', in *Nomina* 26: 93–117.

McIntosh, Angus 1978. 'Middle English word-geography: its potential role in the study of the long-term impact of the Scandinavian settlements upon English', in Thorsten Anderson and Karl Inge Sandred (eds.) *The Vikings: Proceedings of the Symposium of the Faculty of Arts of Uppsala University, June 6–9, 1977.* Uppsala, 124–30; reprinted in Margaret Laing (ed.) (1989) *Middle English Dialectology: Essays on Some Principles and Problems*. Aberdeen: Aberdeen University Press, 98–104.

—— 1994. 'Codes and cultures', in Laing and Williamson (1994) 135–7.

McMahon, April M. S. 1994. *Understanding Language Change*. Cambridge: C.U.P.

—— 2006. 'Restructuring Renaissance English', in Lynda Mugglestone (ed.) *The Oxford History of English*. Oxford: O.U.P., 147–77.

—— and McMahon, Robert 2005. *Language Classification by Numbers*. Oxford: O.U.P.

Meier, Hans Heinrich 1999. 'Imagination and ideophones', in Nänny and Fischer (1999) 135–54.

Meillet, Antoine 1921. *Linguistique historique et linguistique générale*. Paris: Champion.

Mengden, Ferdinand von 1999. 'Französische Lehnwörter im Altenglischen', in Wolfgang Schindler and Jürgen Untermann (eds.) *Grippe, Kamm und Eulenspiegel*. Berlin: de Gruyter, 277–94.

—— 2001. 'Die altenglische Wortfamilie *prūt* und ihre Herkunft', in Thomas Honegger (ed.) *Authors, Heroes and Lovers*. Bern: Peter Lang, 179–98.

Merlan, F. 2006. 'Taboo: Verbal practices', in Brown (2006) XII: 462–66.

The Middle English Dictionary, 1952–2001. Ed. Hans Kurath, Sherman Kuhn, and Robert Lewis. Ann Arbor: University of Michigan Press.

Millar, Robert McColl 2007. *Trask's Historical Linguistics*. London: Arnold; revised edition of Trask (1996).

Minkova, Donka 2002. 'Ablaut reduplication in English: The criss-crossing of prosody and verbal art', in *English Language and Linguistics* 6: 133–69.

—— and Stockwell, Robert 2006. 'English Words', in Aarts and McMahon (2006) 461–82.

Morpurgo Davies, Anna 1978. 'Analogy, segmentation, and the early Neogrammarians', in *Transactions of the Philological Society* 76: 36–60.

—— 1998. *Nineteenth-century Linguistics* (= *History of Linguistics*, ed. Giulio Lepschy, vol. IV; first published in Italian 1992). London: Longman.

Myers-Scotton, Carol 2002. *Contact Linguistics: Bilingual Encounters and Grammatical Outcomes*. Oxford: O.U.P.

Nänny, Max and Fischer, Olga (eds.) 1999. *Form Miming Meaning*. Amsterdam: Benjamins.

Nevalainen, Terttu 1999. 'Lexis and Semantics', in Lass (1999) 322–458.

The Oxford Dictionary of English (revised edn.) 2005. Ed. Catherine Soanes and Angus Stevenson. Oxford: O.U.P.

The Oxford Dictionary of English Etymology 1966. Ed. Charles T. Onions, with the assistance of G. W. S. Friedrichsen and Robert W. Burchfield. Oxford: O.U.P.

The Oxford English Dictionary, 1884–1933, 10 vols. Ed. Sir James A. H. Murray, Henry Bradley, Sir William A. Craigie and Charles T. Onions. *Supplement*, 1972–1986, 4 vols., ed. Robert W. Burchfield; 2nd. edn. 1989, ed. John A. Simpson and Edmund S. C. Weiner; *Additions Series*, 1993–7, ed. John A. Simpson, Edmund S. C. Weiner, and Michael Proffitt; 3rd. edn. in progress: *OED Online*, March 2000–, ed. John A. Simpson, www.oed.com.

Pagel, Mark, Atkinson, Quentin D., and Meade, Andrew 2007. 'Frequency of word-use predicts rates of lexical evolution throughout Indo-European history', in *Nature* 449: 717–20.

Pahta, Päivi and Nurmi, Arja 2006. 'Code-switching in the Helsinki Corpus: a thousand years of multilingual practices', in Ritt et al. (2006) 203–20.

Pierce, Marc 2006. 'The book and the beech tree revisited', in *Historische Sprachforschung* 119: 273–82.

Plag, Ingo 2003. *Word-Formation in English*. Cambridge: C.U.P.

—— 2005. 'The variability of compound stress in English: structural, semantic, and analogical factors', in *English Language and Linguistics* 10: 143–72.

—— 2006. 'Productivity', in Aarts and McMahon (2006) 537–56.

Pokorny, Julius 1959–69. *Indogermanisches etymologisches Wörterbuch*. 2 vols. Bern: Franke.

Pope, Mildred K. 1934. *From Latin to Modern French*. Manchester: Manchester University Press.

Poplack, Shana 2004. 'Code-switching' in U. Ammon, N. Dittmar, K. J. Mattheier, and P. Trudgill (eds.) *Sociolinguistics: An International Handbook of the Science of Language and Society*, 2nd edn. Berlin: Walter de Gruyter, 589–96.

—— and Meechan, Marjory 1998. 'How languages fit together in code-mixing', in *International Journal of Bilingualism* 2: 127–38.

——, Sankoff, David and Miller, Chris 1988. 'The social correlates and linguistic processes of lexical borrowing and assimilation', in *Linguistics* 26: 47–104.

Quinion, Michael 2005. *Port Out, Starboard Home*. London: Penguin.

Redmonds, George 2002. *Surnames and Genealogy: A New Approach*. Bury, Lancs.: Federation of Family History Societies; U.S. edn. (1997) Boston, Mass.: New England Historic Genealogical Society.

Ringe, Donald A. 2003. 'Internal reconstruction', in Joseph and Janda (2003) 244–61.

—— 2006. *From Proto-Indo-European to Proto-Germanic*. Oxford: O.U.P.

Ritt, Nikolaus, Schendl, Herbert, Dalton-Puffer, Christiane, and Kastovsky, Dieter (eds.) 2006. *Medieval English and its Heritage*. Frankfurt am Main: Lang.

Rix, Helmut 2001. *Lexikon der indogermanischen Verben: die Wurzeln und ihre Primärstammbildungen*, 2nd edn. Wiesbaden: Ludwig Reichert.

Robinson, Orrin W. 1992. *Old English and its Closest Relatives*. London: Routledge.

Romaine, Suzanne (ed.) 1998. *The Cambridge History of the English Language*, vol. IV: *1776–1997*. Cambridge: C.U.P.

Ross, Alan S. C. 1952. *Ginger: A Loan-word Study*. Oxford: The Philological Society.

Ross, Alan S. C. 1958. *Etymology: With Especial Reference to English*. London: André Deutsch.

Ross, Malcolm and Durie, Mark 1996. 'Introduction', in Mark Durie and Malcolm Ross (eds.) *The Comparative Method Reviewed*. Oxford: O.U.P., 3–38.

Rothwell, William 1998. 'Arrivals and departures: the adoption of French terminology into Middle English', in *English Studies* 79: 144–65.

—— 2005. 'Preface: Anglo-French and the AND', in *Anglo-Norman Dictionary*, 2nd. edn., vol. I: A–C. London: Modern Humanities Research Association v–xx.

Samuels, Michael 1972. *Linguistic Evolution: With Special Reference to English*. Cambridge: C.U.P.

Sapir, Edward 1921. *Language: An Introduction to the Study of Speech*. New York Harcourt, Brace, and Company.

Saussure, Ferdinand de 1972. *Cours de linguistique générale*, ed. Charles Bally and Albert Sechehaye with the collaboration of Albert Riedlinger; critical edn. by Tullio de Mauro, Paris: Payot. (English edn. (1983): *Course in General Linguistics*, trans. Roy Harris. London: Duckworth.)

Schendl, Herbert 2001. *Historical Linguistics*. Oxford: O.U.P.

Serjeantson, Mary S. 1961. *A History of Foreign Words in English*, 2nd edn. London: Routledge.

Sheard, J. A. 1954. *The Words We Use*. London: André Deutsch.

Shibatani, Masayoshi 1990. *The Languages of Japan*. Cambridge: C.U.P.

Short, Ian 2007. *Manual of Anglo-Norman*. London: Anglo-Norman Text Society.

Silva, Penny 2000. 'Time and meaning: sense and definition in the *OED*', in Lynda Mugglestone (ed.), *Lexicography and the OED: Pioneers in the Untrodden Forest*. Oxford: O.U.P., 77–95.

Simpson, John, Weiner, Edmund, and Durkin, Philip 2004. 'The *Oxford English Dictionary* today', in *Transactions of the Philological Society* 102: 335–81.

Smith, Jeremy J. 1996. *An Historical Study of English*. London: Routledge.

—— 2006. 'Phonaesthesia, ablaut and the history of the English demonstratives', in Ritt et al. (2006) 1–17.

—— 2007. *Sound Change and the History of English*. Oxford: O.U.P.

Smithers, G. V. 1954. 'Some English ideophones', in *Archivum Linguisticum* 6: 73–111.

Stanley, Eric G. 1982. 'The prenominal prefix *ge-* in late Old English and early Middle English', in *Transactions of the Philological Society* 80: 25–66.

Sweetser, Eve E. 1990. *From Etymology to Pragmatics: Metaphorical and Cultural Aspects of Semantic Structure*. Cambridge: C.U.P.

Szemerényi, Oswald J. L. 1979. 'Germanica I (1–5)', in *Zeitschrift für vergleichende Sprachforschung* 93: 103–25.

—— 1996. *Introduction to Indo-European Linguistics*. Oxford: O.U.P. (translation of Szemerényi, Oswald J. L. 1990. *Einführung in die vergleichende Sprachwissenschaft*, 4th edn. Darmstadt: Wissenschaftliche Buchgesellschaft).

Thier, Katrin 2003a. 'Sails in the North: new perspectives on an old problem', in *International Journal of Nautical Archaeology* 32: 182–90.

—— 2003b. 'Sea-lanes of communication: language as a tool for nautical archaeology', in Lucy Blue, Fred Hocker, and Anton Englert (eds.) *Connected by the Sea: Proceedings of the Tenth International Symposium on Boat and Ship Archaeology*. Oxford: Oxbow Books, 210–16.

—— 2005. 'Das Paddel – eine Minikulturgeschichte', in Heidemarie Eilbracht, Vera Brieske, and Barbara Grodde (eds.) *Itinera Archaeologica: vom Neolithikum bis in die frühe Neuzeit*. Rahden: Marie Leidorf, 281–94.

—— 2007. 'Of Picts and penguins – Celtic languages in the new edition of the Oxford English Dictionary', in Hildegard L. C. Tristram (ed.) *The Celtic Languages in Contact: Papers from the Workshop within the Framework of the XIII International Congress of Celtic Studies*. Potsdam: Universitätsverlag Potsdam, 246–59.

Thomason, Sarah G. 2001. *Language Contact: An Introduction*. Edinburgh: E.U.P.

—— 2003. 'Contact as a source of language change', in Joseph and Janda (2003) 687–712.

—— and Kaufman, Terrence 1988. *Language Contact, Creolization, and Genetic Linguistics*. Berkeley: University of California Press.

Townend, Matthew 2002. *Language and History in Viking Age England: Linguistic Relations Between Speakers of Old Norse and Old English*. Studies in the Early Middle Ages 6. Turnhout: Brepols.

Trask, R. L. 1996. *Historical Linguistics*. London: Arnold. (For revised edn. see Millar (2007).)

—— 2000. *The Dictionary of Historical and Comparative Linguistics*. Edinburgh: E.U.P.

Traugott, Elizabeth Closs 1989. 'On the rise of epistemic meanings in English: An example of subjectification in semantic change', in *Language* 65: 31–55.

—— 2006. 'Semantic change: Bleaching, strengthening, narrowing, extension', in Brown (2006) XI: 124–31.

—— and Dasher, Richard B. 2005. *Regularity in Semantic Change*. Cambridge: C.U.P.

Ullmann, Stephen 1962. *Semantics: An Introduction to the Science of Meaning*. Oxford: Blackwell.

Van Langendonck, Willy 2007. 'Iconicity', in Geeraerts and Cuyckens (2007) 394–418.

Verner, Karl 1875. 'Eine Ausnahme der ersten Lautverschiebung', in *Zeitschrift für vergleichende Sprachforschung* 23: 97–130. (English translation in Lehmann, Winfred P. (1967) *A Reader in Nineteenth Century Historical Indo-European Linguistics*. Bloomington: Indiana University Press, 132–63.)

Wales, Katie 1990. 'Phonotactics and phonaesthesia: the power of folk lexicology', in Susan Ramsaran (ed.) *Studies in the Pronunciation of English: A Commemorative Volume in Honour of A. C. Gimson*. London: Routledge, 339–51.

Wang, William S-Y. 1969. 'Competing changes as a cause of residue', in *Language* 45: 9–25.

Wartburg, Walther von 1962. *Einführung in Problematik und Methodik der Sprachwissenschaft*, 2nd revised and extended edn., with the collaboration of Stephen Ullmann. Tübingen: Niemeyer.

—— 1969. *Problems and Methods in Linguistics*, rev. edn. with the collaboration of Stephen Ullmann, trans. Joyce M. H. Reid. Oxford: Blackwell (translation of the second French edition (1963) of von Wartburg (1962)).

Watkins, Calvert 2000. *The American Heritage Dictionary of Indo-European Roots*, 2nd edn. Boston: Houghton Mifflin.

Webster's Dictionary of English Usage 1989. Ed. E. Ward Gilman. Springfield, Mass.: Merriam-Webster.

Weinreich, Uriel 1953. *Languages in Contact: Findings and Problems*. New York: Linguistic Circle of New York. (Reprinted 1964 The Hague: Mouton.)

Wells, John C. 1982. *Accents of English*, vol. 1: *Introduction*. Cambridge: C.U.P.

Wescott, Roger W. 1971. 'Linguistic iconism', in *Language* 47: 416–28.

General index

ablaut 47, 111–114, 252, 288
abbreviation (in medieval
   manuscripts) 193, 235
abrupt sound change 196
accent 19, 112; see also stress
acronyms 121, 122–123, 206
Adams, Douglas Q. 88, 264, 298
Adams, J. N. 11
Adams, Valerie 35, 97, 98, 99, 106, 122,
   130, 297
Adamson, Sylvia 151
affixes, affixation 16, 44, 46, 48, 53, 70,
   94, 95–106, 109, 111, 114, 119, 120,
   125, 129, 151, 191, 200–201, 218, 252,
   253, 277, 278, 281, 288
Afrikaans 9, 139
agreement 38
Aitchison, Jean 48
Albanian 13, 263
Algeo, John 114
allophones 14
amelioration 28, 235, 237–240, 243,
   246, 288
ambiguity 92
analogical change 199, 288
analogical creation 199, 200–201, 219,
   288
analogy 27, 66, 96, 98, 101, 113,
   129, 137, 179, 182, 191, 194, 197–207,
   208, 213, 218–219, 239–240, 271, 276,
   288, 289; see also proportional
   analogy
analysability 44, 45, 48, 49, 51, 53, 54,
   55, 56, 57, 59, 97, 121, 124, 203, 289,
   295
Anatolian languages 13, 180
Anderson, John M. 267, 298

Anglo-French (issues concerning) 5, 6,
   62–63, 149–154, 175–177, 276–277;
   see also French
Anglo-Norman: see Anglo-French
Anglo-Norman Dictionary, The 5, 150,
   152, 172
Anglo-Saxon Chronicle 277
Anglo-Saxons 11, 282–283
animal sounds 126–128
animal names 126–128
ante 7
anti-lexicalization 56, 205
antonymy 105
Anttila, Raimo 91, 198, 297
aphaeresis 117
aphesis 117, 203
apocope 118
apophony: see vowel alternation
apparent exceptions to sound
   changes 182, 184, 208
Arabic 114, 244
Arawakan languages 204
arbitrariness of the linguistic sign 36,
   123–125
Armenian 1, 13, 18
assimilation (type of sound
   change) 195, 196–197, 289
assimilation (type of associative change
   in word form): see contamination
associative change in word form 179,
   194, 197–207, 208, 217, 218, 221, 269,
   286, 289, 290
assonance 129
Atkinson, Quentin D. 159
Augustinians 6
Austrian German 146
Avestan 247

Index of word forms

English (*cont.*)

miaow 126

mice 24

micro-, micrography, microbiology, microskirt, micro, microdress, microcomputer, microwave oven 108–109

microfilm, microfilmer 102

Middle Eastern 102

Middle Europe 135

midshipmate, midshipmite 205

mien 165

mignon 169

Milanese, milaner 281

mile 187, 188

milk of human kindness 43

milliner 276, 281

milord, my lord 133, 137

mindscape 98

minikin 275

minion 169

mimsy 73

min 233–234

mind 100, 233

ministry 80, 81

mint 202

minter 99

mirth 247

miss, mistress 116

mister 80, 81

mockumentary 118, 120

moderate, moderature 139

molten 80

monish 117

monkeyrony 205

monumentary 69

moonscape 98

moot 100

moralize 138

morepork 127

mosquito 196

most 201

motel 118

mother 19, 20, 252

motor 118

mould, moulder 233

moules marinière, moules marinières 177

moult 207

mountain 158

mouse 24, 190, 199

mouth 151

Mr. 81, 238

Mrs. 238

muller, mullered 254

mum, mumble 125

municipal, municipality 44

murmur 125

mushroom 204

must 247

myoneural 103

mystery 80, 81

nape 221

nappy, napkin 117

narco, narcotic 116

naseberry 58, 203, 254–255

naturalize 138

near 158

needle 271

needler 196, 271

neep 203

negotiation 167

-ness 39, 44, 46, 48, 94, 95, 109, 200–201

newt 207

neuristor 119

neuromuscular 103

neurotize 138, 143

neutralize 138

New Christian 135

nick 255, 257

niddle 129

nightscape 98

Nile green 135

nonsensicalness 69

northern 102

noso-, nosology 138, 143

noxious 29

LIBRARY, UNIVERSITY OF CHESTER

LIBRARY UNIVERSITY OF CHESTER